THE ENVIRONMENTAL JUSTICE READER

THE ENVIRON MENTAL JUSTICE READER

POLITICS, POETICS, & PEDAGOGY

edited by

Joni Adamson, Mei Mei Evans, & Rachel Stein

THE UNIVERSITY OF ARIZONA PRESS TUCSON

The University of Arizona Press
© 2002 The Arizona Board of Regents
First printing
All rights reserved

⊛ This book is printed on acid-free, archival-quality paper.
Manufactured in the United States of America

07   06   05   04   03   02   6   5   4   3   2   1

Library of Congress Cataloging-in-Publication Data
The environmental justice reader : politics, poetics, and pedagogy /
edited by Joni Adamson, Mei Mei Evans, and Rachel Stein.
p. cm.
Includes bibliographical references and index.
ISBN 0-8165-2206-5 (cloth : acid-free paper)
ISBN 0-8165-2207-3 (paper : acid-free paper)
1. Environmental justice. I. Adamson, Joni, 1958–
II. Evans, Mei Mei. III. Stein, Rachel.
GE220 .E585 2002
363.7—dc21   2002003308

British Library Cataloguing-in-Publication Data
A catalogue record for this book is available from the British Library.

Publication of this book is made possible in part by the proceeds of a permanent
endowment created with the assistance of a Challenge Grant from the National
Endowment for the Humanities, a federal agency, and in part by a grant from the
Provost's Author Support Fund of the University of Arizona.

CONTENTS

ACKNOWLEDGMENTS

We wish to thank the many people who have contributed in a variety of ways to this project. Firstly, we thank all those in the field who are working for environmental justice through political channels, community organizing, teaching, and the arts. This book is dedicated to your efforts to make this planet a safe and nurturing home for all.

This book has been a collaborative effort of many hands, hearts, and minds, and we sister-editors have learned a great deal from working together and with others during a year in which a number of us also dealt with personal difficulties and tragedies. Working concertedly through these trials has taught us again the preciousness of community. We value the generosity of the many scholar/teacher/activists who have allowed us to include their essays in this volume. We offer thanks to our colleague Kamala Platt, who assisted us in the initial planning stages of this project. We offer a special thanks to Teresa Leal, cochair of the Southwest Network for Environmental and Economic Justice, for sharing her time and knowledge of the movement as we envisioned the shape of this project.

We thank Patti Hartmann, our acquisitions editor at the University of Arizona Press, for her faith in this project and her able guidance as the book took final form. We would also like to thank Steve Hopkins for his excellent, thorough copyediting of the manuscript. We wish to thank Siena College for the sabbatical leave that allowed Rachel Stein to complete this project, and for financial support from the Siena Program for Sustainable Land Use, which funded permission fees and index assistance. We are also grateful for the support of Alaska Pacific University and the Alaska Community Action on Toxics. The two campuses of the University of Arizona—both Main and South—provided generous support for this project. We wish to thank the University of Arizona Provost's Author Support Fund for awarding Joni Adamson a subvention grant to lower publication expenses and make the book more affordable to a wider audience. We are greatly indebted to Susan Glandon, our University of Arizona South student assistant, who completed the technical preparations of this text with computer skills and patience far beyond our own. We also thank Lauri Lindsay for her able assistance with our index. We would also like to thank Sheila Savadkohi and Carol Lehman at the South Campus for providing clerical support as we finished the project. Finally, we wish to thank our friends and colleagues in the Association for the Study of Literature and Environment and the American Studies Association for offering us supportive scholarly communities in which to share and strengthen our work.

THE ENVIRONMENTAL JUSTICE READER

INTRODUCTION

Environmental Justice Politics, Poetics, and Pedagogy

Joni Adamson, Mei Mei Evans, and Rachel Stein

In the fall of 1999, delegations of environmental activists, trade unionists, Buddhist monks, indigenous peoples, and "raging grannies," representing many countries of the world, converged in Seattle, Washington, to protest the World Trade Organization's support of multinational corporate objectives and trade agreements that contribute to the building of a global economy where control over local environments, communities, cultures, education, and health care is no longer in the hands of the people but in the hands of big business. The Seattle protests, and more recently, those in Toronto, Canada, and Genoa, Italy, dramatically recall struggles of the past several decades by such activists as rubber tappers in the Amazon protecting their traditional rain forest homelands, villagers of the Chipko movement in northern India fighting against deforestation, and Ogoni dissidents detained by the military government of Nigeria for their opposition to large-scale oil drilling in fields where they once cultivated yams and cassava. The last quarter of the twentieth century also saw the emergence of similar struggles in the United States: Navajo sheepherders fighting the encroachment of the world's largest open-pit coal mine into sacred lands, women in South Central Los Angeles opposing the siting of a hazardous waste burning facility in their neighborhood, residents of a Memphis, Tennessee, neighborhood calling on the Environmental Protection Agency and the U.S. military to contain and remove toxic substances escaping into the air, water, and soil from an arms storage facility near their homes, and members of several American Indian tribes in the Northwest advocating the removal of dams that threaten their salmon-based cultures.

Each of these specifically located struggles may be said to have contributed to what we today recognize as a global environmental justice movement. This book, inspired by the activists, artists, teachers, and scholars who are working to make social and environmental justice a reality, seeks to examine the issues, events, cultural productions, and educational initiatives emerging from the environmental justice movement worldwide. We define environmental justice as the right of all people to share equally in the benefits bestowed by a healthy environment. We define the environment, in turn, as the places in which we live, work, play, and worship. Environmental justice initiatives specifically attempt to redress the disproportionate incidence of environmental contamination in communities of the poor and/or communities of color, to secure for those affected the right to live unthreatened by the risks posed by environmental degradation and contamination, and to afford equal access to natural resources that sustain life and culture. As members of marginalized communities have mobilized around issues of environmental degradation affecting their families, communities, and work sites, they have illuminated the crucial intersections between ecological and social justice concerns.

In the last several decades, environmental justice movements around the world have grown out of convergences between civil rights movements, antiwar and antinuclear movements, women's movements, and grassroots organizing around environmental issues. One defining moment in the history of the U.S. environmental justice movement was the publication in 1987 of a report sponsored by the United Church of Christ Commission for Racial Justice (UCC-CRJ). The report, a compilation of the results of a national study, found race to be the leading factor in the location of commercial hazardous waste facilities and determined that poor and people of color communities suffer a disproportionate health risk: 60 percent of African American and Latino communities and over 50 percent of Asian/Pacific Islanders and Native Americans live in areas with one or more uncontrolled toxic waste sites. Following publication of the report, the Reverend Benjamin Chavis, then executive director of the UCC-CRJ, coined the term "environmental racism," which he defined as "racial discrimination in environmental policy-making and the enforcement of regulations and laws, the deliberate targeting of people of color communities for toxic waste facilities, the official sanctioning of the life-threatening presence of poisons and pollutants in our communities, and history of excluding people of color from leadership in the environmental movement."[1]

Another watershed moment in the history of the movement, this time international in scope, occurred in 1991, when over three hundred community leaders from the United States, Canada, Central and South America, and the Marshall Islands convened the First National People of Color Environmental Leadership Summit in Washington, D.C. The purpose of the meeting was to bring together leaders from people of color communities worldwide who could shape the contours of a multiracial movement for environmental change founded on the political ideology of working from the grassroots. Delegates took a stand against environmental racism and drew up seventeen "Principles of Environmental Justice" outlining a broad and deep political commitment to pursue environmental justice and "to secure our political, economic, and cultural liberation that has been denied for over 500 years of colonization and oppression."[2]

Environmental justice movements call attention to the ways disparate distribution of wealth and power often leads to correlative social upheaval and the unequal distribution of environmental degradation and/or toxicity. For example, in Chiapas, Mexico, members of the Zapatista National Liberation Army commanded the world's attention when they took over four sizable towns on January 1, 1994, the day the North American Free Trade Agreement (NAFTA) went into effect, and later insisted that Mexico's government bring indigenous peoples into all deliberations affecting their cultural, economic, and environmental futures. Indeed, by calling into question global institutions such as NAFTA, which favor large multinational agribusiness at the expense of small subsistence farmers, the Zapatistas brought the urgency of the issues at the center of the environmental justice movement into international prominence and demonstrated that disgruntled groups of women, farmers, indigenous peoples, or urban city dwellers have the power to confront large governments, corporations, and even global steamrollers such as NAFTA or the World Trade Organization. These groups have also mandated awareness within the mainstream environmental movement to issues of race, class, and gender, among others, as well as within social justice movements to the foundational importance of ecological integrity to a community's sense of well-being.

Although the worldwide environmental justice movement is still relatively young, there is already a vast literature on the subject by scholars in the fields of social science, environmental science, and philosophy. This writing documents the efforts of local groups to organize, mobilize, and empower themselves to take charge of their own lives, communities, and environments. Many of the essays in this volume build upon landmark texts in the movement authored by such scholar/activists as Robert Bullard, Pratap Chatterje, Ward Churchill, Giovanna Di Chiro, Winona LaDuke, Mathias Finger, Laura Pulido, Wolfgang Sachs, Vandana Shiva, and Jace Weaver. Contributors extend the literature by analyzing the connections between different incidents of environmental degradation and economic exploitation while at the same time emphasizing the local, regional, and cultural complexities of the struggles taking place at those sites.

This volume also points to the growing number of expressive writers and artists representing environmental justice struggles in their works. Novelists, essayists, playwrights, and poets as diverse as Jimmy Santiago Baca, Octavia Butler, Ana Castillo, Mahasweta Devi, Linda Hogan, Winona LaDuke, Barbara Neely, Simon Ortiz, Adrienne Rich, Marilynne Robinson, Ken Saro-Wiwa, Leslie Marmon Silko, Helen Maria Viramontes, Gerald Vizenor, Alice Walker, and Karen Tei Yamashita, among others, write about the environmental hazards faced by communities of color and economically and politically disenfranchised communities. They have created a literature that depicts the social, material, and spiritual devastation that results when, for example, hydroelectric projects destroy tribal lands and water, when poisonous and radioactive materials originating at local factories, mines, garbage incinerators, and agricultural areas threaten human health and life, or when traditional agropastoral farmers are unable to compete with corporate agribusiness executives. Other nontraditional literary forms and cultural production including testimonies, oral histories, manifestoes, and street theater are also being used to draw our attention to and enhance our understanding of the experience of living with the effects of environmental racism. Grassroots groups are producing poster graphics, sculpture, murals, and public greening projects. Regional environmental justice issues appear in media arts such as video and film, in Internet web art and computer-generated graphics, and in academic and community scholarship, including lectures, essays, radio programs, field trips, and community flyers.

As Robert Figueroa explains in his essay for this collection, environmental justice is such a contemporary area of concern that those who enter into discussion of this issue have the opportunity to "engage the subject matter while the origin of many terms, meanings, concepts and associated action . . . is in its earliest developmental stages" (see chapter 16). In the environmental justice courses he teaches, Figueroa encourages students "to feel that they are a part of the community of scholars and activists working to clarify these issues by developing ways of articulating the problems and solutions." Like Figueroa, the editors of this volume have as their goal the creation of a text that will encourage teachers, students, and community members to see themselves as part of the global community working to clarify and promote the issues surrounding the environmental justice movement. The book takes a multivocal approach: our collection of activist testimonies, interviews, political analyses, curricular accounts, and literary comparisons emphasizes the dialogic nature of political resolution for environmental social experiences of environmental injustices. Contributors point out the paths that U.S. and international environmental justice movements are taking, articulate the problems and solutions that environmental justice initiatives address, and envision the potentiality of future collaborations between artists, activists, scholars, teachers, and students working toward environmental justice.

The Environmental Justice Reader: Politics, Poetics, and Pedagogy expands the field of environmental justice studies by offering new case studies, including cultural analysis of environmental justice arts, and by providing pedagogical essays that encourage teachers to incorporate these issues and texts into their classrooms. By means of section headings, "Politics," "Poetics," and "Pedagogy," we assert that both teaching and making art are intrinsically political acts. Both require a skillful examination, negotiation, and transformation of the tensions that sometimes manifest in more overtly "political" responses. As illustrated by the roundtable discussion between Simon Ortiz, Teresa Leal, Devon Peña, and Terrell Dixon that opens this book, the separation of these impulses has too often been artificial and unnecessary, and our text is an attempt to join political, poetic, and pedagogical acts of resistance back together.

Politics

In her essay for the Politics section of this book, Valerie Kuletz suggests that, too often, researchers and scholars have been content to simply present a "postmortem of an already disastrous situation." She argues, instead, for a "proactive scholarship" that points out patterns of environmentally destructive and socially unjust activity and that also identifies resistance movements working for community and environmental survival (see chapter 6). Such proactive scholarship points us toward solutions and encourages action rather than hand-wringing, which is exactly the intent of the essays included in the book's first section. The essays assembled in "Politics" expand the limited focus of mainstream environmental movements, explain the interrelationships of environmental problems and social concerns, and explore particular environmental justice struggles that have emerged in the United States and other regions of the world, such as Mexico, Africa, and the Pacific Islands. The essays add new critical perspectives to the existing body of environmental justice scholarship, describe the wide range of issues that may be grouped together under this heading, and examine the different strategies adopted by community groups faced with environmental injustices.

The Politics section opens with a cluster of first-person testimonies in which citizen-activists Doris Bradshaw, Sterling Gologergen, Edgar Mouton, Alberto Saldamando, and Paul Smith speak directly of the grassroots movements that have formed in their regions to address the environmental toxicity endangering their communities and call attention to other environmental threats to their cultural survival as well. Their voices give urgency to the analyses contained in the essays that follow.

Next follow two essays discussing Hispano and Native American environmental justice issues in the southwestern region of the United States. Joni Adamson's "Throwing Rocks at the Sun: An Interview with Teresa Leal" examines the lifelong efforts of one woman to name, fight against, and find solutions to the interrelated problems that threaten women, workers, and the environment in the border region between the United States and Mexico. Devon Peña's "Endangered Landscapes and Disappearing Peoples? Identity, Place, and Community in Ecological Politics" describes the interrelationship of cultural and ecological preservation evidenced within the struggle of traditional Hispano acequia farmers to maintain collective land and water rights in the face of development, logging, and mining interests that threaten both traditional agriculture and culture.

The southeastern United States, an area notorious for toxic waste dumping and exposure within communities of color, gave rise to some of the earliest environmental justice movements in the 1980s. Andrea Simpson's "Who Hears Their Cry? African American Women and the Fight for Environmental Justice in Memphis, Tennessee" focuses upon the difficulties that activist Doris Bradshaw faces as her organization, The Tennessee Concerned Citizens Committee, fights toxic waste sites in a working-class African American community. In particular, Simpson discusses the obstacle of confronting scientific experts who deny residents' claims of environmentally caused illnesses. In a similar vein, but very different locale, Nelta Edwards's "Radiation, Tobacco, and Illness in Point Hope, Alaska: Approaches to the 'Facts' in Contaminated Communities" describes the Atomic Energy Commission's experimentation with radioactive materials near Point Hope, Alaska, in the 1950s and the current efforts of Inupiat people living in that area to link their high incidence of cancer to radiation exposure, despite the negation of scientists. The situation leads Edwards to conclude that environmental justice movements must find ways to argue their claims beyond the limits of the current scientific framework. Examining related issues of nuclear colonialism in the Pacific region, Valerie Kuletz's "The Movement for Environmental Justice in the Pacific Islands" traces the Nuclear Free and Independent Pacific Movement, which has emerged in resistance to decades of nuclear testing, and new plans for storage of nuclear and toxic waste in this extensive region.

Poetics

As Julie Sze suggests in her essay, the environmental justice movement is not only a political movement concerned with public policy, but also "a cultural movement interested in issues of ideology and representation." By calling attention to the importance of cultural productions that offer us insider perspectives on the environmental justice struggles so crucial to building political solidarity, the middle section's examination of environmental justice poetics breaks new ground. This section also functions as a conduit between the sections on politics and pedagogy in its exploration of the many expressive arts used to transform toxic landscapes, to voice community experiences of environmental racism, and to imaginatively convey the issues at stake in environmental justice struggles. The section opens with several essays that explain how environmental justice literature radically expands both the mainstream nature-writing canon and environmental justice discourse. T. V. Reed's "Toward an Environmental Justice Ecocriticism" exposes the limitations of mainstream ecocritics' valorization of wilderness-based, white-authored nature writing, and advocates a more inclusive, class- and race-conscious ecocriticism that articulates the complex human relationships to environment expressed in culturally diverse literature, such as poetry by June Jordan and Adrienne Rich. In "From Environmental Justice Literature to the Literature of Environmental Justice," Julie Sze explains how cultural productions, such as Karen Tei Yamashita's novel *Tropic of Orange*, use metaphors and imagery in ways that expand the social-science orientation of much environmental justice discourse and imaginatively reframe issues of environmental racism.

Contributors to this section argue for an expansion of the canon of environmental literature by focusing upon texts that incorporate racial, ethnic, class, and sexual differences, and that emphasize intersections between social oppressions and environmental issues. Mei Mei Evans's "'Nature' and Environmental Justice" argues that hegemonic U.S. conceptions of racial, gender, and sexual identity have excluded women, people of color, and gays and lesbians from natural space. She reads texts that contest dominant cultural assumptions regarding who may enter "nature" in order to experience its transformative effects. The next two essays examine gendered representations of injustice, illness, and activism. Rachel Stein's "Activism as Affirmation: Gender and Environmental Justice in Linda Hogan's *Solar Storms* and Barbara Neely's *Blanche Cleans Up*" focuses upon women's fictional accounts of actual environmental justice struggles. Their portrayals of the hydroelectric project that destroyed Cree and Inuit homelands in Canada and of lead poisoning of African American children in Boston emphasize how these environmental injustices invade families, put children at risk, and radicalize women to take direct political action against the threats to their communities. In "Some Live More Downstream than Others: Cancer, Gender, and Environmental Justice," Jim Tarter writes as both a literary scholar and as a cancer survivor who has lost family members to this disease. Tarter focuses upon cancer as an environmental injustice in which class and gender are significant risk factors, and his reading of Carson's *Silent Spring* and Steingraber's *Living Downstream: An Ecologist Looks at Cancer and the Environment* analyzes their authorial positions as cancer survivors, scientists, and activists. In a very different neocolonial political context, Susan Comfort's "Struggle in Ogoniland: Ken Saro-Wiwa and the Cultural Politics of Environmental Justice" examines the complex authorial positioning of Saro-Wiwa, whose journalism and fiction tirelessly advocated for the Ogoni communities that have been devastated by oil mining, enclosure, and civil war.

A number of the essays in this collection focus on rural struggles over water and land rights affecting communities of color in varied regions of the United States and Canada. Tom Lynch's "Toward a Symbiosis of Ecology and Justice: Water and Land Conflicts in Frank Waters, John Nichols, and Jimmy Santiago Baca" focuses on writers who portray Hispano struggles to maintain the water and land rights to sustain traditional cultures and agricultures in the Sangre de Cristo watershed. Similarly, in "Saving the Salmon, Saving the People: Environmental Justice and Columbia River Tribal Literatures," Janis Johnson focuses on the efforts of Northwest Indian tribes and environmental groups to remove dams on the Snake River in order to restore the salmon runs so crucial to tribal economies, religions, and identities.

The Poetics section concludes with an essay that focuses upon the transformative power inherent in varied forms of activist art produced within those communities affected by environmental injustice. As Giovanna Di Chiro observes in her interview with Baltimore-area artist/activists Cinder Hypki and Bryant "Spoon" Smith, "Sustaining the 'Urban Forest' and Creating

Landscapes of Hope," community-based environmental art projects confront the following fundamental questions: What counts as "green"? Where is the "environment" located? What are we trying to "sustain" and for whom? Di Chiro argues that the artistic images produced by grassroots groups contest the paralyzing stereotypes of inner-city dwellers as, at best, unconcerned and unproductive, and, at worst, menacing and destructive.

Pedagogy

In the final section, four college professors discuss their strategies for teaching undergraduate environmental justice courses in a range of disciplines and institutions. Soenke Zehle writes that environmental justice education must "translate the mantra of ecology (all is connected) into a web of concrete relations that includes not only ecological but cultural, economic, and political processes." The essays in this section share strategies for this process of translation and raise wide-ranging theoretical questions about the ways in which educational institutions are implicated in environmental racism. They describe the value of expanded programs of environmental studies that encompass environmental justice and transnational environmental issues, and they explain approaches for introducing environmental justice materials into a variety of disciplines, such as environmental studies, philosophy, literature, and women's studies, within a range of college settings.

The first two essays articulate overarching approaches and concepts of environmental justice that might be applicable to a variety of programs and curricula. Robert Figueroa, who teaches interdisciplinary philosophy courses on environmental justice at Colgate University, explains in "Teaching for Transformation: Lessons from Environmental Justice" that the study of environmental justice requires students to understand interconnections between theory and practice. He recommends service-learning projects and case studies that expose students to environmental justice as a social movement. In "Notes on Cross-Border Environmental Justice Education," Soenke Zehle discusses key concepts, such as ecological democracy, subaltern environmentalism, colonialism and commodities, eco-internationalism, and media ecology, that serve as the framework for the interdisciplinary, transnational environmental justice courses that he teaches at SUNY-Binghamton. The last two essays explain pedagogical strategies and curricular materials useful for bringing environmental justice curriculum to different student bodies. In "Changing the Nature of Environmental Studies: Teaching Environmental

Justice to 'Mainstream' Students," Steve Chase describes the successful efforts of graduate students to lobby for courses on environmental justice within the Environmental Studies program at Antioch New England, and he discusses his own pedagogical strategies for generating enthusiasm for this subject among predominantly white, middle-class students who may not at first appreciate its relevance. In "Teaching Literature of Environmental Justice in an Advanced Gender Studies Course," Jia-Yi Cheng-Levine describes the course she offered at the University of Houston's racially diverse downtown campus, in which she emphasized the interrelated effects of colonization and multinational capitalism upon women and the environment. Her curriculum blends study of literary texts, such as those discussed in the Poetics section of this collection, with secondary studies of environmental justice theory and movements.

Conclusion

With the exception of the roundtable discussion that follows this introduction, all of the essays included in this volume are previously unpublished. Their interdisciplinary nature is readily apparent from the varying source documentation one finds from essay to essay. Taken as a whole, this collection moves environmental justice studies in new directions, beyond an exclusive focus on documenting environmental racism. Many of the essays explore intersections between race and other aspects of social identity that are pertinent to achieving justice, such as class, gender, family and community relations, sexuality, cultural and ethnic traditions, transnational economics, and geographic location. The studies highlight the complexity and urgency of environmental justice issues and urge us to expand our perspectives as we articulate the full range of social concerns at stake, and work toward truly just solutions.

This volume also expands our understanding of the wide range of environmental issues that impact communities of color and poor communities. Communities are not only struggling to alleviate various sorts of health-threatening toxic exposures, they are also fighting to maintain access to the natural resources that sustain cultural identities and traditional lifeways in the face of transnational corporate development based on attitudes toward the natural world that are often completely at odds with their own. While environmental justice has often been thought to be an urban issue, a number of essays focus upon rural concerns and struggles over land and water rights. Although our text is primarily based in the United States of America, several contributors also widen the focus of environmental justice studies by analyzing the complex threats posed to communities of color around the world by transnational neocolonial forces.

Furthermore, our text includes the arts and teaching as important aspects of environmental justice work. Essays detail the way that writers and artists voice community concerns and visions, articulate the complexities of righting environmental injustices, and invite outsiders to imaginatively enter embattled communities to experience the issues from within. Art is also a tool employed by activists and community members for community building. As Bryant Smith and Cinder Hypki explain in their interview with Giovanna Di Chiro, people must have visions of possibility in order to shape and guide our struggles for justice and imagine alternatives to current tragedies and blight.

In the roundtable discussion that follows this introduction, Devon Peña touches on a theme that we, as editors, see emerging throughout this book: that as a result of grassroots activism and cultural production focused on environmental and economic justice issues, people are moving beyond the simple critique of environmental racism and the awareness of how globalism is destroying the planet and are now actively recovering and promoting the sustainable alternatives to environmental destruction found in diverse ethnic, tribal, and pastoral cultures. He observes that all over the world, place-based activists and community shareholders refuse to despair over the "end of nature"; instead they experiment with locally controlled, self-managed, community-owned, worker-cooperative-type organizations that are almost entirely unrecognized by the general population. Like many of the other activist, academic, literary, pedagogical voices in this volume, Peña urges us to move beyond a politics of negativism and find a pathway to ecological sustainability and social justice. Perhaps Teresa Leal, cochair of the Southwest Network for Environmental and Economic Justice, best expresses the call for all to work for solutions to our environmental and social problems in her interview in this volume when she says that we all must "throw rocks at the sun." Leal explains that environmental justice workers understand the enormity of the challenge; they know that their fight against giant multinational corporations or local developers or industrial plants may be daunting and that their efforts to stem the destruction of the world's cultures and environments sometimes seems an impossible goal. However, according to Leal, we must continue to keep our eyes on the prize and to aim for the sun because "change comes only when a few brave hearts dare to throw the first rock."

We, as editors, hand you this book as a testament to the brave hearts who have dared to throw the first rocks. We invite you to join with the many worldwide who are working for environmental justice. As huge and hopeless as the task may at first appear, each of us has something to contribute. Let us aim our volleys at the sun.

NOTES

1. Chavis is quoted in Giovanna Di Chiro, "Nature as Community: The Convergence of Environment and Social Justice," in *Uncommon Ground: Rethinking the Human Place in Nature,* ed. William Cronon (New York: Norton, 1996), 304.

2. Ibid., 306. All seventeen Principles of Environmental Justice are reprinted in this article.

ENVIRONMENTAL JUSTICE

A Roundtable Discussion with Simon Ortiz, Teresa Leal, Devon Peña, and Terrell Dixon

Joni Adamson and Rachel Stein

To call more attention to the interrelated social, economic, and environmental issues surrounding the environmental justice movement, the leadership of the Association for the Study of Literature and Environment (ASLE) asked Joni Adamson and Rachel Stein, whose own research and course offerings focus upon environmental justice writings, to organize a roundtable session addressing this topic for the Environment and Community conference held in Reno, Nevada, in February of 2000. The panel brought together Simon Ortiz, Teresa Leal, Devon Peña, and Terrell Dixon, who sat down together to discuss their contributions to environmental justice politics, poetics and pedagogy, and the potential for future collaborations between artists, activists, scholars and teachers within the movement.

To briefly introduce panel members, Simon Ortiz is the author of many collections of poems and essays including *Woven Stone, Speaking for the Generations: Native Writers on Writing,* and *After and Before the Lightning.* His work focuses on the issues, concerns, and responsibilities of Native Americans toward their lands, cultures, and communities. He writes about his experiences working in the early 1960s in the uranium processing industry in Grants, New Mexico, and some of the social and environmental impacts of the mine on the Acoma community in *Fight Back: For the Sake of the People, For the Sake of the Land.*

Teresa Leal is cochair of the Southwest Network for Environmental and Economic Justice (SNEEJ) and is a grassroots representative to the National Environmental Council (NEC), which advises the director of the Environmental Protection Agency. Please see Joni Adamson's interview with Teresa Leal in the Politics section of this collection.

Devon Peña is an activist/environmental anthropologist at the University of Washington who works with the Rio Grande Bioregions Project, an independent research and advocacy network of social and environmental scientists, lawyers, traditional Hispano farmers, and sustainable agriculture activists. His works include *The Terror of the Machine: Technology, Work, Gender, and Ecology on the U.S.–Mexico Border,* and *Chicano Culture, Ecology, Politics: Subversive Kin.* Please see Devon Peña's article in the Politics section of this collection.

Terrell Dixon has been chair and director of graduate studies in his department at the University of Houston and is well known to members of ASLE for his tireless service to the organization. He has published a collection of essays on the grizzly bear, contributed numerous essays and reviews on nature writing to such publications as *The CEA Critic* and *The American Nature Writing Newsletter,* and with Scott Slovic, edited *Being in the World: An Environmental Reader for Writers.* He has presented many papers on environmental justice writings and is currently putting together a volume of essays on toxic literature and another on urban nature.

Joni Adamson: We've brought together Simon Ortiz, Teresa Leal, Devon Peña, and Terrell Dixon, and will begin by asking each panelist to speak about his/her own work and its connection to the environmental justice movement.

Simon Ortiz: Good morning. I'm a poet and writer and storyteller and what I write comes from a community and culture of people who are Native American or the indigenous population of this homeland that we call America or the United States of America. I write about the experience of native people. I'm from Acoma, New Mexico, and as you may know, most of my writing has to do with the Acoma people, and other Native American people, and the experiences of their cultures and communities. That means that my poems and stories have to do with the environmental setting of Acoma, and all of the Americas, where indigenous native people live. When I write, I write as an Indian, or native person, concerned with his environmental circumstances and what we have to do to fight for a good kind of life.

Teresa Leal: Buenos días. I am Teresa Leal, from Nogales, Arizona, on the Mexican border. I am cochair of the Southwest Center for Economic and Environmental Justice. We are celebrating our tenth anniversary this year. We are eighty-five grassroots organizations on both sides of the Mexican border. Some of us are from the Black Beret, Brown Beret, indigenous movement, trade unions. We are focused on creating a network that will communicate among all of these small locally focused organizations in order to develop the indicators that we need to be observant of the impact of industrialization in our lands. This is something that at this time is a worldwide movement. We were at the World Trade Organization meeting and we met with other groups worldwide who had the same issues. We need to enhance our capacity to communicate with them in the future, because there aren't that many differences in what is happening to communities, to the natural environment, the landscape, to all of us. We can work on these issues together.

I started working with Cesar Chavez during the sixties. When the sprayers were spraying pesticides on the pickers, close to Tucson, it was easy for us to get the sprayers out of there and close down the fields and get a boycott on what they were producing. Now the economic issues are so dramatic that we cannot afford to shut down jobs for our affiliates or the people that we are trying to defend. So now our challenge is to find new ways to create a just transition movement with jobs and communities involved. A lot of our organizations are traditionalists and we need to use all the tools that are part of globalization, and to use them ourselves. Part of the principal guidelines of our network is to look for funding and knowledge and training for our affiliates so that they can confront these issues, and not just be confrontational, but be able to propose environmentally friendly substitutes, be able to not have to close jobs for our people, but instead creating a new way of development. At the World Trade Organization meetings, I was very pleased to see that we came together from different areas and groups, the enviros, the trade people, all sorts of people. It created a catalyst so that we realized that we all have to work together. We all got gassed, we all got bullets. That was a novelty for a lot of us from both sides of the fence, the environmentalists and the native peoples, it made us realize that we all have to work together, which will enhance the work that we do in the next ten years.

Devon Peña: When I think of myself as a mestizo or Chicano, I think of myself in terms of being rooted for twelve generations in Native America; one of my immediate ancestors was a full-blooded Cherokee woman by the name of Missouri Anne Berryhill. But I also have roots in the culture that came here from Spain; my family first came to the desert Southwest, to the land grant community of Laredo in 1775.

I teach at the University of Washington, in a Ph.D. program in Environmental Anthropology, which is an extraordinary effort to bring together natural and social sciences at the doctoral level. Environmental Anthropology is not just interdisciplinary research, it is collaborative. You have to collaborate with local cultures to produce the knowledge called Environmental Anthropology. My particular area of research is agroecology. I look at farms and ranches as ecosystems, agroecosystems. The farmers that I work with, in the communities of the upper Rio Grande watershed of northern New Mexico and southern Colorado, are all family farms that have been in the same family for back to twelve generations. When people stay on the ground, in place, they are bound to have learned a little bit about living in place. This knowledge that has been accumulated over generations of people living in place, Hispano and Pueblo farmers in the region, has been typically disqualified, treated as being based on superstition, as being primitive, inefficient, backward and so on. The work that I do focuses on bringing together interdisciplinary collaborative research teams to study farms in both bioregional and political ecological contexts. We just completed a five-year study funded by Ford Foundation, National Endowment for the Humanities, and the Colorado Historical Society, of historic acequia farms in northern New Mexico and southern Colorado. Our team included forty-three people, including a hydrologist, a plant ecologist, a geologist, a botanist, an ethnobotanist, an agricultural historian, a historian, three sociologists, a folklorist. . . . We looked at everything on eight historic sites. These are living farms. The oldest one was founded before the Oñate Entrada [the first Spanish explorer's entry], it is part Indian and they have probably been there for a thousand years, but now there is intermarriage between the San Juan Pueblo family and the Chicano family, so that land has been worked for over a thousand years and yet they have a six-foot soil horizon, and no plough pan: the hydrologist on our research staff says that the gravity-driven earthen work irrigation system or acequias that these farms use, actually create soil, rather than destroy soil, especially when it is a multigenerational art form. When you have multigenerational, place-based knowledge you convert your cultural landscapes into veritable mosaics of habitable spaces for humans and for wildlife.

The work I do with the Colorado Acequia Association, is working to establish a community land and water trust. Because these very old historic farms are being blacktopped for condos, second homes, and the amenities industry, eco and cultural tourism. So, the work that I'm currently doing is on land and water trust acquisitions and conservation easements to insure that these historic cultural landscapes are not converted or dried out. Therefore this is as much about ecological democracy as it is about social equity. This is part of what is happening with the environmental justice movement, which is bringing together the struggles for ecological diversity, ecological democracy, and social equity, and seeking to invent new sustainable ways of inhabitation of our planet earth.

Terrell Dixon: Like the other panelists, I'm shaped by my environment. I grew up in a small town in rural, eastern Oklahoma, the capital of the Creek Indian Nation, reading Thoreau. More recently my environment has been Houston, Texas, and much of what I will talk about today stems from my efforts to come to terms environmentally with the city. Houston has a Texas-size sense of itself; we want to be number one. So far, our development efforts have led us to number one status in one dubious category: air pollution. We've surpassed all the California cities, even Los Angeles. Houston is thus a challenging environment in which to teach environmental literature, but it is also a tremendously interesting cultural locale. As Houston has become one of the major in-points for immigration into the United States, classes at the University of Houston have become wonderfully diverse. When I go into a literature and environment class, I want to work with as many traditions of nature as I can.

What I want for my students comes in two parts. One is an awareness of the natural world, and our individual and cultural connections to nature, even in the city, and the second part is some growth into activism. There are several ways to go about this. I focus when I can on urban nature. This is not an oxymoron. It is a solid, interesting field of inquiry about a subject that my students confront every day. This introduction to urban nature is rarely easy, so that one thing I do is to have students write a history of their family's engagement with nature. Since many of my students are first generation Americans and first generation college students, those histories are often very interesting. They cross borders, they chronicle family changes from rural to urban life, and I always ask that they conclude in Houston with attention to our campus and their lives. Many students see connections to the larger cultural history or urbanization embodied in these family histories. Another way, one that fits well with our discussion today, is to work with what I call the literature of toxicity. I believe that over the last three or four decades, the years since *Silent Spring,* a major theme of American life and literature is our growing concern with toxicity and that this concern appears in many of the diverse literatures that make up contemporary American literature.

Toxicity is also a topic that engages my students living in Houston, breathing Houston air. A third way for me has been to work with graduate students in the development of service learning eco-composition classes. Students who choose these classes do the usual reading and write the usual number of essays, but they also agree to do a number of hours of service for various organizations—the Museum of Natural Science, the Sierra Club, etc.—in the city. Such service becomes part of the course work; it figures in their writing assignments, and it is correlated to their reading. At first students love working this way because it promises practical help through real-world experience and vita building, but they also come to love it for the work they do. Once they are in the Houston Arboretum (last year at this time there were forty of us at work clearing a field in the arboretum for planting with native grasses) or writing a draft for a Sierra Club position paper, they begin to change, to become engaged with environmental issues in ways that deepen and extend their classroom awareness.

Joni Adamson: As Devon and Teresa mentioned earlier, one of the key efforts of the Environmental Justice Movement has been to expand mainstream American environmentalist definitions of "the environment." We'd like to ask each of you to speak to the reasons why this work is so important and explain how you and your groups are redefining what we mean when we say "Nature."

Teresa Leal: We view the environment as where we live, work and play but also where we worship, which is something very important that we need to take into account as we go through the designation of projects and permitting issues that keep us very busy in the network. The Southwest Network for Economic and Environmental Justice has a whole campaign that is dedicated to EPA accountability. We are constantly trying to get the EPA to be more accountable to what is happening. We've got another campaign which is the worker justice campaign. Worker justice campaign is where we work. These workers, if they are involved in some risk management in their work area, take it home with them. That also is something we need to make connections with directly. Then, the border justice campaign includes human justice issues that are often seen as something not connected to the environment. And violence, the human rights issues are directly connected to how we fare socially as well as spiritually, so that does affect the environment. The last one of these campaigns is the youth leadership campaign. The youth leadership campaign is a very important part of our organization because it is a way to take care of preparing the future, bringing the youth into what is happening, not packing it up and writing it in nice books and leaving it in some bookcase for them to read in the future, but for them to walk with us, as they mature, and get them to be more efficient as the elders phase out of this. We've got to hand this to different people but the issues go on and on. We continue to have these problems. So that's the way we envision the environment and it's something that I don't think that we have been able to bridge, that concept as [Terrell] was saying about the differentiation that is often done with the environment, as well as with the urban and the people connected with the environment. For example, in the borderlands, we deal with a lot of collective farmers as well as Indian tribes. They are very alienated, often, when there is a conservation program going, because they are often accused of misusing the natural resources. But they need the water, they need the resources to fend and to survive, and yet they are being denied the use of the land and water rights. So those are the issues to really be pushy about getting on the table.

Simon Ortiz: I am glad that Teresa brought up water. Water is a major element of the natural environment, which means that for the native people of the Southwest, water is a necessary element for continuing life. A farming way of life and economic self-sufficiency is the basis of culture and community for the Pueblo Indian people of New Mexico and Arizona in the Colorado Plateau. That means that, for these people, the struggle for water and the preservation and use and maintenance of water is very important. And yet, we know that because of expanding population in the American Southwest, that water is becoming scarce. But water defines our culture, water from the skies, and groundwaters, which are really part of each other. In terms of religion, the gods and the kachinas bring the water, of course they bring it in terms of the weather forces, the climatic conditions that provide that water.

Today, with the capitalist economy as it is, the native communities and cultures are in many cases no longer able to make a sufficient economic livelihood by farming. So, we find that because of the increasing population and water use of the major cities like Phoenix, Tucson, Albuquerque, El Paso, and Denver, our way of life is under threat. I would say that if we are to find a way in which native communities, Indian people and non-Indian communities are to protect the environment, there must be a workable solution to the way that water is to be dealt with. I know that as a topic for my writing, water is a major feature because it is a concern of the culture, indigenous as well as nonindigenous.

Devon Peña: The farmers that I work with have a saying, *"Sin agua, no hay vida. Sin tierra, no hay paz."* [Without water, there is no life. Without land, there is no peace.] That goes to the heart of what Teresa and Simon, quite right, are saying. The question of water and of indigenous access, equitable access to water is one of the most pivotal political ecological struggles of contemporary times. Under the capitalist system we have a very complex set of struggles that are emerging around the commodification and privatization of water. You see, for the Pueblo Indian and the Hispano Mexicano alike, water was not a commodity. It was not the exchange value that was important, it was the communal and spiritual value that was important. So that water was treated not as a private property right, that you could sell and separate from the land. Rather, water was seen as a communal value and an ecological value that sustained a way of life in place. Fortunately, over the last ten–fifteen years or so, indigenous communities, in New Mexico and Colorado especially, less so in Arizona, although I believe it's starting there, too, have organized acequia associations which are these ancient, gravity-driven irrigation networks, that typically, in Colorado and New Mexico have the oldest adjudicated water rights. But these acequia associations are having to spend a considerable amount of effort in defensive positions because of the growing population, not really the growing population itself, as the industrialization and commercialization of water, the growth of the demand for water.

Right now we are facing a situation in the San Luis Valley where one group, Gary Boyce, a multimillionaire, wants to mine the confined aquifer, which is assumed to have about 3 billion acre feet of water, and he wants to pump this out to the tune of about 250 thousand acre feet a year to sell to Reno and Las Vegas and so on. So whatever you do here, as this population in Reno and Las Vegas grows, people are going all the way to Colorado to this high altitude alpine desert, at 8,000 feet above sea level for their potential water supplies. And of course, this is not a sustainable, regenerative type of irrigation, it's the removal of water from the ecosystem to another place, to a totally different place. It's a repeat of the Owens Valley, and we all know what that story is about. So, this is all very interesting and problematic. Capitalism has unleashed this incredible environmental degradation and our body is an environment. So when I talk about environmental degradation, I am talking about degradation of our bodies, as well, because our bodies are in the environment and they are a microecosystem themselves.

But what about the positive side? Is there an upshot to this? What I see happening within the environmental justice movement, partly as a result of the leadership of the network, SNEEJ and other grassroots organizations, is that environmental justice wants to get beyond the critique of environmental racism, it wants to get beyond the critique of how globalism is destroying the planet and destroying the cultures to sustainable alternatives. What are the alternatives? Experiments in locally controlled, self-managed, community-owned, worker-cooperative-type organizations are visible everywhere. There are thousands of worker-owned cooperatives, and community-owned lands, and emerging land trusts for people of color, and water-rights users' groups that support cooperative farming. Thousands of these alternatives that are almost entirely unknown to the general population. We need to find a pathway to ecological sustainability and social justice. My answer to that is that those ways are already there. In thousands of local efforts to create democratic workplaces, to create production processes that aren't based on the destruction of the environment or the worker. And it's in those lessons, those local models that we can learn a lot about the nature of the alternatives. So I urge my colleagues at the table to think about how environmental justice is, in a way, moving away from the literature of toxicity to the literature of sustainability.

Terrell Dixon: One way to illustrate my view is to talk about working with concepts of degraded nature—toxicity—and community. Students come to the classroom with what seems to me a fairly standard issue sense of toxicity. They get the usual sound bites, the iconographic messages about hazardous wastes. There is a familiar kind of a loop where they, like the rest of us, see the news story, read the news story, worry briefly, and forget about it. One classroom task is to break through that loop and I would like to mention one book that does this very well. It's Helen Maria Viramontes' book, *Under the Feet of Jesus,* a powerful, short novel about migrant workers in California, dedicated to Cesar Chavez, and concerned with pesticides and their effect on the workers. By working with this text, students can move to a stronger understanding of what is at stake with toxicity. I emphasize that what we can call the toxicity chain is not only physical, that the way we have degraded our environment, our own bodies and those of other citizens, also creates a web of mistrust where government and corporations come under suspicion. The result is deep divisions along lines of class, ethnicity, and gender. Once they see how all of this stems from how society works, or fails to work with toxicity, students come to recognize how toxicity fractures the potential for community.

Rachel Stein: We intentionally brought together a varied group, a poet, an activist working on the ground, two scholars working in the academy, all working for environmental justice in different ways. We wondered if you could each speak to what you think you have to offer each other. What might poetry, what might working on the ground, what might the academy offer each other in terms of working towards environmental justice?

Devon Peña: All the teaching I do—which historically during and since my years at Colorado College—involves me in some kind of field work. I have been a sort of "roads scholar"; I hit the road. The most valuable thing that teaching in the field has taught me is to respect and seek to legitimize local knowledge, the knowledge of the people who have knowledge of the place you happen to be visiting. Therefore activists from the Southwest Network (SNEEJ) have always lectured and taught in my classes, farmers, environmental activists, environmental scientists involved in litigation, Forest Service personnel, the list is endless, folk healers, curanderas, native ethnobotanists, if you will, these are the folks that have the on-the-ground, place-based knowledge. And so in my own teaching I try to meld together the experience, the local knowledge of activists, people on the ground. Many of them are poets and therefore open up a whole other vision of the world that cannot be seen through scientific discourse alone or by the intellectual community of students and faculty and researchers alone.

But the other thing that we do is that when we ask local people to teach these courses with us, we sit down and together come up with a problem that is facing the community or a need that exists in the community. And then the students and I work with, say, a local rancher or someone on solving that problem.

Simon Ortiz: I know that to make use of our collective knowledge or individual or personal knowledge or put it into community use is what we are looking for to make positive change. I'd like to offer up some names to everyone, to the universities and colleges and organizations that you work with, people who may be helpful. These are native people. For example, from here, there is an elder man in the Nevada and eastern California community,

Corbin Harney. He's a community leader, a religious elder, with long experience in community organizing. He's part of an intellectual and activist movement, on behalf of native people, but he knows and has experience working with nonnative people as well. Another elder is Grace Thorpe. She's Sac and Fox. Originally from Oklahoma, Grace Thorpe is an antinuclear activist. I think her work as an antinuke began because her people, the Sac and Fox people in Kansas, had been considering a nuclear storage facility, which has affected native communities like the Mescalero people, Apaches in New Mexico, and I think presently the Skull Valley community in Utah. Also her daughter, Dagmar Thorpe, is a very articulate woman, an environmentalist spokesperson, and writer. Winona LaDuke is fairly well known as an environmentalist and feminist spokeswoman, a person who is very concerned about the indigenous, Anishinaabeg communities and culture in Minnesota, her homeland. Another person is Manny Peno. Manny is from Acoma Pueblo. Manny teaches in Scottsdale, Arizona, where he lives. Manny is a younger person who is very knowledgeable about environmental concerns. I think that indigenous peoples and their spokespersons, speaking on behalf of their communities, are obviously necessary to the social and environmental justice movement.

Teresa Leal: Yesterday I was impressed by the circle of people who met to dwell on what writers are doing in order to bring more attention to these issues. This is really very necessary. It is very important to bring more popular education styles into your writings. I think that as economic and environmental circumstances and issues become more necessary for people to read about, and again I am taking the populist position for very obvious reasons, it is very hard for common people to read scholarly journals, or to buy expensive magazines, or specialty magazines, but if they can read it in *USA Today,* or some trashy periodical (laughs), if the issue is introduced in a way that is simple, yet highly, highly informative, it often triggers people's concerns and activism. That has been a concern for me, that writing about the natural environment and on contamination and globalism continues to be very, very elitist and inaccessible. I represent grassroots participation in NAC, which is the National Advisory Council for the North American Commission for Environmental Cooperation (CEC), which advises the Administrator of the EPA. I find that it is the same thing there: Spaces are provided on the NAC for citizen participation, for people to have access to this information, and yet the information is kept highly elitist and secretive and the meetings are scheduled in places where common people wouldn't dream of going or can't afford to go or can't afford to buy. So there should be an effort to disseminate this information in ways that can be understood by all people. The World Trade Organization meetings and protests were another illustration of events that could have been enhanced had there been more writers writing about the environmental concerns that were being raised by the protestors there. Instead, the media focused on the violence and the chaos and the bombings and everything. There should be more effort on the part of the media and scholars to write in ways that compel us to come together to solve environmental and social problems; there should be more writing that is accessible to more people on a broader scale. Make the writing simple, so it will make a mark on people. Don't make the writing so sophisticated that it just goes over people's heads.

Terrell Dixon: Very quickly. I would like to take the very interesting things that have emerged here back to the city. Eighty percent of Americans live in cities, and it is in our cities that our diverse nature traditions intersect. However, when we look at cities, we often tend to see the built overlay, that is the highway loops, the skyscrapers, and all the other kinds of construction on top of the landscape. If we are going to have long-term success in legitimizing local knowledge, and community-based partnerships, a first step is to move away from our easy dismissal of cities as merely replicating collections of McDonald's, Starbucks, and suburban sprawl and to recognize instead the different, local nature of individual cities. Cities are potentially our best sites for truly multicultural interaction with the natural world. Acknowledging that will help us move ahead with many of the things we have talked about today.

POLITICS

I

TESTIMONIES

Mei Mei Evans

The voices that follow are of those speaking from "ground zero" of the environmental justice movement; they are the individual and collective voices of those among us whose lives have been directly affected by the disproportionate incidence of contamination or habitat loss or lack of subsistence opportunities in their communities.

Personal testimonies have been the lifeblood of the environmental justice movement, bearing witness as they do to the material effects of policy-making, not on the corporation's or the government's bottom line, but on human lives. These witnessings, in other words, are not abstractions or analyses; rather, they are the chronicle of the consequences of environmental injustice.

Briefly profiled here are the authors of the testimonies that follow. Each represents a local, community-based response to an environmental inequity and speaks to the same human need to bear witness found in essays collected elsewhere in this volume. (See Jim Tarter's "Some Live More Downstream than Others," chapter 11; Joni Adamson's "Throwing Rocks at the Sun," chapter 2; Susan Comfort's "Struggle in Ogoniland," chapter 12; and Giovanna Di Chiro's interview with Cinder Hypki and Bryant "Spoon" Smith, chapter 15.) The concerns expressed in these testimonies reverberate throughout the entire anthology. Interested readers will find explicit connections following these short biographies.

Like the others, Doris Bradshaw and Sterling Gologergen emerged as activists because they dared to question the authority of the U.S. government to control their respective communities' quality of health. In both of their cases, they have rejected the notion that we must quietly accept the death of loved ones from cancer.

As a working class member of a black community in Memphis, Tennessee, Bradshaw responded to the death of her grandmother by asking questions. She uncovered the likely source of her grandmother's cancer as well as the source of other illnesses suffered by friends and family in the community.

That source—the Defense Depot of Memphis—was a major employer of those who inhabited the Memphis area. Now closed and designated a Superfund site, the Defense Depot is completing its cleanup and is being redeveloped by the city. Founder and president of the Defense Depot Memphis, Tennessee—Concerned Citizens' Committee, Bradshaw seeks acknowledgment that the Depot exposed people to toxins for over thirty years. She wants full disclosure of how these toxins have affected the health of the community. Because the polluter is the U.S. military, which avoids accountability by cloaking its activities in issues of "national security," such disclosure is unlikely to be made. Doris Bradshaw is also an at-large board member of the Military Toxics Project, which seeks enforcement of environmental compliance and disclosure at all military installations. (Department of Defense sites comprise 81 percent of federal sites on the Superfund National Priorities List.)[1]

Sterling Gologergen is a Yupik Eskimo born and raised in the village of Savoonga on St. Lawrence Island, Alaska (sixty miles from Siberia). Like Doris Bradshaw, Gologergen is a mother and grandmother who, along with other islanders, suspects the former Cold War military installation at Northeast Cape on St. Lawrence as the likely cause of the increasing incidence of cancer among villagers there. Gologergen has worked for the Alaska Community Action for Toxics (ACAT) to build public support for the Persistent Organic Pesticides (POPs) Elimination Treaty and now coordinates ACAT's environmental justice project designed to benefit the people of Savoonga. Her text is compiled from different testimonies presented at various POPs Elimination Treaty meetings held worldwide.

Edgar Mouton, President of Mossville Environmental Action Now was born and raised in Mossville, Louisiana. The father of eight children and grandfather of thirteen, he was a carpet layer for ten years before going to work for the Olin Corporation as an operator, retiring from there after twenty-five years. Mouton feels strongly that corporations must be accountable not only to their employees, but to those who live around their manufacturing plants. A deacon of the Mount Zion Baptist Church, Mouton wants to make the environment cleaner and safer—not just in Mossville, but everywhere it's contaminated. In his quest of this goal, he has traveled as far as Geneva, Switzerland, and Johannesburg, South Africa. His testimony is taken from remarks he made in Anchorage, Alaska, in the fall of 2000.

Alberto Saldamando is general counsel for the International Indian Treaty Council (IITC). The IITC was founded in 1974 at a gathering by the American

Indian Movement in Standing Rock, South Dakota, which was attended by more than five thousand representatives of ninety-eight indigenous nations. Its mission, as established by its founders, is to work for the sovereignty and self-determination of indigenous peoples; it seeks, overall, to establish and promote the collective rights of indigenous peoples as peoples within the international community and within the province of international law. Saldamando is in charge of IITC's human rights work; he is responsible for providing training and technical assistance in both Spanish and English to IITC's staff as well as to grassroots indigenous communities on international humanitarian law and human rights law. He also works as a trainer and mentor in IITC's Urban Youth Mentorship Program. His testimony was written for publication in this collection.

Paul Smith is an organic farmer from the Oneida Nation in Wisconsin who has worked for the Heifer Project. His testimony provides biographical background explaining how he came to be an environmental justice activist. Like Mouton's, his testimony was delivered at an environmental justice workshop held in Anchorage, Alaska, on September 18, 2000.

These testimonies intertwine with many of the essays collected in this anthology. For example, Doris Bradshaw is the subject of Andrea Simpson's "Who Hears Their Cry? African American Women and the Fight for Environmental Justice in Memphis, Tennessee" (chapter 4). Readers will find Bradshaw's and Mouton's concerns echoed, as well, in the discussion of Barbara Neely's *Blanche Cleans Up* by Rachel Stein (chapter 10). Nelta Edwards's "Radiation, Tobacco, and Illness in Point Hope, Alaska" (chapter 5) and Valerie Kuletz's discussion of nuclear colonialism in the Pacific (chapter 6) amplify Sterling Gologergen's and Alberto Saldamando's words. Additionally, in her discussion of Linda Hogan's *Solar Storms*, Rachel Stein examines the ways in which environmental justice issues radicalize native women (chapter 10).

Several of the book's essays speak to the concerns on behalf of indigenous pastoralists, raised by Paul Smith and Alberto Saldamando—subjects investigated by Devon Peña in his "Endangered Landscapes and Disappearing Peoples?" (chapter 3) and by Tom Lynch in "Toward a Symbiosis of Ecology and Justice" (chapter 13). Janis Johnson examines issues of subsistence salmon fishing in "Saving the Salmon, Saving the People" (chapter 14).

May the voices of Doris Bradshaw, Sterling Gologergen, Edgar Mouton, Alberto Saldamando, and Paul Smith—like the voices of their many counterparts worldwide—awaken us to the need for environmental justice for all peoples.

Statement from Doris Bradshaw, President of Defense Depot Memphis, Tennessee Concerned Citizens' Committee

My grandmother, Mrs. Susie Hall, died from urinary tract cancer on June 25, 1995. During her illness and after her death, I was extremely distraught. I believed her illness, and subsequent death, was strange and untimely. My grandmother grew all of her own vegetables and neither smoked nor drank. How did she contract cancer? Somewhere along the way I read that these kinds of cancers are environmentally induced. At first I wasn't sure what that phrase meant, since to my knowledge, my grandmother had not been in any unhealthy environments, but that phrase—"environmentally induced"—was in the back of my mind.

Around the time of my grandmother's death, I received a notice from Memphis Light, Gas, and Water notifying residents that certain water wells in our area would be shut down for a while. I wondered why. I began calling the company, but received no response to my questions. I then received a notice from the Memphis Defense Depot announcing that it would be closing and cleaning up certain materials. If we wanted to know more, we had to attend a meeting. I suspected that the shutting down of the wells and the cleanup at the Defense Depot was somehow connected to my grandmother's death. I began to call the Depot, somewhat frantically, to get information on the cleanup. I was not angry or confrontational—I just wanted more information. The response told me all I needed to know. They refused to return any of my phone calls or to talk to me about the impending cleanup.

After a meeting at our neighborhood elementary school about the pollutants that were buried at the Depot, the community was encouraged to organize by state representative Lois DeBerry. I could not let the death of my grandmother go. It inspired me to become a community activist and form the Defense Depot Memphis, Tennessee Concerned Citizens' Committee (DDMT-CCC). In the past, I had always taken a back seat—I never wanted to be up front. Armed with nothing but a high school diploma, I began to educate myself about Superfund sites, chemical pollutants, and brownfields. The Coalition of Black Trade Unionists sent me to a training seminar on handling hazardous materials. I began to travel to workshops and to meet other activists as I received funding from various sources. Through these learning experiences, I came to understand that my grandmother's efforts to feed us healthy foods resulted in her death, and may have affected other members of the family. She was growing her vegetables in tainted soil. I learned that people of color were subjected to poisonous environments all over the country. At one meeting in the Southwest, after learning about the struggle of Native American and Mexican American people, I sat in my hotel room and cried all night. It feels like it's being done on purpose.

In my community, which has middle-class blacks, the educational leaders in our community, people have been dying too young. We have the highest high school dropout rate in the city and unusual levels of ovarian and uterine cancer. After a normal rain, the water flows off Depot property into the many culverts and ditches surrounding the Depot. Then, as the hot sun evaporates the water left standing in the ditches, small particles of lead are left. When the wind blows, the lead is blown into the air. We are breathing in this poison. The community understands that something is wrong, yet officials treat us as if we are ignorant and crazy. They think that we don't notice or don't realize what is happening to us and to our children.

The Memphis Defense Depot refuses to acknowledge that there was off-site dumping in the early 1960s, after which middle-class suburban developments were constructed that housed teachers, principals, and ministers. They have killed some of our most prestigious black people. Yet officials of the Environmental Protection Agency (EPA) and the Agency for Toxic Substances and Disease Registry claim that people in our community have not been exposed to toxic levels of chemicals.

In the past several months during the cleanup of the Depot, there have been several incidents where workers have had severe physical reactions to the removal of substances such as mustard bombs. This has been hidden from the community, and we still do not have the complete story on what happened to these workers and where and how they were treated. The Memphis Depot and all of the officials associated with it feel that they do not have to respect this community. They do not have to give us information because they are in charge. They are in charge of the Depot and they are in charge of our lives because we are African Americans. This is about much more than environmental justice. This is about the struggle for power against institutions that are racist. Government officials may not want to tell us the truth, but I have the kind of faith that is the motto of the DDMT-CCC: "And ye shall know the truth, and the truth shall make you free" (John 8:32).

Statement from Sterling Gologergen, Indigenous Environmental Network/Alaska Community Action on Toxics POPs (Persistent Organic Pesticides) Organizer

Greetings from Alaska. My name is Sterling Gologergen. My Siberian Yupik Eskimo name is Ayalngawen. I am from Savoonga, Alaska, which is located on St. Lawrence Island. We live closer to the Soviet Far East than to the United States. Many of us have relatives over on the Soviet side.

My people depend on the land and the sea for their survival. We hunt for whales, walrus, seals, birds, and also eat various types of fish, seaweed, reindeer, polar bear, edible plants, roots, and greens. We teach our children through "hands on" subsistence activities, things that are not taught in classrooms. We pass on our traditional knowledge by interacting with our children. It is extremely important to keep and maintain our way of life in order for us to have healthy communities. Respect for others, being a contributing member of society, sharing, as well as our language and history are passed on in this way. Statistics show that a community strong in its cultural traditional way of life has significantly fewer social problems such as drug/alcohol abuse, domestic violence, suicide, and dependence on the welfare system. Young people who are engaged in healthy activities and treated as valued members of their family and community grow up with self-esteem and self-confidence.

I work for the Indigenous Environmental Network and the Alaska Community Action on Toxics as the POPs organizer. Together we must take a strong, unified stand in getting an international treaty passed with the ultimate goal of eliminating POPs worldwide. I cannot stress enough the importance of a clean environment to indigenous peoples everywhere.

Because many of our cultural traditions, values, and subsistence activities have been passed down from generation to generation, much of our lifestyle remains intact today, despite the great changes brought about by the western world. In the early 1900s, there was a great loss of lives on St. Lawrence Island. The commercial whalers, fur traders, and missionaries brought with them many fatal diseases, such as tuberculosis and influenza. They traded alcohol for ivory, baleen, and furs. The island men stayed drunk all spring when they should have been hunting and storing up food for the winter. All in all, disease and mass starvation wiped out eight of the ten villages on the island. Of the original ten thousand, we now number fifteen hundred Siberian Yupiks. It would not take much to wipe us out as a people.

As indigenous people, we are environmentally vulnerable. It is now well known that the arctic is a sinkhole for many of the world's pollutants. Because of our way of life and geographic location, we are especially exposed to persistent organic contaminants that accumulate in the food chain.

My two sons are being taught by their elders and uncles how to hunt to provide for the community. My older son is a whaling striker for my father. But today, my family and community is in grave danger of losing not only our traditions, but our lives. At this very moment, people related to me, those whom I have known from birth, are dying of cancer. In my lifetime, there has been a significant increase of cancer on St. Lawrence. We attribute many of the cancer deaths to exposure to toxics from a former military site that remains on our island. The Northeast Cape cold war installation was constructed by the U.S. Army in the early 1950s. This year, my dear uncle John Kulowiyi, who worked for the military there and who conducted subsistence activities at the site, died of cancer. The U.S. government says that cancer in Alaskan Natives is attributable to cigarette smoking, but like many of my other relatives and neighbors who've died of cancer, my uncle never smoked.

We need nationwide support in cleaning up these old military installations wherever they are located. Our traditional and cultural lifeways cannot survive without the elimination of POPs worldwide. The effects of POPs to the male reproductive system and the human immune system are indeed terrifying to contemplate. We must unite to say, "No more!" It is our right to live our lives in a clean environment and to continue our inherently sacred way of life.

I myself spent several years of my childhood at Northeast Cape when my father worked there as a civilian employee. I breast-fed all three of my children; my daughter breast-fed her son. Sometimes I cannot help but wonder if my own family will continue to survive since POPs' effects are passed on to children through breast milk.

Before her own death of cancer last year, my aunt Annie Alowa said, "I will fight until I melt." Please help us work to put an end to the contamination of our Mother Earth so that people everywhere can live healthy lives.

Statement from Edgar Mouton, President, Mossville Environmental Action Now

Mossville, Louisiana, is west of New Orleans and east of the Texas line. Our community numbers about fifteen hundred adults and children. Where I live, there are twenty-two chemical plants in a half-moon-shaped area: Louisiana

Pigment, CITGO, Firestone, PBG, Conoco, W.R. Grace, and so on. There are more chemical plants around New Orleans and Baton Rouge. To give you some idea of how much pollution is put out, Louisiana Pigment alone puts out 3,122,000 pounds every day. We have been fighting to get them to lower their emissions.

We also have a dioxin problem, and we have the third-highest cancer rate in the nation. One of my dear friends, only thirty-five years old, died of cancer only four days ago. Some of my grandchildren have learning disabilities and breathing problems. We have asthma and endometriosis, diabetes, heart disease, blood clots. You name it; we have it. I'm here to share my experience with all of you because the same contamination that affects Mossville is headed your way. If we don't unite as one, we're all in big trouble. The toxins may take a while to reach you, but they fall on me every day.

We're having our children tested now because of the dioxin. We have one of the highest rates of dioxin in the United States—three times the national level. The government doesn't want us to know the extent of the problem, the risks that these chemicals pose; they disqualified the results of a study conducted on our children by Dr. Peter Orris of Chicago.

I myself retired from one of these chemical plants. I worked in one for twenty-five years. I made fertilizer, acid, ammonia, TDI and TDA. I manufactured these things for ten years before the company let us know the effects of working with these chemicals on men's and women's reproductive systems. They always told us that pollution stopped at their fence-line, but of course airborne pollutants don't stop at anybody's fence.

We have what we call a "bucket brigade." We use five-gallon plastic buckets with Teflon liners and vent pipes going in and out. Whenever anyone in the community smells something that doesn't agree with them, they call one of us to come and test the air with a handheld vacuum attached to the bucket. Then we get the contents tested. The evidence speaks for itself. If the company doesn't report the emission to the EPA, we report them, and they get fined. That's one tool we've created that helps us defend ourselves.

Now we are having our children tested. We believe that our children's learning disabilities are directly connected to the dioxins present in Mossville. The school officials want to keep our children on drugs to quiet them down. That ought to tell them something is wrong. Dr. Peter Orris discussed this in his report, but the federal government discredits his findings.

Our civil rights have been, and continue to be, disregarded by the government. We must all come together in protest of the contamination in our communities. We must put pressure on our government. I made my living in industrial chemical manufacturing and I know for a fact that the products that they make today could be produced in a much cleaner manner, but, because it's expensive, the corporations don't want to spend the money. As voters, we should put pressure on our state and local representatives. They work for us. We should be very careful who we select to represent our communities.

In Mossville, when those plants were first built, the land was rich and productive. Now, we can't raise cows or chickens; we can't plant gardens. Our soil, water, and air are all polluted. I was raised up on seafood, but now there are signs posted around the estuary cautioning us to eat no more than one fish a month.

Your part of the world may not yet be as bad as mine, but these pollutants travel all around the world, especially northward. They affect all of us, no matter where on earth we live.

Statement from Alberto Saldamando, General Counsel, International Indian Treaty Council

In spite of the first two World Conferences to Combat Racism, which stated that indigenous peoples have a right to their lands and that their natural resources must be protected, indigenous peoples continue to lose their lands at an alarming rate, seemingly a continuation of the "conquest" of the Americas.

Reuters has reported on a recent contact with the Naua tribe in Brazil, thought to be extinct, who emerged from the Amazon to protest the creation of a national park on their lands. The reaction of Brazilian authorities, as quoted by Reuters, was that the Naua had been found in a national preserve and they would have to be moved: "No humans are allowed in the park, just the forest and the animals."

Ever since Pope Alexander VI's 1493 Papal Bull, the "Inter Caetera," calling for the subjugation of the Americas' "barbarous nations" and their lands, first colonial and then successor states have forcibly and violently destroyed indigenous peoples. To this day, the racial discrimination and cultural denigration established by Pope Alexander VI are engraved in the mentality of mainstream Americans and continue to perpetuate the rationale for racial discrimination against indigenous peoples. The old religious imperatives of conversion and annihilation have been replaced by assimilation and "development" as the most desirable outcome for indigenous peoples. The state, economic elites, and transnational corporations have replaced the Spanish and Portuguese kings and colonists as the beneficiaries of indigenous lands and resources.

We believe, as many United Nations experts have reflected, that the loss of lands and resources is the machine that drives racial discrimination against indigenous peoples. This is also the conclusion of the Committee on the Elimination of Racial Discrimination's (CERD) General Recommendation 23, which describes the loss of indigenous lands and resources as a violation of the Convention for the Elimination of All Forms of Racial Discrimination. Gross and massive, pervasive and persistent violations of human rights and fundamental freedoms, including genocide, ethnocide, forced removal, and forced assimilation are somehow justified by the devaluation of indigenous peoples, their cultures and worldviews. Indigenous peoples have been described as "stone age" by anthropologists and accused of being pagans and practitioners of black magic and witchcraft by dominant religions. Our destruction is perceived as necessary to "progress" by most dominant societies in the Americas.

Among many states, there are policies that have the effect, if not the intent, of forcible assimilation of indigenous peoples. Indigenous peoples continue to suffer forcible and violent mass relocations, as well as denials of our fundamental right to our land and the destruction of our environments. Forced relocation is also caused by the economic need to migrate to urban areas due to loss of lands and territories and loss of our means of subsistence. Once urbanized, indigenous peoples join the great mass of undereducated and unemployed who try to survive without the support of family, community, and culture.

Yet, indigenous peoples seek only to be who we are, to remain on our own lands, and to practice and live our traditional cultures, languages, and religions. These are human rights and fundamental freedoms guaranteed by the United Nations International Bill of Human Rights.

Our very presence is denied, as though we have already been assimilated. Data on the numbers of indigenous peoples is skewed, as some states deny even the existence of indigenous peoples within their borders. The official census of states throughout the Americas grossly undercount, if not ignore, indigenous populations.

In the United States, for example, according to the recent 1999 census, the state of Oklahoma's Native American population rose from 258,000 in 1990 to 263,000 in 1999, a reported net gain of 5,000 people. Yet in that same period of time the Oklahoma State Health Department recorded 56,000 indigenous live births. Even subtracting the 11,000 indigenous deaths recorded by the state for that period there remain 45,000 born in Oklahoma during the decade, 39,000 of whom were not recorded in the census. If the United States with its vast resources so grossly undercounts Indians, the situation can only be far worse in the developing countries of the Americas.

Grossly erroneous numbers such as these have the effect of denying or impairing a great many social, economic, political, and cultural rights. They obscure the great need of indigenous peoples for medical and other culturally relevant state services called for by existing international standards as well as international organizations such as the World Health Organization.

Unreliable data, furthermore, paints a picture of great tracts of underutilized indigenous lands and territories, justifying continued theft, colonization, and settlement by great masses of other nonindigenous poor. Data such as these justify nonindigenous, transnational "development" of indigenous lands and facilitate the destruction of indigenous environments.

Pretending that indigenous peoples no longer exist minimizes the need for protection of indigenous cultures and religions and denies the great need in American states for bilingual and historically accurate education. Inaccurate census data accounts for subtle and deadly racial discrimination by the state against indigenous peoples.

It is no secret that social discrimination against indigenous peoples is deep, pervasive, and rampant in all American societies. In many dominant cultures, to be called an Indian is the grossest form of insult. Popular media throughout the Americas portrays indigenous people as ignorant and so backward as to appear mentally retarded. Even our traditional dress is derided. The professional baseball team, the Cleveland Indians, have as their logo a caricature of a buck-toothed Indian wearing a feather. Even to admit this harsh, pervasive, and racist reality is particularly painful for our people.

These socially ingrained attitudes of racial superiority and inferiority, these historical colonialist attitudes are now burned into the very synapses of America's dominant cultures. The continuing denigration of our cultures and traditions with the tacit complicity, if not the approval, of the state, serves only to damage and destroy our identity, our children, our lands and our future.

All of these factors, from loss of land and culture to deforestation, loss of habitat, and the failure of states to collect reliable data, as well as pervasive discrimination against indigenous peoples, were cited by the World Health Organization as causal factors of the lamentable state of the health of the world's indigenous peoples.

The Convention on the Elimination of All Forms of Racial Discrimination prohibits any distinction based on race that has the purpose or effect of nullifying or impairing the enjoyment "of human rights and fundamental freedoms in the political, economic, social, cultural, or any other field of human rights." Racism not only affects individual rights, such as the right to health, it also profoundly affects indigenous peoples' collective rights, including the right to peace.

From the Gwich'in caribou birthing grounds in Arctic Alaska to Mapuche traditional territories in Antarctic Chile, indigenous lands are subject to pressures today that are comparable only to the historical pressures brought to bear on them by the so-called conquest. Like the Mapuche in Chile, indigenous peoples of Colombia, the Katio Embera, are being displaced from their traditional lands as their rivers are dammed. This brief statement cannot adequately describe the militarization and terror in which indigenous peoples live throughout the continent, particularly in Mexico, Colombia, and now, again, in Guatemala.

There is a reason why the Declarations and Programmes of Action of the first two World Conferences to Combat Racism call upon the member states of the United Nations to respect indigenous lands and cultures as a matter of racial equality. These World Conferences as well as the CERD recognized that land is essential to the survival of indigenous peoples and that a denial of their rights to land is racial discrimination. That land is central to the spiritual and physical well-being of indigenous peoples is now undisputed even in the western understanding of these words. The CERD again came to this understanding when it found that Australian legislation facilitating loss of indigenous aboriginal title violated the CERD Convention.

Existing international standards and emergent norms on the rights of indigenous peoples describe the collective rights of *peoples*. The right to own, keep, and control our lands and natural resources; the right to practice our own cultures, language and religion; the right to our means of subsistence; the right to participate freely in the establishment of our own political relationships, are rights described in the International Bill of Human Rights as the collective rights of peoples.

Yet, with the advent of the Third World Conference to Combat Racism, scheduled for Durban, South Africa, in September of 2001, the member states of the United Nations even now refuse to recognize these collective rights of peoples as the rights of indigenous peoples. Their understanding of international human rights and fundamental freedoms reflected in the first two world conferences appears to have been tempered by historical greed and the liberalization of trade. The now hard refusal of a few powerful states to fully recognize the rights of indigenous peoples serves to underpin, if not justify, the deplorable state of human rights of indigenous peoples.

Some states, including the United States, justify their refusal by telling us that, although they have no problem in recognizing that indigenous peoples are peoples within the full meaning of the term under international law, they are concerned about the disintegration of other states that such recognition might precipitate. The truth is that it was not the recognition of human rights that led to Cambodia, Rwanda, to Bosnia and Ex-Yugoslavia, or Chechnya. It was the *denial* of human rights that precipitated these tragedies.

The positions of these states may change but, many times, the results remain the same. Every Indian that dies in defense of the rain forest dies in defense of every human being's right to breathe. It is not just that historical justice demands the recognition of the rights of indigenous peoples. The survival of our sacred Mother Earth, of our water and our air, depends on it. Until states examine in good faith the basis of their racism and its results, including their visions of so-called "development," indigenous peoples and sacred Mother Earth will be pushed toward the brink of annihilation.

Although Hopi prophecy tells us that we have gone too far and passed the point of no return with regard to the damage inflicted upon Mother Earth itself, this prophecy also tells us that there is still time at least to ameliorate the resultant human suffering. Indigenous peoples continue our struggle for recognition of our rights in the hope that it is not too late to at least accomplish this much. We would urge all who share this hope, including the member states of the United Nations, as well as their citizens, to join us in this struggle.

Statement from Paul Smith, Oneida Nation, Wisconsin

(Address opened with a welcome in his own language.)

Greetings. My traditional name means that I have feet on my shoulders. I belong to the People of the Standing Stone, the Oneida, a part of the Iroquois Confederacy, Six Nations, or Longhouse People.

I'd like to share a little bit about who I am and the ways in which I was raised. I'm not an environmental educator or activist but someone who is a member of a community. This is really the first time that I have spoken out about who we are and our place in the Great Lakes region.

As a young man, one of the primary staples of our diet was fish. Seasonal fishing carried us through the winter. We can no longer safely eat the fish.

Not only can we not eat as little as one a week, or one a month, but the tributaries within our region are so polluted that we can eat no fish at all. As a farmer, I am today entrusted with the preservation of twenty-three Iroquoian varieties of bean alone, as well as many species of squash and many forms of our indigenous corn. I've worked with these foods for most of my life.

As subsistence people, it was important for us to regard other forms of life as relatives, to live with them as relatives. Part of my job is the responsibility of a warrior to respect and maintain what the women of our matriarchy have determined is necessary to the preservation of our life and culture. It is the women who decide what is important to put in place for the future. The women decide what is necessary. We don't look just to this generation or even the next. They call us the Seventh Generation thinkers and planners, so when the women look forward, they can call me in at any time to ensure the implementation of their vision for the future. I've been asked to put in place traditional food systems to help preserve those things in our world to the best of my ability.

We have fourteen major paper mills in the community that I come from: Proctor and Gamble, Kimberly-Clark, Fort James, Fort Howard, and so on. The effluents from the paper mills, along with municipal sewage sludge, are converted into fertilizer. These fertilizers are then sent back into our rural communities and onto our agricultural land. Many of the minerals they contain are beneficial nutrients for the soil, but they also contain heavy metals, lead, arsenic, and dioxins. These persistent organic pollutants bioaccumulate; they leach into our aquifers. In my community now, all the wells are capped. We can't drink the water. Unfortunately, those things also run off and affect our ability to fish and to live the way that we used to.

Along with that, we also have many of the petrochemical by-products, such as herbicides, insecticides, fungicides, and other pesticides, that are applied to our lands and are creating many problems in our part of the world. What's going on right now in our community is that minimally 50 percent of our people will be diabetic, and there are estimates that 80 percent or more of us will be diabetic by the time we're eighty. We have increased rates of cancer. Over 30 percent of our children in the school system right now are on some type of drug to control neurological disorders: attention deficit disorder, hyperactivity. We haven't got the data yet on the dropping levels of IQ in our community. A lot of those types of health issues have been very, very recent and are becoming a major concern.

The reason why I'm here is to talk about the source of the contamination, the pesticides and the fertilizers and the paper mills, and the impact of these things. But most importantly, what I want to stress is that everyone, world-wide, eventually will be affected by all this contamination, whether they are right now or not. We have to consider our relationship to all of the earth's systems.

Most of us think of the earth as our mother; we talk to the waters, to the big plant world and the little plant world, the four-leggeds. There are proper ways for us to treat them, to acknowledge them, to work with them so that all of us may coexist. I was raised with the understanding that I had to be very conscious of these life forces and I see in recent times that people are concerned about their health and nutrition, so I became organically cer-tified as a farmer. Now the issue in our community is that of dioxins from the chlorine-based paper processes. But there are alternative processes. The dioxins get into the food chain and even now, our organic dairy products, our milk, butter, and cheese, carry dioxins because it is transported through the fatty tissues of the cows.

I look around our community at the poorer people who receive public as-sistance. They receive a lot of milk, butter, and cheese from the federal government to supplement their diets. We have a ten-year moratorium in our community on environmental issues because the paper mills decided to ne-gotiate the cleanup of tributaries by going outside of the EPA. Industry must be made to be accountable. It's my hope that somehow the citizens of the world can appeal to governments and industry to please reconsider their use of these pollutants, and to eliminate entirely those that are the most toxic.

NOTE

1. Retrieved 25 June 2001 from Military Toxics Project (www.miltoxproj .org).

2

THROWING ROCKS AT THE SUN

An Interview with Teresa Leal

Joni Adamson

Teresa Leal began her activist work as a high school student in the 1960s, working in the cotton fields surrounding Tucson and Sahuarita, Arizona, with Cesar Chavez and other members of the United Farm Workers Union (UFWU). She went on to organize Comadres, a binational group of women that addresses social, environmental, labor, and toxicity issues related to the build-up on the U.S.–Mexico border of the *maquilas,* notorious for exploiting their workers and polluting their surrounding environments. Leal is currently cochair of the Southwest Network for Environmental and Economic Justice (SNEEJ), a group of eighty-five grassroots indigenous and labor groups. She is also working to organize an alliance of groups to protect the Santa Cruz River, which flows from Mexico past Nogales, Arizona, and toward Tucson, Arizona.

One week before my interview of Teresa, she was my guide for a tour of the industrial parks south of Nogales, Sonora, where workers employed in the multinationally owned maquilas make luggage, electronic and industrial parts, locks, and other products. She then took me through the dusty, crowded squatter villages, or *colonias,* teeming with children playing in the streets. Here, maquila workers live in houses made of cardboard, wooden pallets, or cinder blocks. These houses lack basic public services and the people must have their water delivered from urban Nogales wells which Teresa reports have been contaminated by industry with high levels of arsenic and heavy metals. Everywhere in the colonias, we saw women standing outside their houses washing their dishes and clothes in barrels filled with this contaminated water.

We then drove twenty minutes south, to the mountains overlooking Nogales, where we ate a lunch of bagels, apples, and bottled water in a sun-dappled grove of scrub oak and wild walnut trees. There, Teresa talked of her life and work. Pointing in the direction of a spring bubbling up from the ground, she directed my vision along the steep canyon through which the water flows before it joins the Mambutu River. Her Opata and Mayo grandparents, she explained, were descendants of the tribal peoples who had lived in these canyons long before Spanish conquest. They brought her to this spring as a child, told her the stories of her ancestors' migrations through these mountains, and taught her to love and respect her traditional homeland. She, in turn, brought her own small children to the same spring for picnics in order to instill in them a love for their birthplace.

When I asked how a mother of eight found time to battle for the environment on so many fronts, she told me she is descended from a long line of "reactionaries." Her Chinese grandfather was a member of a group who called themselves "Righteous and Harmonious Fists" and who attempted to oust foreigners from Chinese soil in 1900. The so-called "Boxer Rebellion" was put down by American and European forces and Leal's grandfather was forced to flee to Mexico, where he helped to build the railroad. Leal's father, a trained engineer who helped build Mexico's first desalinization plant but who quit his job to become a revolutionary after being inspired by Leon Trotsky in the 1940s, taught her that we must learn to live with our environment without depleting our resources. Imprisoned during certain times of his life for his work to organize laborers in the mines of Cananea, Mexico, and peasant farmers agitating for land reforms, Leal's father occasionally stole away from his work to visit his young daughter who was living with her mother just north of the international border in the United States. Leal, who had surprised her mother and the local Catholic priest by learning to read at three years old and speak English by the age of five, lovingly remembers her father's visits to her schools and never forgot the example of principled struggle he set.

Any conversation with Terèsa Leal is engaging, informative, and full of good humor. Our picnic in the mountains above Nogales lasted an enjoyable two hours. However, every fifteen minutes or so, one or more large semitrailers filled with domestic refuse from the city and industrial waste from the maquilas rumbled up the road on which we had come, drowning our talk and filling the air with dust. Though the view towards Nogales was a breathtaking vista of forested mountains and lush canyons, we had only to turn around to be confronted by the "sanitary landfill." On the ground behind us, bits of refuse—toilet paper and food wrappers and aluminum cans—were scattered through the brush and clinging to the wildflowers. Teresa told me that chemicals dumped by the maquilas at the landfill seep into the water of her beloved spring, then flow into the Mambutu River. From there, the

Mambutu winds five kilometers south before being pumped into a system that sends the water north to be recharged into the Nogales water system. Thus, Teresa is concerned about the spring not only because it is associated with ancestral traditions and happy family memories, but also because the water and the chemicals in it are being sent back to Nogales where they are consumed by residents. Teresa regularly sends samples from the spring to a lab so that the chemicals dumped by the maquilas and seeping from the landfill into the spring water can be identified and measured.

With all these things in mind, I went to Teresa's home, located just a few blocks north of the international border in Nogales, Arizona, on July 17, 2000. The following transcript is a condensed version of our six-hour conversation, which concentrated on Teresa's lifelong work as an activist.

Joni Adamson: Can you describe your early experience working with Cesar Chavez and the UFWU and speak to how it informs your activist work today?

Teresa Leal: Back then, we didn't call what we were doing "environmental activism." We just called it "survival." I remember when I started working with the UFWU in the cotton fields in what is now Sahuarita, Arizona. The issues of course were very much tied to chemicals, the planes that would spray the people that were bent over picking the cotton with pesticides. It was both a human rights issue and a toxicology issue. Yet, we did not call it an environmental movement; it was just the *"movmeniento de la raza."*

I would get out of high school and I would go into the fields to distribute flyers to the workers. I would question the pilots of the little sprayer planes to see when they would be spraying and often they would share their schedules and that is the information I would put on the flyers. So that was a way to form a straight line between the spraying schedules and the people because we could not get the bosses to tell the people when they were going to spray. They would never commit to giving us forewarning about when they were going to spray. So we were all constantly on the go.

We also tried to get the workers to speak up for themselves. We would tell them, "Go and ask the boss, ask the supervisor, will you spray in the early morning or in the late afternoon?" We encouraged the workers to protect themselves. But for economic reasons, the workers needed to keep on picking as much cotton as time would allow. They were afraid of being fired. By staying in the fields and quote "protecting" themselves with handkerchiefs and some cover, they believed they could continue picking while the spraying was going on. They didn't understand how dangerous it was. Because they would go home contaminated with chemicals, the barracks where they lived with their families, with their children, were also contaminated. It was a human rights issue, definitely.

However, people who are barely surviving rarely have the luxury of haggling over terms. They can't afford to call it "just" an environmental movement or "just" a social movement, just green stuff, just brown stuff. We call it "survival at its finest." In retrospect, I know that this was a very environmentally based operation. But our movement was interconnected with human rights, labor rights, gender rights, and environmental rights and this reality—of interconnectedness—still guides our actions and campaigns today.

Joni Adamson: What were the events that led you to become active in the fight to improve living and working conditions for maquila workers and organize Comrades, a grass-roots organization of women struggling to empower women and children in the barrios of Nogales?

Teresa Leal: At first, when I was still a young mother, people started coming to me to ask me questions because I was educated and could speak English. They would ask, "Do you know what chemical this is that I am working with at the factory? The label is written in English." They wanted me to translate. My desire to help grew into an idea we call, "Comadres." *Comadres* actually means "co-mothers." As Latina women we've always been told that women are "smaller and weaker than men." Also, in our culture, comadres are put down by the machos; they are considered *mitoteras*. Mitoteras comes from *mitote*, which means "gossip." Mitoteras are gossipy. But we are changing the meaning of "gossip" from negative gossip to positive gossip. We put out the good mitote, or good gossip. We get out the news about what's going on in the villages, or colonias, and in the factories. We share information.

Some comadres are individuals helping individuals. But other comadres are community-based comadres. They're the comadres that help not only individuals, but also share the results of their efforts with their community. They're scavengers; they find materials that can be used to help build shelters for workers who have just come to the community. They scavenge food, clothes. The people who are seeking aid see what the comadres are doing and go to them for help. The type of women who tend to be attracted to this type of organizational work are what I call "macro-comadres"! [laughter] They're the ones challenging the system, challenging the government, and trying to stop the railroad tanker cars filled with toxic materials that roll through our communities. They're yelling about the fact that there's no water, no electricity, no police, no safeguards. Some comadres in the colonias are well versed in one skill and others in another. Some are very good at getting electricity introduced into their community. Some are good at making people aware of the chemicals that are in the barrels that the people scavenge from the factories to hold their water. They tell people that the barrels have previously held toxic substances that contaminate their drinking water. They tell people they must line the barrels with concrete or heavy plastic to keep their water from becoming contaminated. They give people that kind of information.

Joni Adamson: How did Comadres first become aware of the ways in which toxins were affecting maquila workers and other members of the community and getting into the water supply?

Teresa Leal: I remember the story of one comadre. Her situation was one of the first that got us involved with the issue of toxics. Her name was Panchita. That was in '72 and she was working for Samsonite making suitcases. She was working at the maquila and going to Comadre meetings in the colonia where she lived. She called me aside one day. "I know this has nothing to do with the colonia," she said, "and I don't want to take much of your time but I want to know, since you speak English, if you could tell me what this label says." She brought me some of the material she was handling. Since she couldn't read English, she didn't know what it was. She said, "Something in this material that I'm handling is giving me a lot of problems. Not just me, but a lot of other women." I looked and read the label and the material was fiberglass. The workers in the Samsonite factory had to sew fiberglass material. She was sewing fiberglass with four needles at the same time; that's how they made the liners for the suitcases. I explained to her how sewing through that material created microscopic little shards of glass that fly through the air and into her clothes and body. That's why she had all these rashes.

Some days her legs would bleed so bad that her pants would stick to her legs. She said she had taken her complaint to the company doctor. He told her to take down her pants and he doused alcohol on her legs to put out the bleeding and then, despite her pain, sent her back to the line. She told me, "It's getting worse and worse, it's not getting any better. The doctor tells me that this is mange. And that's the reason why I wanted to talk to you in private because mange is a dirty dog's disease." The doctor told her, "You don't clean your house; you live in the dump and that's why you have mange. Because your hygiene is so bad." She told him, "I take a bath every day." She was very embarrassed because he said that she had mange. She got suspicious when the same doctor told her friend that the bleeding was the result of cirrhosis. You know, from alcohol, the disease you get when you drink. Her friend didn't drink.

Later, these two women started talking about it quietly to friends, and then another woman came up and said that the doctor had told her she probably had leprosy. That's when they all said, "We're going to ask Teresa about this." We started making a lot of noise and of course having Comadres meetings in the colonia. That's how we began getting involved in toxicology issues. So you see the beauty of word-of-mouth strategies, of mitote, of gossip. Once it starts going, you can't stop it. That's how Comadres uses the power of "gossip."

Joni Adamson: Can you tell me a little more about your work in the colonias?

Teresa Leal: Colonias are a phenomenon that developed simultaneously all along the U.S.–Mexico border. When the maquilas came in, they did not have a social agenda; maquila officials didn't give a hoot about the influx of people or where they were going to live.

When people first come to the border looking for work in the maquilas, they can get a job right away because of the high turn-over rate in the maquila work force. They get the job, but they may not have a house, they may not have furniture, they may not have a car, all of which makes it possible to keep a job. They can't count on the maquilas to provide housing either. So they start looking for ways to obtain housing, but they will not have any money for one month because the maquilas keep their first two weeks pay until they quit or get fired. So, the workers don't get paid until they have worked their second two weeks. Imagine coming here with nothing and trying to survive for a month without housing or money!

Article 27 of the Mexican Constitution says that every Mexicano has a constitutional right to a piece of land. My father and my uncle spent half their lives in prison for teaching people about the use of this constitutional right, which came about because of the Agrarian Reform of 1917 and Emiliano Zapata. I knew about Article 27 because of my family and my education. I began to see that we could use Article 27 as an organizational tool and I began to counsel people on how to do that. Of course Article 27 was watered down during the presidency of Salinas but not repealed; collective farms are no longer administered collectively and land can be owned individually. This means that a giant corporation like Green Giant can (and does) come in and offer individual members of a communal farm money for their land, and the individuals have the right to sell. But Article 27 was never fully dismantled because the idea of communal land ownership is so dear to the Mexican people. It is still legal for a community of people who do not own land to challenge huge landowners or *"latifundisios"* for a plot of land because Article 27 forbade owning too much land. So Article 27 can still be used as a basis for squatter's rights. If a squatter stays on his or her land for five years, they can achieve ownership.

Using Article 27 as our authority, we began to take over small plots of unoccupied land—ten by twenty meters—wherever we could find it, being careful to only select plots owned by latifundisios. We call these takeovers, "invasions." People set up little shacks made out of wooden pallets, cardboard, and plastics in order to be able to shelter themselves. Eventually, when they have more time and are working, they build something more concrete—cinder block is the most popular. Comadres gives people the organizing skills and knowledge they need to accomplish these invasions, to start working on things, and Article 27 gives them the legal right to do so. When a group of people come together for a planned invasion, the result is a small squatter village, or colonia.

Today there's some incipient planning by the government and by the maquilas in order to stem the incredible turnover of the workforce. So one of the ways that many of these maquilas have found to entice workers into their fold and to retain them is to "invest" in training them for peak production and quality. Also, the maquilas have moved to provide housing for their workers. They are developing "satellite cities" that provide everything: the school, the church, the grocery store.

Joni Adamson: Could you describe the events that resulted in the creation of SNEEJ and explain how so many diverse groups and people find common ground on which to work for common goals?

Teresa Leal: In 1991 we had the First National People of Color Environmental Summit which resulted in the realization that the issues that were affecting people of color were also affecting low income people. But at that time, there weren't any significant groups or movements within this grassroots network of people of color which were effectively influencing decisions about economic development, trade, and the environment. Greenpeace and the Sierra Club—the mainstream environmental groups—were doing it, but they were doing more conservation and preservation. Very green ecology, save the whales, you know. But the mainstream groups were not speaking to the issues that concerned people of color—water rights in Colorado, uranium mining in the sovereign Indian nations, for example. We realized we had to do something about it.

What this movement is really about is people speaking for themselves. We came out of the summit and here, in the Southwest, we formed a network of labor groups, indigenous groups, and community groups. We stress that movements do not exist if there isn't a democratic process, a permanent rotation of information and leadership. One of our first campaigns as a network was a leadership development campaign. In fact, our biggest endeavor is training. We don't do politicking or lobbying; we do training and teach people how to organize.

Joni Adamson: Can you describe some of the training workshops you've run?

Teresa Leal: We are working on what we call a "just transition," which is not about "free trade," but "just trade." We try to prepare workers for globalization so they will not be victims of globalization. The real problem with globalization is that it threatens people's cultures and identity, and an identity is necessary for people to consider that they have something to fight for, that they have something to defend, that they have something to care for. Our workshops teach people about things that can help them defend and protect their cultures, identities, and lifestyles. We also teach them about legal systems, about lawyers, and about lawsuits. We teach in a way they can understand so they can do something about the things that threaten their identities and environments. We teach them how to work together, to network, and to access resources. We also teach them about sustainable economic development in their communities. Economic development is a thing that we've needed. In order to afford to stay in the movement, you have to be self-sustaining.

Joni Adamson: What are your goals as cochair of SNEEJ?

Teresa Leal: My goal is to continue helping the network. We have worked very traditionally before, much as we did in the 60s. Now we need to use technology, we need to work with other networks through this technology. We need to develop life schools or leadership schools in different areas to teach our youth and our local groups how to defend the defendable. And that's something that's a real challenge because instead of becoming macro, such as the corporations do when they become macro, we've got to come back to the local groups, but use new models that interface with high technology. And that's a real challenge because it takes money, technical expertise, and training.

My last goal as cochair is very important and has to do with gender. The movement has always been mostly women. It's been very, very balanced. And of course being a woman, "very balanced" means three women to one man! That's very balanced. [laughter]

Joni Adamson: So your goal is to keep gender balance?

Teresa Leal: Not just to keep that balance, but to have our organization give even more support to women. As time goes on and economics get worse and politics move even more to the right, women are getting booted out of the system. Our network has to be intentional about helping the women who are getting booted out of the system, for example, with food stamps. I myself am very [pause] "decapitalized" not "poor"! I like the word "de-capitalized" so much better than "poor." [laughter] But it has never occurred to me to go out to ask for food stamps. I would be very embarrassed to ask for food stamps. I'd rather live under a tree. But women who are now receiving food stamps are limited to a certain amount of years. The government gives you help, then they tell you to learn to live without it. But if you're getting food stamps from the U.S. Department of Economic Security (DES) and you start working—say you start earning a small weekly wage—immediately, DES tells you, "We're gonna cut off your food stamps." It's like castigating people for trying to get out of the urban poverty cycle. So people shy away from getting a part-time job and from getting more education because they believe they are gonna be punished for it. So my quarrel with food stamps is that they keep you poor. People like to see you under the boot, on drugs, being flagellated by a husband, or mired in prostitution; then they'll warm up to you and take care of you. But if they see you getting on your feet, then you're no longer important. These kinds of issues affect women much more than they affect men and that's the reason why I'd like to see SNEEJ working to support women in a very committed way.

Joni Adamson: You recently traveled to Seattle to participate in the protests staged at the World Trade Organization's meetings. This demonstration has been described as a protest against globalism. Can you speak to the significance of the fight against globalism for the environmental justice movement in general?

Teresa Leal: SNEEJ participates in very few political events. Events are good to prove a point, but it's not the everyday work we do. We did feel that it was important to go to Seattle, however, because of the significance of how global institutions such as North American Free Trade Agreement (NAFTA) and the World Trade Organization and multinational corporations are attempting to take over the agendas of local peoples and regions and create these umbrella agendas which sidestep local/regional legal requirements. Moreover, institutions like the World Trade Organization want to control local and regional health and education policies. Corporations like Monsanto want to take over natural life, create genetic warehouses, control the production of seeds, even indigenous seeds. We have to stop this at any cost. In Seattle, we wanted to join forces with other environmentalist groups, with the turtle people, the whale people, with the monks from Tibet, with the "Raging Grannies."

Joni Adamson: The Raging Grannies?

Teresa Leal: Oh, they were so neat! They were out there yelling, "You're spoiling the earth for our grandchildren. We want our grandchildren to eat apple pie without pesticides!" [Laughter] They were from everywhere; Raging Grannies from here, from Argentina, from every country; they're the mothers of victims of violence, but they're getting older now. So, now they're the grannies! The Buddhist monks were also there, with their big flowing robes, which they were using to protect people from the tear gas. They were picking up the canisters and throwing them to the side. Some of them were carrying bags full of water and they would get the tear gas canisters and put them into the water, which neutralizes the gas. There were some contemplative friars who, with their arms crossed as if they were praying, were forming barriers so that the military couldn't get past them to reach the demonstrators. There were Indian tribes that were playing their drums. There were turtle people who had come to advocate for the rights of turtles worldwide. They were dressed as turtles, with these big shells on their back. They were using their shells to protect people from the rubber bullets being shot by the police. Bob Marley music was playing, so we were singing, "Get up, get up, stand up for your rights." For me, the most impressive realization that emerged from this event was, "This is what democracy looks like."

The grannies—and all the other groups which gathered in Seattle—were there to show that people need to become involved. I came back from Seattle convinced that we have to come out of our little trenches. We get so entrenched and we don't want to share our trenches or causes with anyone else. That has to stop; we have to work together. We are overcoming a lot of the barriers that have kept us insulated from each other, not agreeing with each other, and not agreeing with those with green agendas. So the fight against globalism has united a lot of diverse groups that previously never worked together or that ignored each other.

Joni Adamson: From your perspective, why do all these groups need to come together to fight against global imperatives?

Teresa Leal: The air is for all of us; the water is for all of us. Shit and pollution, toxic substances, do not ask for permission to come into your house; they do not need a passport to cross the border. Without permission, these substances come into our lives. We can't say, oh that person has cancer because they're poor. No, cancer hits everybody. People are dying all over the world, in part, because cancer can result from the release of POPs, or Persistent Organic Pollutants, into the environment. These toxins can find their way into everyone's house, whether they're rich or poor.

I learned about this reality very early in my life. I remember when I was working with the UFWU, I was cautious about warning women who were picking in the fields about their babies. I was very proud to see them so bent on breast-feeding. At the same time, Nestle was just as bent on corporate profiteering and on replacing mothers' milk with formula. And while I was happy to see that women wanted to breast-feed their babies, I knew that they would often carry their babies on their backs even when the sprayers would come along. So the babies would get the chemicals that way and they would get it in the breast-milk, too. Even if a mother has cholera, the cholera doesn't go through the mother's milk, but POPs do go through the mother's milk. So, on the one hand, I wanted to encourage breast-feeding and discourage people from enriching the Nestle Corporation, but on the other hand, I knew the babies were being affected by the toxins.

There is plenty of research to suggest that POPs are released into the environment by industrial processes, and by the spraying of pesticides, etc. These toxins are flowing through intercontinental airways. Do you know what that means? They're spreading all over the planet! Why don't we stop it? Because corporate profiteering is paramount; people don't seem to be able to live without exorbitant profits. So different groups need to come together to fight the corporations. No one group can do it alone.

Joni Adamson: You are not only involved in fighting on the global and regional level, but also on the local level. Could you speak briefly about your lawsuit against the City of Nogales, the Environmental Protection Agency (EPA), and the International Boundary and Water Commission?

Teresa Leal: Nogales, Arizona, and Nogales, Sonora, share a binational wastewater treatment plant. The wastewater treatment plant is financed by both countries. It treats the water, the sewer, or runoff water on both sides; it treats and recharges it back into the Santa Cruz River. The problem is that over the last ten years the treatment facility has had very serious violations of treatment. In other words, not treating enough of the flow of the gray or residual waters. And it's pumping lots of raw sewage into the Santa Cruz River.

The EPA itself knows that the raw sewage is going into the river—their own data shows this—yet they have not acted on those violations, which is why I, and my partner in this suit, the Sierra Club, are suing the EPA. We are also suing the International Boundary and Water Commission because they are the ones that operate the plant. We are suing the city of Nogales, Arizona, because they have been informed of all these violations over the past ten years yet they have done nothing about it. So we're not suing them to do any miracles, we're suing them to do their job.

Joni Adamson: Over the past few decades, environmental justice activists have often had a very problematic relationship with mainstream environmentalist groups like the Sierra Club, the Nature Conservancy, and Greenpeace. Do you see this lawsuit, and your partnership with the Sierra Club, as an example of how diverse groups can work together for common social and environmental goals?

Teresa Leal: Yes. The plaintiffs are the Sierra Club and me. People of color groups have had very serious problems with the Sierra Club in the past because they have often been at odds with our agendas. For example, in working to preserve natural landscapes, they often ignore or deny that some people need to LIVE off the land, and depend for their survival on natural resources. That blind spot definitely does not set us up to be good neighbors. But in a world increasingly affected by globalism, we can not afford to work against each other. This lawsuit, in which the Sierra Club and I are working together for a common goal, puts us in a wholly different relation to each other than we have been in the past. We're coming from different perspectives and yet we are working toward a common goal.

Joni Adamson: You are also involved in projects on the local level that look more like those carried out by mainstream environmental groups. Can you speak briefly about your work for the Santa Cruz River.

Teresa Leal: The Santa Cruz River Project is an effort to create a coalition of people concerned for the health of the river. The reason I'm helping to organize this is because there are a lot of groups out there—each one working at different levels for different things. As a result, there is also a lot of in-fighting, a lot of people refusing to work with each other. I believe we can transcend that. I plan to propose a series of goals for the river. All these goals do not have to be assumed by any one group, but all of them are in agreement with those goals. We will each go and work on these goals as much as we can and then we can meet once in a while, and, hopefully, engage in the kind of training that will make us all more effective at reaching our goals.

For example, I would like the Friends of the Santa Cruz River group to offer to teach others how to do inventories or to do water testing, which is something that group has been doing very well for quite some time. Or as a group, we could ask the EPA to give us some funding to do some training on other skills that could help us in our fight for the river. To me, the most ambitious goal would be to take the river, sector by sector, and do an inventory of the aquatic life, the flora or the fauna, you know, the natural wildlife of the river so that we could create a holistic plan with the individual sectors classified, so that we can better understand what the river is about.

Joni Adamson: In 1988, you ran for mayor of Nogales. You lost that election but have been quoted as saying that you are going to continue to "throw rocks at the sun." What did you mean by that?

Teresa Leal: Well, when I ran for mayor, it was mostly so that there would be a candidate running opposite the PRI (Institutional Revolutionary Party) candidate. The PRI has been the ruling party in Mexico for over eighty years. Opposing parties have to have their candidates. They have to have a historical background so that people in the future can say, yes, we recognize that party, they have existed, and people have voted for them before and will vote for them again. We needed a candidate that was well known here, somebody who could be shameless and talk about things in a political way. You know, to shake hands and say, "Thank you, thank you, thank you." I thought the race was going to be much easier; just go through the motions and say, "Democracy" at all the right times. But it was very hard because my campaign management crew convinced me that, to be successful, I had to talk about myself. I had to be able to say, "Please vote for ME because I'M the one who thinks and does, and I'VE done this in the past and I'M doing this now and I'M the mother of eight perfect kids." I just couldn't do it! But despite all of that, we did very well at the polls, and I think the campaign showed that democracy can work.

The democratic process never works fast enough but it is always in a process of evolution. So, you know, many of the things that we did in that election were just initial efforts, very open efforts to keep on throwing rocks at the sun. Throwing rocks at the sun is not bad, because, if you keep it up, sooner or later you will hit it! [laughter] We have to teach people, this is the way you throw rocks at the sun, despite the fact you know you're not always going to hit it, despite the fact you are not always going to win. If we were only stimulated by the sure shots, we would never get anywhere; we would be very behind. Change comes only when a few brave hearts dare to throw the first rock.

3

ENDANGERED LANDSCAPES AND DISAPPEARING PEOPLES?

Identity, Place, and Community in Ecological Politics

Devon G. Peña

In 1852, the *hispano mexicano* settlers of the land grant village of San Luis de la Culebra, located in what is now south-central Colorado's San Luis Valley, completed the construction of their first *acequia madre,* the San Luis Peoples Ditch. Over the next two decades, the Rio Culebra villagers constructed more than twenty of these communal irrigation ditches. This was in keeping with the customary practice established in 1598 and the digging of the first New Mexico acequias in the vicinity of San Juan Pueblo, about one hundred miles downstream from San Luis on the Rio Grande. The construction of communal irrigation ditches was the first task of the Spanish and Mexican land grant settlers. Acequias—the gravity-driven, earthen-work irrigation networks handed down from late antiquity—remain the pivotal material basis and ecological precondition for the existence and sustenance of a four-hundred-year-old bioregional culture.

The acequia irrigation system is based on the use of water released by the gradual melting of winter snowpack during the spring and summer months. The capture by humans of this renewable energy, like beaver works, concentrates ecological processes that expand the riparian life zone, creating new habitat and movement corridors for native flora and fauna. The snowmelt cycle of the mountain headwaters sets the underlying pulse for agroecological livelihoods in the irrigated bottom lands. In return, acequia irrigators provide a variety of ecological services to the watershed, including the formation of wildlife habitat. The patchy long-lot mosaics and wetlands resulting from subirrigation are renowned examples of anthropogenic wildlife habitat. Other important ecosystem benefits of the acequias include the maintenance of water and soil quality and the preservation of agrobiodiversity through heirloom seed-saving (Peña 1998, 2001a; Peña and Martínez 2000).

One ethnoecologist recently described the acequia as characterized by "an almost compulsive need to link up and connect" (Nazarea 1999, 17). The capillary networks of acequias create a veritable landscape mosaic that extends the native riparian life zone within an expanded circulatory system where the natural element of water is used to create biomass and is then returned to in-stream flows. The acequia network typically follows a natural dendritic pattern, in which water webs spin off the natural contours and water courses of the locality. But there is a reiteration within each acequia resulting in a pattern of branching and rebranching. Each acequia consists of several different types of ditches. The acequia madre, or mother ditch, is the principal diversion canal that links the ditch network to the water source, which is typically a snow-fed creek. At different points along this mother ditch, each *parciante* (water user) has *compuertas* (headgates) that are used to divert water from the acequia madre to the fields, row crops, and orchards. These ditches are called *laterales* or *linderos* (lateral ditches). In the middle of the irrigated long-lots is another ditch that carries water to the fields furthest from the acequia madre. This middle ditch is usually called the *espinazo,* or spinal ditch. Flowing off the lindero and espinazo ditches are the *sangrias,* or bleeding ditches, which divert water into *melgas* (sub-sections) of irrigated fields and row crops.

Over the generations, the dendritic networks of earthen-work ditches have created a veritable landscape mosaic pattern wherever they are found in the upper Rio Grande bioregion. The agroecological landscapes of acequia fields and farms have melded with the natural landscapes of the montane water-sheds. The acequia is a profound accomplishment because it exemplifies the possibility that local cultures sometimes fulfill "keystone" functions in eco-systems by providing habitat for numerous species of native flora and fauna (Peña 1998, 1999, 2001a; Rívera 1999; Peña and Martínez 2000).

The acequia landscape mosaic is also highly endangered. Blacktopping of farm land driven by the ruthless subdivision, second home, and tourism amenity industries is resulting in the loss of these historic cultural land-scapes. Industrialized logging and mining are degrading the watersheds and affecting the ability of the irrigators to operate their acequias (Curry 1995; Peña 1998). The loss of this agroecological landscape may seem a bit more poignant if one compares the messy diversity of the acequia farms with the neat, orderly, and legible crop circles produced by agro-industrial monocul-tures in other parts of the interior or intermountain West. The circles are the fossil fuel by-products of mechanical center-pivot irrigation sprinklers that spray chemically treated water on genetically altered hybrids. To operate the modern monoculture, the grower must reduce the topographic and biological diversity of the natural landscape to polka-dot uniformity. The destructiveness of agriculture is starkly revealed to be driven by the mad, crazy desire to impose the grid, reduce trophic complexity, and commodify nature more efficiently.

Acequia institutions in the Rio Arriba have always expressed political power in the form of collective social movements. But contemporary expressions of such struggles derive from a deeper source. This chapter explores the roots of the localized civic culture that continues to organize as a watershed commonwealth for self-governance. These *are* the famed autonomous irrigation municipalities championed by General Vallejos in California at the end of the eighteenth century. The acequia is a communally managed institution that is organized under the authority of local customary practices. Historically across the Rio Arriba, the acequia as a civic institution for local self-governance has emphasized three normative principles: (1) the use value of water to the community, (2) mutual aid, and (3) cooperative labor. It is largely through the institution of the acequia, that the hispano-mexicano irrigators have persisted in place for so long, against the odds and despite the doctrines imposed by the over-layering of Anglo water law.

The biophysical persistence of the acequia communities is a profound keystone accomplishment. While the water webs provide keystone services to local ecosystems, the endurance of the acequias derives more from the civic and cultural institutions of place-based custom and practice. And yet, the sustainable inhabitation rendered by the acequias is not just a static by-product of some everlasting and mystical local cultural balance with the "natural environment." The success of the acequias has always been under siege and any legal or political power vested in acequias is completely a result of hard-fought battles over the control of land and water rights deemed essential to the persistence of right livelihoods. The history of conflict generated by power, inequity, enclosure, and legal changes is an equally persistent feature of the acequia communities. These battles involve a collision between the making and remaking of places in localized sites of contested socio-spatial power (Peña 2001b).

The place-centered identity of the acequia farmers is apparent in the rich and complex ritual life of the community. The melding of ritual and agricultural calendar cycles is evident in many acequia communities. The Feast Day of San Isidro, the patron saint of the farmer, falls on May 15. This date is also the start of the annual spring ditch clean-up, an event that brings the community together in an act of cooperative labor. Each parciante must donate his or her labor to the task of clearing out the ditches in preparation for the spring and summer irrigation season. But in some places, like the Culebra watershed, the hard work of ditch maintenance is integrated with the ritual observation of the patron saint feast day in which the local priest blesses the land and water during a long procession along the edge of the acequias and fields. A celebratory mass is followed by a communal dinner consisting entirely of foods prepared with ingredients harvested from the local lands during the previous year. The religious historian, Rowena Rívera, documented the May 15 feast day celebration in San Luis de la Culebra (Rívera 1998). She recorded the prayers, including an oration by one of the acequia irrigators participating in the liturgical service:

> Aquí nos juntamos todos pa' rezarle al sol, a nuestra madre tierra, y al agua que nos dan vida pa' recibir el amor que nos da Dios, pa' amarnos los unos a los otros. Recémosle, entonces, a Nuestro Padre Jesús, que es la naturaleza divina y a nuestro San Isidro Labrador, que es nuestro protector y intermediario pa' que nos den nuestros alimentos y el modelo pa' nuestra vida terrenal y espiritual. Así sea. En el nombre del Padre.
> [Translation: We gather here to pray to the sun, to our mother earth, and to the water that provide us with life so we can receive God's love and so that we can come to love one another. Let us pray, then, also, to Saint Isidro the Laborer, who is our protector and intermediary so that with his help and that of God, we may receive our food and the model to follow in our earthly and spiritual life. And thus it shall be. In the name of the Father.] (Anonymous, Interview with Rowena Rívera, San Luis, Colorado, 13 May 1995)

The acequia is not just a sustainable, regenerative, and renewable irrigation technology. It is a political and cultural institution that intersects with the place-centered identities and environmental ethics of the local community. The acequia is the material and spiritual embodiment of people making habitable places. But it is not without its antithesis in the degradation of homeland by the forces of modernity and maldevelopment.

Disturbing Place

On June 20, 1996, an unusual protest group blocked logging trucks attempting to enter the Taylor Ranch, the enclosed common lands of the Sangre de

Cristo Land Grant. The protestors included three generations of a local ranching family, a group of nine college students with their professor on a field trip, and a large contingent of eco-activists from Earth First!, Ancient Forest Rescue, and Greenpeace. Watching over the blockade was a group of elder farmers and ranchers who came to be fondly known as the "Wise Old Dudes for Wilderness."[1] The Maestas family members present at the sit-down protest included the grandmother, Olivia Maestas, her daughter-in-law, and two grandchildren (Derick and Aubin Maestas). Another local youth was present, Edwin Sanchez, the son of Adelmo Kaber, one of the "Wise Old Dudes for Wilderness," and Veronica Sanchez. The events that brought such an unlikely group of protestors together have been discussed elsewhere (see Peña and Mondragon Valdéz 1998; Peña 1998, forthcoming). The protest was a response by the acequia community and its allies to a massive logging operation initiated by Zachary Taylor on the enclosed and contested common lands. Zach, "Junior," was the second-generation owner of the Taylor Ranch and a direct descendant of President Zachary Taylor, himself notoriously well known to us as the army general who led the war against Mexico in 1845–48.

For many reasons this was no ordinary timber sale, and not just because of the depth of its historical background, the "long shadow" cast by the 1848 treaty (see Weinberg 1999). First, the volume of the cut was staggering. This has turned out to be a world-class example of massive deforestation on "privately held" land. There are no regulations for logging on private lands in Colorado, so Taylor developed a voluntary timber plan based on "overstory" removal (in which every tree larger than thirteen inches diameter breast height (dbh) was removed and the smaller trees left for "natural" reseeding). Taylor misrepresented the logging as a "watershed improvement and management plan," but it involved more than 200 million board feet (mmbf) of timber cuts over ten years on a mere 34,000 acres of land with "merchantable" trees. This made it the largest timber sale on private land in twentieth-century Colorado history and among the top ten largest such private timber sales in modern Southwestern environmental history.

Second, the property rights to the land in question remain legally and politically contested. The current round of litigation occurs under a persistent "little cloud over the title" and a series of judicial mishaps and irregularities.[2] In 1960, "old man" Jack Taylor bought the "Mountain Tract" and closed it to the local acequia communities which had used the land as a commons (for hunting, fishing, wildcrafting, fuel wood, construction materials, etc.). The Taylor enclosure involved some 77,000 acres of common land. The historic use rights of the land grant heirs (acequia farmers) are the subject of continuing legal action in the renowned *Rael v. Taylor* land rights lawsuit (Peña and Mondragon Valdez 1998). So the land in question is still subject to litigation over the historic use rights of the acequia community, including their rights to water runoff from the winter snowpack.

Third, the volume of the logging is rendered more complicated by the misuse of Montana Best Management Practices, which are ill-suited for the unique hydrological and climate regimes of the southern Rockies biome. The ill-advised "overstory" removal timber practices exposed the remnant seed trees to massive blow-down and other disturbances (Curry, Soulé, Peña and McGowan 1996). The misuse of the Montana Best Management Practices was particularly troublesome because of the effect that removal of the canopy trees had on the snowpack and runoff patterns.

For the acequia association, this is the most profound problem facing the community in the wake of industrial-scale logging. The cumulative effects of logging involve changes in the rate at which snowpack turns into in-stream flow during the spring and summer runoff season. This is precisely the effect that has been documented for irrigated bottom lands located downstream from twenty- to thirty-year-old timber cuts (Curry 1995; Colorado Acequia Association 2000). Hydrologists call this an altered "stream hydrograph slope." Because of overstory removal, the snowpack is exposed to more sun and to spring and summer "rain-on-snow" events that accelerate the runoff rate. Acequias rely on gravity from the runoff to power their dendritic water webs. But they also rely on a sustained snowmelt that extends the irrigation season from May through early October. The ever-expanding open gaps in the canopy caused by the logging operations are affecting the length of the runoff, shortening it by as much as three to five weeks (Curry 1995, Colorado Acequia Association 2000).

The Taylor Ranch is perceived by the place-based acequia communities as a multivalent disturbance. Enclosure involves biophysical and hydrological disruptions and perturbations. It is associated with the long-standing legal battles that counterpose common and private property regimes. It is thus a social and political disturbance, involving claims for moral, legal, and economic actions to restore the justly and historically asserted land and water-use rights of the land grant heirs. But it is also a disturbance of the community's sense of place, a disturbance in the biophysical realm that disrupts the place-based identities of the community.

From a Sense of Place to a Senseless Place?

To appreciate the persistence of the land grant struggle, one must examine the history of ecological politics in the bioregion. However, it is also necessary to explore the changing environmental ethics of the acequia communities. The recovery of hispano mexicano environmental ethics has been one of the more fascinating and serendipitous aspects of this study. Too often, previous scholars have assumed that hispano mexicanos lacked a "conservation ethic." Or worse, hispano mexicanos are thought to live an insurmountable contradiction between a strong emotional attachment to the land and rampant ignorance of the science of ecology (for critical interpretations, see Peña 1992, 1999; Peña and Mondragon Valdéz 1998; Peña and Martínez 1998).

There is considerable evidence showing that acequia farmers are knowledgeable of the ecological limits imposed on agriculture by the environmental conditions of the bioregion (Peña and Martínez 1998). Hispano mexicano understanding of ecological limits is perhaps best demonstrated by the marvelous sixty- to ninety-day white roasting corn cross-bred from various land race varieties by the acequia farmers of San Luis. The development of this land race variety was an effective response to the dry and short growing season on farms that, after all, are located in a cold desert biome, the Upper Sonoran, at an elevation of eight thousand feet above sea level. While this focus on the behavioral ecology of hispano mexicanos is quite instructive about successful strategies of adaptation to the limits imposed by the natural conditions of agricultural production, I also felt that research on material culture was incomplete without an accounting of the values and norms associated with these practices. This led me into exploration of the land and water ethics of acequia communities.

During the field research, the farmers began to narrate memories that were clearly organized according to a set of cognitive maps—mental pictures of their home places. This led me to explore the knowledge of local ecological interactions, for example between land and water, by asking farmers to draw mental and figurative maps of these processes in the context of their own local watersheds and farming landscapes. I found that the acequia farmers in each watershed have very precise local knowledge of the landscape and that this knowledge goes well beyond familiarity with place names or with areas identified with pasture, hunting, or specific plant communities. The Hispano farmers also have deep experiential knowledge of the workings of watersheds. An important aspect of this "watershed consciousness," to borrow a phrase from hydrologist Robert Curry, is recognition of the ways in which human disturbance is often harmful to plants, animals, humans, and water courses. Thus, the maps drawn by Joe Gallegos, of the Culebra watershed before and after industrial-scale logging operations, gently bring your focus unto the violent transformation from undisturbed emerald homeland to a radically disturbed and industrialized landscape (see Peña forthcoming). Joe Gallegos' painful drawings remind us that the "uniform and legible" forest invented by the first German scientific forester, Johann Gottlieb Beckmann, is dead and well in the Culebra in the aftermath of Taylor's industrial and "fiscal" forestry (cf. Scott 1999).

The acequia farmers weave these cognitive maps into the tapestry of a "resistance identity": Place-based knowledge of locality is combined with critical consciousness of the threats posed by the modernist projects of a globalized political economy (Peña 2001b). The farmers' livelihoods are too directly affected by the actions of transnational corporations for them to not develop awareness of the contradictions between the local and the global. Thus, the land ethics of Hispano farmers seem to revolve around the critique of the global economy to the extent that it manifests as a threat to the well-being and integrity of the local community (Peña 2001b).

Fermin Arguello's description of contemporary ecological politics in the Taos-area national forests is quite instructive here. He states that the problem with the relationship of Chicanos to the Forest Service and the environmentalists is that "they want to follow the rules over there, by the book. We want to follow it over here by the nature." He wonders how policy can be fashioned in a place as far away as Washington, D.C. by people who have never been on the land.[3] Fermin's map of this violated world offers a poignant cultural affirmation of local knowledge and a call for cultural resistance to encroachment by corporations and environmentalists alike (Rubine 1998, 84). At the root, hispano mexicano environmental ethics seem governed by an intense and even militant attachment to place (and to staying in place) and therefore by an unwavering commitment to the principle of local autonomy. The environmental ethics of hispano mexicanos are thus an ethics of place and are derived from localized identities (see Wilkinson 1992).

But the environmental ethics of hispano mexicanos are in fact in the midst of a radical transition. I once asked a San Luis–area farmer how the enclosure of the common lands had affected him. His short, yet terribly pithy and painful, reply was, *"Perdimos la libertad, nos encercaron."* ["We lost our liberty, they fenced us out."] The enclosure of the commons, the fencing of the land to prevent locals from exercising their traditional use rights, becomes an act of violence because it deprives people of their liberty. The barbed-wire fence is invoked as a symbol of the loss of an open landscape that was once an undisturbed part of the community's identity.

Joe Gallegos responded to the same question by explaining how it had resulted in nothing less than a fracturing of his identity: "How can I ever be the same in this place? Taylor has raped the mountain. He has logged it until the soil bleeds, until the land flows off the mountain and right into the creeks and acequias like so much debris and sediment. I am torn up by this violence against the trees. Taylor has clear-cut my soul."[4] The destruction of the Culebra forests is the extirpation of a man's soul, a rupturing of his spiritual connection to the land, mountains, and water. His sense of place is violently disturbed by the industrial exploitation that radically altered the landscape of his childhood. The actual biophysical anchors of memory are displaced, producing a sense of being violated and emptied of spirit. In another interview, Joe Gallegos explained how his first memory of La Sierra was that his father, Corpus A. Gallegos, had told him to "tip-toe across the [Taylor Ranch] headquarters road," since they were now trespassing on what had suddenly and surreptitiously been transformed from common into private property (Peña forthcoming). These personal memories are imbued with a sense of loss, of dis-placement. As an environmentalist from Ancient Forest Rescue, who now works for the acequia association in San Luis, put it: "This is not a sense of place, it is a senseless place."[5]

Hispano mexicano land ethics are thus profoundly affected by the loss of the qualities that allowed people to define a place as the corresponding biophysical anchor of local identities. When places are violated in this way, by the destructive forces of industrial extraction and other forms of mal-development, local people feel the changes intimately and personally as a loss that touches their sense of being in a most deeply troubling and disquieting manner. One farmer, Adelmo Kaber, even described this loss as a type of *susto,* a term that refers to an illness defined in ethnomedical folklore as a form of fright so intense and profound as to lead to the "loss of the soul." *"Me dio susto ver como cambio la sierra. Siento que perdí mi alma."* ["I got fright to see how the mountain has changed. I feel I lost my soul."] Ecological devastation is the same as the malaise of "soul-flight," susto.

Acequia Environmental Ethics

The acequia farming communities have not accepted this ecological devastation and cultural displacement by succumbing to the fitful display of a stereotyped behavior like fatalism. I have never heard anyone say, *"Pues, así lo manda Dios."* ["Oh well, that is the way God wills it."] Instead, the communities, invariably, have developed what Castells (1997) calls "project identities" and organized struggles to restore, defend, and protect the enclosed commons. To understand the nature of these struggles, their ideological underpinnings and organizational forms, it is important to take stock of the historical basis of environmental ethics in the Rio Arriba. I found that those ethics are grounded, more than anything else, in the customary laws of the acequia.

In his wonderful book, *Acequia Culture: Land, Water, and Community in the Southwest,* José A. Rívera provides an insightful analysis of the historical and cultural roots of acequia customary law (1999, 25–48). While Roman and Arabic legal systems and technologies shaped the acequia institution in Spain, Rívera correctly notes that the evolution of the acequia in its New Mexico context proceeded more by means of local needs and adaptations. Over a period of four hundred years (1598–1998), hispano mexicanos developed the acequia as a bona fide indigenous environmental management institution.[6]

My study, agreeing with Rívera's take, demonstrates that the acequia customary law derives from three interlinked ethical concepts: (1) the value of water as communal riparian property with associated usufructuary rights, (2) the principle of mutual aid, and (3) the principle of cooperative labor. First, following Islamic traditions as transplanted to Spain, the customary law of the acequia defines water as community property. It is not treated as a commodity value, which is the case with the Anglo doctrine of prior appropriation (also see Brown and Ingram 1987). A related principle of water as communal property is the fundamental rule of the acequia: one does not separate water from the land. This homespun riparian doctrine is related to the concept of usufruct: Irrigators do not own the water, they have the right to use it, and only as long as their practices do not damage other irrigators. The significance of usufruct in this context is in the explicit linking of use rights with ethics governing both social equity and environmental protection. In this case, environmental justice is not just a late-twentieth-century social movement; it is a deep and replicating idea spawned by the local civic culture over many generations.

The second principle, mutual aid, is the basic organizational ethos governing the management and maintenance of the acequia. *Mutualistas* (mutual aid societies) have a long and rich history within Mexican and Chicano cultures. These societies emerged, partly, as a response to the exclusion of poor people from funeral homes and cemeteries. In the case of the Rio Arriba, the mutualista tradition was organized into the well-known Sociedad Protectora Mutualista de Trabajadores Unidos, the Protective Mutualist Society of United Workers or SPMDTU.[7] The SPMDTU is still active in many of the land grant villages and in some places, such as Antonito, Colorado, is actually experiencing a resurgence with growing membership. Mutual aid practices, however, are not limited to the formal civic associations like the SPMDTU. Mutualist values, in fact, permeate the entire cultural and social fabric of the "irrigation municipality." In the case of the acequia, mutual aid principles are most fundamentally expressed in the rules governing the maintenance of the ditch and the allocation of water for irrigation. *Parciantes* define mutual aid in very concrete and specific terms. For example, the customary law of the acequia requires that in times of drought the irrigators share in the scarcity of water. Everyone uses less so that all can have access to water. However, the imposition of the doctrine of prior appropriation has sparked battles on acequias related to "priority calls," whenever the holders of "senior" water rights issue "calls" for water during drought (see Hicks and Peña forthcoming).

The third principle involves the institution of cooperative labor in the maintenance and operation of the acequias. The traditional spring ditch cleaning is usually done within a week of May 15, which is the Feast Day of San Isidro Labrador, patron saint of the farmer. This work is a fine example of a cooperative labor process. Each of the parciantes (farmers with a water right) must share in the work of ditch maintenance, although one can hire a *peón* (in this context, replacement worker) to participate in the cooperative labor.

The ethics of communal property, use rights with attendant obligations to protect and conserve the land and water, mutual aid, and cooperative labor are the original autochthonous cultural source of hispano mexicano environmental ethics. There are, however, local concepts of ecological interaction that merit further discussion here. Research scholars have already verified and explained the existence of Spanish colonial and Mexican laws governing environmental protection (see Ebright 1994; Peña 1992, 1998, 1999, forthcoming; Peña and Martínez 1998, 157–59). Rivera continues this effort by drawing attention to acequia rules that expressly prohibited pollution of the water courses and ditches:

> The laws of 1868 and 1872, enacted for the communities in Valencia and Socorro counties, authorized local *mayordomos* to levy fines against persons who befouled acequia waters by washing dirty cloths, bathing, or allowing swine to wallow inside the ditch. By the turn of the century, a series of general laws had been enacted, in 1880, 1897, and 1899, that applied to all acequias of [New Mexico] territory. These laws prohibited the pollution of streams, lakes, and ditches by any number of means or the discarding of objects that would endanger the public health of the community. The penalties, upon conviction, were gradually made more severe, up to one hundred dollars and/or a sixty-day jail sentence in the 1897 laws. (1999, 30–31)

Similar laws early on were expressed throughout the Rio Arriba at the local level. The town ordinances of San Luis, Colorado, formulated in 1852, for example, expressly forbid the discarding of garbage in view of the public and in any area of common use, including acequias. The 1911 rules adopted by the Acequia de Margarita in Lincoln County, New Mexico are another example:

> "Nadien tendrá derecho de destruir los bordos de la acequia madre a modo que [h]aiga peligro de que se rompa la acequia [h]acerse perjuición a si mismo al vecino." (Our translation: No one shall have the right to destroy the banks of the mother ditch in such a manner that there will be danger of the acequia overflowing which would become an injury as such to the neighbor.) . . . Rules have also been crafted by the irrigators to protect and enforce water quality standards in the ditch. (The 1911 rules) of the Margarita Ditch . . . charged the mayordomo with enforcing the *"Reglas de Limpiesa"* (Rules for Cleanliness). These rules prohibited anyone from discarding junk in the community ditch, namely "garras, cajetes, puercos cueros, barriles o otras porquerillas que sean en perjuicio de la salubridad de los ha[b]itantes." (Translation: rags, tubs, pig hides, barrels, or other filthy objects which might endanger citizen health.) (Rívera 1999, 31–32)

Hispano mexicanos clearly took their ethics seriously, especially when it came to protecting the integrity of the acequia and of equity in social exchange relations on the ditches. The resulting laws requiring protection and preservation of environmental values like water quality and sanitary conditions were of critical import and should be seen as practical expressions of deeply rooted environmental ethics.

But my research also focused on the threats posed by "modernization" to the ancient customary law. These threats are principally derived from fundamental value conflicts between the customary law of the acequia and the Anglo-imposed doctrine of prior appropriation. Under this doctrine, the law treats water not as a community but as a commodity value (see Brown and Ingram 1987). An unfortunate and ill-conceived aspect of this doctrine is that water can be severed from the land. Defying the logic of gravity, property rights interpretations of water rights allow individual land owners to convey water rights to others, even if that means one moves water over mountains toward money. In fact, for the acequias many problems have emerged from the imposition of the doctrine of prior appropriation. In Colorado, the state individualized what historically had been defined as collectively held water rights. But the water rights of individual parciantes do not derive from the priority lists of the doctrine of prior appropriation. Instead, these are usufructuary rights derived from the context in which the community "husbanded" and created the watershed-wide stock of natural assets that are used by the acequias to operate the ditch networks as a collective affair (see Hicks and Peña forthcoming).

Anglo industrialization and commercialization of the region's water resources have been driven by the marketization of the communal and ecological value of water (see Peña 1998, forthcoming). The conflict between acequia law and the doctrine of prior appropriation is a complex affair and has filled volumes of case law in New Mexico and Colorado water courts (see Crawford 1988; Peña 1998, especially 249–78). This conflict resulted in the emergence of acequia associations as political organizations. Acequia farmers have responded, in a largely successful manner, to the legal contradictions by sustaining customary practices and affirming their lawful status under both state and federal statues (see Peña and Martínez 2000; Hicks and Peña forthcoming).[8]

The Persistence of the Disappeared

The disappearance of the "Other" is a recurrent theme in much of anthropology. This is equally true of the conventional literature on the rural hispano mexicano cultures of the Upper Rio Grande. The cultural geographer, Alvar Ward Carlson, has predicted that "this way of life will disappear rather quickly" (1990, 233). My own study would seem to confirm a prognosis of a "disappearing" culture. I could argue that the endangered landscapes violated by enclosure, logging, and mining can no longer sustain place-based identities. That the violent transformation of the biophysical landscape not only displaced hispano mexicanos from the common lands, it is leading to the loss of practical, or working, knowledge. The decline of traditions such as the wildcrafting of *remedios* is one of the most clear examples of a process of convergence between the destruction of biodiversity and the extirpation of local knowledge. I could further argue that the degradation of the enclosed common lands has biophysical and spiritual qualities. Landscapes are not just degraded in a material sense—that is, the loss of habitat for rare plants used in local ethnobotany. Damaged landscapes are also degraded as the material basis of place-based identities. The clear-cuts of the legible forest rupture the memories people have embedded in place over generations.

But displacement and dislocation are often followed by a process of "re-inhabitation." Displacement may be followed by regeneration and resurgence. This point cannot be overemphasized. Despite enclosure, every community in this study has a rich history of subaltern resistance in which displaced persons continue to exercise historic use rights. People still hunt, fish, gather wild plants, collect fuel wood, or simply ride horseback on a favorite trail. They do so either by means of "trespass" or by negotiating new arrangements with the managers of private and public lands. In either case, local residents continue to gain access to the common lands.

However, often the circumstances *have* changed and favorite "witness trees" or grazing meadows may have been altered or even destroyed since childhood. When such threatening disturbances occur, people find ways to redefine their relationship to place. Keith Basso (1996) suggests that a sense of place may become more salient and obvious to members of a local culture during times of crisis and dramatic change. There is nothing like a new threat to make people more aware of their attachment to place:

As normally experienced, sense of place quite simply is, as natural and straightforward as our fondness for certain colors and culinary tastes, and the thought that it might be complicated, or even very interesting, seldom crosses our minds. Until, as sometimes happens, we are deprived of these attachments and find ourselves adrift, literally dislocated. . . . On these unnerving occasions, sense of place may assert itself in pressing and powerful ways. . . . It is then we come to see that attachments to places may be nothing less than profound, and that when these attachments are threatened we may feel threatened as well. (Basso 1996, xiii–xiv)

The emergence in the acequia communities of concerted resistance to displacement and environmental degradation is one of these examples of the profound recollection and rearticulation of a sense of place by local cultures that see themselves to be unjustly endangered by globalization and its discontents. It is here that the contested terrain of cultural studies meets the equally turbulent and contentious ground of ecological politics. But to surmise that enclosure, modernization, and globalization displaced local cultures, rendering these susceptible to disappearance because of the expropriation and rape of the land, is a conceptual and practical stretch of the evidence. "You have to change, but you don't have to die," is the eloquent way Joe Gallegos has put it (Peña and Martínez 2000).

James C. Scott, in a recent book, *Seeing Like a State,* observes that "high modernism" has always been preoccupied with the displacement of local practical knowledge, what he calls *mètis,* through the imposition of universal and standardized techniques. Such efforts have consistently failed because "no forms of production or social life can be made to work by formulas alone—that is, without *mètis*" (1999, 335). He notes with respect to the case of traditional peasant farming in Malaysia that the expert knowledge of the agricultural extension service workers could not work or completely displace the local knowledge of peasant communities:

It is hard to imagine this [practical] knowledge being created and maintained except in the context of lifelong observation and a relatively stable, multigenerational community that routinely exchanges and preserves knowledge of this kind. . . . the social conditions necessary for the reproduction of comparable practical knowledge . . . at a minimum, would seem to require a community of interest, accumulated information, and ongoing experimentation. (Scott 1999, 334)[9]

From this vantage, we can see that mètis has technical and sociocultural dimensions. The practical knowledge in a given locality is not just the sum of local knowledge a community creates to produce a range of right livelihoods located in place. Mètis includes knowledge related to expressive oral traditions and these nearly always encompass moral and not just technical qualities. I am ultimately brought back to an infinitely "thick" moment when a rancher taught his daughter how to ride bareback on a horse. This represents the transmission of practical, working knowledge, of mètis, to the next generation in an act of conscious resistance against high modernist imperatives. The emergence of resistance identities in violently disturbed places is in this manner intimately linked to the reproduction of mètis and the *re-emplacement* of local cultures against the odds. But Scott further notes that: "Some forms of *mètis* are disappearing every day. As physical mobility, commodity markets, formal education, professional specialization, and mass media spread to even the most remote communities, the social conditions for the elaboration of *mètis* are undermined (1999, 335)." Perhaps the most violently wrenching manifestation of this is the sense of displacement caused by deforestation and other forms of ecological degradation of enclosed homeland commons. But even here we find local hispano mexicanos re-inventing their relationship to the landscape in order to re-establish their place-based identities. More than that, the most significant turn of events involves the resurgence of the land grant movement, only this time organized with an explicitly environmental justice agenda.

The link between the persistence of place-based identities and the resurgence of the land grant movement as a "new social movement" for environmental and economic justice, cultural survival and local self-governance marks an important departure from the usual business of imperial initiatives designed to produce "disappeared" others. The process of modernization and commodification does not easily erase every last vestige of the autochthonous cultures. This seems particularly the case wherever aspects of the autochthonous civil society are legitimized within the new administrative regime of power. The legal affirmation of acequias, both as vested water rights and as autochthonous forms of self-governance, under state and federal law, provides ample evidence of the conditions necessary for the reproduction of "disappeared" local knowledge (Hicks and Peña forthcoming). Even the best efforts of the scientific experts who serve capitalist enclosure cannot destroy these "disqualified" forms of local knowledge.[10]

The historic acequia communities of the Rio Arriba have produced significant legal, political, and economic struggles to restore common lands and protect their headwaters. These new social movements have been based on numerous strategies—for example, land grant litigation, the persistence of subaltern and informal use, legislative action, litigation, land use planning and zoning, direct action and other forms of civil disobedience—but they all share one thing: This is the persistence of a strong sense of place that is accompanied by the resurgence of place-based identities. I see these struggles as involving a shift from "resistance" to "project" identities (cf. Castells 1997). The act of "trespass" by an individual rancher asserting her claim to historic use rights on the enclosed common lands is an example of resistance identity. The act of organizing a legal campaign to restore the land grant to local community ownership and control is an example of project identity. And it is the latter which is becoming more extant, and politically visible, in the Upper Rio Grande. It represents a more conscious articulation of an environmental justice agenda (see Peña 2001b).

Joe Gallegos's lament, that he cannot "ever be the same in this place," must be understood in the context of the broader horizon of organized struggles for environmental and economic justice unfolding in each of the historic acequia communities. The emergence of the acequia associations (for example, the Taos Valley Acequia Association, New Mexico Acequia Association, and Colorado Acequia Association) in the 1980s and 1990s, as bona fide agencies of organized resistance, suggests that the battle over the politics of place is not a finished chapter. These struggles focus on the defense and protection of the acequias through litigation related to the re-adjudication of water rights. New strategies of resistance are focused on the establishment of community land and water trusts that seek, as their political objective, to prevent the transfer of land and water to speculators, developers, and other non-traditional users (see Peña 1998, 2001a, 2001b, forthcoming). The acequia associations have also played a critical role in strategies to empower local communities to manage their private and public lands. The successful efforts by the Culebra acequias to establish a "watershed protection zone" and the equally successful efforts by the Taos Valley Acequia Association and the Acequia de San Antonio to impose and enforce land use regulations are both illustrative of these new organizational forms and strategies of resistance.

The acequia farming communities of the Rio Arriba are experiencing disproportionate adverse impacts from the cumulative effects of logging, mining, and subdividing. The struggles to restore land and water rights are explicitly linked to social and economic justice ethics. The historic acequia communities are not disappearing. On the contrary, they are actively reinventing themselves out of the ruinous rubble brought about by late high modernity. These struggles by the "disappeared" are possible because the multigenerational transmission of local knowledge and place-based identities persists. It is the persistence of place-based memories and identities, in light of the real and often radical biophysical and sociocultural transformations, that gives me pause. Clifford Geertz recently noted that "it is still the case that no one lives in the world in general. Everybody, even the exiled, the drifting, the diasporic, or the perpetually mobile, lives in some confined and limited stretch of it—'the world around here.' . . . The ethnography of place is, if anything, more critical for those who are apt to imagine that all places are alike than for those who, listening to forests or experiencing stones, know better" (1996, 262). The people of the acequia farming communities are among those who listen to the forests and experience stones. Their intimate working knowledge of the watersheds is giving rise to a new social movement that aims to put an end to the "placeless amnesia" that afflicts contemporary society. In the process they are restoring their own place-based identities while struggling to reinhabit disturbed places. The reinhabitation of violated places is a fundamental objective of the environmental justice movement, which "affirms the need for urban and rural ecological policies to clean up and rebuild our cities and rural areas in balance with nature, honoring the cultural integrity of all our communities, and providing fair access for all to the full range of resources."[11]

NOTES

1. Over the course of the three years of anti-logging protests at the Taylor Ranch, the "Wise Old Dudes for Wilderness" were present to observe and protect the protestors from abuse by law enforcement officials. The group of local elders, all of them acequia farmers, included Corpus A. Gallegos, Donaldo Maestas (husband of Olivia Maestas), Adelmo Kaber, Cornelio Arellano, and Ramon Maestas (for more discussion see Peña forthcoming).

2. These mishaps and irregularities range from crude racist statements by judges to explicit violations of basic constitutional rights to due process. For example, the original district court judge overseeing the case rejected the concept of common property use rights and said, "It is time to bring these Mexicans into the 20th Century" and into the world of private property. A 1994 Colorado Supreme Court decision found that the due process rights of the land grant heirs were in fact violated during the original quiet title action by Taylor and ordered a new trial which took place in 1998 (see Peña and Mondragon Valdez 1998).

3. Fermin Arguello, interview by Erica Rubine, Ranchos de Taos, New Mexico, June 1996.

4. Joe Gallegos, interview by author, San Luis, Colorado, June 1998.

5. Mike McGowan, personal communication to author, San Luis, Colorado, June 2000.

6. There are three different perspectives on the granting of water rights within Spanish and Mexican law in the New Mexico context. The first view is that water was a private property right that arose by grant and was a separate added interest (to landed property rights) requiring severance from the royal or public domain. A second view is that water required a separate private claim to sever it from the sovereign (public domain). In both of these views, water rights are not seen as riparian as the old common law used that term. A third view is that water rights did not require an explicit or implicit grant from the governmental authority but derived from local customary practice and use. A critical difference is that the third perspective views water as inseparable from the land and thus envisions a riparian rights doctrine at the level of local customary practice (see Hall 1990). My perspective is consistent with the third view.

7. Regional Anglo folklore has it that SPMDTU stands for "Some Poor Mexican Died Toes Up" or "Some Poor Mexican Died Tied Up." Other than the racist connotations, this also oddly confirms the emergence of mutualistas as a response to the need for funeral insurance, particularly among widows.

8. The emergence of "modern" acequia organizations, such as the Taos Valley Acequia Association, the New Mexico Acequia Association, and the Colorado Acequia Association, is a topic deserving its own study (see Peña forthcoming).

9. A similar argument was actually made much earlier by Douglas Harper (1987) in *Working Knowledge* and by Devon Peña (1997) in *The Terror of the Machine.* Harper focused on a rural case study of an automotive mechanic to argue that working knowledge, interacting with local community discourses about change and continuity, can contribute to the persistence and evolution of skill over time, creating conditions that allow for the survival of older forms of artisan and craft knowledge despite the predominance of Taylorist and Fordist regimes in the surrounding urban areas. Peña focuses on how "deskilled" assembly line workers in the border maquiladora factories acquire working knowledge of the production process which they combine with practical local knowledge to create new forms of struggle on the shop floor and in the community. Scott seems to reduce mètis to its technical, or practical, components. But practical knowledge is more than the sum of practices generated and sustained by generations of firsthand observation. But as I suggest in my study of *maquila* (assembly-line factory) workers' struggles:

the knowledge produced by the maquila workers in the context of the workplace is not limited to technical know-how derived from firsthand observation of labor processes. Much of their "technique" is also combined with other forms of knowledge, especially local knowledge . . . of tacit social and cultural skills. Local knowledge, when coupled with the inventive force of working knowledge, can engender the circulation of struggle, promoting discourses that link with the activities of informal . . . networks and other organizational forms. This link occurs because the discourses provide a common cultural framework for collaboration in struggle. (1997, 202)

10. For environmental justice activists, the task is to actively assist in the recovery, re-emplacement, and thus re-empowerment of mètis. Whenever political struggles over environmental protection become particularly intense, researchers are obligated to respond to the call by locals for research that is meaningful and useful to community-based struggles for environmental justice. In this case, the farmers' sense of place, and the contingency of the need to directly confront ecological degradation, constantly forced me to shift the focus of the study to include new problems. In this case, the effects of logging on stream hydrograph slope or the ecological services of the acequias are two important examples.

11. This is Principle 12 of the 1991 Principles of Environmental Justice, as cited in Bullard 2000, 3.

WORKS CITED

Basso, K. H. 1996. *Wisdom sits in places: Landscape and language among the Western Apache*. Albuquerque: University of New Mexico Press.

Brown, F. L., and H. Ingram. 1987. *Water and poverty in the Southwest*. Tucson: University of Arizona Press.

Bullard, R. D. 2000. *People of color environmental groups: 2000 directory*. Flint, Mich.: Charles Stewart Mott Foundation.

Butzer, K. W., J. F. Mateu, E. Butzer, and P. Kraus. 1985. "Irrigation agrosystems in eastern Spain: Roman or Islamic origins?" *Annals of the Association of American Geographers* 75 (4): 479–509.

Carlson, A. W. 1990. *The Spanish-American homeland: Four centuries in New Mexico's Rio Arriba*. Baltimore: Johns Hopkins Press.

Castells, M. 1997. *The power of identity*. Volume 2 of *The information age: Economy, society and culture*. Oxford: Blackwell.

Colorado Acequia Association. 2000. *Cumulative watershed assessment: The state of the Culebra and its tributaries*. Report submitted to the Environmental Protection Agency. San Luis, Colorado (December).

Crawford, S. 1988. *Mayordomo: Chronicle of an acequia in northern New Mexico*. New York: Anchor Books.

Curry, R. 1994. "Letter to Devon G. Peña." Rio Grande Bioregions Project, Vertical File Collection. Department of Anthropology, University of Washington, Seattle.

———. 1995. "The state of the Culebra watershed: The impact of logging on the southern tributaries." *La Sierra: National Edition* 2: 10–11.

Curry, R., M. Soulé, D. Peña, and M. McGowan. 1996. *Critical analysis of Montana best management practices sustainable alternatives*. Technical consultants' report presented to the Costilla County Land Use Planning Commission. Costilla County Conservancy District and La Sierra Foundation, San Luis, Colorado.

deBuys, W. 1985. *Enchantment and exploitation: The life and hard times of a New Mexico mountain range*. Albuquerque: University of New Mexico Press.

Deutsch, S. 1987. *No separate refuge: Culture, class, and gender on an Anglo-Hispanic frontier in the American Southwest, 1880–1940*. New York: Oxford University Press.

Ebright, M. 1994. *Land grants and lawsuits in northern New Mexico*. Albuquerque: University of New Mexico Press.

Forrest, S. 1989. *The preservation of the village: New Mexico's Hispanics and the New Deal*. Albuquerque: University of New Mexico Press.

Geertz, C. 1996. "Afterword." In *Senses of place*. Ed. S. Feld and K. Basso. Santa Fe: School of American Research.

Hall, G. E. 1990. "Shell games: The continuing legacy of rights to minerals and water on Spanish and Mexican land grants in the Southwest." *Rocky Mountain Mineral Law Institute* 36: 1–44.

Harper, D. 1987. *Working knowledge: Skill and community in a small shop*. Berkeley: University of California Press.

Hassell, M. J. 1968. *The people of northern New Mexico and the national forests*. Report prepared for Region 3, United States Forest Service, Department of Agriculture, Washington, D.C.

Hicks, G., and D. G. Peña. Forthcoming. "A conflict of parallels: Customary law, prior appropriation, and distributive justice in the legal evolution of the Colorado acequia system." To be submitted to *Ecology Law Quarterly*.

Hurst, W. D. 1968. "Memorandum, report on follow-up actions." Forester's Office, Region 3, Santa Fe, New Mexico (21 August).

Levi-Strauss, C. 1963. *Structural anthropology*. New York: Basic Books.

Libecap, G. D., and G. Alter. 1982. "Agricultural productivity, partible inheritance, and the demographic response to rural poverty: An examination of the Spanish Southwest." *Explorations in Economic History* 19 (April): 184–200.

Martínez, M. 1998. "The Martínez ranch: Background on the grant which included the lands in San Acacio Viejo." Paper prepared for the conference on "Four Hundred Years of Acequia Farming in the Rio Arriba Bioregion: A Cultural and Environmental History, 1598–1998," sponsored by the Ford Foundation, Colorado College, and Rio Grande Bioregions Project. Oñate Cultural Center, Alcalde, New Mexico (7–10 August).

Nazarea, V., ed. 1999. *Ethnoecology: Situated knowledge, located lives*. Tucson: University of Arizona Press.

Peña, D. G. 1992. "The 'brown' and the 'green': Chicanos and environmental politics in the Upper Rio Grande." *Capitalism, Nature, Socialism* 3 (1): 79–103.

———. 1997. *The terror of the machine: Technology, work, gender and ecology on the U.S.–Mexico border*. Austin: University of Texas Press.

———. 1999. "Cultural landscapes and biodiversity: The ethnoecology of an Upper Rio Grande watershed commons." In *Ethnoecology: Situated knowledge, located lives*. Ed. V. Nazarea. Tucson: University of Arizona Press.

———. 2001a. "Rewarding investment in natural capital: The acequia commonwealth of the Upper Rio Grande." In *Natural Assets and Environmental Justice: Democratizing Environmental Ownership*. Ed. J. K. Boyce. Beverly Hills: Sage Publications.

———. 2001b. "Globalization of the environment and local communities of resistance." In *Just sustainabilities: Development in an unequal world*. Ed. J. Ageyman, R. D. Bullard, and B. Evans. Cambridge: MIT Press.

———. Forthcoming. *Gaia en Aztlán: Endangered landscapes and disappearing peoples in the politics of place*. Tucson: University of Arizona Press.

———, ed. 1998. *Chicano culture, ecology, politics: Subversive kin*. Society, Place, and Environment Series. Tucson: University of Arizona Press.

Peña, D. G., and R. O. Martínez. 1998. "The capitalist tool, the violent, and the lawless: A critique of recent southwestern environmental history." In *Chicano culture, ecology, politics*, op. cit.

———. 2000. *Upper Rio Grande Hispano farms: A cultural and environmental history of land ethics in transition, 1598–1998*. Final report. Grant

RO-22707-94, National Endowment for the Humanities. Rio Grande Bio-regions Project, Department of Anthropology, University of Washington (January).

Peña, D. G., and M. Mondragon Valdéz. 1998. "The 'brown' and the 'green' revisited: Chicanos and environmental politics in the Upper Rio Grande." In *The struggle for ecological democracy: Environmental justice movements in the United States.* Ed. D. Faber. New York: Guilford Press.

Peña, D. G., H. Rothman, and E. Arellano. Forthcoming. *Four hundred years of acequia farms in the Rio Arriba bioregion: Cultural and environmental histories.* Tucson: University of Arizona Press.

Rívera, J. A. 1999. *Acequia culture: Land, water, and community in the Southwest.* Albuquerque: University of New Mexico Press.

Rívera, R. 1998. The sacred origins of agriculture. Paper prepared for the conference on "Four Hundred Years of Acequia Farming in the Rio Arriba Bioregion: A Cultural and Environmental History, 1598–1998," sponsored by the Ford Foundation, Colorado College, and Rio Grande Bioregions Project. Oñate Cultural Center, Alcalde, New Mexico (7–10 August).

Rothman, H. 1989. "Cultural and environmental change on the Pajarito Plateau." *New Mexico Historical Review* 64 (2): 185–212.

Rubine, E. 1998. "Conversations. Habitus, the Arellano family, the Arguello family, and the power of then and now." Paper prepared for the conference on "Four Hundred Years of Acequia Farming in the Rio Arriba Bioregion: A Cultural and Environmental History, 1598–1998," sponsored by the Ford Foundation, Colorado College, and Rio Grande Bioregions Project. Oñate Cultural Center, Alcalde, New Mexico (7–10 August).

Salmon, E. 1998. "The ethnobotany of the acequia: Recognition, identification, and uses of plants in the Rio Arriba of southern Colorado and northern New Mexico." Paper prepared for the conference on "Four Hundred Years of Acequia Farming in the Rio Arriba Bioregion: A Cultural and Environmental History, 1598–1998," sponsored by the Ford Foundation, Colorado College, and Rio Grande Bioregions Project. Oñate Cultural Center, Alcalde, New Mexico (7–10 August).

Sandoval, D. 1995. "Final report: Costilla County." Rio Grande Bioregions Project, Vertical file collection, Department of Anthropology, University of Washington, Seattle.

———. 1998. "Final report: Taos County." Rio Grande Bioregions Project, Vertical file collection, Department of Anthropology, University of Washington, Seattle.

Scott, J. C. 1999. *Seeing like a state: How certain schemes to improve the human condition have failed.* New Haven: Yale University Press.

Steinel, A. J. 1922. *History of agriculture in Colorado.* Ft. Collins: State Agricultural College Press.

Valdéz, A., and M. Valdéz. 1990. *The Culebra River villages of Costilla County: Village architecture and its historic context, 1851–1940.* Denver: Colorado Historical Society.

———. 1992. "La Capilla de Todos los Santos." *The Adobe Journal* 13: 12–23.

Weber, K. R. 1992. "Necessary but insufficient: Land, water, and economic development in Hispanic southern Colorado." *Journal of Ethnic Studies* 19 (2): 127–42.

Weinberg, B. 1999. *Homage to Chiapas.* London: Verso Books.

Wilkinson, C. F. 1992. *The eagle bird: Mapping the new West.* New York: Pantheon Books.

Wilmsen, C. 1995. *Fighting for the forests.* Ph.D. diss., Department of Geography, University of Wisconsin, Madison.

Wolf, T. 1994. *Colorado's Sangre de Cristo Mountains.* Niwot: University Press of Colorado.

4

WHO HEARS THEIR CRY?

African American Women and the Fight for Environmental Justice in Memphis, Tennessee

Andrea Simpson

> *And ye shall know the truth, and the truth shall make you free.*
>
> —John 8:32, inscription printed on newsletter published by Defense Depot Memphis, Tennessee Concerned Citizens' Committee

On Thursday, July 20, 2000, community members sat and listened to presenters explain the results of testing for toxic wastes on and around the site of the Memphis Defense Depot, a facility built in 1942 as a storage and maintenance facility for the army's engineering, chemical, and quartermaster corps. Doris Bradshaw, Restoration Advisory Board member, environmental justice activist, and president of the Defense Depot Memphis, Tennessee Concerned Citizens' Committee (DDMT-CCC), was not present. She had known in advance that the two experts scheduled to review their research, one from the Environmental Protection Agency (EPA) and the other from CH2M Hill, an engineering firm, were going to report they had found little evidence of toxicity on the grounds of this 642-acre facility, and no evidence that the toxins that were present had seeped into the surrounding residential neighborhoods. Rather than attend the meeting, Bradshaw instead chose to stay at home to begin planning new strategy and dealing with the emotional letdown she felt over the findings of the EPA and CH2M Hill report.

For the staff of the Memphis Depot and the EPA, this meeting was the end of a long, hard battle with the mostly African American community members living in the areas affected by the Memphis Depot, and with Bradshaw's organization, the DDMT-CCC. The battle was over the possibility of toxic poisoning from the Depot that affected the health of residents over a number of years. This was a battle waged largely by one woman, Doris Bradshaw, and her husband, Kenneth Bradshaw, who charged the Memphis Defense

Depot with environmental racism. According to the EPA's own reports, the South has more states with environmentally hazardous sites than any other region (see figure 4.1). Texas, Louisiana, Alabama, Florida, and North Carolina are excessively contaminated, and Tennessee, in particular, is one of the most environmentally toxic states in the nation. The South also continues to be the region where most African Americans reside.

In *Dumping in Dixie: Race, Class, and Environmental Quality* (1990), Robert Bullard focuses on the inability of black communities to mobilize and block the location of hazardous industries in their communities. In attempting to explain the obstacles to mobilization, scholars of social movements focus on the effects of *political opportunities, mobilizing structures,* and *framing processes* in the emergence and development of movements (McAdam, McCarthy, and Zald 1996). These scholars define political opportunities as changes in institutional structures and formal and informal power relations that create a climate favorable to social change. They define mobilizing structures as mediums through which people organize and participate in collective action. Framing processes refer to the meanings devised by movement actors that develop a consciousness that there are shared grievances that they can solve collectively. In this chapter, by focusing on the single case of Doris Bradshaw and the DDMT-CCC, I will examine how contemporary urban regimes limit political opportunities for environmental justice activists. I will also examine how race, class, and gender status play a role in hampering the success of environmental justice leaders in accessing mediums through which to tell their story.

I come to this project because I grew up in Memphis, Tennessee, in the 38114 zip code, one of the areas affected by the Memphis Depot. A witness to the leadership of women in the civil rights movement and education, I am committed to understanding the work of such women in this city of stark contrasts. As a former Memphian, this case both attracts and repels me. The opportunity to learn and write about this movement in an intimately familiar setting attracts me. The intractability of racism, sexism, and classism in the place I still call "home" repels me. Memphis, a city of conflict and cooperation, racial distance and intimacy, is an ideal context in which to examine the elements of one struggle in the environmental justice movement.

Women of color are a significant percentage of the leadership in the environmental justice movement. Often neglected in the literature on social movements, black working-class women offer inspired leadership for the younger women and girls in the community. However, most environmental

Fig. 4.1. Map showing relative concentration of listed environmentally hazardous sites by state. The darker the shade, the more hazardous sites that are present. (Map used with the permission of the EPA and retrieved from the EPA website at http://maps.epa.gov/environmapper)

justice activists in urban settings face institutional structures committed to economic development, even at the costs of citizens' health and well-being. Cities across the country are facing the political and social fallout of gentrification and the return of mostly white and wealthy people to urban centers. These changes have much to do with how local governments respond to the working-class communities of color who are complaining of environmental threats and hazards.

How does race, class, and gender status constrain the ability of activists to mobilize followers? If framing the cause of environmental justice requires access to the media, and the media grants legitimacy to those who they label "experts," then the media will deny access to environmental justice activists who lack the requisite training or organizational associations. The story of Doris Bradshaw illustrates how the media denies access to those who lack traditional credentials. The main newspaper, *The Commercial Appeal,* has never recognized her efforts, nor have some in the Memphis television and radio news media.

The Memphis Case

The Defense Distribution Depot of Memphis, Tennessee (DDDMT) was built in 1942 in what was then a rural area of Memphis, Tennessee. From 1954 through the 1970s, various toxic and nontoxic substances were handled and buried on this 642-acre facility. The community surrounding the DDDMT is part of South Memphis and is nearly 100 percent African American. The median income is $19,786, a figure reflecting the number of retirees who are on fixed incomes. Two of the main zip codes that contain the DDDMT are 38106 and 38114. Community members often use the zip code designation to describe the physical boundaries of the contamination area (see figures 4.2 and 4.3). Both zip codes are almost 100 percent African American. They contain middle-class to upper-middle-class homes as well as working-class neighborhoods and poor neighborhoods. The community is home to many retired schoolteachers, principals, and school administrators, once the elite class among African Americans.

In the 38106 zip code, 30 percent of the residents did not complete high school. While slightly over half of the black population own their own homes, nearly half are renters. One third of the households are female-headed households and one third are nonfamily households. One third of residents work in the service industry. In the 38114 zip code, almost half of the housing units are rentals; almost 90 percent were built prior to 1970 and 65 percent in 1950 or before. Over half of the households are female-headed households with children under six years of age. More than four in ten residents do not have a high school diploma—less than 1 percent have a college degree.[1] These data indicate a community in decline—its educated populace aging, its younger citizens struggling in single-parent homes. In addition to the DDDMT, the 38114 zip code was home to a Quaker Oats plant and is still home to a Kellogg's Cereal plant. As children growing up, we could often detect the odorous emissions from these industries throughout the entire neighborhood. As the maps indicate, these zip codes have numerous sites of hazardous materials.

Doris Bradshaw is a resident of the 38106 zip code and resides very near the Depot. She became involved in this movement because of the death of a loved one. There is a wide body of literature on how personal suffering may be politicized—prompting citizens to take action. M. Kent Jennings, in an address to the American Political Science Association, presented four sources of political activism that flow from pain and loss: accidents, disease,

Fig. 4.2. Map of the 38106 zip code area of Memphis, Tennessee, with squares indicating hazardous sites and toxic releases. (Map used with the permission of the EPA and retrieved from the EPA website at http://maps.epa.gov/environmapper)

human action, and natural disasters.[2] Interestingly, Jennings places environmental justice issues in the "accident" category. He uses Love Canal as an example of a case in which bodily harm from an accident motivated Lois Gibbs to start a movement against environmental polluters (Jennings 1999). According to Jennings, an example of activism stimulated by disease would be the AIDS movement. Activism stimulated by human action would include that of parents who advocate for public notification of where convicted child molesters are residing. Human action is a stimulant that seeks to assign blame for the pain and suffering felt by the activists and their families. This combination of sources; disease and the need to find a causal agent, spurred Doris Bradshaw to act. The death of her grandmother, Susie Hall, inspired her evolution from a shy stay-at-home mom to political activist. Hall died of a cancer so aggressive and devastating that doctors were unsure about its origins. Bradshaw believes that it began with bladder cancer, and says that she found literature indicating that this kind of cancer is "environmentally induced."[3] She explored the origins of her grandmother's cancer because of Susie Hall's dedication to natural foods and healthy living. Mrs. Hall did not smoke or drink alcohol. Around the same time of Susie Hall's death,

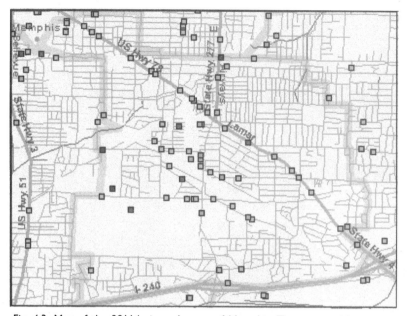

Fig. 4.3. Map of the 38114 zip code area of Memphis, Tennessee, with squares indicating hazardous sites and toxic releases. (Map used with the permission of the EPA and retrieved from the EPA website at http://maps.epa.gov/environmapper)

Bradshaw received a notice announcing a public forum on environmental contaminants at the Depot.[4]

After receiving the notice, Bradshaw began phoning Depot officials for answers. She could not get anyone to speak with her or to return her phone calls. It was this failure to respond that eventually led Bradshaw to suspect the Depot, the U.S. Army, and, ultimately, the federal government as the culprits in the death of Susie Hall. As the timeline indicates, Bradshaw made her discovery during the same time that the EPA chose to place the Depot on its priority list of sites to clean up.

The question of toxic poisoning from the Depot was a long time in coming to the fore, in part because the Depot was a major employer of people living in the community and paid higher than average wages. Table 4.1 provides a list of the events that brought the Defense Depot to the attention of the surrounding community.

One area of concern is a network of drainage ditches that flow from the Depot site. Because the Depot became an inactive facility just before the Gulf War, the ditches do not currently have high levels of contaminants. No one can answer the question of whether or not high levels of contamination

Table 4.1. Timeline of Events Leading to Memphis Depot Conflict

DATE	EVENT
February 1992	DDDMT is proposed as a candidate for the EPA National Priority List and is eligible for Superfund resources.
October 1992	DDDMT is added to the National Priority List.
November 1993	Pentagon reports that the DDDMT may contain chemical weapons or chemical warfare contamination.
June 1995	DDDMT slated to close. Approximately 600 jobs will be lost. 80 percent of the workers are African-American.
October 1995	Doris Bradshaw forms the Defense Depot of Memphis, Tennessee Concerned Citizens' Committee (DDMT-CCC).
December 1995	The City of Memphis looks forward to acquiring and redeveloping the Depot site. A Memphis Depot Redevelopment Agency is formed.
March 1997	Commissioners approve the Memphis Depot Redevelopment Plan. The plan proposes light industrial and public use of the land.
September 1997	DDDMT closed.
January 1998	Memphis Park System announces new $302 million dollar plan to develop 88 acres of the Depot property.
March 1998	Community perceives that the area is a cancer cluster. Neighbors are concerned at the mounting deaths from cancer.

existed in the past. Health data on the residents who live near the Depot are not available before 1989. There is also the possibility that records of disposal methods for various toxins—where and how they were buried—are not accurate. In 1994, the Agency for Toxic Substances and Disease Registry (ATSDR) determined that the level of contamination was too low to cause health problems for people living near the Depot.

Epidemiologists, environmental engineers and other experts do not dispute the fact that contaminants from the Depot have seeped through the surrounding residential area. The question is: Have these contaminants been in doses lethal enough to cause serious health problems? Cancer data examined by ATSDR and state officials showed no excessive rates of cancer among residents living near the facility. However, these data were from 1990–1996 only, and covered broad census tracts—not just the areas near the Depot. Methods employed by ATSDR have been scrutinized in a number of environmental justice cases. The Military Toxics Project reports that the agency routinely fails communities because its studies are characterized by "inadequate contact with the populations being studied, reliance on inappropriate testing techniques, reliance on statistical methods unsuitable for small or mobile populations, contracting with biased researchers, and studying the wrong types of illnesses." For example, residents of Whidbey Island, Washington, requested a health assessment to determine the effects of aircraft noise on residents. Whidbey Island is the home of the Whidbey Island Naval Air Station. Rather than conduct an independent assessment, ATSDR relied on information provided by the Navy and the county.[5]

Anecdotal evidence from community members is available—stories of lung cancers in nonsmokers and nonsmoking residences, children with leukemia, teenaged girls and boys with cancers of the reproductive organs, and numerous cases of kidney failure in early adulthood. A main source of the frustration experienced by the Memphis Depot community, as well as other communities, is that medical professionals do not keep records of exposure of their patients to toxic substances, therefore, the history of the exposure and possible combinations of exposures is lost. Cancers take a long time to develop, and without knowledge of possible exposures, citizens cannot secure accurate health assessments. Additionally, in cases where there are a number of conditions present, for example, obesity, tobacco use, and residing near toxic waste, it is difficult to isolate the cause of illness. The obstacles presented by current paradigms of scientific inquiry are prompting citizens to resist with evidence of their own and their neighbors' experiences. As Kroll-Smith, Brown, and Gunter (2000) write: "One simple but powerful assumption that citizens make in designing their research is that human experience is a valid mode of knowing the world. Normal science begins by discounting the importance of the individual's sensory understanding of the world. Subjectivity, in other words, must be rigorously excluded from the research design. Citizen science . . . privileges the human senses, according them an important place in the overall work to understand the problem" (19).

Doris Bradshaw is working with Howard University medical students in trying to conduct an assessment that might reveal patterns of illnesses specific to the Depot neighborhood. She is particularly concerned about the occurrences of reproductive organ cancers in the women in her community. The problem is that Bradshaw is working for social change in an era antagonistic to such ideas. She needs resources and methods of getting her story out to a wider public. In the following section, I will point out how the lack of political opportunities and the ability to effectively frame this problem have hampered Bradshaw in her quest for environmental justice.

Contemporary Obstacles to Social Justice Movements: Changing Times, New Political Objectives, and Access to the Public

PROSPERITY IDEOLOGY: THE NEW BLACK POLITICS   Traditionally, social movements flourish in times of socioeconomic change. In this era of un-precedented economic growth for the country, one would expect to see the formation of movements around various social issues. Yet, while we have seen protests staged on behalf of the environment, animal rights, and global economic policies, none of these issues have attracted the attention of a significant number of citizens in the United States. One explanation may be that growing income disparities are a feature of our current economy. While the majority of American citizens enjoyed the post–World War II economic boom, a more select group of Americans have benefited from the boom of the last six or so years. Memphis, a major point of struggle in the Civil Rights Movement, is experiencing, as many other major cities are, the flight of middle-class blacks to the suburbs and the return of middle-class whites to the city. As one scholar demonstrates in a study of Atlanta, these patterns promote conservative pro-growth policies on the part of city leaders (Banks 2000). A conservative pro-growth agenda is not friendly toward the concerns of environmental justice activists, as I will discuss in more detail in the following pages.

The Memphis city population is 61 percent black, with many residents living in declining neighborhoods south of the city. The city has committed to rebuilding its fading downtown and restoring its housing projects, some of which are so dilapidated that it is hard to believe that people live in them. People living in working-class communities of modest single-family homes are falling between the cracks as city leaders pursue dreams of building a metropolis for the new millennium.

Political rivals have accused the mayor, Willie Herenton, of neglecting black Memphians in favor of white business leaders (Kilborn 1999). However, as Clarence Stone pointed out in *Regime Politics: Governing Atlanta* (1989), the business elite and other elite groups are cultivated by public officials because these groups have the resources, material and social, to enhance officials' capacity to govern and to get things done. Black Memphians had high expectations for Herenton, a product of South Memphis and the former school superintendent. However, the result of his historic election in 1991 is that those who are in a position to invest in and start businesses are doing better, while the working-class and poor struggle to catch up.[6] One of the areas of tension is the city's desire to develop the land on which the Depot is located to increase opportunities for both businesspersons and members of the community.

If we define political opportunities as a shifting of power relations that create a climate ripe for social change, this shift has not taken place yet in Memphis. I mentioned the concept of pro-growth conservative policies earlier in this section. Scholars define a pro-growth conservative agenda as one that relies on market forces to solve problems, values the "private" over the "public," and is punitive toward the poor and those on public assistance (Banks 2000; Simmons 1998). Banks's study demonstrated that Atlanta's politically active black middle-class population was essentially trading places with the politically active white population, with the latter group becoming the urban dwellers. He convincingly argues that the increased voting power of these urban dwellers, who tend to be more conservative, is an important factor in pursuing a conservative agenda.

A similar pattern has developed in Memphis. The Center City Commission of Memphis boasts on its website that "from 1990 to 2000, Downtown Memphis had the largest percentage increase of non-Hispanic white populations of any downtown area in the United States." In an excerpt from the Commission's Strategic Plan, the site lists as one of its goals "to create a guide for the prioritization and allocation of resources so that public money can leverage private funding to achieve the maximum positive results."[7] These statements indicate a commitment to economic development and those citizens who can participate in this vision. New directions in urban political agendas mean that activists for social change will need powerful mediums through which to direct their efforts. The pro-growth agenda does not serve the environmental justice movement, because environmental issues are often in conflict with economic incentives.

Memphis mayor Herenton won his second and third elections by aligning himself with business interests. The development of the 642-acre Depot site will be an accomplishment that will serve him well in future bids for elective office. Doris Bradshaw claims that when she finally met Mayor Herenton at a meeting about airport noise in the community, he accused her of causing "public hysteria" about the Depot. He then said, "I'm not going to have it." Putting his face closer to hers, he repeated, "Do you understand? I'm not going to have it."[8] One wonders if it would matter more if Bradshaw could marshal forces opposing Herenton in the next election.

DISMISSED AND DISRESPECTED: NO ONE HEARS THEIR CRY The 1980s and 1990s were decades of retrenchment and advancement for African Americans. The Reagan-Bush years introduced the American electorate to a new political dialogue—the coding of racial issues that served to give racial conservatives the moral and political advantage in public debate (Edsall and Edsall 1992). Republicans replaced the language of civil rights with terms such as "special interests," "taxes and big government," "quotas," "reverse discrimination," and "welfare"—terms weighted with racial implications. Politicians talked about, and people responded to, "welfare queens" and others who would not work and were living off the hard-earned wages of working Americans. The Republicans were largely successful in framing the debate about race, poverty, and inequality in ways that captured the minds and hearts of those people who were feeling left out of a rapidly changing economy. The Democratic Party, liberal activists, and black organizations have not been successful in challenging this new frame. In failing to recast the debate in terms that citizens can understand, Democratic and liberal leadership have retreated and moderated, rather than strengthened, their argument.[9] The result has been a climate that is hostile to social justice arguments. While conservatives complain of a liberal media, scholars have shown that this is a myth. A conservative perspective dominates media, and liberal arguments are not popular (Hellinger 2000; Parenti 1995).

How groups frame their grievances so that they can bind themselves to the cause and recruit followers requires that they have access to public forums and media. When access is stymied, it becomes difficult to sustain the core of a movement and more difficult to recruit followers. Scholars have discovered that marginalized groups have tremendous difficulty in accessing media to air their views. According to one article: "journalistic routines and practices favoring official sources and those holding institutional power are often intractable. The tendency of some journalists to define politics solely as a domain of elites significantly hinders the ability of social movement organizations to shape news stories . . . American journalism rarely presents people as citizens, capable of articulating their views and providing an understanding of the forces that shape their lives" (Ryan, Carragee, and Meinhofer 2001).

Other scholars have found that a credible framing of issues, or one that is effective in gaining empathizers and followers, has three components: consistency, empirical credibility, and credible claimsmakers. The latter component is the one that concerns me in this work, and leads to the question of how claimsmakers, or social movement activists, establish credibility. Scholars say that claimsmakers need status, knowledge, and a legitimizing organization (Benford and Snow 2000). Being black, female, and working class compromises the status of the claimsmaker. A lack of formal education compounds the problem. If she does not represent an organization that has established itself, then her credibility as a claimsmaker, at least in the American journalists' eyes, is questionable.

Media framing and the nature of political discourse make matters worse. In the previous section, I discussed the way in which the term "welfare queen" became salient for the public. The public discourse is fraught with language that characterizes African American women who are poor as undeserving. According to a study by Franklin Gilliam: "media coverage of America's welfare reform process perpetuates racial myths that dominate ethnic relations. Analysis of published stories reveals a predominant theme that most welfare recipients are African-American females, and are couched in ambiguous language that implies the individuals are to blame for their condition through lack of perseverance and uncontrolled fecundity . . . the notion of the welfare queen [has] taken on the status of common knowledge." (Gilliam 1999). This means that every African American woman of poor or working-class status has the specter of a "welfare queen" over her head. If status is crucial to credibility, and credibility is crucial to getting your voice heard, then women such as Doris Bradshaw will have a steep hill to climb in their battle against institutions and corporations. However, Bradshaw, her husband, and members of the DDMT-CCC are fighting negative media portrayals and winning some victories.

Doris Bradshaw wants Depot officials to acknowledge that they have harmed the community. She does not want the city to develop and use the property until they are certain that all of the toxins have been identified and cleaned up. Bradshaw began publishing a newsletter that documented her efforts on behalf of the community. Some feel that this protest is halting economic progress for both the city and the community; however, the DDMT-CCC feels otherwise. In their January 2000 newsletter, they write: "DDMT-CCC has worked closely with the Depot officials to bring jobs to Memphis that pay a decent living-wage and that are safe to work. But, the good jobs that Depot officials promised never occurred. It's the same old stuff—the local residents get maximum-production-at-minimum-wage jobs while people from outside of the area get the high paying jobs with good benefits" (DDMT-CCC 2000a).

The Defense Logistics Agency, which is the agency responsible for the Depot cleanup, is charged with communicating with the surrounding community about both the toxins and the plans for cleaning them up. They hired a community relations firm based in Canada, Frontline Communications, to facilitate meetings, send out press releases, and produce the monthly newsletter called *EnviroNews*. They also supported a move to place Doris Bradshaw on the Restoration Advisory Board (RAB) as a way of neutralizing her efforts. Ulysses Truitt, RAB member and former environmental manager of the Depot, claimed that it was his idea to nominate her to the RAB so that she would "quiet down."[10] Truitt believes that Bradshaw is sincere but misguided, because if there were any dangerous toxins that seeped into the community from the Depot, he would know about it and he would not still live in the area.

Depot officials formed the RAB soon after the EPA designated the Depot as a Superfund site. The purpose of these boards is to serve as representatives of community and governmental interests at the sites. The board has no real power, though it is supposed to encourage community involvement in the cleanup process. Depot officials, along with the staff of Frontline, facilitate the RAB meetings and rigidly adhere to parliamentary rules of order. The fact that most of the RAB members as well as attendees do not know or understand these rules limits their ability to put certain items on the agenda for discussion. Moreover, a hierarchy of Army officials must clear reporters and scholars seeking interviews with Depot officials. Officials demand that scholars and reporters submit a list of questions in advance, after which they decide whether or not to give the reporter or scholar access to technical experts and Depot officials.[11] These processes stymie the information flow between the community, Depot officials, and the various technical consultants.

Depot officials allocated time at RAB meetings for the public to ask questions or make comments about the toxins identified at the Depot and the cleanup effort. Doris Bradshaw took advantage of these opportunities to speak out about what she believed was the intentional poisoning of the community by the U.S. Army. The minutes of the RAB indicate that Depot officials frequently did not take Doris Bradshaw's contributions seriously. For example, during the ATSDR presentation of the health study of cancer incidents in the community, Doris Bradshaw responds to the study's five-year limit by stating that her organization wanted a twenty-year analysis, because "you can't tell anything about no five years." Shawn Phillips, the Depot official who ran the meeting, simply responds, "Okay. Thank you."[12] The expert goes on to explain why twenty-year data is not available, but Depot officials never address the concern. In a discussion of the removal of mustard gas bombs on the property, Doris admonishes Depot officials to prepare for public hearings. They respond that after a removal plan is prepared, they will deposit the plan in the "Information Repository," which is a reading room on the Depot grounds, for public view. Bradshaw wants public hearings, and mentions that she has filed an Environmental Justice complaint against the Defense Logistics Agency in the past for moving ahead with cleanup procedures without warning the community:

> And I want to know that if something happens with this mustard gas bomb that is like what happened with the dieldrin, we won't have time to file no complaint.[13] So, you better get our fears and concerns taken care of in the beginning, or you are going to have a problem with the community. Now, you can kind of stonewall and try to play and make it pretty like this is absolutely harmless, and we know that chlorine will probably be in the air and different levels of it after they start digging. You better. I am warning you, because you already got the community in a frenzy already, and you are going to have to answer to that.

Shawn Phillips simply responds, "Okay. I guess we'll move along with the agenda-update of the TAPP Grant, questions and comments from the January meeting."[14]

Bradshaw and the DDMT-CCC have implemented a number of strategies to get the attention of city and Depot officials. They contact media on numerous occasions but receive minimal coverage. They attend all of the RAB meetings, which they did even before Doris was appointed, and vigorously protest the move to redevelop the land. Dick Gregory, the famous comedian and activist, as well as officials of environmental justice centers around the South attended a protest march organized by DDMT-CCC. Numerous environmental justice complaints to the EPA have gone unanswered. Due to scarce funds, the newsletter, "The Truth is the Light," is published sporadically. Although the Bradshaws travel extensively to meet with other environmental activists, they have yet to recruit a sizeable number of residents and/or nonresidents to their cause. The reasons for this are varied and complex—the community is poor with few resources that allow for activism; the issue is a "hard" one, difficult to understand and more difficult to substantiate; and the class strata within the community are barriers to fomenting a unified identity.

The only daily newspaper in town, *The Commercial Appeal,* has not covered the organization or Bradshaw. It has published only two articles on the concerns of citizens in the area. One of the alternative papers, *The Memphis*

Flyer, did do a cover story on the Bradshaws and their efforts; however, the tone of the story cast them as sincere but uneducated and misinformed:

> It's not passion the Bradshaws lack, it's diplomacy and savvy. The media have a hard time with the clumsy name of their organization (DDMT-CCC, standing for "Defense Depot of Memphis, Tennessee-Concerned Citizens Committee), of which 44-year-old Doris is president. At 49, Kenneth thinks nothing of giving interviews in the middle of the day while he eats cereal and forgoes the use of a shirt. Neither Bradshaw has a problem using phrases like "a pack of lies" in their newsletters and calling for the various resignations or terminations of almost every government environmental technocrat they've encountered on the Depot issue. (Campbell 1998)

In the same story, the reporter identifies Larry Smith, a white male, as "the city's most notable environmentalist." The Bradshaws sometimes confronted this former member of the RAB during meetings. The article states that:

> According to Doris Bradshaw, Smith wasn't helpful because he doesn't live in the Depot community; he was lackluster at best during meetings, in secret agreement with government officials at worst. According to Smith, the Bradshaws would make wild assertions, then fail to back them up with proof. One time, he says, Doris claimed to have had maps of Depot property showing that hazardous materials existed where Depot officials said nothing existed. Smith says he asked for copies of the maps. She never produced. (Campbell 1998)

Doris was disappointed in the way the reporter characterized her in the article. She was also appalled at the cover photograph of her and her husband (figure 4.4). According to Doris, the photographer asked her and Kenneth to look as serious and confrontational as they could, and they complied. She took it all rather lightly at first, not realizing that this would be on the cover with the title "The Agitators." The result is a likeness that does not at all resemble the attractive and soft-spoken Doris Bradshaw.

Bradshaw is frustrated in her attempts to get Depot officials to acknowledge her concerns. She charges racism, but is ambivalent about seeking legal solutions to the problem. In its opening volley for the year 2000, the DDMT-CCC newsletter begins with an essay entitled "Militarism, Army Racism, and Capitalism." In the essay, the group attempts to legally connect

Fig. 4.4. Doris and Ken Bradshaw pose for a Memphis news article. They were asked by the reporter to look "serious and confrontational." (Photograph by Trey Harrison)

issues of environmental racism to slavery and Jim Crow. They also explain why they believe the legal system is failing them: "DDMT-CCC is not anti-legal. The American legal system is one of the best in the world. Yet, this fine legal system has always tolerated racism. And, no system in the world can be trusted to regulate itself. Just as slavery and Jim Crow segregation were legal institutions in the USA, environmental racism is imbedded in the American legal system" (DDMT-CCC 2000a). In the next newsletter, the language of rights is stronger and more specific. The entire newsletter is describing the "Days of Outrage" protest and its goals: "The Days of Outrage was a concerted four-pronged attack upon the right-wing cabal in general and the Defense Depot in particular. The right-wing cabal has been trying to roll back the clock on the Title VI Civil Rights legislation of 1964 and the Presidential Executive Order #12898 that guarantees Poor and People of Color Communities participation in Environmental Clean-up" (DDMT-CCC 2000b). The Days of Outrage took place on April 1–3, 2000, and included a tour of the Depot community; a Sunday service held at New Sardis Baptist Church; a press conference at Macedonia Baptist Church; and a mock funeral procession through the neighborhood. The mock funeral procession symbolized the deaths activists attribute to Depot toxic waste. Only one local television station, a minor one, Channel 24, covered this event.

Bradshaw has had some victories. She has taken advantage of the growing network of national activists in the environmental justice movement to help galvanize her supporters. She has been able to secure small grants from foundations and has formed relationships with the National Congress of Black Churches, the Coalition of Black Trade Unionists, Greenpeace USA, and the Military Toxics Project. Her perseverance convinced Depot officials that they needed an African American community relations liaison and resulted in the hiring of a person, Alma Moore, with close ties to the Memphis Depot community. This was a significant accomplishment. Moore, a public relations specialist and member of the community, makes access to public documents much easier for community members and scholars. Bradshaw has also forced the Depot to respond to requests for information and for additional testing. Her travels and associations with other activists around the country have strengthened her resolve, but she has been unable to halt the development of the Depot site. As of this writing, Depot officials have released a report on groundwater contamination at the Depot site. The next section is a brief overview of the progress of environmental litigation and the possibilities for the Memphis case.

Civil Rights and Environmental Justice

In 1994, President Clinton issued Executive Order No.12898, Federal Actions to Address Environmental Justice in Minority Populations and Low-Income Populations. It requires federal agencies to establish procedures for addressing issues of environmental justice. While it is not a legal remedy, it is significant in that it recognizes environmental justice as an issue, which had been, and to some extent still is, under dispute. It also forces agencies to establish policies that include public participation and provide avenues for airing disputes.

Litigants applied the Equal Protection Clause of the Fourteenth Amendment in past cases involving environmental justice. However, in *Washington v. Davis* (1976), the Supreme Court ruled that plaintiffs must establish discriminatory intent in order to prevail on equal protection grounds.[15] Title VI of the Civil Rights Act of 1964, particularly sections 601 and 602, eliminates the need (at least formally) to establish discriminatory intent, and has become the current basis for contesting environmental inequity. Section 601 prohibits discrimination under any program or activity receiving federal financial assistance. Section 602 requires agencies to develop and carry out regulations that effectively sustain the directive in Section 601. The EPA has adopted a disparate impact standard in its Title VI regulations that specifically addresses discriminatory effects, unless these effects are justified, and an alternative, which would not have disparate impact, is unavailable.

Courts, however, have held to a "discriminatory intent" standard in most environmental justice cases, and have ignored the concept of discriminatory effects. When African American residents of Pollocksville, North Carolina, for example, challenged the location of a wastewater treatment plant on land settled by freed slaves in 1870, the U.S. Court of Appeals for the Fourth Circuit ruled that the town and the U.S. Department of Agriculture "provided substantial legitimate nondiscriminatory reasons for its site decision."[16] They also ruled that alternatives were given due consideration, and none were found. What is clear is that intent to discriminate must accompany disparate impact.

In a case involving the Federal Highway Commission and the disparate impact of a highway bypass through an African American community, the U.S. Court of Appeals for the Fourth Circuit ruled that the plaintiffs were barred from filing against federal agencies by sovereign immunity.[17] These strict standards involving complaints of environmental injustice make the

Memphis case a hard one. The Depot community is 97 percent African American, which helps in legitimizing a civil rights claim. The problem comes in meeting the standard of proving that the resulting health effects, even if established, were intentionally inflicted. The U.S. Army and the Defense Logistics Agency might claim that while the outcomes have not been ideal, as a matter of security for the nation they had little choice. Were there less discriminatory alternatives? Perhaps—when the military built the Depot, there were few people populating the area, although South Memphis is a historically black section of town. One could assume that blacks would move into the area once jobs became available at the facility.

There are other legal challenges:

- Any damage to the community wrought by Depot dumping happened over a twenty-five- to thirty-year period. Assessing how, when, and where Depot officials buried toxic wastes, and the process by which they might have contaminated the community, is difficult.
- There are other sources of contaminants in the community that offer an alternative source for the health problems perceived by the community.
- Risk assessments for toxic substances as well as health assessments have found no evidence of the claims made by community members.

Clearly, Bradshaw and the DDMT-CCC are aware of the applicability of Title VI. However, they are also aware of the challenge facing them in disproving the results of the professional assessments obtained by the EPA and Depot officials.

Conclusion

Ignored and dismissed as reactionary, Doris Bradshaw does not have the support of the black political leadership in Memphis or the media in her fight against the Memphis Depot. She is waging her battle in a city that, in spite of its efforts to become progressive, has not yet exorcised racism, sexism, and classism from the local culture. Those who believe that she has no right to speak, try to silence Bradshaw, but she continues to advocate for her community. Bradshaw believes that carcinogens have contaminated the drinking water. Tests conducted by the U.S. Army Corps of Engineers have found contaminated soil and groundwater beneath the Depot. The contamination comes from the use of pesticides, solvents, fuels, and other hazardous compounds, some of which are cancer-causing agents. However, officials assert that the contamination is restricted to a shallow aquifer, and has not reached the Memphis Sand aquifer, which supplies the city's water. Bradshaw and her followers do not trust the Army officials or the EPA, and believe that liability concerns drive their conclusions. They believe that the community is a cancer cluster, and that the toxins buried at the DDDMT are responsible.[18] The lack of official support or scientific evidence of a cancer cluster in the Depot community does not mean that there are no health problems present. Citizens in the area surrounding the DDDMT believe that community residents have suffered more than their share of deaths from cancer, although most residents hesitate to speculate as to how this may have happened.

In order to halt the continuing development of the Depot, Bradshaw and her followers must find ways to broker their political power, organize, and frame their issue. We know that in any social movement, conditions must be ripe for the group to be heard. My research indicates that at least in one urban setting, conservative pro-growth policy along with the race, class, and gender status of environmental justice leadership are barriers to environmental justice victories. Doris Bradshaw and the DDMT-CCC continue to struggle while the Memphis Depot continues with the planned cleanup of toxic areas and the leasing of land and buildings to tenants. As of today, thirteen light industrial businesses have located on the property. The director of the Memphis Depot Redevelopment Corporation, a private entity, believes that a botched deal with a local community college to purchase the main building on the site is due to publicity generated by DDMT-CCC.[19] He is confident, however, that eventually all of the property will be leased and the creation of new businesses will provide jobs and income for the City of Memphis.

NOTES

1. 1990 U.S. Census Data, U.S. Census Bureau (homer.ssd.census.gov).

2. M. Kent Jennings presented this work in his presidential address at the 1998 annual meeting of the American Political Science Association. The address was later published in the *American Political Science Review,* March 1999.

3. According to the University of Pennsylvania's Oncology Link, the incidence of bladder cancer in men is three times that in women. They cite cigarette smoking, exposure to chemicals called arylamines (used in the textile

and rubber industries), and a parasite as possible causes. Retrieved 19 February 2001 from *Oncolink* (www.oncolink.upenn.edu/disease/bladder).

4. Doris Bradshaw, interview by author. Memphis, Tenn., 4 March 2000.

5. Exchange between Bradshaw and Phillips as recorded in the Minutes from the Restoration Advisory Board (RAB) Meeting of 18 February 1999, Memphis, Tenn.

6. Memphis was the last city with a majority-black population to elect a black mayor. For a detailed analysis, see Wright 2000.

7. Retrieved 12 July 2001 from *Definitely Downtown* (www.downtown memphis.com).

8. Doris Bradshaw, interview by author. Memphis, Tenn., 16 December 2001.

9. The Black Radical Congress, founded in 1998, has environmental justice issues as one of its main agenda items. There is hope that this new organization may emerge as a leader in the environmental justice movement.

10. Ulysses Truitt, interview by author. Memphis, Tenn., 25 July 2000.

11. I was denied access to Depot officials and directed to use public documents as sources of information for this paper and the subsequent book manuscript.

12. Exchange between Bradshaw and Phillips as recorded in the Minutes from the RAB Meeting of 21 January 1999, Memphis, Tenn.

13. Dieldrin was a popular pesticide used from the 1950s to the early 1970s as soil and seed treatment and in public health in the control of mosquitoes and tsetse flies. A study by Danish researchers found a link between Dieldrin and breast cancer in women. Other researchers have contested these findings.

14. Exchange between Bradshaw and Phillips as recorded in the Minutes from the RAB Meeting of 18 February 1999, Memphis, Tenn.

15. African American applicants to the Washington, D.C. police department claimed that the written personnel test administered by the department was discriminatory in that it excluded a high number of African Americans and bore no relationship to job performance. The Court ruled that the respondents had to establish discriminatory intent in order to prevail in this case.

16. Retrieved 18 June 2001 from *ABA Network* (www.abanet.org). See also *Goshen Road Environmental Action Team v. U.S. Department of Agriculture*, No. 98-2102 (4th Cir., 1999).

17. See *Jersey Heights Neighborhood Association v. Glendening*, 174 F.3d 180 (4th Cir., 1999).

18. According to a National Institutes of Health website, along with at least six other websites from health organizations, cancer is most often a random occurrence, even clusters of cancers in communities. Incidences of cancer are difficult to link to environmental causes, especially when researchers and epidemiologists are seeking statistical proof of the existence of such clusters. Yet, these experts admit that there is often not enough data—not enough cases, and not enough medical history, to confirm or reject a community's claim of environmentally induced cancers. This means that there can never be enough "proof" to support such claims.

19. Jim Covington, interview by author. 28 July 2000, Memphis, Tenn.

WORKS CITED

Banks, M. E. II. 2000. "A changing electorate in a majority black city: The emergence of a neo-conservative black urban regime in contemporary Atlanta." *Journal of Urban Affairs* 22:3 (Summer): 265–79.

Benford, R. D., and D. A. Snow. 2000. "Framing processes and social movements: An overview and assessment." *Annual Review of Sociology* 611.

Bullard, R. 1990. *Dumping in Dixie.* Boulder: Westview Press.

Campbell, P. 1998. "The agitators." *The Memphis Flyer,* 26 November–2 December.

DDMT-CCC. 1998. "Toxic anguish." *The Truth is the Light,* 12.

———. 2000a. "Militarism, army racism, and capitalism." *The Truth is the Light,* 1 January: 7.

———. 2000b. "Days of outrage." *The Truth is the Light,* 1–3 April: 9.

Edsall, T. B., and M. D. Edsall. 1992. *Chain reaction.* New York: Norton.

Gilliam, F. 1999. "The 'welfare queen' experiment." *Nieman Reports* 53 (2): 49.

Hellinger, D. 2000. "Conservatives constructed myth about liberal media." *St. Louis Journalism Review* 30 (230): 20.

Jennings, M. K. 1999. "Political responses to pain and loss: Presidential address, American Political Science Association, 1998." *American Political Science Review* 93 (1): 1.

Kilborn, P. T. 1999. "Memphis blacks find poverty's grip strong." *The New York Times* 5 October: A14.

Kroll-Smith, S., and H. H. Floyd. 1997. *Bodies in protest: Environmental illness and the struggle over medical knowledge.* New York: New York University Press.

Kroll-Smith, S., P. Brown, and V. Gunter. 2000. "Knowledge, citizens, and organizations." In *Illness and the environment: A reader in contested medicine.* Ed. S. Kroll-Smith, P. Brown, and V. Gunter. New York: New York University Press.

McAdam, D., J. D. McCarthy, and M. N. Zald. 1996. *Comparative perspectives on social movements.* Cambridge: Cambridge University Press.

McCann, M. 1994. *Rights at work.* Chicago: University of Chicago Press.

Parenti, M. 1995. "The myth of a liberal media." *The Humanist* 55 (1): 7.

Ryan, C., K. M. Carragee, and W. Meinhofer. 2001. "Theory into practice: Framing, the news media, and collective action." *Journal of Broadcasting and Electronic Media* 45 (1): 175.

Simmons, L. 1998. "A new urban conservatism: The case of Hartford, Connecticut." *Journal of Urban Affairs* 20: 175–98.

Stone, C. 1989. *Regime politics: Governing Atlanta.* Lawrence: University Press of Kansas.

Washington v. Davis, 426 U.S. 229 (1976).

Wright, S. D. 2000. *Race, power, and political emergence in Memphis.* New York: Garland.

5

RADIATION, TOBACCO, AND ILLNESS IN POINT HOPE, ALASKA

Approaches to the "Facts" in Contaminated Communities

Nelta Edwards

I use this case study of environmental contamination near the Alaskan Inupiat community of Point Hope to discuss an impasse that presents itself in cases of contaminated communities. I describe and exemplify three approaches common to activists and/or scholars: doing better science, investigating the potential distortion provided by scientific language, and treating scientific language as the construction of reality. I suggest an alternative "ironic stance" toward the "facts" through the use of a conceptual tool called "mobile ontologies" in order to address this impasse and to progress toward an ecologically sound epistemology.

Introduction

Point Hope sits on a narrow gravel peninsula that stretches westward into the Chukchi Sea off the coast of present-day Alaska. Located some 130 miles north of the Arctic Circle, this area has been called "remote," "isolated," and even "barren" by outsiders. However, anthropological evidence indicates that Point Hope is one of the oldest continuously occupied communities in North America. For more than two thousand years this location has proven ideal for hunting, fishing, and gathering.[1]

Traditional food acquisition activities remain paramount for the people of Point Hope despite the influence of Western culture introduced by European whalers, traders, and missionaries. These activities signify much more than just survival or even merely a way of life. Alaska Native people consider them inextricable from belief systems and self-identity. The yearly food procurement cycle provides the social structure that helps to maintain spiritual and cultural values, such as mutual respect, sharing, and resourcefulness as older generations teach skills to younger generations.[2]

In 1957, far away from Point Hope, nuclear scientists at the Atomic Energy Commission (AEC) established Project Plowshare, a national program to explore "peaceful" uses of nuclear bombs. Plowshare intended "to highlight the peaceful application of nuclear explosive devices and thereby create a climate of world opinion that [was] more favorable to weapons development and tests." In order to create favorable world opinion Plowshare advocates proposed the use of nuclear bombs for civilian construction projects. Nuclear bombs could improve a "slightly flawed planet" to allow for easier extraction of natural resources and to create waterways.[3]

The Panama Canal represented a waterway in need of improvement according to the Plowshare advocates. They lamented that the series of locks in the Panama Canal slowed travel and might prove problematic as world-shipping needs increased. To remedy this, Plowshare advocates recommended using nuclear bombs to level the canal, thus eliminating the need for the locks. However, because the use of nuclear explosives for an underwater project had not been tested it might have been difficult to convince the Panamanians to agree to it.[4]

In order to demonstrate the feasibility, both nationally and internationally, of using nuclear bombs for civilian projects, Plowshare advocates looked for a place in the United States where they could test their ideas. They preferred a coastal area to determine the shape of post-detonation underwater cratering. They also sought a sparsely populated area due to the danger of radiation.[5] Based on these criteria, they settled on Cape Thompson, Alaska, which is located approximately 30 miles south of Point Hope. The Atomic Energy Commission called the plan to create the harbor at Cape Thompson "Project Chariot." The original Project Chariot plans called for the equivalent of 2.4 million tons of TNT to excavate the mile by half-mile harbor and the mile by quarter-mile entrance channel, an amount of TNT 160 times that which was dropped on Hiroshima.[6]

People in Point Hope opposed Project Chariot from the start. Alaskan environmentalists supported their views, as did environmental groups from outside Alaska. Some of the scientists contracted to do the preliminary work also came to question the safety and practicality of the proposed blast. Due to this pressure, and the economic unfeasibility of the project, the AEC canceled Project Chariot even though several years of preparatory work had taken place.[7] Before the AEC officially cancelled Project Chariot, they contracted with scientists from the United States Geological Survey (USGS) to conduct radioactive tracer experiments near the Project Chariot site. The AEC wanted to know how radioactive materials dispersed through the local waterways. To find out, the USGS scientists constructed twelve plots demarcated with two-by-fours. On some of the plots they sprinkled the radioactive sand transported to Alaska from the Nevada Test Site. The sand contained ten millicuries of undefined fallout from the July 1962, Sedan explosion. On other plots the scientists sprinkled pure forms of radioactive isotopes—five millicuries of iodine 131, five millicuries of strontium 85, and six millicuries of cesium 137. The scientists watered the plots, caught the runoff in jars, and later took the jars to a laboratory in Denver for testing. Upon finishing the experiments the scientists instructed a worker to bulldoze the contaminated test plots' soil and surrounding soil into a mound, thereby producing 15,000 pounds of contaminated soil. The amounts of strontium 85 and cesium 137 in this soil exceeded that permitted by federal regulations by 1000 times.[8] Neither the scientists nor their agencies told the local Inupiat people about the radioactive mound, in spite of the fact that it was well known that people from the nearby communities of Point Hope and Kivalina used the area extensively for subsistence activities.[9]

Unaware of the contamination, people from Point Hope and Kivalina continued to use the Cape Thompson area for traditional food-gathering activities. Over the years, the community in Point Hope, which by the 1990s had a population of about six hundred, began to perceive a sharp increase in the diagnosis of cancer.[10] People also noticed a decline in the health of the wildlife they used for subsistence. A Point Hope elder, Helen Tuzroyluke, told of a red fox that she and her husband trapped in 1987 near the (undisclosed) tracer experiment site. When her husband skinned the fox, a patch of growth on the fox oozed liquid. Mr. Tuzroyluke cut off the head and discarded the fox. By the time they got back to Point Hope, Mr. Tuzroyluke had broken out in sores and shortly thereafter began to suffer from chronic nausea. Mrs. Tuzroyluke believed that touching the carcass of the fox caused her husband's subsequent liver problems. Others told of animals that they hunted that could not be brought home because of apparent illnesses.[11] Elder Irma Hunnicutt told of caribou with strange lumps and "different looking meat," sick whales, and oddly scarred fish. Although community members did not know about the tracer experiment, stories began to circulate in Point Hope about the relationship between cancer in the village, the decline in the health of the wildlife, and the possibility of buried poisons left by the Project Chariot scientists.[12]

Community leaders relayed fears about buried poisons to state and borough public health officials. In response to the concern coming from Point Hope, public health agencies undertook two epidemiological studies of the North Slope Borough, the borough that includes Point Hope.[13] These studies found that the overall cancer rate in the North Slope Borough did not differ from the U.S. standard rate but that the types of cancer differed. Both studies concluded that the most effective means of reducing the cancer rate would be through improved cancer screening and the elimination of tobacco use.[14] Many people in Point Hope remained unconvinced by the epidemiological findings and continued to discuss the possibility of buried poisons.

Alarm continued among community members in Point Hope when, between 1988 and 1990, eight people were diagnosed with six different kinds of cancer. These included two lung, two cervix, and one each of stomach, colon, bone, and testicle cancers. In response to the renewed community concerns, the Centers for Disease Control (CDC) analyzed data from North Slope Borough communities, including Point Hope. This study, using data from 1984 to 1989, found the age-adjusted cancer rate in Point Hope to be 38 percent higher than the national average. However, because this rate was based on a small number of cancer cases in a small population it was not deemed statistically significant. Because this 38 percent difference did not achieve statistical significance, the CDC author considered the rate substantively insignificant as well.[15]

In August of 1992, Dan O'Neill, who was working on a history of Project Chariot, learned of the tracer experiments while combing through AEC documents obtained through the Freedom of Information Act. O'Neill passed this information on to village leaders in Point Hope. Upon learning about the tracer experiments, community members in Point Hope, although furious about the deception, felt vindicated, for they had long suspected that buried poisons left by scientists had caused their cancer.[16]

In the flurry of activity following the disclosure of the radioactive tracer experiment, community members and public officials scrambled to assess the situation. At an early public meeting, officials assured community members that the amounts of radioactive materials used in the tracer experiment had never really presented a danger and certainly could not be responsible for any perceived change in the rate of cancer.[17]

Like other cases of contaminated communities, what happened in Point

Hope follows a familiar story line: community members notice health problems that they link to suspected or known contamination or pollution. They report their suspicions and evidence to the local/regional/national agencies or authorities. Sometimes these agencies use existing epidemiological data and sometimes they collect new data to study the problem. The studies often "prove" that there is no environmental problem. However, people in the local community still believe that their health is being affected and may believe that the agencies that are supposed to protect and aid them fail to do so. Meanwhile agency officials may believe that they have done the best job possible and dismiss the concerns of community members as alarmism fueled by ignorance of science. Neither community groups nor the people in agencies who are supposed to help them are satisfied with the outcome. It is precisely this impasse that I address in this essay using data gathered by interviewing the scientists involved in the Point Hope situation, watching videotapes of public meetings held in or pertaining to Point Hope, and by analyzing the documents produced before and after the tracer experiments.[18]

Doing Better Science

One way to overcome this impasse is for one side or the other to do more or "better" science; that is, science that adheres more closely to the methodological norms of science. Grassroots environmental organizations have criticized federal public health agencies, such as the CDC, for consistently failing to protect public health due to their poor practice of the scientific method. Methodological problems lead to inconclusive results, which in turn insure that public health agencies will not be compelled to intervene to halt current pollution or to make previous polluting entities responsible for cleanup and/or compensation.[19]

Sometimes communities can marshal the resources to conduct their own study that, ostensibly, would adhere more closely with the methodological norms of science, thereby assuring that the "truth" of the matter would emerge. People in Point Hope, with the help of the North Slope Borough, were able to do this. The North Slope Borough, the borough that encompasses Point Hope, commissioned their Health and Human Services doctor, Ron Bowerman, to examine the existing data and to collect new data. Rather than adhering to methodological norms, Bowerman used nonstandard methods that, while they made sense to the people in the community, went outside of the norms of accepted epidemiological method. Using this method,

Bowerman found that the Point Hope cancer rate was significantly different than the U.S. rate and, unlike the previous studies, concluded that this difference could not be attributed to personal behaviors such as diet and tobacco use.[20] In a subsequent study, Bowerman and Point Hope community members collected more data. They found that people who lived in Point Hope in 1962, the year of the tracer experiments, were significantly more likely to contract cancer than those who did not live in Point Hope in 1962.[21]

Again this case follows a familiar story line: differing interpretations of similar evidence, contradictory evidence, new evidence and yet community members who believe their lives and bodies are still being affected by contamination. One way out of this deadlock of dueling scientists might be to collect even more data in hopes that the "truth" of the matter would emerge. However, the impulse to collect more data relies on two myths—the myth of rationality and the myth of the power of science. The myth of rationality holds that gathering as much relevant information as possible can reduce uncertainties and that occasionally uncertainties will disappear altogether, leaving a predominantly, if not wholly, obvious answer. The myth of the power of science maintains that science has the capacity to provide all of the relevant information and that the direction of research can be changed without introducing intolerable delays.[22]

Collingridge and Reeve recommend that the myth of rationality and the myth of the power of science be dispelled in favor of an approach that recognizes the limitation of the human intellect to analyze data and of science to provide information in a usable form. In addition, supporters of the precautionary principle have pointed out that delays to collect data in order to determine the harm caused by pollution usually benefit the polluter at the expense of public health. Polluters are allowed to keep polluting while data is collected to prove that the pollution is harmful.[23] Finally, the impulse to collect more and more data privileges science as the superior way of knowing about the world. In Western culture science is widely held as the most esteemed way of knowing.[24] However, there are other legitimate ways of knowing. For example, in this case, the people of Point Hope have an ancient and successful knowledge system based on their traditional lifestyle practices.

Investigating the Distortion Provided by Scientific Language

A second way out of the impasse is to focus on the language of science to uncover the way that language can be used to distort the "truth." This distortion may stem from the politics of public health that demand that even well-meaning public health officials minimize the number of hazards identified. Public health professionals prefer to minimize the number of hazards identified because of the potential for public disruption often caused by disclosure of environmental hazards. For example, news of an environmental hazard may put pressure on government agencies to take action and may also make them subject to public criticism about how the hazard came into being in the first place.[25] Distortions in Point Hope included equating statistical nonsignificance with public health nonsignificance, focusing on personal tobacco use, and trivializing the risk presented by the tracer experiment materials.

As mentioned above, the 1990 CDC study found that the cancer rate in Point Hope was 38 percent higher than the U.S. standard rate. Because of the small population rate, which makes statistical difference unlikely, this 38 percent difference did not attain statistical significance and was dismissed as substantially insignificant as well. Using statistical significance in this way means that what is statistically significant *is* what is there; if it is not statistically significant then it is not there. In other words, if application of the scientific method does not "find" statistical significance, then a problem does not exist. In this way statistical significance as a marker of "reality" can be seen to equate findings based on the scientific method with "truth." This is a powerful way of making the problem go away insofar as the problem is said never to exist in the first place. But this result is all too easy to achieve, especially with small populations and standard statistical practices.

Another example of distortion is the way that public health officials will often focus on lifestyle issues, especially personal tobacco use, to avoid talking about environmental carcinogens. Public officials may suggest that the exposed group smokes more than the general population and that, thus, any differences in disease rate can be attributed to smoking.[26] Nearly all of the epidemiological studies completed before the disclosure of the tracer experiment at least mention lifestyle variables. Many, however, highlighted personal tobacco use. The 1990 CDC report represented an especially egregious example of the overemphasis on smoking. In the first three paragraphs of the introduction the author emphasizes the role of cigarettes in cancer causation while dismissing the identification of environmental carcinogens as akin to "finding a needle in a haystack."[27] Ozonoff and Boden conclude that, "[t]he effects of confounding variables like smoking are a serious technical issue, but they seem never to be invoked to explain non-positive results: Failure to find a problem is never ascribed to the fact that the control population may smoke more than the control group."[28]

In addition to equating statistical nonsignificance with public health nonsignificance and focusing on lifestyle variables, public health officials often trivialize the risk at hand by making comparisons to things with which community members might be more familiar and thus more comfortable. In Point Hope, trivialization included emphasis on the naturalness of radiation, emphasis on the beneficial medical uses of radiation, and minimizing the amounts of radioactive material used in the Project Chariot tracer experiment.

Authors of the texts produced in conjunction with the cleanup of the tracer experiment and presenters in Point Hope public meetings often compared man-made radiation to naturally occurring terrestrial and cosmic radiation. For example, a representative of the outside consulting agency hired by the North Slope Borough opened her presentation by explaining that radiation "is natural, and you are exposed to it, just as I am, and everybody else is, all of the time. It's just a matter of how much and what we can do about dealing with it."[29] The speaker uses the word "natural" when first describing radiation, even though later in her presentation she distinguishes natural from man-made radiation, but her implication is that *all* radiation is at least somewhat natural. She further discounts the radiation used in the tracer experiment, emphasizing the ubiquity and inevitability of radiation, by stating, "There's radiation in the human body, in the foods we eat, in the water we drink."

Another way that the authors of the scientific documents and officials in public meetings at Point Hope trivialized the radioactive contamination was to point out the beneficial medical uses of radiation. One presenter, for example, pointed out that both Barbara and George Bush received radioactive iodine for treatment of Graves Disease. In another public meeting, in response to a question from a community member asking about the relationship between cancer and the cesium 137 in the tracer experiment soil, an Indian Health Service representative responded by saying, "One of the things that we do for people who have overactive thyroids is we give them radioactive iodine to partially destroy the thyroid. It's an accepted treatment. And interestingly enough the dose we give them, it doesn't destroy the thyroid, just calms it down, is 29 millicuries. This mound, on the day it was buried had about 26 . . . just to give you an idea of how very little was in that mound at the beginning.[30] In addition to highlighting the beneficial medical uses of radiation, the speaker also discounts the amount of radiation used in the tracer experiment.

Discounting the amounts of radiation in the tracer experiment was also accomplished by pointing out how much more radioactive material was used in other places, at other times. For example, one presenter in a public meeting at Point Hope stated that "we have thousands of acres at the Nevada Test Site that are 10 times more contaminated than what was buried there [Cape Thompson] and other cities all over the country too."[31] One of the documents produced in conjunction with the eventual clean-up of the tracer experiment site offered that "[t]he dose received by the people of Point Hope and Kivalina from the ingestion of caribou meat today and in the early 1960s did not approach those received in Norway after Chernobyl."[32] Discounting the amount of radiation left in Cape Thompson suggests that the people in the nearby communities ought to be *grateful* that the USGS left so little radioactive material, especially in light of the massive amounts of radiation left in Nevada or the radioactive contamination spread by the Chernobyl accident.[33]

Investigating the distortion provided by scientific language reveals poor reporting of science rather than poor methodology, as in the first approach. However, this approach still privileges science in its implication that language is the problem, not science. Both the call for improved science and the investigation into the distortion provided by scientific language lead activists and scholars to try to debunk the official explanations of what happened in contaminated communities by showing how they are variously "unscientific," biased, misleading, incomplete, and/or politically motivated. The erroneous version can then be replaced with a "truer" or more scientific version.

Both of the above approaches rely on a particular ontology, or understanding of reality. They rely on a realist ontology that assumes a reality to be discovered "out there," even though this reality may be hidden or distorted. This is also the ontology of science. Scientists set out to "discover" an already-existing, or an objective, reality.[34] Those who wish to deconstruct knowledge from within this realist frame look for truth under a layer, or even layers, of distortion.[35] Because it identifies bad science, not science as usual, as the problem, this approach does not challenge the existing methodological norms of science. However, it does deeply subvert the notion of objectivity in that it challenges the notion that the social position of a particular scientist is irrelevant to the research results.[36]

Treating Scientific Language as the Construction of Reality

A third way to address the impasse comes from the sociology of scientific knowledge and argues that language cannot be separated from the reality it purports to describe. This approach maintains that scientific discourse is the *construction*, rather than the *representation*, of scientific fact.[37] It suggests that language *actively* organizes and defines human social life, in contrast to the realist approach, which maintains that language is a *passive* structure of syntax, semantics, and phonetics available to human agents.[38] This approach employs an antirealist ontology: there is no reality to be discovered "out there"; instead the world is a place of flux and discord. Rather than looking for truth underneath layers of distortion, this approach assumes that disguise comes in layers upon layers. Indeed, this strategy implies that the world may be nothing but distortion, containing no truth at its core.[39]

Using this approach, social constructivists look at the way that scientists produce facts discursively through the use of simple organizational features that encourage readers to read the text in particular ways. For example, sociologists look at the way that authors use sequencing devices to cut out or background other potential paths and other potentially relevant events. Because nonspecialists do not know the range of things that could have been included in the account, they rely on the author, as well as others s/he may evoke, to present the "right" information.[40] In the Point Hope case, I found that authors used sequencing devices when talking about "safe" levels of radiation exposure.

The matter-of-fact way in which officials spoke about "safe" levels of radiation exposure belie the disagreement surrounding it. Some health physicists maintain that all ionizing radiation, even the smallest doses, even naturally occurring, causes cellular damage. Thus, there is no tolerance level of radiation exposure under which zero damage to cells occurs. Because of this, standard-setting agencies set "safety levels" according to a series of value judgements—for example, the tradeoff between exposure for the patient and the diagnostic uses of x-rays. What, then, is referred to as "safe" levels of exposure is actually a permissible level of exposure.[41] However, not everyone agrees with the notion that all radiation is dangerous. Others suggest that low doses of radiation may be beneficial as they increase cell growth and development, increase mean life span, stimulate immune reactions, and even decrease cancer mortality.[42]

In addition to opposing beliefs about the effects of low levels of radiation, the measurement of radiation itself is complex for at least four reasons. First, radiation science uses several measures of radiation that are not comparable. Second, elements have varying powers of penetration; elements stay radioactive for widely varying amounts of time. Third, elements that have been ingested have widely varying amounts of time they will stay in the body. Fourth, radiation effect differs according to the part of the body exposed. The above list suggests only some of the complexity involved in measuring radiation; Bertell warns that, in measuring radiation effects, "living systems are too complex for such an approach to provide anything more than a good guess."[43]

Finally, some have argued that the standard-setting boards have been heavily peopled by those who have an interest in deprecating the effects of low levels of radiation—those who want unlimited use of diagnostic x-rays and those with ties to the nuclear establishment. Thus the levels of "safe" exposure have been increased even when the empirical evidence indicated that safe exposure levels should be decreased.[44]

When authors of texts or speakers in public meetings sequence or cut out discussion of "safety" levels they imply that radiation safety levels are undisputed, simple, and nonpolitical matters of empirical evidence. However, as mentioned above, "safe" levels of radiation exposure are social negotiations rife with political interests and based on complex and, thus, empirically controversial evidence. The social constructivist approach, unlike the previous approaches, is not looking for "truth" under layers of distortion; rather, it demonstrates that peeling off the layers of distortion may reveal more layers rather than an essential "truth." In this way the social constructivist approach demonstrates the claim that "safety" levels are a product of language rather than a product of an objective reality.

The focus on language and the denial of any objective truths leads to at least two criticisms, each of which come from a realist ontology. First, deconstruction of the rhetorical practices of scientists involves its own use of rhetorical practices. In this essay I use rhetorical strategies more similar to than different from the rhetorical strategies used by the scientists. My claim that scientists construct reality through the use of simple organizational tools seems invalidated by my own use of these tools. However, to slip into absolute relativism and claim that everything is rhetoric misses the point of this approach. The aim of this approach is not to ascertain any transcendental truth; rather it is to reveal the subjective and constructed nature of the world through language. Revealing the constructed nature of scientific knowledge by pointing out rhetorical strategies, even while using those same rhetorical strategies, does not debunk science and replace it with a better or truer version of reality. Instead, it is a way of recognizing that science is firmly embedded in, and a product of, language.

The second critique of this approach points out that if scientific language creates "facts," then the "fact" of illness must also be a product of language.

In this case, cancer and radiation must also be seen as products of discourse. Again, the temptation is to slip into absolute relativism. However, this approach does not require ignoring material realities. Rather, it recognizes that material realities, such as illnesses, are embedded in cultural practices and social structure and do not have an independent existence removed from social structure and culture. For example, whether low levels of radiation are safe is not only a matter of empirical negotiation but also one of interpretation, trade-offs, and influence.

Why, if the social constructivist position is so easily misunderstood and likely to be dismissed, have I invoked it in this essay? I do so because it may be the realist ontology of science that portends ecological destruction. According to Wright, science is ecologically incoherent, or irrational, because it does not take into account the goal of sustaining life. In addition, science is conceptually incoherent because of its realist ontology.[45] Despite the incoherence, scientific knowledge gained ascendancy in Western culture because of its claim of neutral observation, which did not oppose Christian epistemology, and because of its technological successes. However, technological success does not necessarily point to a superior theory of knowledge. Ancient sailors had the technology to successfully navigate the oceans although they used incorrect assumptions about the rotation of the planets. That is, they were successful at navigation with flawed epistemology. The numerous technological successes brought about by the application of the scientific method does not guarantee the soundness of scientific epistemology, namely, the assumption of an objective reality. More importantly, and referring to the first incoherence, we ought to be more critical about what technology we consider "successful." Nuclear power plants are technically successful in that they produce power; however, they also produce highly dangerous and long-lasting wastes that threaten sustainability and, in the ecological sense, are not successful at all.

To remedy the ecological destruction and the threat to sustainability precipitated by scientific objectivist knowledge, Wright recommends making knowledge "wild." Wild knowledge would replace the scientific referent to objective nature with a referent to language because it is language that makes human social life and thus human knowledge possible.[46] For wild knowledge, validity would become an issue of sustaining social life, rather than an issue of technological success or the objectivist method. That is, the validity of knowledge would depend on its social impacts and consequences in addition to its predictability, reliability, and technical success.

If the dominant epistemology of Western culture were already wild, then it is less likely that technologies that contaminate communities and threaten sustainability would be developed. In this case, the "instant" harbor at Cape Thompson would never have been proposed and the tracer experiment would not have been undertaken. Since we cannot click our heels and wish ourselves into a different epistemology, how might we begin to move toward an epistemology that includes a commitment to sustainability? I suggest that we can begin to move toward it on at least two levels—the political and the theoretical.

Mobile Ontologies

On the political level we can do several things, the most important of which may be involving community members in the research process as Ron Bowerman, the North Slope epidemiologist, did. Local citizen involvement provides energetic and intellectual resources and improves the design and performance of the study.[47] "Popular epidemiology" incorporates lay ways of knowing into the investigation and interpretation of environmental health hazards and may eventually lead to increasing generalizability and/or a paradigm shift. This approach to epidemiology moves away from the narrowly mechanistic and individualistic findings intrinsic to risk factor epidemiology to a more ecological and democratic approach. Democratic epidemiology includes the recognition and inclusion of the perspectives and interests of community members rather than only the interests and perspectives of those who control the economic, academic, and information institutions. Democratic epidemiology also recognizes that education between scientists and the public takes place in both directions. Among other things, democratizing science means that community members and scientists decide on the measurement standards before the study begins and then they work together to collect the data and analyze it. This approach would elucidate the difficulties and uncertainties of performing and interpreting epidemiological studies and, while it erodes some of the authority of science, it is more realistic about the kind and quality of information that science can provide in these situations.

Democratic science exposes science as a social production, like other social productions, rather than as a method and a body of knowledge that exists apart from social influence. In the Point Hope case, a few of the scientists, in an informal setting, recognized the fallibility of scientific knowledge and were not willing to equate scientific evidence with "truth."

Wider participation in science might lead nonscientists to a similar conclusion. Of course, one of the ways that scientists protect the power of science is by policing what counts as scientific knowledge and authorizing the legitimate producers of that knowledge.[48] Individual scientists and scientific institutions might thus resist moves to democratize science. Nonetheless, it is a political agenda we should undertake.

The concomitant move toward making knowledge wild might also take place on the theoretical level. Rather than synthesizing approaches, Ferguson advocates the use of "irony" to simultaneously maintain multiple approaches without insisting that they resolve into larger wholes.[49] This use of irony encourages ongoing and contentious conversations, making it possible to operate within unstable theoretical space, which in turn may lead to new ways of thinking about the world.

Ferguson maintains realist and antirealist approaches to subjectivity in feminist theory with a conceptual tool she calls "mobile subjectivities."[50] Mobile subjectivities are not constrained by the theoretical constraints of either a realist or antirealist ontological position and, thus, they lead to imagining other possibilities for subjectivity that might further the feminist agenda. I would like to suggest a similar conceptual tool that could promote the move toward Wright's "ecologically coherent epistemology." "Mobile ontologies" would allow us to talk about material realities while always maintaining an awareness that our understanding of their "reality" may be wrong. This would allow an antirealist stance toward "facts" while concurrently taking the contradictory realist stance that "facts," or an objective reality, does exist. Engaging both realist and antirealist approaches simultaneously allows recognition of the materiality of the body—people get sick—while considering the discursive production of the things that are said to act (or not act) on the body.[51] This strategy allows one to simultaneously align with certain categories of the truth, while at the same time questioning, disrupting, and perhaps even rejecting these categories. In Point Hope, it means looking at the rhetorical structure of what scientists say as well as accepting what they say as "truth."

What might the application of mobile ontologies mean in the case of Point Hope? To begin with, it would mean that we could accept that both radiation and tobacco cause cancer while simultaneously acknowledging the physiological, philosophical, and political issues inherent in cancer causation. It would mean recognizing that there are legitimate knowledge systems other than science, those based on subsistence lifeways, for instance. It would mean taking into account the preference public health agencies may have for not identifying public health hazards. It would mean questioning the practice of using statistical significance as a marker of "truth" as well as scrutinizing the tendency of public health agencies to emphasize personal behaviors, such as tobacco use, rather than to consider hazards such as radiation. It means considering the empirical evidence of radiation exposure as well as attending to the differing interpretations of that exposure and the political motivations of those who set "safety" levels. Mobile ontologies maintain antirealist *and* realist ontological positions. This allows for the possibility of expanding logical space, and thereby appeals to courage and imagination rather than ostensibly neutral criteria. In this way, mobile ontologies, like mobile subjectivities, are not only about epistemology but also about the value of living in an ecologically sustainable culture.[52]

NOTES

I would like to offer a special thanks to Mei Mei Evans for her encouragement and assistance.

1. Asatchaq, *The Things That Were Said of Them: Shaman Stories and Oral Histories of the Tikigaq People,* trans. Tukummiq and Tom Lowenstein (Berkeley: University of California Press, 1992), xxvii.

2. Thomas R. Berger, *Village Journey: The Report of the Alaska Native Review Commission* (New York: Hill and Wang, 1985), 48–72.

3. Dan O'Neill, *The Firecracker Boys* (New York: St. Martins, 1994), 25.

4. Ibid., 24–28.

5. Ibid., 28.

6. Ibid., 41.

7. Ibid., 239–57.

8. James Magdanz, "Northern Exposure?" *Anchorage Daily News,* 22 November 1994, F7–F10.

9. O'Neill, *The Firecracker Boys,* 75, 280. In a public meeting held in Point Hope in October of 1992, Tom Gerusky of the Department of Energy stated that copies of the correspondence between the USGS and the AEC concerning the tracer experiment had been made available to the state thirty years previously. He offered no explanation for why none of those who had knowledge of the tracer experiment had failed to notify the local people. Videotapes of the public meetings held in Point Hope, Kivalina, and Kotzebue in 1992, 1993, and 1994 are available in the film archives at University of Alaska, Fairbanks library.

10. Edith Turner, "Native Reaction to Nuclear Contamination: The Social Aspects" (paper presented at the Annual Meeting of the Alaska Anthropological Association, Anchorage, Alaska, 8–10 April 1993).

11. Dimitra Lavrakas, "Point Hope's Suffering, Anger Pour Out Over Experiment" *Anchorage Daily News,* 17 October 1994, B1.

12. Magdanz, "Northern Exposure," F10–F11.

13. Ibid., F11.

14. B. Ireland and Anne Lanier, "Report on the Incidence of Cancer in Alaska Eskimos" (report for State of Alaska Department of Health and Human Services, Anchorage, Alaska, 1986); Jennifer Williams, Elizabeth Carey, Renee Pelowski, and Anne Lanier, "North Slope Borough Cancer Study 1984–1985" (report for State of Alaska Department of Health and Human Services, Anchorage, Alaska, 1986).

15. Matthew T. McKenna, *Cancer in the North Slope Borough 1984–1989* (Atlanta: Centers for Disease Control, 1990). The 95 percent "confidence" interval from 219.8 to 998.6 cases per 100,000 was so large as to be virtually meaningless. The age-adjusted Point Hope cancer rate was 505.6 per 100,000 while the U.S. standard rate was 366.4 per 100,000. Because the U.S. standard rate fell into the confidence interval, the 38 percent difference was considered to be due to chance (8).

16. Magdanz, "Northern Exposure," F11.

17. Project Chariot Tracer Cleanup: Public Meeting held in Point Hope, Alaska, 23 February 1993. Community member, and later mayor, Ray Koonuk asks Robert Nakamura, head of the Indian Health Services in Alaska, about the safety of the drinking water and eating animals. Nakamura responds, "If we're talking about exposure from this stuff from Russia or from other heavy exposures, I would be real concerned, if we're talking about the exposure to the amount of stuff that's in the mound. No, no problem. And all I can do is tell you what my best scientists are telling me is true. They are the ones who are much more knowledgeable than me and they're telling me that it's O.K. What's in there is not, not a problem."

18. This information was collected for Nelta M. Edwards, "Cancer in Point Hope, Alaska: Science, Language and Knowledge" (Ph.D. diss., Arizona State University, 2000).

19. See for example, Sanford Lewis, Brian Keating, and Dick Russell, *Inconclusive by Design: Waste, Fraud and Abuse in Federal Environmental Health Research* (Boston: National Toxics Campaign Fund and Environmental Health Network, 1992); Dan Fagin and Marianne Lavelle, *Toxic Deception: How the*

Chemical Industry Manipulates Science, Bends the Law, and Endangers Your Health (Secaucus, N.J.: Birch Lane, 1996).

20. Ron Bowerman, "Cancer in Point Hope: An Epidemiological Overview for 1969–1992" (report for North Slope Borough Health and Social Services, Barrow, Alaska, 1994). In this study Bowerman compared the number of people who had migrated out of Point Hope with the number of people who had migrated out of a control community. He found the out-migration patterns were similar for both villages, but that the cancer rate among former residents of Point Hope was much higher than the cancer rate among the former residents of the control village. Bowerman then added the resident to the non-resident cancer cases, which he called the "expanded" Point Hope cancer cases. This approach certainly makes sense from the point of view of current Point Hope residents who count among the cancer victims former-resident friends and family members. However, Bowerman's use of the "expanded" cancer cases is problematic because it is not the standard way that epidemiologists measure residency and thus this rate cannot be compared to other rates that are compiled using standard residence criteria. Bowerman's treatment of the expanded population also fails to take into account the number of people who left Point Hope who did not get cancer and thus inflates the cancer rate.

21. Ron Bowerman, "Cancer in Point Hope II—a Case-Control Study" (report for North Slope Borough Health and Social Services, Barrow, Alaska, 1995). The study matched those who did not have cancer with those who did (including the deceased). Residence in Point Hope in 1960 was statistically significant with a probability of 0.035, while "burning coal inside" approached significance with a probability of 0.16, however, smoking and other lifestyle variables all had probability values greater than 0.5 (10–12). A portion of this study was subsequently published as "A Case-Control Study of Cancer Risk Factors in the Alaskan Arctic: Responding to Village Cancer About Environmental Radiation," *Arctic Medical Research* 55 (1996): 129–34.

22. David Collingridge and Colin Reeve, *Science Spears to Power: The Role of Experts in Policy Making* (New York: St Martin's, 1986), as cited in John Hannigan, *Environmental Sociology* (London: Routledge, 1995).

23. Brian Wynne and Sue Mayer, "How Science Fails the Environment," *New Scientist* 138 (June): 32–35.

24. See for example, Stanley Aronowitz, *Science as Power: Discourse and Ideology in Modern Society* (Minneapolis: University of Minnesota Press,

1988), vii–viii, 3–34; Hilary Lawson, "Stories About Stories," in *Dismantling Truth: Reality in the Post-Modern World,* ed. Hilary Lawson and Lisa Appignanesi (London: Weidenfeld and Nicholson, 1989), xi–xxviii; Will Wright, *Wild Knowledge: Science, Language, and Social Life in a Fragile Environment* (Minneapolis: University of Minnesota Press, 1992), 23–42.

25. David Ozonoff and Leslie I. Boden, "Truth and Consequences: Health Agency Responses to Environmental Health Problems," *Science, Technology and Human Values* 5 (1987): 70–77.

26. Ibid., 75.

27. McKenna, *Cancer in the North Slope Borough,* 2.

28. Ozonoff and Boden, "Truth and Consequences," 75–76.

29. Joyce Spellman of Foster Wheeler, consultants to the North Slope Borough. Public meeting, Point Hope, 23 February 1993.

30. Jim Berner of the Indian Health Services. Public meeting, Point Hope, 23 February 1993.

31. Joel Ecker of Westinghouse Corporation, a Department of Energy contractor. Public meeting, Point Hope, 22 February 1993.

32. Alaska Department of Environmental Conservation, Northern Regional Office, *Report on Project Chariot Removal and Assessment Actions in August 1993* (Fairbanks: Alaska Department of Environmental Conservation, 1994), 67.

33. This sort of logic is absurd, akin to telling a woman whose partner physically abuses her that she ought to be glad that he does not kill her. That there are worse instances of abuse, or contamination, cannot be used to discount the instance at hand. In a world of limited resources for environmental cleanup, or at least the political unfeasibility of funds appropriation for cleanup, it may be pragmatic to rank, by degree of severity, which problem ought to be addressed first. In fact, contamination sites are commonly ranked by degree of severity based on a number of criteria. This is not a reason to suggest, however, that contamination problems less severe are anything to celebrate. Additionally, this attempt at a "hierarchy of oppression" is divisive as it suggests a reductionism capable of differentiating the worst cases from the not-so-bad cases. It also suggests that social problems such as environmental contamination are discrete problems and not related to other social justice issues such as poverty and racism.

34. See Steve Woolgar, *Science: The Very Idea* (New York: Tavistock Publications, 1988), 55–66.

35. See Kathy Ferguson, *The Man Question: Visions of Subjectivity in Feminist Theory* (Berkeley: University of California Press, 1993), 27.

36. Sandra Harding refers to this approach as "feminist empiricism" in *The Science Question in Feminism* (Ithaca: Cornell University Press, 1986), 24–26.

37. For a humorous, though now dated, discussion on the sociology of scientific knowledge, see Malcolm Ashmore, *The Reflexive Thesis: Wrighting Sociology of Scientific Knowledge* (Chicago: University of Chicago Press, 1989), 1–25.

38. Wright, *Wild Knowledge*, 16–17.

39. Ferguson, *The Man Question*, 10, 27.

40. Dorothy E. Smith, "K Is Mentally Ill: The Anatomy of a Factual Account," *Sociology* 12 (1978): 23–53.

41. See for example, Rosalie Bertell, *No Immediate Danger: Prognosis for a Radioactive Earth* (London: Women's Press, 1985), 42; John W. Gofman, *Radiation-Induced Cancer from Low-Dose Exposure: An Independent Analysis* (San Francisco: Committee for Nuclear Responsibility Book Division, 1990).

42. This is the theory of radiation hormesis. For more on this see Thomas D. Luckey, *Radiation Hormesis* (Boca Raton: CRC Press, 1991); and the May 1987 special issue of the journal *Health Physics*.

43. Bertell, *No Immediate Danger,* 36.

44. See Karl Z. Morgan, "ICRP Risk Estimates—An Alternative View," in *Radiation and Health: the Biological Effects of Low-Level Exposure to Ionizing Radiation,* ed. Robin R. Jones and Richard Southwood (Colchester: John Wiley & Sons, 1987), 125–54.

45. Wright, *Wild Knowledge,* 1–22.

46. Ibid., 20.

47. See Ozonoff and Boden, "Truth and Consequences"; Phil Brown, "Popular Epidemiology and Toxic Waste Contamination: Lay and Professional Ways of Knowing," *Journal of Health and Social Behavior* 33 (1992): 267–81; Steve Wing, "Whose Epidemiology, Whose Health?" *International Journal of Health Services* 28 (1998): 241–52; Connie Ozawa, "Science in Environmental Conflicts," *Sociological Perspectives* 39 (1996): 219–30.

48. See Barry Barnes, *About Science* (Oxford: Basil Blackwell, 1985); Thomas F. Gieryn, "Boundary-Work and the Demarkation of Science from Non-Science: Strains and Interests in the Professional Ideologies of Scientists," *American Sociological Review* 48 (1983): 781–95.

49. Ferguson, *The Man Question,* 30.

50. Ibid., 154.

51. I am thinking here of Judith Butler's discussion of materiality in *Bodies That Matter* (New York: Routledge, 1993).

52. See Ferguson, *The Man Question,* especially chapter 6, for a more detailed discussion about the political commitments attached to mobile subjectivities. See Richard Rorty "Feminism and Pragmatism," in *Pragmatism,* ed. Russell B. Goodman (New York: Routledge, 1995), 125–148 for a discussion about expanding moral boundaries to achieve political commitments.

6

THE MOVEMENT FOR ENVIRONMENTAL JUSTICE IN THE PACIFIC ISLANDS

Valerie Kuletz

> *There is no choice for us. We don't know what our future is going to be.*
> *Maybe there is only the choice to live in our contaminated land and die.*
> *But we don't want our friends and neighbors around the world having the*
> *same problems that we are facing . . . We have to look forward; we do not*
> *have to look back. Forward is already being damaged. I do not have to*
> *look back for the damage. I have to look forward, to reach out to my*
> *friends around the world.*

—Lijon Eknilang, Rongelap, Marshall Islands

> *The Polynesian land, our fenua maohi, has been defiled by man's apoca-*
> *lyptic folly . . . Our society has become tough, cruel, merciless and we are*
> *dominated by a new desire to make individual profits. To continue along*
> *this road is sheer nuclear prostitution.*

—Jacqui Drollet, Secretary General of the Ia Mana party,
speaking at a rally to commemorate Bikini Day 1984

Future Scenarios

Since the advent of nuclear testing after World War II, Pacific Islanders have
endured the use of their oceans and islands as testing arenas for the global
powers' nuclear weapons. This environmentally and socially destructive activity, which has far-reaching implications for the future of the region, was
inextricably bound to colonialism. Today—in a period of so-called postcolo-
nialism and globalization—the same regions that were used for nuclear
testing have been targeted by some nuclear powers for the disposal of nuclear

and toxic wastes (a trade represented by nuclear states and industry as a form of development). The current global trade in nuclear and toxic waste targeted at impoverished Pacific Island countries is held largely at bay by local, regional, and international resistance, but it remains an ongoing struggle.

This essay explores the environmental justice movement, known as the Nuclear Free and Independent Pacific movement (NFIP), that has emerged in response to the above forms of nuclear colonialism. This essay is proactive in the sense that it seeks to identify a potential problem by interrogating the signs for future inequity, and further to develop insights into how environmentally destructive and socially unjust development might be alleviated. Of central concern is the targeting of Pacific Islands for socially and environmentally destructive practices (such as toxic waste burial). Identifying such activity shows the possibility of these practices to be a clear and present danger. The task is to highlight these signs before they coalesce into irreversible reality. Focusing on targeting then is a form of proactive scholarship as opposed to doing a postmortem of an already disastrous situation. Of equal importance is the identification of Pacific Islander resistance to this activity; thus, this essay illuminates the strengths and weaknesses of the NFIP as a form of resistance to these developments.

Overview

The Pacific Island region is a geopolitical and multicultural region consisting of three major island areas: Micronesia in the northwest, Melanesia in the southwest, and Polynesia in the south. The Hawaiian islands, which are in the mid-Pacific, are included in this domain. This region consists of vast oceanic space punctuated by thousands of islands and atolls, which host many different cultures. Despite its centrality the region is not part of the celebrated Pacific Rim economy. Due to its distance from most of the dominant global powers, it is an "edge" region in most senses of the word: politically, economically, and geographically. Indeed, its distance from the centers of power was one of the key reasons for its use as a nuclear testing site. When asked about the nuclear testing program in the Marshall Islands, former U.S. Secretary of State Henry Kissinger is reputed to have stated: "There's only 90,000 people out there. Who gives a damn?"

The history of nuclear colonialism (in the form of nuclear testing programs) has put in place social, political, economic, and environmental structures that make Pacific Islanders (newly independent and colonized) vulnerable to the recent pressure placed upon them by various groups to accept nuclear and toxic waste. Political independence in the wake of nuclear testing comes with a legacy of dependence. As noted by many activists, the business of nuclear and toxic waste storage as a form of "development" makes independence a problematic term, since accepting such inherently destructive materials becomes an option only considered when there is a lack of economic independence. Environmentally sustainable economies, then, are among the most important forms of resistance, although, because nuclear and conventional testing regimes have disrupted traditional practices, sustainable economies (sustainable both environmentally and culturally) are not so easily revived.

The NFIP is a multidimensional social response to the use of the Pacific as a testing laboratory for nuclear weapons, the colonial and postcolonial militarization of the region, and to globalization as it manifests in the nuclear and toxic waste trade in particular, and the acceleration of the Western neoclassical development agenda in general. In other words, it is a largely (although not exclusively) indigenous response to colonialism, neocolonialism, and certain aspects of the globalization project. As such, this movement includes within it strong place-based identity politics; although because it is also a broad network of activism it has, in some ways, redefined Pacific Island identity to move beyond its separate local arenas.

The NFIP is also a multitiered movement that functions on three distinct levels of resistance and practice: the local, the regional (composed of differently situated states), and the transregional (or global). These levels of activity are not evolutionary in the sense that one level inevitably evolves into another (such as the local into the global). Rather, movement between the levels is multidirectional. This spatial dimension of the movement makes it a promising model for other regions confronted with problems associated with the new reorganization of global power. More than simply a resistance movement, the NFIP is also a campaign that promotes "independence . . . and true economic and social development, and environmental concerns."[1] In many ways, particularly because it has successfully mobilized intercommunity cooperation, the NFIP can be described as globalization from below.[2]

Nuclear and Military Colonialism

Within the post–World War II Pacific "theater" colonial regimes of power came hand in hand with the nuclear bomb. Under colonialism the Pacific

Island region has been used as the First World's nuclear weapons laboratory and intercontinental ballistic missile testing range for over fifty years. Nuclear activity—consisting of hundreds of nuclear detonations—has occurred almost continuously from 1946 to 1996, and intercontinental missile testing continues today. In the 1940s and 1950s the United States and Great Britain tested nuclear weapons in Micronesia, Australia, and the Line Island Chain. As a result of the testing, six islands were vaporized and fourteen others were left uninhabitable. Hydrogen bombs, such as Bravo, were over a thousand times more powerful than those used on Hiroshima and Nagasaki. Needless to say the impact of such testing has had profound consequences for Pacific Islanders and their descendants. As Darlene Keju-Johnson, a Marshall Islands woman, explains: "Since the testing . . . we have this problem of what we call 'jelly-fish babies.' These babies are born like jelly-fish. They have no eyes. They have no heads. They have no arms. They have no legs. They do not shape like human beings at all."[3] Similarly, Marshall Islander Lijon Eknilang notes: "I know first hand what the devastating effects of nuclear weapons are over time and over long distances, and what those effects mean to innocent human beings over several generations. I plead with you to do what you can not to allow the suffering we Marshallese have experienced to be repeated in any other community in the world."[4]

From the 1960s to the late 1990s France conducted nuclear tests in Polynesia at the atolls of Moruroa and Fangataufa in the Tuamoto Archipelago (the administrative center for nuclear operations being located in the city of Papeete on Tahiti).[5] Throughout the last fifty years, as well as today, the region has been essentially deterritorialized and reterritorialized not only into a nuclear laboratory, but also into a strategic militarized space, most recently for the U.S. Star Wars project (the center of which is located on Kwajalein Atoll in the Marshall Islands).

Such reterritorialization of Pacific space includes the reconstruction (at least in part) of traditional Islander identity through subjugation. For example, with the American nuclear weapons program, Marshall Islanders became American "subjects" in two ways: politically as colonial subjects, and experimentally in studies of nuclear science and the effects of radionuclides on both ecological communities and human communities. The post–World War II nuclear testing regimes in the Marshalls were in many ways typical of a colonial occupation. The difference was in the kind of raw material that was taken from the colonized site and brought back to the colonial mother country. Instead of gold, timber, or sugar, the Americans obtained scientific knowledge about radiation and nuclear weapons. Such knowledge was a valuable commodity in the Cold War era. Radiation-contaminated Bikini and Enewetok Atolls functioned as laboratories for an array of scientific studies. They were important sources of information in the development of eco-systems analysis, specifically the formulation of the energetic basis of eco-systems. Distinguished ecologist brothers Howard and Eugene Odum con-ducted ecosystems studies in these irradiated landscapes.[6] And irradiated human subjects were studied to learn more about how the human body reacted to acute and prolonged radiation exposure. As noted by the Brook-haven National Laboratory in the U.S. Atomic Energy Commission's 1957 three-year report on the Marshall Islands of Rongalap and Utirik: "Even though . . . the radioactive contamination of Rongelap Island is considered perfectly safe for human habitation, the levels of activity are higher than those found in other inhabited locations in the world. The habitation of these people on the island will afford most valuable ecological radiation data on human beings."[7]

Human contamination was described by the Atomic Energy Commission and the Department of Defense as a regretful but unavoidable consequence of the tests. However, according to the Greenpeace report "Pacific Paradise, Nuclear Nightmare," 1994 releases of classified information about the test program in the Marshalls confirmed that not only has the United States been lying for forty years about the extent of contamination, but the United States deliberately exposed the Marshallese people to radiation as part of a medical experiment code-named Project 4.1.[8] Islands have always been seen as good laboratory sites because of their isolation within vast oceanic re-gions. Here the "inputs" and "outputs" of the organic system are perceived as being more easily observed and controlled.

In Tahiti, the French nuclear testing program, called the CEP or the Pacific Experimentation Center (Centre d'Expérimentation du Pacifique), itself be-came the economic foundation of the Tahitian region—far surpassing tour-ism. The CEP's bureaucratic center in Tahiti stimulated migration of Islanders throughout Polynesia, drawing large numbers of workers into the city of Papeete. Islanders were also used extensively for low-level work at the nu-clear testing sites themselves (the atolls of Moruroa and Fangataufa).[9] To-day, as the nuclear testing program pulls out, the Tahitian region (like the Marshalls) is left with significant environmental and social problems.

The environmental and social cost of this form of colonialism (known as nuclear colonialism) is severe and multiple: displacement of local tribes from home islands in order to conduct nuclear tests and to free up missile corridors; total destruction of some tribes' homelands; nuclear weapons–

based economies replacing traditional self-sufficient, sustainable, and culturally appropriate economies; loss of indigenous languages, customs, and independence; disruption of community and family ties; loss of health and accompanying increases in radiation-caused child deformities, cancer, and miscarriages; increases in poverty-related illnesses such as alcoholism and suicide; severe pollution; serious overcrowding in urban centers due to mass migrations to testing centers and removals from homelands; the introduction of Western consumption desires and practices resulting in increased dependence on the colonial regime; and so forth. Most severely affected have been the Marshall Islands in Micronesia (Aelōñ In Majeļ) and the Tahitian region in French Polynesia (Te Ao Maohi). The effects are strikingly visible among the shack ghettos in the gullies of paradise in these post-nuclear economies.[10]

Second-Order Nuclearism

It is against this background of nuclear colonialism and its aftermath that we need to understand recent efforts by representatives of the global nuclear powers and private commercial operatives contracting with nuclear states to use the Pacific as a dumping space for nuclear waste, the incineration of chemical weapons, and continued missile defense testing. It is against this background that we need to understand globalization in this region and resistances to it. Here globalization is about providing space—both isolated space and strategic space. If, as Gayatri Spivak suggests, globalization is the post–Soviet era transformation of colonialism, then the way nuclear testing under colonialism threatens to be transformed into nuclear and toxic waste disposal under the current period of globalization must be a prime example of this trend. Here, at different times, the previous colonizers and others in the nuclear arena (governments and commercial operatives) have proposed that nuclear and toxic waste be thought of by Pacific Islanders as a form of development—as a way to enter the global economy. It has been presented as their niche market, as they say in globalization discourse. Others, however, describe it as "environmental apartheid."[11]

Examples of such targeting are numerous, although difficult to get a handle on because of their secrecy, mobility, and because those doing the targeting come from different places on the globe (many of which are not as monitored as, say, nuclear waste operatives in the United States). Private companies, such as the New York investment firm called KVR, have attempted to obtain use of islands (Palmyra and Wake) for disposal of Russian and U.S. plutonium wastes. A U.S.-based firm called Babcock and Wilcox Environmental Service Inc., as well as Taipower (the state-run energy corporation of Taiwan) have each attempted at different times to gain use of previously contaminated islands in the Marshalls for nuclear waste disposal.[12] France has already used the boreholes of nuclear detonations as nuclear waste dumps before sealing them over, and French parliamentarians have suggested using these same atolls for future wastes.[13] The Pangea Corporation, from the United States, and British Nuclear Fuels Ltd. have initiated a joint feasibility study for an international nuclear waste repository in an area known as Billa Kalina in Aboriginal Australia (and aboriginal land—specifically the site of Jabaluka—is also now being used for uranium mining). In 1997, Tonga was targeted by Korean businessmen for a disposal operation reputedly named the "Nuclear Waste Complete Burning Technology Research and Experimentation Center in the Kingdom of Tonga," and the list goes on, including the current problem of transboundary shipments of plutonium across Pacific waters. (France and Japan, who are the hosts of these shipments, do so in defiance of regional conventions against such activity.) What we see here are mostly private companies—transnational corporations—that are beginning to respond to an emerging global market in highly toxic materials. Most people in the United States aren't aware of these attempts to dispose of nuclear and toxic wastes—including many who consider themselves specialists in nuclear studies. This is because, first, scholars more often focus on nuclear weapons issues as opposed to waste; second, many people in the United States forget that countries such as Taiwan, Russia, and others have generated large amounts of nuclear waste; and finally, because the trade itself is fairly new (which makes a focus on targeting practices essential).[14] Indeed, because our nuclear culture now faces a nuclear waste crisis, the global trade and disposal of nuclear materials promises to be one of the most important "growth industries" in the coming decade and beyond. Thus, studies on the targeting of different regions (not just the Pacific Islands) as sites for disposal are urgently needed.

The Space of Activism: The Nuclear-Free and Independent Pacific Movement (NFIP)

In the 1950s, 1960s and 1970s it was nuclearism and its role in maintaining a communist-free Pacific that legitimated possession of Pacific Islands by the great colonial powers—particularly the United States and France. In the case of French Polynesia, nuclearism reinforced earlier forms of colonial rule.[15] However, beginning in 1975 and certainly by the 1980s, this same nuclearism (or nuclear colonialism) becomes the source of a countervailing movement. It becomes a locus for anticolonial consciousness and identity, and it becomes the source of a combined environmental and social justice movement that sweeps across the Pacific Island region in the form of the NFIP. Indeed, it is nuclearism itself that forges the links of resistance between Pacific Island nations—so much so that a pan-Islander identity politics emerges in the late 1970s, peaks during the French nuclear tests in 1996, and continues today as an active resistance to nuclear and toxic waste targeting.

My own introduction to the NFIP is a good example of the global dimension of this movement. It wasn't in the Pacific Islands that I first became aware of the NFIP but in the American western desert, at the Nevada Test Site, during an annual protest (this one held in the mid-1990s) organized by the Western Shoshone Indians of the Great Basin and Mojave Deserts. As they had done with Kazakhs, who had been the victims of the Soviet Union's testing program, as well as other indigenous nuclear subjects, the Western Shoshone had invited a large contingent of Pacific Islanders (composed of people from different island nations) to join them in protest over nuclear colonialism, and to support indigenous sovereignty movements globally. (The Western Shoshone's traditional homelands have been used for over nine hundred nuclear detonations.) What I witnessed at the protest was essentially the workings of a Fourth World indigenous network, something I was to see on numerous occasions in my work with the Western Shoshone in the American Southwest—the American nuclear landscape.[16] Thus, from the beginning I was aware of a larger field of inquiry and indeed, a larger field of transregional identity—one linked to the international network of indigenous rights and sovereignty. This global alliance serves as a foundation or a support network for local resistance practices in the Pacific. This larger field is in some ways reminiscent of Akhil Gupta's "non-aligned movement," or imagined community, described in "The Song of the Non-Aligned World."[17] Indigeneity in this transregional, global sphere is, of course, constructed as an alternative to American and European colonialism. It is, in Derridean discourse, the maligned second term to the European/American first term within colonialist hierarchical dualism.

The NFIP also functions to inform formal governance at the regional level. Both Tahiti and the Marshall Islands—the two most prominent postnuclear cultures and economies in the Pacific—along with many other island nations, are part of a transnational Pacific Island regional network called the South Pacific Forum, which is a body of representatives from different island states that meet periodically to contend with interisland issues (in Melanesia, Micronesia, and Polynesia) relating to trade, environment, and other transisland concerns. Prompted by the growing power of the NFIP, the 1997 South Pacific Forum meeting in Rarotonga directly stated that its members opposed the "use of the Pacific as a dumping ground for others' wastes." To ward off such activities the Forum also adopted what they call the Waigani Convention, which is essentially a comprehensive ban on the importation of nuclear wastes to the region. As early as 1985, Forum members had adopted the South Pacific Nuclear Free Zone Treaty, and subsequently a separate regional organization negotiated the South Pacific Regional Environment Program, which is a comprehensive program meant to prevent nuclear dumping in the South Pacific. So what we see here is regional action. Rather than waiting for global multilateral agreements and conventions for the regulation of toxic wastes (such as the Basel Convention, which, in any case, has not been ratified by some of the most polluting states, such as the United States), Island states are attempting to address the issue of toxic dumping as a regional block. This constitutes a deliberate reconstruction of Pacific space—a weaving together of separate Island nations and cultures into a postcolonial regional community.

The state, of course, is the primary actor at this level of governance, and the state is not without complications. Constituting the regional body are independent, semi-independent (the Marshalls), colonized (French Polynesia), and colonial settler states (New Zealand and Australia). Differences between these differently situated governments and peoples create what could be described as stress fractures within the regional body. It is here, within the heterogeneous regional body, that differences threaten to dissolve alliances for environmental justice. It is therefore a site that requires particularly strong focus for the NFIP. For instance, indigenous independence is fundamentally threatening to white-settler colonial countries like New Zealand and Australia, both of which constitute the most powerful members in the South Pacific Forum, as well as other regional assemblies and the Pacific Island arena in general. Because of these differences, the NFIP, which strongly supports indigenous rights and sovereignty, is perceived by some as a positive force but also a negative force. Colonial states (such as New Zealand) take great pride in the antinuclear stance of the movement and actively align themselves with it, however they do not accept the issue of independence when it is related to indigenous peoples. This part-acceptance/part-resistance to the NFIP by colonial states is consonant with the divisions between indigenous and nonindigenous environmentalism in other parts of the world where the issue of indigenous sovereignty, which is inextricably tied to indigenous environmentalism, is not always embraced by nonindigenous environmentalists. The result of this tension among Pacific Island states is a weakening of the NFIP. Even so, and in spite of these tensions, the power here of indigenous communities (through the NFIP) to influence regional interstate policy is exceptional and therefore a noteworthy model for other indigenous groups struggling with nation-states in different parts of the world.

Local Activism: Tahiti and the Marshalls

However important the above global and regional levels of activism are, the real foundation of the NFIP exists at its local sites where it is grounded in the practice of survival. The following are two examples that show the power of the local level in this movement, one very positive and one very problematic.

TAHITI   The Tahitian NGO called Hiti Tau (Dawn of the Bird of Peace) exemplifies the dynamic way the Pacific movement functions at the community level. I recently spent time in the town of Taravo on the island of Tahiti, at the Hiti Tau Secreteriate, to observe some of the alternative development projects in which the Maohi (Polynesians) were engaged. Here alternative development is a self-conscious form of resistance to colonialism and globalization in the form of the nuclear and toxic waste trade, as well as in the form of mass tourism controlled by transnational corporations. For without sustainable economic alternatives the people of Tahiti are left with few options for a secure economic future. (Mass tourism and toxic waste are not considered by most Tahitians as sustainable, neither environmentally nor culturally.) This is why one Tahitian woman, Mareva Neti de Montlue, describes Hiti Tau as a source of hope: "Hiti Tau . . . for us it truly represents hope. This organization is giving people the opportunity to get themselves in hand to no longer be beneficiaries."[18]

Hiti Tau's development projects are community identified and organized. Their goal is to create a flexible self-sufficiency that is culturally and environmentally sustainable at the local level, as well as to engage in various projects that might be successful at the regional and sometimes transregional levels. They are engaged in a variety of land/ocean-based sustainable economic ventures: growing vanilla beans using traditional rain forest planting techniques, small-scale environmentally sustainable tourism, black pearl cultivation, and the production of scented flower oils, which is controlled exclusively by women who are thus provided an avenue to reenter the production sphere—a sphere lost to them under colonialism. Hiti Tau exists on the island of Tahiti itself, as well as in outlying island communities—knitting the islands of Polynesia (Te Ao Maohi) together through sustainable environmental practices. Hiti Tau is thriving, although, according to leaders that I spoke with, it is no easy task to stimulate or reactivate semitraditional practices, even when they are clearly more sustainable than colonial practices. Tahitians have altered their lifestyles under the French primarily because of the cash economy that reorganized subsistence in the region toward French imports and that restructured desire and consumption practices during the French nuclear testing program. For Gabriel Tetiarahi, one of Hiti Tau's leaders and a leader in the broader NFIP movement, it is the minds of the Maohi people that have become imprisoned by colonialism, particularly in the creation of new desires and the loss of traditional practices.[19] Thus, "independence" for him is self-sufficiency, economically as well as in terms of Tahitian identity. In the case of Hiti Tau, self-sufficiency and true independence are linked to environmental sustainability, which is itself inseparable from cultural sustainability. Part of this cultural independence is also expressed in a recognition of intersubjective relations between humans and nonhuman nature—a very different construction of the subject than is found in Western liberal discourse, and a fundamental aspect of their conceptions of environmental and social activism. None of this can be called strictly essentialist indigenous identity politics, including strategic essentialism. Rather we need to see it as the local space and practice of autonomy, which calls upon traditional knowledge—practical knowledge—but not to the exclusion of contemporary knowledge when it is of use to them. I would describe this as an attempt to develop "flexible traditional knowledge," which is capable of expanding to include new practices and ways of knowing, or, conversely, of contracting to exclude Western influence—on a case-by-case basis. As noted in item four of the Preamble to the NFIP Peoples' Charter: "We, the peoples of the Pacific reaffirm our intention to extract only those elements of Western civilization that will be of permanent benefit to us. We wish to control our destinies and protect our environment in our own ways."[20] Such goals have not always been realized but they nonetheless continue to instill vitality into activism at the local level.

This focus on alternative sustainable and appropriate development exists in Hiti Tau in conjunction with active anti-nuclear sentiments. For these Islanders the two cannot be separated. For example, along with local development Hiti Tau also supports a relief program for the victims of the French nuclear tests. As Tetiarahi notes: "We were very active against nuclear testing because we considered nuclear testing to be a violation of human rights. . . . If nuclear testing has gone from the region its effects remain and will cause uncertainty for thousands and thousands of years. Hiti Tau has thus created Foundation 2001 for the Polynesian victims of French nuclear testing."[21]

THE REPUBLIC OF THE MARSHALL ISLANDS (RMI)   One of the weak links on the regional level in this largely successful multidimensional environmental and social movement is found in Micronesia at the local and state levels in the Marshall Islands. Specifically, one of the more serious pressure points in the movement comes in the form of the formal relationship that Marshall Islanders have accepted with the United States, which is called a "Compact of Free Association." As both discourse and practice, the Compact of Free Association effectively disrupts the unity of the Pacific Islands regional mosaic of resistance and self-sufficiency by inserting into that region the powerful and overbearing presence of the American military. Further, the compact maintains a dependency relationship with the Marshall Islands, which inhibits local economic alternatives. For a price, under the Compact of Free Association, the Marshallese give up the right to determine military access of non-Marshallese to their oceans and atolls. The United States exercises complete control over who is allowed access to the region militarily and who is not. The Marshallese have also given up (for a price) the right to sue for future health injuries—miscarriages, deformities, cancer—resulting from the U.S. nuclear testing regime. (This is problematic since contamination by radionuclides, which themselves alter human genetic structure, creates intergenerational illness.) Under the Compact of Free Association, the Marshallese are pushed to rent the Kwajalein Atoll to the United States and only the United States, allowing the United States to reconstruct their region into the world's premier theater defense missile center. (Indeed, some have suggested that if Kwajalein military base were to close down, half the momentum for the global arms race would be lost.) And the Marshallese give up the right to stop the United States from any activity it deems necessary for its national security, which could conceivably include the stockpiling and even the testing of nuclear weapons on their atolls (at some future time).[22] For this relinquishment of true sovereignty the Marshallese are given money, Western goods, access to the United States, and the discursively problematic claim to "independence." And the money is not substantial. The Marshallese remain among the poorest of the Micronesian peoples. As the late Amata Kabua, President of the RMI, said after signing the Compact: "We lost many things in that Compact, we regret many things, but what can you do? I mean when you grow up with your brother and he's a lot bigger than you and he slaps you . . . what can you do?"[23]

We need to see this situation spatially because it is quite literally a reorganization of space (not to mention identity) linking the Marshalls to the United States and thereby breaking the unity of Pacific Island resistance to Western neocolonial power. Space here is organized along missile corridors, training theaters, and restricted zones, as well as the construction of radioactive contamination zones, such as the Bikini Atoll or the Kwajalein lagoon, which has been polluted by depleted uranium as a result of the missile tests.

In the period of formal post–U.S. colonization, the Marshallese have very little to sustain them, which is why they have actively entertained proposals to use their islands for nuclear waste disposal (and because of this they have been subject to strong criticism by other Pacific Island states). The late president, Kabua, himself has said: "It's better to earn some money out of the situation [islands left uninhabitable due to radiation contamination from nuclear testing] than having nothing."[24] The logic of accepting nuclear waste because one's islands have been used for nuclear testing is precisely the logic of second-order nuclearism.

What the Marshallese do have as postcolonial peoples are newly created Western desires and consumption practices, and economic and psychological dependence on the United States. Any walk down the trash-filled roads of Majuro Atoll confirms the ubiquity of Western consumer products—diapers, soda cans, and Styrofoam containers, among other things, are everywhere. In fact, one could argue that it is "independence" (or the discursive double-speak of independence deployed by the United States) that allows the United States to now justify their continued militarization of the region, and to maintain a relationship of dependency. One compares the two postnuclear local situations (Tahiti and the Marshalls) with a good deal of irony. The Tahitians are formally colonized but, in some ways, are more truly independent than the "independent" Marshallese. The Marshallese are nominally independent but in some respects more vulnerable to continued colonial exploitation. This is clearly a problem concerning nuclear and toxic wastes, since their dependence on the United States keeps them from developing true sustainable economic alternatives and makes them vulnerable to targeting by a variety of nuclear states and operatives.

While this may sound like a hopeless situation, the Marshallese are not only defeated victims, first of nuclear colonialism and then of neocolonialism. There are RMI groups and individuals, such as those quoted in this essay, who actively align themselves with the NFIP, and who engage in other forms of resistance. For instance, in the 1980s the Marshallese conducted what they called "sail-ins" to reoccupy their land and to protest forced relocation from their islands by the U.S. military. In dark humor they called the sail-ins "Operation Homecoming," a play on "Operation Crossroads," an earlier U.S. nuclear testing series in the Marshalls. But as with many postcolonial environments in other parts of the world, colonialism has not simply disappeared with the creation of an indigenous independent government. The Marshallese have been the subjects of severe and life-threatening colonization. Neither do they have an abundance of options (environmentally) for sustainable developments. Their atolls are small with limited space and vegetation—a situation quite different from French Polynesia, which has larger islands for cultivation. Aside from the possibility of a sustainable fishing industry (which has not, in any case, been developed adequately, although there is some movement in that direction), the RMI situation is a decidedly difficult one. While they have decided against taking in nuclear waste as a form of development for now, according to my informants in the Marshalls, they also have not completely rejected that option as a possible future development scheme.

Conclusion

In this brief introduction to environmental justice in the Pacific Islands there are three main issues that emerge as central to postcolonial, postnuclear Pacific resistance and the advancement of justice in this region:

- The first concerns the recognition of the continuation of colonialism within the so-called postcolonial era and its link to the discourses and practices of globalization. Here, nuclear and toxic waste is represented as a form of development by nuclear states and private transnational corporations as they target islands for their enterprises.
- Second, we can understand the environmental and social justice movement—the Nuclear Free and Independent Pacific movement (NFIP)—as

one that addresses injustices at multiple levels of practice and governance. I think this model is an encouraging one as we search for new ways to contend with the negative aspects of the new free-trade market economy. The NFIP gets its strength from the local grassroots. This is where resistance in the form of alternative practice is most realized, such as in the Hiti Tau example; but the NFIP also functions on the regional and transregional levels, forming new blocks of resistance and strength when confronting the new block-alliances of the globalizing market, as well as strengthening global indigenous alliances and networks.

- Third, we need to be aware of the power and the problematic nature of the discourse of independence and how it can compromise regional Islander resistance to second-order nuclear colonialism. In the case of the RMI, the problematic nature of independence is represented by the Compact of Free Association, which is deployed both discursively and with active reterritorialization practices in the Marshalls' domain. As a discursive and legal form of legitimization the Compact of Free Association allows the United States to enter the Pacific region to disrupt the formation of pan-Islander resistance, to disrupt the Pacific mosaic of alliance. The compact is problematic for these reasons and because Marshallese are divided on its usefulness to their country. While it does allow the Marshallese a form of political independence and does provide more autonomy than under colonialism, it is also controversial and contested from within the RMI.

For many Pacific Islanders their status is peripheral economically, they feel the constant pressure of the nuclear powers, they have a history of nuclear sacrifice, and—for complex cultural reasons—Western development strategies have not always proved successful in providing them with sustainable economic alternatives. This is why the example of Hiti Tau is so important, since it provides a model for appropriate sustainable and socially just development. And, while not as apparent as in Tahiti, there are Marshallese who are working to move in this direction.

The question for these countries concerns whether or not there are viable alternatives to accepting nuclear and toxic wastes or entering Compacts of Free Association that continue militarization in their homelands. Supporters of the NFIP are aware of this and ask: how can the people of the Pacific be truly independent in the shadow of nuclear contamination and outside militarization? The NFIP has done an impressive job of keeping nuclear and toxic wastes out of their region. But as the demand for new sites of disposal increases, they will have to continue to be vigilant, and continue to press for independence without nuclearism. In this way we might better understand why the environmental justice and independence movement in the Pacific is called the *"Nuclear-Free* and Independent Pacific Movement." For supporters of the NFIP there can only be independence in a nuclear-free environment.

NOTES

1. This assessment of the NFIP comes from my own interviews with members of the movement, as well as from correspondence with representatives at the Pacific Concerns Resource Center, which is the NFIP Secretariat in Suva Fiji. The quotations are taken from NFIP informational materials.

2. By "globalization from below" I mean to call attention to the way in which the NFIP forms a coherent and relatively recent regional block (made up mostly of minor economic players) in order to address both colonialism and the new power blocks usually associated with transnational markets and "globalization from above."

3. Zohl dé Ishtar, ed., *Pacific Women Speak Out for Independence and Denuclearisation* (Christchurch, Aotearoa/N.Z.: Women's International League for Peace and Freedom; Christchurch: Disarmament and Security Centre; Annandale, NSW, Australia: Pacific Connections; Christchurch: Raven Press, 1998), 24.

4. Ibid., 26.

5. Enumeration of times and places of nuclear tests in the Pacific is taken from Donald Denoon and Stewart Firth, eds., *The Cambridge History of the Pacific Islanders* (Cambridge: Cambridge University Press, 1997). Especially helpful in understanding the history of Pacific testing is chapter 10, "A Nuclear Pacific." See also, Stewart Firth, *Nuclear Playground: Fight for an Independent and Nuclear Free Pacific* (Honolulu: University of Hawaii Press, 1987).

6. See Howard Odum and Eugene P. Odum, "Trophic Structure and Productivity of a Windward Coral Reef Community on Eniwetok Atoll," *Ecological Monographs* 25 (1955): 291–320.

7. Susie Cohn et al., *Pacific Paradise/Nuclear Nightmare: Women Working for a Nuclear Free and Independent Pacific* (London: CND Publications, 1987), 37.

8. Greenpeace, *Pacific Paradise, Nuclear Nightmare: A Critique of the Pro-*

posal to Use the Marshall Islands as a Nuclear Waste Dump (Auckland, New Zealand: Greenpeace, 1994).

9. For more on the French nuclear testing experiment center see Peiter de Vries and Han Seur, *Moruroa and Us: Polynesians' Experiences During Thirty Years of Nuclear Testing in the French Pacific* (Lyon, France: Centre de Documentation et de Recherche sur la Paix et les Conflits, 1997). This book documents, with qualitative and quantitative analyses, the impact of the CEP on the lives and the environment of the region.

10. In 1999 I traveled to Tahiti, the Republic of the Marshall Islands, and Guam to research postnuclear economies and cultures, as well as the NFIP. The information in this essay on both Tahiti and the Marshalls is, in part, the result of my interviews and observations in the field.

11. Vandana Shiva has used the term "environmental apartheid" when describing the toxic waste dumping practices of the North on the South, particularly in India. See her "Ecological Balance in an Era of Globalization" in *Global Ethics and Environment,* ed. Nicholas Low (London/New York: Routledge, 1999), 47–69.

12. Greenpeace, *Pacific Paradise, Nuclear Nightmare.*

13. This suggestion appeared in a report presented on 17 December 1997 by Socialist Party Member of Parliament Christian Bataille. Report no. 541 to the French National Assembly.

14. Such focus on nuclear weapons has been required by the urgency of Cold War nuclear politics. Consequently, because of the Cold War spectacle of apocalypse, the very serious problem of mounting nuclear wastes has taken a backseat in nuclear studies. However, not all scholars focus on weapons to the exclusion of waste. Scholarly work has been done by Shrader-Frechette, Makhijani, Kuletz, Hanson, and others.

15. The term "nuclearism" is a way of designating various aspects of nuclear or radioactive activities in one word, so as not to have to list nuclear testing, radiation experiments, nuclear development, waste burial, and uranium mining (or any combination of the above) each time I refer to more than one aspect of nuclear activity. The term also implies the structures—administerial, military, political, scientific—that surround and support nuclear activities of various kinds.

16. See Valerie Kuletz, *The Tainted Desert: Environmental and Social Ruin in the American West* (New York: Routledge, 1998).

17. Akhil Gupta and James Ferguson, *Culture, Power, Place: Explorations in Critical Anthropology* (Durham, N.C.: Duke University Press, 1997).

18. This quote is from the 1998 video, *Hiti Tau,* a collaboration between

the NGO Hiti Tau and the World Council of Churches' Pacific Desk (as well as other Pacific NGOs).

19. Taped interview with Gabriel Tetiarahi by author; Hiti Tau Secretariet in Taravo, Tahiti; 20 November 1999.

20. This quote from the MFIP Peoples' Charter can be found on the MFIP website (www.pasifika.net/pacific-action/nfip.html).

21. Quote from *Hiti Tau* video.

22. For more on the complicated nature of the Compact of Free Association between the United States and the Republic of the Marshall Islands see David Hanlon, *Remaking Micronesia: Discourses over Development in a Pacific Territory, 1944–1982* (Honolulu: University of Hawaii Press, 1998). Greenpeace has argued that the Compact of Free Association specifically guards against the use of the Marshalls as a U.S. nuclear waste dump. However, others—such as Hanlon—suggest that the complexity of the Compact legal document includes problematic language and cross-referencing that actually allows such practices.

23. This quote is from an unidentified U.S. news segment videotape and is cataloged in the Department of Geography at the University of Canterbury, N.Z.

24. Ibid.

POETICS

7

TOWARD AN ENVIRONMENTAL JUSTICE ECOCRITICISM

T. V. Reed

I want through this essay to encourage the growth of an emerging field I call "environmental justice ecocriticism." In coining this label, I hope to co-alesce existing work and help foster new work that understands and elaborates the crucial connections between environmental concerns and social justice in the context of ecocriticism. I'll begin by pointing up some problematic features of much current ecocriticism, and then suggest some ways to further develop an environmental justice strand of ecocriticism. My problem with much past and current "ecocriticism," a term whose necessarily imprecise contours I will try to sketch below, is less what it is than what it is not (yet). While the field of ecocriticism is in many respects very broad, it has not often dealt seriously with questions of race and class, questions which I and many others believe must be at the heart of any discussion of the history and future of environmental thought and action.

Both the problem and some hints towards its solution can be found in the collection of essays entitled, *The Ecocriticism Reader: Landmarks in Literary Ecology,* edited by Cheryll Burgess Glotfelty and Harold Fromm.[1] As the title itself might suggest (*the* ecocriticism reader, not *an* ecocriticism reader), this volume had designs to be the defining text for its field, and to a large degree it has served that role. As the introduction puts it, "These are the essays with which anyone wishing to undertake ecocritical scholarship ought to be familiar" (xxvi). While there are some gestures noting the incompleteness of the project of ecocriticism, mention of its "evolving nature" for example, to the extent that this text is representative, it suggests that ecocriticism is in danger of recapitulating the sad history of environmentalism generally, wherein unwillingness to grapple with questions of racial, class, and national privilege has severely undermined the powerful critique of ecological devastation. While the field has evolved since *The Ecocriticism Reader* was originally published in 1996, judging by conference programs and the main journals featuring ecocriticism, the anthology remains representative of what many consider the main concerns of the field; and those most recent works that acknowledge environmental justice concerns do not like those concerns to fully reform ecocriticism.[2] I want to argue that the center of concern needs to shift significantly for ecocriticism to truly represent the range of connections among culture, criticism, and the environment. Where a certain type of ecocritic worries about "social issues" watering down ecological critique, mounting evidence makes clear that the opposite has been the case, that pretending to isolate the environment from its necessary interrelation with society and culture has severely limited the appeal of environmental thought, to the detriment of both the natural and social worlds. Any serious environmentalist must now realize that for decades the worst forms of environmental degradation have been enabled by governmental and corporate policies of dumping problems on communities of color, poor whites, and the Third World. This process was inadvertently aided and abetted by mainstream environmentalists whose not-in-my-backyard focus led to more sophisticated corporate and governmental efforts at environmental cover-ups that mollify the middle classes while intensifying distress in poor communities in the United States and around the world.[3]

The problem I am addressing can be seen clearly in a remark in the section of the introduction to *The Ecocriticism Reader* entitled, "The Future of Ecocriticism." There, coeditor Cheryll Burgess Glotfelty names the problem and exhibits it in the same breath. She writes: "Ecocriticism has been a predominately white movement. It will become a multi-ethnic movement when stronger connections are made between the environment and issues of social justice, and when a diversity of voices are encouraged to contribute to the discussion" (xxv). Notwithstanding the good intentions no doubt present in this statement, it is a remarkably complacent and politically insensitive one. Offered as a series of passive constructions, there is clear recognition that the "whiteness" of the movement can appear to be a problem, but there is little sense of urgency about making connections between "the environment and issues of social justice." We are presumably to wait until those connections "are made" (as if they had not been made for years by environmental justice workers), and there is more than a hint that we will have to wait for those connections to be made after "a diversity of voices is encouraged to contribute to the discussion." Again, why do "we" have to wait? Why does Glotfelty not feel an urgent need not merely to encourage but actively to seek out "those" voices for the collection? And why are issues of racial justice not seen as a "white" problem, rather than one that must await diverse voices? A vast body of literature now available on the racialization of "whiteness" is utterly ignored in that formulation. The content of the rest of the volume unfortunately reinforces the problems and gaps in this initial formulation.

There is not a single essay in the volume that deals seriously with environmental racism. The two essays that seem most clearly chosen to introduce something of the "diversity of voices" Glotfelty mentions are essays by mixed-race American Indian authors Paula Gunn Allen and Leslie Silko. Both articles attempt to elucidate aspects of Native American relationships to the natural world and, however admirable each may be on its own terms, in context it seems to me they play into the syndrome wherein Indians of the past are noble, in this case noble keepers of the land, while contemporary Indians remain invisible or useful only as symbols of a degraded present. I hasten to add that this is not an attitude I attribute to Gunn Allen or to Silko, but rather to the discursive context in which they are set in the absence of serious environmental justice perspective.

Before continuing my discussion of what is missing from ecocriticism, I think it helpful to try to define and sketch the terrain it covers in order to help locate these problematic dimensions within the wider space of the field. The introduction to the volume offers two somewhat competing definitions of ecocriticism. The first, relatively narrow definition reads as follows: "Ecocriticism is the study of the relationship between literature and the physical environment" (xviii). But immediately after this, a larger, more inclusive set of questions expands the scope of ecocriticism beyond "literature" to include more general questions of "representation" that would entail looking at "U.S. government reports, corporate advertising, and television nature documentaries," among other things (xix). This larger definition is greatly to be preferred, in my view, since a wider sense of relevant "texts" will be crucial to the elaboration of an environmental justice ecocriticism; though as I will try to suggest, there is much that has been and can be done in this respect with regard to "literature" defined narrowly.

Let me offer the following typology of ecocritical schools, approaches, or tendencies as a way of briefly mapping the field. Like all typologies, of course, it is a crude device, and I should say quickly that much, if not most, ecocriticism in practice combines two or more of these "schools." The schools listed are meant to correspond roughly to major sectors in the history and present of environmental movements. Since all of these schools are still relatively undefined, I find the best way to characterize each is through a list of the typical questions it seeks to address, rather than definitive positions it takes.

Conservationist Ecocriticism

Typical questions: What can literature/nature writing and criticism do to enhance appreciation and improve attitudes toward the natural environment? What can literature and criticism do to help preserve and extend wilderness, protect endangered species, and otherwise assist in the preservation of the natural world? How can literature and criticism strengthen the transcendent dimension of the human/nature spiritual relationship?

Ecological Ecocriticism

Typical questions: How can the ecosystem idea (or metaphor) be extended to a poetics of the literary system in relation to nature? How can literature and criticism be placed within ecosystems, or be used to elucidate the nature and needs of ecosystems? How can a sense of rootedness in place, in particular ecosystems, bioregions, etc., be enhanced when examining literary works? How can the insights of the "science" of ecology be used in the analysis of literary texts and other representations of the natural world in ways that better connect people to environments?

Biocentric/Deep Ecological Ecocriticism

Typical questions: How can literature and criticism be used to displace "man" and place the biotic sphere at the center of concern? How can literature and criticism be used to show the limits of "humanism"? How can the independent existence and rights of the nonhuman biotic and abiotic realms be protected and extended through literary and critical acts? How can a deeper, biocentric spirituality be furthered by literature and criticism?

Ecofeminist Ecocriticism

Typical questions: How have women and nature been linked in literature and criticism? How has nature been "feminized"? How have women been "naturalized"? In what other ways has the gendering of nature been written and with what effects? How are the liberation of women and the liberation of nature linked? How do interrelations of race, class, and sexuality complicate the imagined and real relations between women and nature? Is there a separate, different history of women's "nature writing" and other writings about nature?

Environmental Justice Ecocriticism

Typical questions: How can literature and criticism further efforts of the environmental justice movement to bring attention to ways in which environmental degradation and hazards unequally affect poor people and people of color? How has racism domestically and internationally enabled greater environmental irresponsibility? What are the different traditions in nature writing by the poor, by people of color in the United States and by cultures outside it? How can issues like toxic waste, incinerators, lead poisoning, uranium mining and tailings, and other environmental health issues, be brought forth more fully in literature and criticism? How can issues of worker safety and environmental safety be brought together such that the history of labor movements and environmental movements can be seen as positively connected, not antagonistic? How can ecocriticism encourage justice and sustainable development in the so-called Third World? To what extent and in what ways have other ecocritical schools been ethnocentric and insensitive to race and class?

All these strands can and should be woven together into a multifaceted field. But it is clear that the last of these, environmental justice criticism, remains the least considered, least developed approach. Two articles, set back-to-back in *The Ecocriticism Reader* neatly stage the problem and point to solutions I see emerging. The first is an essay by Scott Russell Sanders entitled, "Speaking a Word for Nature" (182–202). The presumptuousness of the title is matched by the content of the essay, which in essence condemns virtually all of contemporary American literature as un- if not antinatural. Sanders cites a number of examples of this alleged unnaturalness, but one will suffice to point to the issue I wish to raise. Sanders writes: "In Don DeLillo's *White Noise*—the most honored novel of 1985—the only time you are reminded that nature exists is when his characters pause on the expressway to watch a sunset, and even the sunset interests them only because a release of toxic gases from a nearby plant has poisoned it into technicolor" (193). For Sanders these facts point up the utter lack of appreciation for, or sense of connection to, "nature" in DeLillo's novel. Tellingly, this passage comes soon after Sanders reports that his own attempt to view a lovely sunset in the Great Smoky Mountains has been interrupted by a rumbling camper van that clearly reminds him of the gross insensitivity of city folks to nature. From Sanders' ecological ecocritical perspective, DeLillo's "unnatural" novel is a tragedy and a travesty. But looked at from an environmental justice perspective, quite a different sense of *White Noise* emerges.

Clearly in part what is at stake here is what counts as "nature" or "the environment." Sunsets apparently count, while toxic gases do not. It would be hard to find a more succinct statement of the problem in much ecocriticism. DeLillo's novel brilliantly shows how the toxic gas cloud aesthetically "improved" the sunset, a biting critique of the limits of an aestheticizing, pastoral form of environmentalism. The problem with Sanders' perspective is not that it is ecological, but that it is not ecological enough. The ecosystem and "Nature" seem to end at the edge of the city or the national park or the wilderness. Sanders argues that much contemporary literature is superficial because it does not treat seriously human connectedness to nature. But his own analysis remains equally superficial in that it fails to connect the social realm to the "natural" (defined too narrowly), including what those toxic gases are doing to all of us but to low-income communities especially. It remains deeply embedded in a romanticist notion of nature as the non-human, and the relatively pristine.

What are left out, of course, are human beings as connected to nature, not only as appreciators but also as destroyers. To privilege the first without dealing seriously with the second is a recipe for continued ecological disaster. The kind of nature appreciation writing Sanders thinks we need more of has, in fact, been the dominant form at least since the Transcendentalists. Despite the great virtues of this tradition, it is not the primary source of modern environmentalism. That source is work like Rachel Carson's, which brought to the world's attention the link between human damage to nature and human damage to humans. The toxic chain she traces is powerful in its evocation of a silence(d) spring, but it is placing people in that chain, I would argue, that accounts for the ultimate power and impact of the book. Even the route to biocentrism must pass through the human.

The next essay in the ecocriticism collection also discusses *White Noise,* but in a very different, more useful way. Cynthia Deitering's "The Postnatural Novel: Toxic Consciousness in Fiction of the 1980s" places *White Noise* in the context of numerous works in the last several decades in which the traditional "wasteland" literary trope has been made more concrete and specific in the form of works pointing to various kinds of real waste—toxics, garbage, landfills, industrial debris, etc.—that are so much a part of the contemporary "landscape" (196–203). Where Sanders saw DeLillo's novel as unnatural, if not antinatural, Deitering's essay sees DeLillo as pointing us toward and trying to bring into greater public awareness a toxic environment that is leading us toward further disasters. This seems to me the beginning of a better understanding of a work like DeLillo's, but an environmental justice ecocritic would push the analysis further in two importantly interrelated ways.

First, Deitering's essay misses the opportunity to raise more directly the nature and causes of the toxic crisis. And second, in doing so, it would be crucially important to see that crisis related in part to the whiteness of the world depicted in *White Noise*. "Noise" in technical jargon is that which distorts communication. And the "white noise" that is the background or subtext of U.S. culture is a not accidentally racially coded distortion of environmental reality. The whiteness of the world in DeLillo's novel is one studded with privilege and the capacity to bury consciousness of toxicity along with all other signs of human vulnerability. The novel is in part about flight from death and the search for reality in a wholly simulated environment. The sunset whose observation Sanders mocks is part of an ecosystem of commodified representations parodied most directly in tourists flocking to photograph "the most photographed barn in America." The commodification of this picturesque rural America is merely an extension and condensation of an ideology of the picturesque that has pervaded European and American apprehension of "Nature" since the late eighteenth century. And that process of commodification has been inadvertently furthered by the kind of aestheticization found in much ecocriticism. What the environmental justice ecocritic would bring to the fore here is the invasive, pervasive effects of corporate capitalism on this process, and the racial-class dynamic that has enabled that process to continue. Aesthetic appreciation of nature has not only been a class-coded activity, but the insulation of the middle and upper classes from the most brutal effects of industrialization has played a crucial role in environmental devastation. Aesthetic appreciation of nature has precisely masked the effects of environmental degradation. In the case of this novel, that dynamic can be seen most richly in the way in which the white suburban characters have been so protected by privilege that they literally cannot see the toxic danger in front of them—the "airborne toxic event" is something that happens only to others, to lower-class people in ghettos or inner cities or squalid Third World villages.

Let me turn now to sketch some directions in which the further development of an environmental justice ecocriticism might go, and then offer two more brief examples of how such an approach might be brought to bear on texts not obviously primed for such a reading. In her introduction to *The Ecocriticism Reader*, Glotfelty offers an ecocritical gloss of Elaine Showalter's feminist gloss of Houston Baker's gloss of the stages through which black literary critical history evolved. She suggests that a similar structure of stages is occurring in the development of ecocriticism. I think this is a useful model that can in turn be transferred to describe the development of an environmental justice criticism. But I would drop the chronological "stages" metaphor and speak rather of three prime "levels" of work: 1) identifying images/stereotypes; 2) uncovering and mapping traditions; and 3) theorizing specific approaches within the field. I think environmental justice ecocriticism is proceeding and should continue to proceed on all these fronts simultaneously.

With regard to level one, we can continue looking especially for relations between racial and environmental stereotypes (a task underway in some ecofeminist work, among other places, and which can learn much from ecofeminist analysis of gender stereotypes in nature literature).[4] Such work would range from tracing the history of racist metaphors like "savage wilderness" or "urban jungle," to examining the class and racial cultural biases that disallow the environmental knowledge produced by nonelites.[5] Since the vast majority of environmental justice workers are women, questions of gender also need to be addressed in this work. This will also include incorporating a rich body of work in racialist biology that analyzes ways in which the racialization of science played into the racialization of environmental science.[6] More directly, we can examine the cultural assumptions in various environmental rhetorics, both texts that have helped enable racism, and texts that have called attention to instances of environmental racism.[7]

Level two will include further attempts to define other than white traditions in nonfiction nature writing generally, as well as tracing the specific literature on environmental justice in fiction, poetry, and other cultural forms, including the visual arts, theater, and pop culture.[8] As Patrick Murphy has pointed out, a preference for nonfiction "nature writing" has limited the range of literary ecocriticism generally.[9] This limit is especially problematic with regard to writers of color, both in the United States and around the world, who have for the most part been excluded from or felt alienated from the Euro-American male-centered tradition of natural history writing and the nature-experience essay.

This work would include a long-range study of how nature has been figured in different cultural traditions within the United States. American slaves, for example, saw the "wilderness" not as the Puritans had as a place of evil, but rather as a place of refuge from captivity, or as a frightening territory that had to be crossed to achieve freedom.[10] More recently and directly, there are those cultural texts that Joni Adamson has called the "literature of environmental justice."[11] Adamson uses the word "literature" with intentional ambiguity, pointing us primarily to a body of poetry and fictional prose directly treating environmental justice issues, but also keeping open the wider meaning of literature as any writing on a given subject. Fiction and poetry by a range of U.S. writers including Ana Castillo, Leslie Silko, Toni Cade Bambara, Octavia Bulter, Winona LaDuke, Audre Lorde, Linda Hogan, Ursula LeGuinn, Gerald Vizenor, Alice Walker, Simon Ortiz, Barbara Kingsolver, Joy Harjo, Karen Yamashita, among many others, fits the first definition. With regard to the larger meaning of literature, environmental justice ecocritical work could also include reading the nonfiction writing about environmental justice, from movement manifestos to Environmental Protection Agency documents, with an eye towards their cultural meanings, contexts, and influence.[12] This work can be of real political usefulness in that the environmental justice movement, as currently constituted, has often worked with a rather thin sense of culture and has not utilized cultural workers as much as it might.

In addition to looking for the most direct sources for an environmental justice ecocriticism, theoretical imagination should encourage us to approach texts where the links are not immediately present. Mary Wood, for example, offers an imaginative reading of immigrant writer Mary Antin's "natural history" of mice in her early-twentieth-century tenement as a reflection on gender, ethnicity, racial privilege and the coding of nature.[13] Wood asks seriously playful questions about what counts as nature and natural history. Why does the idea of studying the habits of urban mice seem risible to us, while observing more "wild" creatures is seen as the utmost in enlightenment? From another angle, the recent novels of "toxic consciousness" Deitering describes could also be enhanced by an environmental justice approach. One might also extend this process to a rereading of such classics of "toxic nonfiction" as Carson's *Silent Spring* in light of racial issues and class difference.[14] In a similar vein, Giovanna Di Chiro has contrasted the aestheticized mode of "ecotourism" that in many ways parallels traditional ecocriticism with the "toxic tourism" organized by some environmental justice groups.[15]

Lastly, level three would seek to bring together theoretical tools from political ecology, cultural studies, racial formation and critical race theory, postcolonial theory, "minority" literary theory, among other sites, as well as from other schools of ecocriticism, to develop further the theoretical bases for extending environmental justice ecocritical analysis in new directions. Works by Laura Pulido and Devon Peña, for example, are highly suggestive of ways to bring environmental justice issues together with a theorized "cultural poetics" sensitive to dimensions of race, class, gender, and sexuality.[16] Cultural studies approaches to environmental issues are many and varied, and often bring critical questions to bear from postmodern theory.[17] One key facet of this work is theorizing other sites as "natural" that are more often coded only as "cultural." There is, for example, a growing body of urban ecocriticism that makes the crucial but often ignored point that the natural environment does not end at the edge of cities.[18] Since suburbia, from which a great many wilderness lovers hail, has proven a far more environmentally destructive place than cities, we need also to develop a sense of suburban ecologies and theorize more fully their role in environmental, gender, class, and race politics. There is also a body of work in political ecology that links up national and transnational questions of culture and environmental justice in crucial ways, and could provide the basis for comparative environmental justice ecocritical work sensitive to varied cultural traditions, political economic conditions, and geopolitical contexts.[19] The potential usefulness of postcolonial theory is suggested in *The Ecocriticism Reader* itself in David Mazel's essay, "American Literary Environmentalism as Domestic Orientalism." Mazel's insights might well be adapted to link environmental colonialism to racialized and gendered colonialism more fully and extensively, thereby joining other work that has pointed out the political dangers of a romanticized, feminized, othered Nature.[20] Just as a reformulated environmentalism may well prove to be a movement capable of bringing into coalition a wide array of progressive social movements nationally and internationally, environmental justice ecocriticism could do much to overcome what Chicana feminist critic Chela Sandoval has called the "apartheid" of theory that has divided related academic discourses also aimed at supporting vital social and environmental change.[21]

Let me end with two brief examples of the kind of synthesizing work that an environmental justice perspective could bring to bear on texts and issues now lying outside the realm of ecocriticism. How for example, might an environmental justice ecocritic comment on these lines from June Jordan's powerful "Poem about My Rights"?

<pre>
                         I am the wrong
sex the wrong age the wrong skin and
suppose it was not here in the city but down on the beach/
or far into the woods and I wanted to go
there by myself thinking about God/ or thinking
about children or thinking about the world/ all of it
disclosed by the stars and the silence:
I could not go and I could not think and I could not
stay there
alone[22]
</pre>

Jordan here is asserting, with and against the Thoreauvian tradition, a "right" to enter the literal and literary "woods" of America as an equal partner, free from the fear of rape attendant upon her race, her class, her gender. Where, she asks, does the gendered part of her being begin and the racialized part end? Where does her natural body enter into its cultural moment? How does the nature of colonialism reinforce the colonization of nature? How might a privileged enjoyment of wilderness blind the seer to the nature of injustices inflicted on the less privileged? Jordan reminds us throughout the poem that her "natural" body is a colonized site, one colonized *with* and *as a part of* the natural world, that the rape of an African country, an environment, an African American woman's body, are all entwined, that each violation of rights shapes each of the others, reinforcing mutually. Just as surely she reminds us that only a mutually reinforcing resistance on all these levels will bring liberation to any part. To revise a famous bumper sticker: If you want a sustainable environment, work for justice.

   Or how might an environmental justice ecocritic look at a quite different, equally influential poem, like Adrienne Rich's "Trying to Talk with a Man"? The poem, about a disintegrating love relationship, is set on the Nevada nuclear test site:

Out in this desert we are testing bombs,

that's why we came here.

Sometimes I feel an underground river
forcing its way between deformed cliffs
an acute angle of understanding

moving itself like a locus of the sun
into this condemned scenery.

. . . .

Coming out to this desert
we meant to change the face of

. . . .

surrounded by a silence

that sounds like the silence of the place
except that it came with us

. . . .

talking of the danger
as if it were not ourselves
as if we were testing anything else.[23]

A new critic or a psychological critic would approach this setting as a mere metaphor, an externalization of a barren relationship (and surely it is that, in part). Feminist critics have read it well as a critique of patriarchal power embedded in the verbal reticence of the male character. What could ecocritics add? Ecological ecocritics could link lack of respect for the delicate desert ecosystem with the other character flaws suggested in the poem and with the violence of the state embodied in nuclear weapons. Ecofeminist critics would extend this to the patriarchal power and arrogance that threatens the world with the bombs being putatively "tested" on this landscape.

An environmental justice ecocritic would use these analyses of power, and then point also to what is left out of the poem. S/he would work, for example, to re-place the indigenous Paiute and Western Shoshone back onto this Nevada Test Site region, for it is they who have suffered most directly the effects that the patriarchal military-corporate-scientific complex have inflicted on this particular landscape.[24] They are present as the absence that calls this place a wasteland. Seeing that this wasteland is inside the "man" of the title, allows an opening toward what "he" does not see—the desert and the people who have lived on it for several thousand years. The poem can be made to reveal the hidden link between gender and racial identity that has rationalized environmental devastation in "national sacrifice zones," even as it has also made barren interpersonal relations and the possibilities of cross-cultural communication.[25] An environmental justice ecocritic would "feel" the "underground river" that Rich evokes, as it forced its way between the "deformed cliffs," would feel a new possibility emerging into this "condemned scenery," and in response would develop an "acute angle of understanding" to remind us that such sites sacrifice us all, beginning with the most vulnerable, already exploited populations.

I end with this composite reading because my goal is not to suggest that environmental justice ecocriticism supplant these other approaches. Rather, I want to suggest that it adds a vital dimension to the important work done by Glotfelty, Sanders, and others, just as surely as the environmental justice movement adds an absolutely crucial dimension to our understanding of environmental problems and solutions. But this is not mere addition. Bringing environmental justice into ecocriticism entails a fundamental rethinking and reworking of the field as a whole, just as environmental justice theory and practice is leading to a fundamental rethinking of all environmental movements. Ecocriticism, like the environmental movement generally, cannot afford to be seen as a domain structured by white privilege, as a place where white folks go to play with wilderness, while others are locked into urban "jungles" (as the racist construction of inner cities was often phrased). The alliances between labor and environmentalists at the World Trade Organization demonstrations in Seattle in late 1999 made clear beyond a doubt how much more powerful an environmental critique can be when it works with, not against, working people and people of color, at home and around the world.

The lack of a strong environmental justice component within the field of ecocriticism should be felt as a deep crisis, one that should be addressed seriously at all levels of the field, from conferences, to journals, to associations, to public statements, in published work, and in direct political action. There are signs all around us of many people of goodwill working to resolve this crisis. This timely anthology is itself a prime artifact of efforts underway to shift focus. But we will need to do more, much more, to overcome the problematic legacy of an incomplete ecocriticism and to create a field in which the modifier "environmental justice" will not be needed because ecocriticism will have a concern for economic, racial, and gender justice at its heart, alongside its deep concern for preservation of the natural world that is utterly entwined with these social concerns.

NOTES

1. Glotfelty, Cheryll Burgess, and Harold Fromm, eds., *The Ecocriticism Reader* (Athens: University of Georgia Press, 1996).

2. A close look at the Association for the Study of Literature and Environment conference programs over that last few years, or a look at recent issues of the association's journal, *ISLE: Interdisciplinary Studies in Literature and Environment,* makes clear that most ecocriticism remains within the paradigms laid out in *The Ecocriticism Reader.* A book like Lawrence Buell's recent *Writing for an Endangered World* (Cambridge: Belknap of Harvard University Press, 2001) is at once encouraging in that a critic with clear ambitions to define the terrain of ecocriticism moves beyond his earlier, largely Thoreauvian paradigm to include environmental justice issues in his scope, and discouraging in that those concerns aren't fully engaged and don't fundamentally transform even his much-expanded paradigm of the field. Among the anthologies and other book-length studies that do expand ecocriticism in various ways, are: Rachel Stein, *Shifting the Ground: American Women Writers' Revisions of Nature, Gender, and Race* (Charlottesville: University Press of Virginia, 1997); Greta Gaard and Patrick D. Murphy, eds., *Ecofeminist Literary Criticism: Theory, Interpretation, Pedagogy* (Urbana: University of Illinois Press, 1998); Michael P. Branch et al., eds., *Reading the Earth: New Directions in the Study of Literature and Environment* (Moscow: University of Idaho Press, 1998); Michael Bennett and David W. Teague, eds., *The Nature of Cities: Ecocriticism and Urban Environments* (Tucson: University of Arizona Press, 1999); John Tallmadge and Henry Harrington, eds., *Reading Under the Sign of Nature: New Essays in Ecocriticism* (Salt Lake City: University of Utah Press, 2000); Patrick Murphy, *Farther Afield in the Study of Nature-Oriented Literature* (Charlottesville: University of Virginia Press, 2000); David Mazel, *American Literary Environmentalism* (Athens: University of Georgia Press, 2000); and Glynis Carr, ed., *New Essays in Ecofeminist Literary Criticism* (Lewisburg, Pa.: Bucknell University Press, 2000).

3. The literature on environmental racism and environmental justice is vast. Among the works most useful in an ecocritical context are: Robert D. Bullard, ed., *Confronting Environmental Racism: Voices from the Grassroots.* (Boston: South End, 1993); Robert D. Bullard, *Dumping in Dixie: Race, Class, and Environmental Equity* (Boulder: Westview, 1990); Al Gedicks, *The New Resource Wars: Native and Environmental Struggles Against Multinational Corporations* (Boston: South End, 1993); Robert D. Bullard, *Unequal Protection: Environmental Justice and Communities of Color* (San Francisco: Sierra Club, 1994); Annie L. Booth and Harvey M. Jacobs, "Ties That Bind: Native American Beliefs as a Foundation for Environmental Consciousness," *Environmental Ethics* 12, no. 1 (1990): 27–43; Laura Pulido, *Environmentalism and Economic Justice: Two Chicano Struggles in the Southwest* (Tucson: University

of Arizona Press, 1996); Devon Peña, *Chicano Culture, Ecology, Politics: Subversive Kin* (Tucson: University of Arizona Press, 1999); Devon Peña, *The Terror of the Machine: Technology, Work, Gender, and Ecology of the U.S.-Mexico Border* (Austin: University of Texas Press, 1997); Giovanna Di Chiro, "Nature as Community: The Convergence of Environment and Social Justice," in *Privatizing Nature: Political Struggles for the Global Commons,* ed. Michael Goldman (New Brunswick, N.J.: Rutgers University Press, 1998), 120–43; Daniel Faber, ed., *The Struggle for Ecological Democracy: Environmental Justice Movements in the United States* (Guilford, Conn.: Guilford, 1998).

4. See, for example, Noël Sturgeon, *Ecofeminist Natures* (New York: Routledge, 1998). This book examines the effects of racial stereotyping and other racial dynamics in undermining the effectiveness of ecofeminism and other radical environmental efforts.

5. For an example of this latter approach, see Giovanna Di Chiro, "Local Actions, Global Visions: Remaking Environmental Expertise," *Frontiers: A Journal of Women Studies* 8, no. 2 (Fall 1997): 203–31.

6. See, for example, Londa Schiebinger, *Nature's Body: Gender in the Making of Modern Science* (Boston: Beacon, 1995). Also see Donna Haraway's books, *Primate Visions: Gender, Race, and Nature in the World of Modern Science* (New York: Routledge, 1990); *Simians, Cyborgs, and Women* (New York: Routledge, 1991); and *Modest_Witness@Second_Millennium* (New York: Routledge, 1996).

7. One rich example of this kind of analysis can be found in Timothy Luke, *Ecocritique: Contesting the Politics of Nature, Economy, and Culture* (Minneapolis: University of Minnesota, 1997).

8. For examples of environmental justice art other than literature, see John O'Neil, "For Generations Yet to Come: Junebug Productions; Environmental Justice Practice," in *Reclaiming the Environmental Debate: The Politics of Health in a Toxic Culture,* ed. Richard Hofrichter (Cambridge: MIT Press, 2000), 301–12; and Giovanna Di Chiro's essay/interview in chapter 15 of this volume.

9. Murphy, *Farther Afield in the Study of Nature-Oriented Literature.*

10. For examples of this kind of criticism, see Kristin Hunt, "Paradise Lost: The Destructive Forces of Double Consciousness and Boundaries in Toni Morrison's *Paradise,*" in *Reading Under the Sign of Nature: New Essays in Ecocriticism,* ed. John Talmadge and Henry Harrington (Salt Lake City: University of Utah Press, 2000; and Penny Hall, "Nature and Culture in Three Slave Narratives" (paper presented at the "Culture and Environment" online conference, Washington State University, June 1997).

11. See Joni Adamson, *American Indian Literature, Environmental Justice, and Ecocriticism: The Middle Place* (Tucson: University of Arizona Press, 2001).

12. When I first coined the term "environmental justice ecocriticism" in the context of an early version of this essay in 1997, I was naming a largely nonexistent field. Today I am happy to report that the kind of work I was calling for is well underway. Perhaps the best sustained example of "environmental justice ecocriticism" to date is Adamson's *American Indian Literature, Environmental Justice, and Ecocriticism*. Her book combines excellent close readings with accessible theoretical insights and a personally grounded narrative connecting theory, movements, and experience. I have no desire to police the boundaries of environmental justice ecocriticism, but among the work that I think contributes to this evolving critical practice are: Kamala Platt, "Ecocritical Chicana Literature: Ana Castillo's 'Virtual Realism,'" in *Ecofeminist Literary Criticism,* ed. Greta Gaard and Patrick D. Murphy (Urbana: University of Illinois Press, 1998), 139–57, as well as her essay "Chicana Strategies of Success and Survival: Cultural Poetics of Environmental Justice from the Mothers of East Los Angeles," *Frontiers: A Journal of Women Studies* 18, no. 2 (1997): 48–72; Valerie Kuletz, *Tainted Desert: Environmental and Social Ruin in the American West* (New York: Routledge, 1998); Joni Adamson, "Toward an Ecology of Justice: Transformative Ecological Theory and Practice," in *Reading the Earth: New Directions in the Study of Literature and Environment,* ed. Michael P. Branch et al. (Moscow: University of Idaho Press, 1998); Krista Comer, *Landscapes of the New West: Gender and Geography in Contemporary Women's Writing* (Durham: University of North Carolina Press, 1999); Bennett and Teague, *The Nature of Cities,* especially the interview with Andrew Ross, and the article by Kathleen Wallace; Carr, *New Essays in Ecofeminist Literary Criticism,* see especially the essays by Julie Sze on Karen Yamashita, Benay Blend on Chicana writers, Charlotte Walker on Alice Walker, and Greta Gaard on Linda Hogan and Alice Walker. And, of course, see the other essays in the "Poetics" section of this book.

13. Mary Wood, "Spiders and Mice: Mary Antin, Immigrant 'Outsider' Identity, and Ecofeminism" (paper delivered at the Pacific Northwest American Studies Association meeting, 10–12 April 1997).

14. Another example of toxic nonfiction nature writing is Robert Sullivan's wonderfully perverse *The Meadowlands: Wilderness Adventures at the Edge of a City* (New York: Scribner's, 1998). With humorous seriousness, this book uses Thoreauvian tropes to explore a profoundly polluted "wilderness." While

missing opportunities to provide deeper social critique, *The Meadowlands* suggests a host of possibilities for a whole new body of nature writing focused on sites that have been de-natured by the nature-writing canon.

15. See Giovanna Di Chiro, "Bearing Witness or Taking Action? Toxic Tourism and Environmental Justice," in *Reclaiming the Environmental Debate: The Politics of Health in a Toxic Culture,* ed. Richard Hofrichter (Cambridge: MIT Press, 2000), 275–300.

16. See Pulido, *Environmentalism and Economic Justice;* Peña, *Chicano Culture, Ecology, Politics;* and Peña, *The Terror of the Machine.*

17. Theoretical issues at the interface of cultural studies and ecocriticism can be gleaned, for example, in the following: William Cronon, ed., *Uncommon Ground: Toward Reinventing Nature* (New York: Norton, 1995); Jane Bennett and William Chaloupka, eds., *In the Nature of Things: Language, Politics and the Environment* (Minneapolis: University of Minnesota Press, 1993); Luke, *Ecocritique;* and two books by Andrew Ross, *Strange Weather: Culture, Science and Technology in the Age of Limits* (London: Verso, 1991), and *The Chicago Gangster Theory of Life: Nature's Debt to Society* (London: Verso, 1995).

18. Bennett and Teague, *The Nature of Cities* contributes to the field by underscoring the fact that "nature" does not stop at the edge of the city, and by exploring a variety of ways in which urban environments, race, and class intersect.

19. See, for example, Richard Peet and Michael Watts, eds., *Liberation Ecologies: Environment, Development, Social Movements* (New York: Routledge, 1996); Bron Raymond Taylor, ed., *Ecological Resistance Movements: The Global Emergence of Radical and Popular Environmentalism* (Albany: State University of New York Press, 1995); and David Harvey, *Justice, Nature and the Geography of Difference* (Cambridge, Mass.: Blackwell, 1999). Ramachanda Guha offered the classic early analysis of the limits of mainstream U.S. environmentalism from a Third World perspective in his essay "Radical American Environmentalism and Wilderness Preservation: A Third World Critique," *Environmental Ethics* 11, no. 1 (1989): 71–84.

20. In *American Literary Environmentalism,* Mazel expands this notion some, and offers a number of other provocative, theoretically informed readings.

21. See Chela Sandoval, *Methodology of the Oppressed* (Minneapolis: University of Minnesota Press, 2000).

22. June Jordan, "Poem about My Rights," in *Naming Our Destiny: New and Selected Poems* (New York: Thunder's Mouth Press, 1989), 102.

23. Adrienne Rich, "Trying to Talk With a Man," in *Diving into the Wreck: Poems, 1971–1972* (New York: Norton, 1973), 3–4.

24. For a rich environmental justice reading of this Western nuclear landscape, see Kuletz, *The Tainted Desert*.

25. Given her own antiracist work, I like to imagine that Rich would welcome such a reading of her poem. For a related perspective, see also Rachel Stein's reading of Rich in "'To make the visible world your conscience': Adrienne Rich as Revolutionary Nature Writer," in *Reading Under the Sign of Nature: New Essays in Ecocriticism,* ed. by John Tallmadge and Henry Harrington (Salt Lake City: University of Utah Press, 2000).

8

FROM ENVIRONMENTAL JUSTICE LITERATURE TO THE LITERATURE OF ENVIRONMENTAL JUSTICE

Julie Sze

Introduction

Environmental justice is a political movement concerned with public policy issues of environmental racism, as well as a cultural movement interested in issues of ideology and representation. Environmental justice challenges the mainstream definition of environment and nature based on a wilderness/preservationist frame by foregrounding race and labor in its definition of what constitutes "nature." It places people, especially racialized communities and urban spaces, at the center of what constitutes environment and nature. Currently, the dominant discourse of environmental justice privileges a sociological analysis of communities of color and community-based organizing to the exclusion of other kinds of inquiries, such as cultural and textual analyses. Literature offers a new way of looking at environmental justice, through visual images and metaphors, not solely through the prism of statistics. This new way of looking references the "real" problems of communities struggling against environmental racism, and is simultaneously liberated from providing a strictly documentary account of the contemporary world. It allows for a more flexible representation of environmental justice, one with a global view and historical roots. Cultural texts, such as novels, broaden the emerging academic field of environmental justice studies by enhancing our understanding of the experience of living with the effects of environmental racism in the United States in the 1980s and 1990s, and connecting environmental justice with other intellectual and activist fields.

As an activist[1] and scholar interested in how ideas of "race" and "nature" affect the culture and politics of the urban environment, I use Karen Tei Yamashita's novel *Tropic of Orange,* as a case study of how to "read" environmental justice perspectives, and as a way to expand environmental justice discourse from its sociological roots. The novel's insights about globalization, immigration, and labor highlight how contemporary struggles are linked to the historical exploitation of nature and people of color.

Set in and along the highways of Los Angeles, the novel highlights the global geography of neoliberalism in the built and natural environment, including that of human labor. Karen Yamashita's *Tropic of Orange* illuminates our understanding of the geography of free trade, the gender politics of environmental justice, and the role of racialized and classed people in the postindustrial city. *Tropic of Orange* offers a new and unique window into environmental justice, a world that is simultaneously farcical and tragic, contemporary and colonial, "real" and unknowable. As studies of nature writing gain acceptance in university literature departments, it is doubly important now to resist the exclusion of people of color from the literary canon of environmental studies, which occurs when utilizing narrow definitions of nature. Thus, it is key to recognize what the literature of environmental justice looks like, and to teach individual texts to raise key themes and issues of the environmental justice movement.

Narratives of Environmental Justice

The emergence of the environmental justice movement in the 1980s resulted from a confluence of events and reports that brought the discourse of "environmental racism" and "environmental justice" to the fore. One key event was the 1982 direct action in a poor, predominantly black community in Warren County, North Carolina, when demonstrators protested the building of a Polychlorinate Biphenyl (PCB) landfill facility.[2] Through case studies of other community struggles like that in Warren County,[3] various early essays identify key issues, terms, principles of the environmental justice movement. Key among these is that environmental justice fuses environmental and social justice issues by focusing on environmental racism in communities of color. The environmental justice movement considers itself "more ideologically inclusive than more traditional ecology groups" because it integrates social concerns around public health with traditional environmental issues and ecological concerns (like air, land, and water).[4] Environmental justice defines the environment as a site where people live, work, and play. This definition rejects the mainstream representation of environment—as green empty space—as ahistorical, classist and antiurban.

Various studies from the United Church of Christ, *National Law Journal,* and U.S. General Accounting Office documented the disproportionate risks that people of color face from environmental pollution as well as their "unequal protection" from this pollution by local, state and national regulatory agencies. According to the 1987 report *Toxic Wastes and Race,* race proved to be the most significant among the variables tested in association with the location of commercial hazardous waste facilities.[5] These studies showed that race is an analytic and social category separate from class, and that environmental racism cannot be subsumed within a general critique of antidemocratic environmental practices. Such writings shaped the public discourse of environmental racism and environmental justice in the late 1980s and 1990s, and facilitated the entry of these terms and concepts into mainstream political discourse (which culminated in the passage of President Clinton's 1994 Executive Order on Environmental Justice).[6]

Environmental justice is, as an emergent academic field, located primarily in sociology, natural resource policy, and environmental law, though environmental justice writings also appear within the disciplines of philosophy and environmental ethics, geography, and radical political economy. The founding environmental justice texts are largely associated with sociologist Robert Bullard.[7] The methodological tools in the sociological and community studies on environmental justice use demographics and statistics stemming from the movement's political need to quantify, measure, and prove that environmental racism exists by public policy standards. The early emphasis of the early environmental justice anthologies on community-based struggles, environmental justice activist/organizations and multiracial coalitions is both legitimate and common, and mirrors the emphasis of the movement.[8]

Yet, I suggest that these methodological tools are not the only way to understand the "nature" of environmental justice. Other methods, such as narrative analysis of cultural texts, offer an alternative strategy to analyzing the roots of environmental racism. Communities in crisis have an understandable and deep-seated resistance to analyses and frameworks that are seen as obstructing the immediate remediation of life and death situations.[9] This attitude explains, in part, why the activist environmental justice movement focuses on corporate polluters and government permitting and regulatory agencies at the federal, state, and local levels. Though environmental justice is theorized when advocates identify its principles and distinctions from the mainstream environmental movement, the environmental justice literature generally does not substantively address the historical constructions and cultural discourses of mainstream environmentalism's representations of "nature."[10] However, placing environmental justice studies in conversation with critical discourses and movements (ecofeminism, elements of science and environmental studies) can deepen our understanding of the origins of environmental racism.

The current singular emphasis on public policy and on remediation of environmental harms necessarily narrows environmental justice as an analytic frame because it truncates theory and action/practice.[11] The separation between ideas and practice is a false one, because the cultural realm (discourses, philosophies and ideologies) does impact what kinds of public and corporate policies are enacted. Environmental justice is an already interdisciplinary and multimethodological field of knowledge that needs to be further broadened into areas such as social theory, literary analysis, and intellectual history that are currently viewed with a raised eyebrow by movement activists. These fields offer a new way at looking at "real world" problems in the contemporary moment, a perspective rooted in a broader time scope of history that links contemporary environmental racism to older exploitation of race, gender, and nature.

Historians of science have documented that ideas—such as the construction of race, gender, and nature—and practices—such as institutionalized racism, gender domination, and environmental exploitation—are intimately linked.[12] Environmental racism must be understood historically and discursively. While environmental justice as a political movement is connected to other radical environmental activist movements—practically, theoretically, and historically (Third World political ecology and the critiques of free trade and globalization)[13]—the current framing of environmental justice studies makes it difficult to see and make these connections.[14] However, the connection between environmental justice and other movements, particularly with the anticorporate globalization/fair-trade organizing, run deep, as an analysis of *Tropic of Orange* shows.

Overview of *Tropic of Orange*

Karen Yamashita's novel *Tropic of Orange* is a vitally important text for the environmental justice movement and the intellectual field of environmental justice studies. This text discusses environmental justice themes of race, labor, and natural exploitation through a primarily nonrealist mode of expression. *Tropic of Orange,* written in the wake of the North American Free Trade Agreement (NAFTA) and published in 1997, critiques the discourse of corporate globalization, described as "free trade," and its impact on people of color, women, and the environment through Yamashita's depiction of chaos in Los Angeles. This is an extremely difficult book to write about, as there are seven main characters and a myriad of themes and subplots. My analysis focuses primarily on Yamashita's representation of the impacts of corporate globalization, particularly on people of color, women, and the environment.

Yamashita's two previous novels, *Through the Arc of the Rain Forest* (1990) and *Brazil-Maru* (1992), broadened the definition of "American" Literature to include the entire Americas. Set in the Brazilian rain forest, *Through the Arc of the Rain Forest* deals explicitly with "nature" and environment in the traditional sense of the words through her account of rain forest destruction. Her second book about a Japanese utopian commune led by a dangerously charismatic leader, is also set in the rain forest. The setting of *Tropic of Orange* is the ultimate anti-"nature" locale—the streets and highways of Los Angeles. Rather than focusing on the rain forest, this novel traces the geography of neoliberalism and free trade. The novel is organized around international movement of goods and peoples into and out of Los Angeles. Rather than acting as a passive setting to the action, "the City of Angels" is central to the novel. Yamashita puts race and class conflict at the center of her definition of Los Angeles through her depictions of social struggle and the race and class war raging in the city. Her representation of Los Angeles rejects the older view of the city as a "natural" and utopic escape from the problems of urbanization and humanity that plague the older cities of the Eastern and Midwestern United States.[15] By emphasizing the environmental justice view of Los Angeles as a city of domination and unequal power relations, Yamashita complicates the definition of nature as uninhabited wilderness, of nature as Edenic "escape" from history, untainted by human touch.

Set in what Yamashita calls "perhaps the recent past" of Los Angeles, *Tropic of Orange* explores the lives of seven characters over the span of seven days. The main characters in the book are all people of color linked to each other through a network of relationships. The Chicano journalist Gabriel Balboa and his Japanese American television-producer girlfriend, Emi, are the central characters. Manzanar, a homeless man, is Emi's grandfather. Buzzworm, a black neighborhood activist and Gabriel's news source from the streets, "tells it like it is." Rafaela Cortes, a Mexican-American married to

Bobby, a Chinese Singaporean janitor, is Gabriel's housekeeper who watches his house in Mexico. A character named "Arcangel," who may or may not be an angel, is a wrestler who goes by the name "El Gran Mojado."[16] The characters represent Los Angeles and its wildly diverse demographic reality. The complex, interconnected structure of the novel takes this diversity to its apogee, with improbable events leading to one another, triggered by the chaos of globalization. Globalization, Yamashita shows, alters traditional values of place, life, and meaning into an orgy of capitalist excess in a landscape of power, hierarchy, and domination.

Environmental Justice and Globalization

The events in the novel are triggered by crises of globalization in a post-NAFTA era. The NAFTA, trumpeted by President Clinton, passed in 1993, and entered into full force in 1994, reduced tariffs between Canada, Mexico, and the United States. NAFTA passed with tremendous hype by free-trade boosters and under intense criticism by labor unions and environmentalists for its weakening of labor and environmental regulations. This book was written in a political context where the benefits of globalization were overly hyped by boosters and economic elites, and among intense xenophobia, which saw immigrants as overutilizing "American" resources. Rather, *Tropic of Orange* emphasizes the human and natural costs of globalization.

Tropic of Orange criticizes the intensification of corporate globalization where worker (labor) and environmental protection (nature) are seen by multinational capital as unnecessary added costs, given the global geography and division of labor.[17] Yamashita's critique of corporate globalization is represented by key objects: oranges, human body parts, and highways. These disparate "things" are linked in that each is transformed into commodities or is central to the movement of commodities in the global market. Polluted oranges (the orange in the title "Tropic of Orange") travel from Brazil to Los Angeles. Rafaela's baby is kidnapped, possibly for baby organ smuggling. El Gran Mojado travels from Mexico to Los Angeles for the "Ultimate Wrestling Championship" fight with a wrestler named "Supernafta." These seemingly unconnected events come to a violent climax on the Harbor Freeway, where homeless people have taken refuge in cars left on the road by drivers fleeing massive car and truck explosions. This homeless assembly is attacked by the militaristic might (Army, Navy, Air Force, federal, state, and local police, etc.) and Emi is killed by a sniper. That the final violent climax takes place on the freeway is no accident. Los Angeles, long known for its auto dependence and freeways, is paralyzed when the roadway is blocked.

The image of a clogged freeway and the hyper-violent response by the State to force the homeless out of their newfound homes suggest a major central reality of free trade: the "right" to the free movement of goods, and for corporations to move factories to low-wage nations, is accompanied by the restricted movement of people, and xenophobia.[18] The events in the novel represent a world where, "Everything is for Sale."[19] In a world where life, land, and labor have been commodified, the highways are an economic lifeblood whose clear passage is guaranteed by the power of the state. Manazar, the homeless man who lives by the highways, notes that he "knew the frustration of the ordinary motorist wedged between trucks—the nauseous flush of diesel exhaust and interrupted visibility—but he also understood the nature of the truck beast, whose purpose was to transport the great products of civilizations: home and office appliances, steel beams and turbines, fruits, vegetables, meats and grain, Coca-Cola and Sparkletts, Hollywood sets, this fall's fashions, military hardware, gasoline, concrete and garbage" (120).

The global movement of natural resources made into commodities—whether organs, oranges, or drugs—initiates the chaos and destruction in the book. This era of free trade has thrown traditional notions of place haywire, leading to acts of individual and state violence, like the attack on the homeless on the Freeway. The central feature of the global economy, where goods and manufacturing travel freely across national borders while labor migration is restricted, is referenced throughout the novel. Additionally, as a black activist character notes, the U.S. urban black community is also impacted by free trade, in the loss of black manufacturing jobs in the inner city.[20] The decay of the inner city is not a result of personal choices (the infamous "culture of poverty" thesis advanced in the 1980s, which blamed black poverty on welfare dependency and single, teenage motherhood), but of structural economic change. The experiences of people of color in the United States, Asia, and Latin America are linked through the history of violence and labor exploitation, a point that Yamashita repeats through the mouthpiece of her diverse characters.

Environmental Justice: Temporality and Truth

Novels such as *Tropic of Orange*, unlike academic writing on environmental justice, offer complex, multilayered analysis that can interweave a dizzying array of images and issues. They reference "real" problems, but are not limited to a realist mode of representation. For example, the diversity of the network of relationships between Yamashita's characters, and the range of plots and subplots, both mirror and alter the complexity of our contemporary world and the temporal order (or the relationship of this present to a colonial past). We are never quite certain what is "real" in this book: whether the oranges are a drug-smuggling scheme gone awry—spiked with cocaine from Brazil, or "rain forest Russian roulette oranges" containing an unidentified natural hallucinogen—is never exactly clear; after Rafaela's son is kidnapped, she battles the villain masterminding the organ smuggling—who may or may not be a real person. The destabilization of what is real in the text is not an escape of "real" issues, but of a realist and singular interpretation of time, events, and peoples. This destabilization expands our understanding of how the current battles over corporate globalization are linked to past injustices.

Rafaela is the central character who exemplifies the rejection of strict realism and temporality. For example, in the beginning of the novel, Rafaela notices a line across Gabriel's property, "finer than the thread of a spiderweb . . . perhaps it was something like a thin laser beam or light passing through and [sic] optic fiber. Rafaela was not sure" (12). At the end of the novel, she finds a "silken thread she knew so well, the one that would lead to the orange and hopefully to Sol" (255). Is this line "real" or "metaphoric"? The distinction between the real or the metaphoric is negligible for Yamashita, who suggests that this boundary between real and nonreal is somewhat arbitrary and limiting in its worldview.

Another example of the limits of this strict boundary of real and nonreal is in Yamashita's conception of time. The novel explores the *historical* and *contemporary* relationship between natural resource and gender exploitation. In a passage when Rafaela battles the villain for her kidnapped son, Yamashita writes:

> The villain pressed Rafaela's elbow into the small of her back and jerked her head back by the hair. The sound of her screams traveled south, but not north. . . . Springing upon her writhing body, he clawed her throat and pawed her breasts, tearing her soft skin. Her writhing twisted her body into a muscular serpent—sinuous and suddenly powerful. . . . Battles passed as memories.
> . . . And there was the passage of 5000 women of Cochibama resisting with tin guns an entire army of Spaniards . . . of one hundred mothers

pacing day after day the Plaza de Mayo. . . . But that was only the human massacre; what of the ravaged thousands of birds once cultivated to garnish the trees of a plumed potentate, the bleeding silver treasure of Cerro Rico de Potosi, the exhausted gold of Ouro Preto, the scorched land that followed the sweet stuff called white gold and the crude stuff called black gold, and the coffee, cacao and bananas, and the human slavery that dug and slashed and pushed and jammed it all out and away, forever. (222–23)

Here, Rafaela interweaves the human and the nonhuman, and the present and the past, in a battle that is both literal and metaphoric. Her screams "travel south but not north," following the direction of violence from the colonizing north, to the colonized global south. She embodies the memory of this violence against women and the land. The first half of the passage places her within a lineage of resistance to the violence of European colonialism. The second half of this passage evocatively references the environmental cost of colonialism—the extraction of environmental resources, the maldistribution of land, the spread of disease that massacred the indigenous people. This history is aptly documented by colonial environmental historians and feminist critics of this genealogy as it relates to modern discourses of "development." Contemporary critics argue that the current crisis of corporate globalization is the newest manifestation of "old" problems: the first wave, colonialism, and the second, development. The extraction of natural and labor resources links these disparate political, geographic and economic contexts. This jumping between time periods, and the author's refusal to embrace a single verifiable truth, enables the reader to understand the contemporary politics around free trade and globalization in an ideological and historical context. The relationship of contemporary corporate domination cannot be separated from historical colonialism. This novel retains this historical memory of activism and resistance against power, domination, and violence.

This excerpt of Rafaela's battle also suggests tantalizing links between the social constructions of race, gender, and nature, building upon the writings of prominent ecofeminists.[21] This passage shows, as ecofeminists have documented, that violence against women, the land, and enslaved racial populations, are linked to one another. Metaphors of racial and gender difference are conceptualized in relation to one another, through a similar history of social domination. The relationship between a number of philosophical oppositions originated with the Great Chain of Being doctrine that flourished in the age of colonial exploration.[22] Central among these are: white over black, man over woman, and human over nature.[23] The degraded half of these oppositions—nature, body, woman, nonwhite, periphery, primitive—are rendered deviant and pathologized as essentially lacking control and disrupting social order. Environmental justice studies, with the help of literature, can go much farther in terms of understanding and representing the origins of environmental racism, and how it is linked to colonialism and gender oppression.

The necessity of understanding the past and its relationship to the present is further reiterated by El Gran Mojado before his Ultimate Wrestling Championship bout with Supernafta. He responds to Supernafta's speech where he accuses El Gran Mojado of "not wanting progress." Supernafta appeals to the crowd to get "Just twelve percent. That's your ticket to freedom. Kids, it's about freedom and the future." Supernafta's charge of antitechnological Luddism echoes the argument made by pro-NAFTA (and other free trade) advocates: that to dispute the terms of corporate globalization is to deny the future. El Gran Mojado responds to the charge of obstructing progress with the following:

> Noble people, I speak to you from the heart
> There is no future or past . . .
> What is archaic? What is modern? We are both.
> The myth of the first world is that
> Development is wealth and technology progress.
> It is all rubbish.
> It means that you are no longer human beings
> But only labor.
> It means that the land you live on is not earth
> But only property.
> It means that what you produce with your own hands
> Is not yours to eat or wear or shelter you
> If you cannot buy it.
>
> (261)

By rejecting a linear narrative of "development," El Gran Mojado shows what links the "archaic" and the "modern": the processes of commodification of land, labor, and life. He then proceeds to kill Supernafta in a bloody battle, but not before Supernafta launches a missile into his heart. This violent and ambiguous ending highlights the bodily and physical violence that the subjugated must endure, while also reiterating the necessity of battle and struggle.

Conclusion

Karen Yamashita's *Tropic of Orange* illuminates our understanding of the geography of free trade, the origins of environmental racism, and the gender politics of environmental justice. This novel makes numerous linkages between past and present and between global and local struggles for justice. *Tropic of Orange* makes clear the social and environmental costs of corporate globalization. But more broadly, it offers a critique of hierarchy and domination, and the particular burden it places on women, nature, and people of color.

Environmental justice is complex and multilayered, occupying more than parameters of race and community in the discourse of quantitative sociology. Environmental justice can be read and understood not only through the narrow grid of public policy, but through the contours of fantasy, literature, and imagination as well. In this evocative passage, Yamashita paints a picture of life as a series of patterns and connections, of layers and linkages, connecting the weather with race: "Life is the prehistoric grid of plant and fauna and human behavior . . . the historic grid of land usage and property, the great overlays of transport . . . a thousand natural and man-made divisions, variations both dynamic and stagnant, patterns and connections by every conceivable definition from the distribution of wealth to race, from patterns of climate to the curious blueprint of the skies" (57). This excerpt, like the novel at large, evokes complex and interesting images and concepts in a striking way that retains descriptive power long after the initial reading. The novel exemplifies the emerging literature of environmental justice and signifies an important new way to understand the roots of environmental racism. Literature offers a significant tool to the emerging field of environmental justice studies—a tool that opens up critical avenues of understanding. Literature, through its testing of the boundaries of realism and temporality, is not a route of escapism from the lived experience of environmental racism in the contemporary moment. Rather, environmental justice needs literature to better understand why and how the exploitation of people of color, women, and the environment are linked, historically and systemically. Through the exhortation that human beings and the earth have more value and meaning then the market value, Yamashita is passionately arguing against the idea that the expansion of corporate capitalism enables human freedom. Rather, she shows that the hyper-commodification of natural resources, land, and labor leads to chaos and destruction—with origins in colonialism. Despite these deep roots, Yamashita's vision is to show how ordinary people, and the people more affected by these changes, resist these forces with conviction and by facing death if necessary. The impulse to fight these forces represents a more authentic path to human freedom and to restoring the balance of nature.

NOTES

1. I have worked with the New York City Environmental Justice Alliance, and Community/Academic Partnership for the Environment, as well as having consulted for other environmental justice groups.

2. See Cole and Foster, 19–21. The protests represented the first time people went to jail to stop a toxic waste landfill and are important because the *direct action* character of the protests suggest linkages between the civil rights and antinuclear movements.

3. These community struggles took place in Virginia, Alabama, New Mexico, Southern Colorado (see Bullard, *Confronting Environmental Racism*), and Georgia, Alabama, Texarkana, West Dallas, Louisiana, South Central and East Los Angeles, Oakland, Navaho and Hopi Reservations in the Southwest (see Bullard, *Unequal Protection*).

4. See Phoenix 77–92; and Moses 161–78. These concerns include, but are not limited to lead and pesticides.

5. See Lavelle and Coyle "Unequal Protection." According to "Investigation on Race and Protection from Environmental Hazards," their *National Law Journal* report that looked at penalties for environmental pollution, the disparity under the toxic waste laws occur by race alone, not income. Penalties at sites having the greatest white population were 500 percent higher than penalties with the greatest minority population. Three out of five African Americans and Hispanic Americans and approximately half of all Asians, Pacific Islanders, and Native Americans lived in communities with uncontrolled toxic waste sites (Lee 48–49).

6. This order mandated that cabinet-level federal agencies generate an agency-specific strategy to address health and environment of minority populations.

7. Bullard wrote *Dumping in Dixie: Race, Class, and Environmental Quality*

(1990) and edited *Confronting Environmental Racism: Voices from the Grassroots* (1993), and *Unequal Protection: Environmental Justice and Communities of Color* (1994).

8. Many of the essays in these early environmental justice anthologies texts read as a step-by-step description of a particular community of color, the unfolding of a campaign, obstacles overcome, lessons learned, and advice for organizing. See especially, Part II, "Surviving Environmental 'Sacrifice' Zones" and Part III, "Networking and Coalition Building" in Bullard's *Unequal Protection*. Bullard writes, "The environmental justice movement is alive and well in diverse communities across the nation" (xxii).

9. As Reverend Ben Chavis, former executive director of the United Church of Christ Commission for Racial Justice, and coiner of the phrase "environmental racism," says: "The discussion of environmental justice is *not* a philosophical debate. . . . the issue of environmental justice is an issue of life and death" (Bullard, *Unequal Protection*, xii). Bullard agrees with Chavis on this point: "Environmental Justice advocates have moved beyond the questioning stage and are seeking solutions" (xix).

10. Historians have documented how mainstream environmentalism's wilderness/preservationist conceptions of the environment as "nature," as a pristine green space devoid of people, was derived from Romantic and Transcendental ideals and reflected class and racial biases (see Darnovsky, 35). Important exceptions to this trend include: Westra and Wenz, *Faces of Environmental Racism;* Taylor, "Can the Environmental Movement Attract and Maintain the Support of Minorities," and Peña and Gallegos, "Nature and Chicanos in Southern Colorado."

11. While Bullard does write about the root cause of environmental problems traceable to "imperial ethics," and about "toxic colonialism," these areas are not fully investigated in considerable depth.

12. See the works of Merchant, Harding, and Schiebinger.

13. The contemporary links between occupational health and environmental justice become increasingly relevant as more multinational corporations move their factories to countries with little or no worker or environmental protections. Asian countries such as Indonesia, Singapore, Vietnam, Thailand, and China are low-wage countries where legions of women work in horrific conditions.

14. This difficulty in linking environmental justice with other radical environmental movements is also rooted in the critique of racism within these other movements.

15. See Mike Davis' *City of Quartz* and *Ecology of Fear.*

16. These seven characters and seven days are organized in a forty-nine-chapter grid in the front of the book, entitled "Hypercontexts." The seven days in the novel are no ordinary days, as a series of seemingly unrelated events converge and explode in Los Angeles. Their individual chapters follow certain themes that reflect each character's defining trait. For example, Rafaela's chapters are titled around times of the day (Midday, Morning, Daylight, Dusk, Dawn, Nightfall, Midnight); Bobby's reflects the economic hardship of life (Benefits, Car Payment Due, Second Mortgage, Life Insurance, Visa Card, Social Security); Emi's are television segments (Weather Report, NewsNow, Disaster Movie Week, Live on Air, Promos, Prime Time, Commercial Break); Buzzworm's are radio shows (Station ID, Oldies, LA X, You Give Us 22 Minutes, AM/FM. The Car Show, Hour 25); Manzanar's are on traffic themes (Traffic Window, Rideshare, The Hour of the Trucks, Lane Change, Jam, Drive-By, SigAlert); Gabriel's reflect his journalistic identity (Coffee Break, Budgets, The Interview, Time and a Half, Overtime, Working Weekend, Deadline); and Arcangel's are the basic elements of life (To Wake, To Wash, To Eat, To Labor, To Dream, To Perform, and To Die).

17. As such, the argument follows that laborers in "Third World" nations (with the exception of the internal Third World elite) do not need/justify/ deserve the same protections as those in the "First World" and that, in fact, to pursue these goals would be to destroy a competitive advantage of low cost.

18. Exemplified by, for example, the 1994 passage of Proposition 187 in California, which prohibited public school services to those who cannot establish their status as a U.S. citizen, a lawful permanent resident, or an "alien lawfully admitted for a temporary period of time." It also limits attendance at public schools to citizens and lawful aliens.

19. This phrase is borrowed from Robert Kuttner's 1997 book, *Everything for Sale: The Virtues and Limits of Markets.*

20. This argument is made most prominently by sociologist William Julius Wilson.

21. Feminist philosophers of science have identified the fundamental dualisms that shaped the structure of Western thought and science—culture vs. nature; rational mind vs. pre-rational body/irrational emotions and values; objectivity vs. subjectivity; public vs. private, science vs. nature. These dualisms, which philosopher Sandra Harding terms "contrast schemas," are linked to racial representations: white vs. "Other"; modern vs. primitive; and colonial center vs. periphery.

22. The Great Chain of Being was the central doctrine that governed the

eighteenth century. It found that species were immutable entities arrayed along a fixed and vertical hierarchy stretching from God down to the lowliest sentient beings, and which perfectly matched social hierarchies of nation, race, and gender.

23. Colonial environmental histories have examined imperial conquest, with particular attention paid to the ideological underpinnings behind the conquest of nature, and natural resource extraction—including the link between slavery/labor extraction and land/natural resource exploitation. Ecofeminist historians, such as Carolyn Merchant in her classic *The Death of Nature: Women, Ecology, and the Scientific Revolution,* focus on historical and discursive connection of notions and identifications of woman with nature. Her history examines the values associated with the images of women and nature as they relate to the formation of the modern world. Her intellectual history examines images to support her argument of the age-old link between women and nature, and that the modern world degrades both women and nature. The link between women, nature, and race is further suggested by colonial environmental histories. In Michael Adas' 1989 study of European perceptions of India, China and Africa, *Machines as the Measure of Men: Science, Technology, and Ideologies of Western Dominance,* he argues that the hierarchies of man meant that some peoples were seen as closer to nature. The civilizing mission is linked to the project of the "mastery of nature" which is further related to a discourse of "social efficiency" (214–16).

WORKS CITED

Adas, Michael. *Machines as the Measure of Man: Science, Technology, and Ideologies of Western Dominance.* Ithaca: Cornell University Press, 1989.

Been, Vicki. "What's Fairness Got to Do with It? Environmental Justice and the Siting of Locally Undesirable Land Uses." *Cornell Law Review* 78 (1993): 1001–85.

Bryant, Bunyan, ed. *Environmental Justice: Issues, Policies, and Solutions.* Washington, D.C.: Island, 1995.

Bryant, Bunyan, and Paul Mohai, eds. *Race and the Incidence of Environmental Hazards.* Boulder: Westview, 1993.

Bullard, Robert D. *Dumping in Dixie: Race, Class, and Environmental Quality.* Boulder: Westview, 1990.

———, ed. *Confronting Environmental Racism: Voices from the Grassroots.* Boston: South End, 1993.

——. *Unequal Protection: Environmental Justice and Communities of Color.* San Francisco: Sierra Club Books, 1994.

Capek, Stella. "The 'Environmental Justice' Frame: A Conceptual Discussion and an Application," *Social Problems* 40, no. 1 (February 1993): 5–24.

——. "Environmental Justice, Regulation, and the Local Community," *International Journal of Health Services* 22, no. 4 (1992): 729–46.

Cole, Luke W., and Sheila R. Foster. *From the Ground Up: Environmental Racism and the Rise of the Environmental Justice Movement.* New York: New York University Press, 2001.

Crosby, Alfred W. *Ecological Imperialism: The Biological Expansion of Europe 900–1900.* Cambridge: Cambridge University Press, 1986.

Darnovsky, Marcy. "Stories Less Told: Histories of U.S. Environmentalism," *Socialist Review* 22, no. 4 (October–December 1992): 11–54.

Davis, Mike. *City of Quartz: Excavating the Future in Los Angeles.* New York: Verso, 1990.

——. *Ecology of Fear: Los Angeles and the Imagination of Disaster.* New York: Metropolitan Books, 1998.

Epstein, Barbara. "The Environmental Justice/Toxics Movement: Politics of Race and Gender," *Capitalism, Nature, Socialism* 8, no. 3 (September 1997): 63–87.

Field, Roger. "Risk and Justice: Capitalist Production and the Environment," *Capitalism, Nature, Socialism* 8, no. 2 (June 1997): 69–94.

Grove, Richard. *Green Imperialism: Colonial Expansion, Tropical Edens and the Origins of Environmentalism, 1600–1860.* Cambridge: Cambridge University Press, 1995.

Harding, Sandra. *Is Science Multicultural: Postcolonialisms, Feminisms and Epistemologies.* Bloomington: Indiana University Press, 1998.

——. *The Science Question in Feminism.* Ithaca: Cornell University Press, 1986.

——. *Whose Science? Whose Knowledge? Thinking from Women's Lives.* Ithaca: Cornell University Press, 1991.

——, ed. *The "Racial" Economy of Science: Toward a Democratic Future.* Bloomington: Indiana University Press. 1993.

Hartley, Troy. "Environmental Justice: An Environmental Civil Rights Value Acceptable to All World Views," *Environmental Ethics* 17, no. 3 (Fall 1995): 277–89.

Hofrichter, Richard, ed. *Toxic Struggles: The Theory and Practice of Environmental Justice.* Philadelphia: New Society, 1993.

Krieg, Eric. "The Future of Environmental Justice Research: A Response to Gould and Weinberg," *Sociological Forum* 13, no. 1 (March 1998): 33–34.

Kuttner, Robert. *Everything for Sale: The Virtues and Limits of Markets.* New York: Knopf, 1997.

Lavelle, Marianne, and Marcia Coyle. "Investigation on Race and Protection from Environmental Hazards," *National Law Journal* Special Section (21 September 1992): 51–56.

———. "Unequal Protection: The Racial Divide in Environmental Law." In *Toxic Struggles: The Theory and Practice of Environmental Justice,* edited by Richard Hofrichter, 136–43. Philadelphia: New Society, 1993.

Lee, Charles. "Beyond Toxic Wastes and Race." In *Confronting Environmental Racism: Voices from the Grassroots,* edited by Robert D. Bullard, 41–52. Boston: South End, 1993.

Martinez Alier, J. "Environmental Justice (Local and Global)," *Capitalism, Nature, Socialism* 8, no. 1 (March 1997): 91–107.

Merchant, Carolyn. *The Death of Nature: Women, Ecology, and the Scientific Revolution.* San Francisco: Harper and Row, 1980.

Moses, Marian. "Farmworkers and Pesticides." In *Confronting Environmental Racism: Voices from the Grassroots,* edited by Robert D. Bullard, 161–78. Boston: South End, 1993.

Peña, Devon, and Joseph Gallegos. "Nature and Chicanos in Southern Colorado," In *Confronting Environmental Racism: Voices from the Grassroots,* edited by Robert D. Bullard, 141–60. Boston: South End, 1993.

Phoenix, Janet. "Getting the Lead Out of the Community." In *Confronting Environmental Racism: Voices from the Grassroots,* edited by Robert D. Bullard, 77–92. Boston: South End, 1993.

Pulido, Laura. "A Critical Review of the Methodology of Environmental Racism Research," *Antipode* 28, no. 2 (April 1996): 142–59.

———. "Multiracial Organizing among Environmental Justice Activists in Los Angeles." In *Rethinking Los Angeles,* edited by Michael J. Dear, Eric Schockman, and Greg Hise, 171–89. Thousand Oaks, Calif.: Sage Publications, 1996.

Schiebinger, Londa. *Mind Has No Sex? Women in the Origins of Modern Science.* Cambridge: Harvard University, 1989.

———. *Nature's Body: Gender in the Making of Modern Science.* Boston: Beacon, 1993.

Shiva, Vandana. *Staying Alive: Women, Ecology and Development.* London: Zed Books, 1984.

Taylor, Dorceta. "Can the Environmental Movement Attract and Maintain the Support of Minorities?" In *Race and the Incidence of Environmental Hazards: A Time for Discourse,* edited by Bunyan Bryant and Paul Mohai, 53–63. Boulder: Westview, 1992.

United Church of Christ Commission for Racial Justice. *Toxic Wastes and Race in the United States: A National Report on the Racial and Socio-Economic Characteristics of Communities with Hazardous Waste Sites.* New York: Public Data Access, 1987.

U.S. General Accounting Office. *Siting of Hazardous Waste Landfills and Their Correlation with Racial and Economic Status of Surrounding Communities.* Washington, D.C.: Government Printing Office, 1983.

Weinberg, Adam. "The Environmental Justice Debate: A Commentary on Methodological Issues and Practical Concerns," *Sociological Forum* 13, no. 1 (March 1998): 25–32.

Wenz, Peter. *Environmental Justice.* Albany: State University of New York Press, 1988.

Westra, Laura, and Peter Wenz, eds. *Faces of Environmental Racism: Confronting Issues of Global Justice.* Lanham, Md.: Rowman & Littlefied, 1995.

Yamashita, Karen Tei. *Brazil-Maru: A Novel.* Minneapolis: Coffee House, 1992.

———. *Through the Arc of the Rain Forest: A Novel.* Minneapolis: Coffee House, 1990.

———. *Tropic of Orange: A Novel.* Minneapolis: Coffee House, 1997.

Yandle, Tracy, and Dudley Burton. "Methodological Approaches to Environmental Justice: A Rejoinder," *Social Science Quarterly* 77, no. 3 (September 1996): 520–27.

———. "Reexamining Environmental Justice: A Statistical Analysis of Historical Hazardous Waste Landfill Siting Patterns in Metropolitan Texas," *Social Science Quarterly* 77, no. 3 (September 1996): 477–92.

9

"NATURE" AND ENVIRONMENTAL JUSTICE

Mei Mei Evans

> *suppose it was not here in the city but down on the beach/*
> *or far into the woods and I wanted to go*
> *there by myself thinking about God/ or thinking*
> *about children or thinking about the world/ all of it*
> *disclosed by the stars and the silence:*
> *I could not go and I could not think and I could not*
> *stay there*
> *alone*
> *as I need to be*
> *alone because I can't do what I want to do with my own*
> *body and*
> *who in the hell set things up*
> *like this*
>
> —June Jordan, "Poem about My Rights"

As with other ideological representations, popular U.S. American cultural constructions of "nature" serve to empower some members of our society while simultaneously disempowering others. Ideas of "nature," like representations of race, gender, sexuality, and class, are never neutral; they themselves create and perpetuate particular meanings. (Indeed, these *social* categories cannot even be understood without an understanding of constitutive ideas of "nature" and what—or who—is "natural," but that is the subject of a different discussion.)

It is not my goal here to theorize how, or even why, the idea of Nature has had and continues to exert such a tenacious grip on the U.S. American cultural imagination. Suffice it to say that it does. Rather, the intent of this essay is to demonstrate, by means of a variety of examples, the ways in which particular constructions of nature and/or wild(er)ness serve to promote the interests of a select few to the exclusion of all "Others." Western European conceptions of nature, imported into the "New World," have proven particularly useful for preserving hegemonic entitlements in North America for more than half a millennium.

The entire realm of earthly life is of course not a creation or invention of Western hegemony. But *ideas* of what is "natural," "wild," in need of taming or domestication, and so on, are most decidedly products of culture.[1] The lack of interrogation of such terms as "nature" and "wilderness," for that matter, is perhaps nowhere as conspicuous as in present-day discourses of "environmentalism" and "ecology," thus necessitating the many counter-hegemonic challenges that we have come to refer to collectively as environmental justice.

Before proceeding, I wish to make a distinction between what I mean by nature—that is, the entire realm of the actual living world—and Western cultural conceptions of (a mostly nonhuman) Nature. In my use of the upper and lower case, I follow philosopher Neil Evernden's lead of adopting "the convention of speaking of 'nature' when referring to the great amorphous mass of otherness that encloaks the planet, and [of] speak[ing] of 'Nature' when referring specifically to the system or model of nature which arose in the West several centuries ago."[2]

For purposes of this discussion, I have chosen to focus on the enduring and persistent, but nevertheless unstable, conception of wilderness or Nature in U.S. American popular culture as the site *par excellence* for (re)invention of the self. Locating oneself, or being located, in Nature is a thoroughly cultural activity: when actual subjects in the United States set forth to experience "the call of the wild," they are accompanied always by cultural expectations that the encounter may change or consolidate their identity in some meaningful way.

Representations of Nature and representations of social identities have often been deployed side-by-side in U.S. literary narratives in order to suggest ideas about particular subjects' place in the national landscape while simultaneously consolidating conceptions of the place of Nature and/or wild(er)ness in our national imagination. Most often in these narratives, Nature is encountered (and subsequently conquered) by a (white) male figure, who then wrests from the confrontation an instatement or reinstatement of his hegemonic identity. Nature is proffered in these representations as an unproblematic reality, when in fact it is a cultural product designed to serve an ideological function: having conferred upon him his hegemony, Nature is reified as that thing which has the power to do so.

The theme of (heterosexual white) men doing battle against Nature in order to achieve "real man"hood has been and continues to be so widely enacted in U.S. popular culture as to scarcely bear mention. In the tradition of Cooper's Leatherstocking, Hemingway's Nick Adams, and Faulkner's Ike McCaslin, for example, young and old U.S. American men continue to enact the ritual encounter with Wild Nature in order to claim or reclaim their manhood. Some examples from recent years include Doug Peacock's memoir, *Grizzly Years,* Jon Krakauer's bestsellers *Into the Wild* and *Into Thin Air,* and feature films such as *The Edge* and *The Thin Red Line,* to name just a few.

This ideological construction creates a representational paradigm whereby heterosexual white manhood (i.e., "real men") is construed as the most "natural" social identity in the United States: the "true American," *the* identity most deserving of social privilege.[3] It's my contention that strategic deployments of representations of Nature or the "wild" have been "naturalizing" and thus privileging straight white men in U.S. society since "discovery." According to this epistemological paradigm, those who have been socially constructed as Other (i.e., not white and/or not straight and/or not male) are viewed as intruders or otherwise out of place when they venture into or attempt to inhabit Nature. In other words, we can see the way that representations of U.S. Nature as a physical location are overdetermined as white, male, and heterosexual when we look at what happens to people who are *not* white, male, and/or straight when they attempt the same sort of transformative experience in nature. The same paradigm has led to notions of some folk as being less deserving than others not only of access to nature but of the right to clean, uncontaminated environments in which to live and work. I argue here that U.S. Nature or wilderness as *culturally constructed* locations have been foreclosed to women, people of color, and gays and lesbians. This foreclosure has had material consequences for those belonging to these social identities, as I shall show.

What's at stake when Nature is culturally determined to be the province of white heterosexual masculinity? How can those Others in opposition to whom this category of humankind has constructed itself—and only itself—as "natural," (re)claim entitlement to autonomous inhabitation of nature? What kinds of discursive strategies might such reclamation or recuperation use and to the achievement of what ends? What kinds of perspectives might narratives created by and about socially identified U.S. American Others—that is, those who are not male and/or not white and/or not straight—as they seek to engage with nature offer us as to both the role of nature and one's role in society? I hope here to illuminate the ways in which representations of Nature and representations of social identities work to create, reinforce, perpetuate, and sometimes unsettle one another. Specifically, I examine the ways in which three narratives place a black woman, a black man, and a gay man, respectively, in U.S. Nature.

When it is said that women are "by nature" maternal, that people of color are "naturally" more in tune with nature, or that it is "unnatural" for people of the same gender to be sexually attracted to one another, what role is being assigned to nature? What is the work of culture, of human-constructed relations, that nature is being asked to perform in these equations? What is at stake for these groups of human beings, and what is at stake for nature itself?

Many have contested the cultural conflation of "woman" with "nature"—a conflation that safeguards and promotes the hegemonic sovereignty of straight white men. Evelyn White interrogates and complicates this conflation in her essay "Black Women and the Wilderness" by rhetorically gendering *and* racializing the human subject.[4] By representing "wilderness" or nature as the site of both personal and group loss *and* recuperation, White challenges as well the mainstream U.S. cultural ideology of wild nature as a site equally available to all citizens.

In this autobiographical piece, the author immediately foregrounds how white hegemony has excluded blacks from unproblematic recreational enjoyment of nature. By emphasizing her own subject position as an African American woman, she brings to bear on the enjoyment of nature by blacks in general, and by black women in particular, the historical legacy of institutionalized racial oppression. Although considerations of gender are implicit to her discussion, it is primarily by emphasizing her racial identity that White contextualizes this argument.

She opens her essay with the acknowledgment that she had never felt at ease in, let alone enjoyed, the experience of being "in nature." A San Franciscan, she writes of her participation every summer in an Oregon women's writing workshop. Describing her apprehensiveness about being in nature, White says, "For me, the fear is like a heartbeat, always present, while at the same time, intangible, elusive, and difficult to define. So pervasive, so much a part of me, that I hardly knew it was there" (377). She discusses her desire to move outside the city; however, "[e]ach house-hunting trip I've made to the countryside has been fraught with two emotions: elation at the prospect of living closer to nature and a sense of absolute doom about what might befall me in the backwoods" (378).

What does "living closer to nature" signify to her? Juxtaposing her desire against her fear, enjoyment of the out of doors thus comes to represent both that which, as a black woman, she feels she has been deprived of *and* (therefore) that which can liberate her from that internalized oppression. She feels compelled to reimagine herself in relationship to the physical environment she temporarily inhabits each summer in Oregon, describing her initial experience at the writing workshop:

> When I wasn't teaching, eating in the dining hall, or attending our evening readings, I stayed holed up in my riverfront cabin with all doors locked and windowshades drawn. While the river's roar gave me a certain comfort and my heart warmed when I gazed at the sun-dappled trees out of a classroom window, I didn't want to get closer. I was certain that if I ventured outside to admire a meadow or to feel the cool ripples in a stream, I'd be taunted, attacked, raped, maybe even murdered because of the color of my skin. (378)

The realization of the lengths to which she has gone to avoid encounters with nature leads White to question her actions and to offer the following rationale: "I believe the fear I experience in the outdoors is shared by many African American women and that it limits the way we move through the world" (378). She links her own fear to various "memories" of racial violence, including a "genetic memory of ancestors hunted down and preyed upon in rural settings" (378). Her construction of a race-based representation of human subjects in U.S. Nature directly contradicts hegemonic representations of wilderness idylls: "I imagine myself in the country as my forebears were—exposed, vulnerable, and unprotected—a target of cruelty and hate" (378). Recalling particularly the 1963 bombing of a Birmingham church that resulted in the deaths of four young black girls, and the 1955 lynching of fourteen-year-old Emmett Till in rural Mississippi, White writes, "In [Emmett's murder] I saw a reflection of myself and the blood-chilling violence that would greet me if I even dared to venture into the wilderness" (380).

Although she never mentions it, it's a matter of record that the Oregon Territory in 1849 passed an exclusionary act making it illegal for "negroes and mulattoes" to live there, an act which was among the most restrictive of such laws then in existence in the United States and one which remained in the Oregon Constitution until 1926. As for acts of violence against blacks in the rural United States, the dragging death of James Byrd Jr. in Jasper, Texas, in 1998 is but one gruesome reminder of their continuing frequency.

"For several Oregon summers," White writes, "I concealed my pained feelings about the outdoors until I could no longer reconcile my silence with my mandate to my students to face their fears" (381). Deciding that only direct personal experience of nature can liberate her from her fear, White determines to accompany a group of white women from the writers' workshop to rent a rowboat at a nearby lake, only to be refused a boat by "the boathouse man." As there appear to be an abundance of boats, White is disquieted by the possibility that he has denied them one because she is black.

Despite this initial setback, White resolves to participate in a river raft trip with the other women. She writes that she was "[d]etermined to reconnect myself to the comfort my African ancestors felt in the rift valleys of Kenya and on the shores of Sierra Leone":

> About an hour into the trip, in a magnificently still moment, I looked up into the heavens and heard the voice of black poet Langston Hughes: "I've known rivers ancient as the world and older than the flow of human blood in human veins. I bathed in the Euphrates when dawns were young. I built my hut near the Congo and it lulled me to sleep. I looked upon the Nile and raised the pyramids about it. My soul has grown deep like the rivers." Soaking wet and shivering with emotion, I felt tears welling my eyes as I stepped out of the raft onto solid ground. (382)

It is by mobilizing this "strateg[y] of essentialism" (in the words of Gayatri Spivak)[5] that White effectively counters the would-be hegemonic white "ownership" of U.S. nature and creates an opening for herself and other nonwhites to move into an enjoyment of nature. The essay gestures triumphantly toward a recuperated nature, a location in which blacks as well as whites, and women as well as men, can "come home."

White's narrative implicitly acknowledges the historic foreclosure of natural locations in the U.S. to blacks, while explicitly insisting on the right of African Americans to (re)claim such places as ones to which they, *as well as* whites, have inalienable rights. Evelyn White suggests here that it is important for blacks, especially black women, to be able to situate themselves without fear in U.S. wilderness or nature in order to realize full liberation from racial and gender-based oppression. Her essay, in its very resistance of that inscription, implicitly acknowledges how over-inscribed as white and male U.S. Nature is.

Like Evelyn White, Eddy Harris is someone who undertook to fulfill a personal quest in nature—a quest, like hers, involving a journey down a river. Unlike White's afternoon adventure, however, Harris canoed, solo, the length of the Mississippi—despite the fact of never before having paddled a canoe, that he lacked the equipment for such a journey, and that he is African American. In spite of his gender, as a *black* man seeking to enact a culturally sanctioned rite-of-passage for men in nature, Harris encounters the same kinds of obstacles as White.

Mississippi Solo—A River Quest[6] begs comparison with Twain's *Adventures of Huckleberry Finn*, if for no other reason than the fact that both narratives concern the journeys of black men on the preeminent U.S. waterway. One way to contextualize Harris's memoir is to note that, a century after the publication of *Huckleberry Finn*, "Jim" finally achieves narrative voice. The causes of the pronounced time lag should be understood as the same that made Harris's journey most challenging: the history of institutionalized racism in the United States.

Lacking precedents, in literature or in life, Harris struggles to find the appropriate representational forms for a contemporary U.S. American black man venturing forth into U.S. Nature. As we shall see, his self-identity is subjected to much indeterminacy: he is never entirely free of the restraints imposed on his mobility by virtue of geopolitical boundaries. Were he a fugitive from justice, his narrative might provide a contemporary spin on fugitive slave narratives, for example; as it is, as Evelyn White observed, there have been few if any cultural scripts for those black persons who would go forth freely in recreational enjoyment of U.S. nature.

Unlike White, who is ready, willing, and able to foreground the role of race in her experience of nature, Harris is initially reluctant to do so: "I promised myself early on that I would not make race an issue out here. I would try to live my life on the river as I so far have lived my real life; I would not make my being black a part of my success or failure or too great a factor in how I perceive things" (67).

Despite his resistance at the outset to acknowledging the role that race might play in others' perceptions of him as he sought to canoe the length of the Mississippi, Harris nevertheless observes when he arrives at the river's headwaters in Minnesota:

It is perhaps startling to realize that there are places blacks don't much go to. . . . Blacks aren't often found cruising the bazaars in Bangkok, or sliding down the ski slopes. Finances could be a problem, but the travel magazines seem not to want blacks to travel, or think that blacks don't travel, or maybe just don't care. . . . And why aren't there very many blacks in Minnesota? Too cold in winter? Safety in numbers? Small town conservatism and bigotry? More jobs in the major industrialized urban centers? Or are there some more subtle rules being worked? . . . You don't find many blacks canoeing solo down the Mississippi River and camping out every night. Why not? (14)

One senses that Harris is merely being rhetorical when he asks if there are "some more subtle rules being worked," but it is exactly this concern that I seek to address. The "rules" are in fact not subtle at all; the cultural overdetermination of U.S. Nature as the province of white men has had material and metaphoric consequences for those not belonging to that single social group.

At the start of his journey, then, Harris seems not to have considered the significance that his racial identity would hold either for himself or for others in the context of his enterprise. In a curious way, however, his efforts to minimize his racial identity serve instead to render it more conspicuous. When he remarks, "Racism—sure it exists, I know that. But its effect and effectiveness depend as much on the reaction as on the action" (69), he seems to be saying that if *he* doesn't let race be an issue, then it won't be. One suspects that as a heterosexual U.S. American male, Harris would like to slip unproblematically into the ample cultural space allotted "men in nature."

Instead, simply because of the color of his skin, his endeavor invites the question, "What *is* he doing out here?" and is this thing he seeks to accomplish as independent of racial overtones as he would have us, and himself, believe? Surely it requires a real act of will to erase the fact of Harris's racial identity in the historical context of this very geographically particular odyssey. And indeed, as he ventures further down the river, his consciousness of race assumes more prominence. He finds it less easy to push the thoughts away.

It's interesting to see how Harris's heightened awareness and subsequent admission of the importance of race correlates to his latitude on the river. In the "North," he downplays any significance others might attach to his skin color, but once he enters the "South," he confronts its resonance more directly: "When I was a kid . . . I hardly knew I was black. Through innocence I missed the turmoil. . . . An attitude was forged that the outcome of my life would be my doing alone. How wonderful for me, but so shallow to think even for a moment that such is the case for all" (104).

When Harris goes ashore at one point in Kentucky, he finds a parked van painted with a Confederate flag, to which he responds with a purely visceral reaction: *"Uh-oh!"* (159). Then, in Mississippi, he has a terrifying encounter with two shotgun-toting "rednecks" who approach his campsite and address him as "boy." Fearing for his life, Harris breaks his tooth in the process of fleeing them. His determined enjoyment of his river adventure has been seriously undermined by the encounter and now he just wants "to get out of there and far away and off this damnable river and out of this idiot adventure" (210). What began for him as something "innocent" and uncomplicated—an enactment of masculine endeavor in the out of doors—has now become inflected with racial overtones that may be life-threatening.

Despite, or because of, this event, Harris discursively constructs himself as an "ecological" being: "To drive the senses alive and then to calm them. . . . To become one with the river, but more to become one with life. The river, the trees, the animals, the men and women, the wind. To feel it all rushing through my veins and to love it. To know that they are me and I am them. . . . There is no color that separates us, no race, no issue deeper than humanity to bind us" (221). Onto this tablet of Nature-as-blank-slate, Harris wants to write himself as a "natural" human, but the ideological process whereby U.S. social identities become "naturalized" proves as obstacle-strewn for him as for Evelyn White. The problem, as Eddy Harris has discovered, is that what constitutes Nature in the U.S. is largely determined and dominated by white hegemony. As such, it is not a "space" easily entered by a black man, no matter how "sweet," "happy," or "kind" one is. Unlike White, who reaches for an ancestral claim to nature, Harris's solution is to seek "naturalization" from the location of a colorless, genderless, "ecological" self.

For both Evelyn White and Eddy Harris, then, there would seem to be a great deal at stake for them as not just U.S. Americans, but very specifically as *black* Americans, in their quest to freely inhabit nature. By insisting on their rights to full agency in that U.S. space, they must push hard against what is shown to be an arena in which full rights and freedoms for dark-skinned Americans remain to be won.

Complicating the ideas of nature-as-proving ground for U.S. American masculinity, William Haywood Henderson's 1993 novel *Native* is founded on the premise that gay men in rural Wyoming risk both social ostracism and violence to their persons should they exercise their sexual desire for one another.[7] (This premise was brought chillingly to life in 1998 when Matthew Shepard, a gay college student, was brutally beaten, bound, and left to die on a deserted stretch of road in Lander, Wyoming.)

At the novel's outset, ranch manager Blue Parker finds himself torn between his love for the Wyoming wilds and his love for his new ranch-hand, Sam. The dramatic tension consists of Blue's realization that to deny either passion is to deny who he is. Presumably, he and Sam could pursue a relationship within an urban environment insulating gays from homophobia, but to do so would entail the loss of the rural ranch life he loves. Similarly, to continue to choose that ranch life very likely means that he will never realize a fulfilling love with Sam or any other man.

By means of the title *Native*, Henderson suggests that native-ness and "natural"ness are linked. The book begins and ends with italicized passages describing the actions of an antelope in a mountain domain, the wild and elusive—but vulnerable—quarry of (male) hunters. The animal is gendered as male, suggesting a conflation with Blue. Like the novel's ensuing descriptions of Blue's minute familiarity with his community and its surrounding wild environment, it is a way of discursively emphasizing Blue's incontrovertible "native-ness": like the antelope, Blue *belongs* here. Like the antelope, he's "natural" to this environment. However, both Blue and the antelope are revealed to be at risk, no match for the heterosexual men who would destroy them. (Indeed, it is the character Derek, a man who has hunted and killed a cougar—a creature representing to Blue something mythical and precious because of its implied wildness—who later beats Blue's lover Sam to within an inch of his life.)[8]

Blue overestimates the social capital he's accrued in this ranching community he's inhabited since boyhood; he mistakenly thinks that his general popularity and reputation for hard work will buy acceptance of his homosexuality. He learns just how badly he has misjudged the tolerance of his neighbors when he discovers that here, at least, normative heterosexual masculinity is compulsory, nonnegotiable. The rancher for whom he works fires him when he embarks on a relationship with Sam, and he is summarily ostracized by the rest of the town.

Another rhetorical representation of native-ness that Henderson explores is the figure of the Native American berdache. The persistent presence of Gilbert, a twice-displaced homosexual Indian, further complicates notions of who belongs or is native (i.e., "natural") here. Gilbert's indigenous presence as social Other is a contradiction that both haunts and taunts Blue, who, in his hegemonic whiteness, is accustomed to entitlements that have been denied Native American men, but who, as a gay man, is as much spurned by his society as Gilbert. The literary conflation runs the risk of collapsing the material differences in the social oppressions engendered by homosexuality and those engendered by nonwhiteness, but the point is made that both gay men and/or those raced as Other are excluded in a social hierarchy privileging straight white men. Taken together, the two men's respective victimizations raise important questions about who has the right to freely inhabit natural space in the United States: which Americans are most entitled to experiencing Nature?

The choice Blue seems to be offered upon his firing—either Sam *or* membership in his community, but not both—is unacceptable to him. Instead, he heads for the hills. His instinct at this moment of crisis to enact a back-to-nature sojourn is a comment on the power accorded the role of nature in American society to naturalize or re-naturalize the male identity. But because this cultural construct applies only to heterosexual white men, Blue's ritual enactment of retreating to nature changes nothing upon his return. Indeed, nature fails utterly to provide reconsolidation or reinstatement to any of the gay men in this novel. Nature, in fact, is part of their problem insofar as its over-inscription as the rightful domain of straight white men casts gay men as outsiders.

Interestingly, at novel's end, we find Blue wandering the environs of Yellowstone, the nation's first national park. It's a significant gesture on Henderson's part: Can Yellowstone's enshrinement and nationalization of Nature confer upon Blue the "naturalization" he so desperately needs? Can Nature (writ large) succeed in restoring his social identity where the previous sojourn in "regular" nature failed to do so? The novel's conclusion is inconclusive; Henderson fails to convince us that even the representational might of Yellowstone is sufficient to naturalize Blue's queer identity.

I offer these readings to underscore my assertion that, not only is the hegemonic concept of Nature a masculinist social construction, but one that is racist and heterosexist as well. Given the over-equation of U.S. Nature with "real" (i.e., heterosexual white) men, those socially identified as Other in our society go into nature at their own risk. Whereas straight white men look to nature to offer up something—the "elements" or large mammals with big teeth—against which they can prove themselves; women, people of color, and gays and lesbians go into nature in fear of encountering straight white men. U.S. Nature is assumed to be a location removed from culture, a space that is open to all, but one has only to look at what happens to those who are not male, not white, and/or not straight when they attempt a transformative experience in nature to see what they risk. One way of understanding the culturally dominant conception of what constitutes "nature" in the United States is to ask ourselves who gets to go there. Access to wilderness and a reconstituted conception of Nature are clearly environmental justice issues demanding redress.

NOTES

I wish to gratefully acknowledge the assistance of Nelta Edwards, Malcolm Griffith, Rachel Stein, and Priscilla Wald.

Epigraph is an excerpt of June Jordan's "Poem about My Rights," in *Naming Our Destiny: New and Selected Poems* (New York: Thunder's Mouth Press, 1989) 102.

1. As Raymond Williams remarks in "Ideas of Nature," in *Problems in Materialism and Culture: Selected Essays* (New York: Verso, 1980), "the idea of nature contains, though often unnoticed, an extraordinary amount of human history" (67). He elaborates, "What is often being argued . . . in the idea of nature is the idea of man; and this not only generally or in ultimate ways, but the idea of man in society, indeed the ideas of kinds of societies" (70–71). Following Williams, Andrew Ross, *The Chicago Gangster Theory of Life—Nature's Debt to Society* (New York: Verso, 1980), writes, "[I]deas that draw upon the authority of nature nearly always have their origin in ideas about society" (15).

2. Neil Evernden, *The Social Creation of Nature* (Baltimore: Johns Hopkins University Press, 1992), xi.

3. The masculinist framework for what we think of as Nature has cast women, by virtue of their procreative biology, as more closely linked to nature than men, and therefore in need of taming or domestication by patriarchal culture. Women are understood to be *too* natural for their own and society's good. Racist patriarchy has cast people of color, particularly dark-skinned people, as more closely akin to animals than "white" people, thereby justifying multiple practices of institutionalized oppression (for example: Indian "Removal," slavery, the Tuskegee syphilis experiments, and nuclear testing in the Arctic and the South Pacific). Finally, heterosexism has cast gay and lesbian sexuality as "un-natural"—contrary to or opposed to nature.

4. Evelyn C. White, "Black Women and the Wilderness," *The Stories that Shape Us—Contemporary Women Write About the West,* ed. Theresa Jordan and James Hepworth (New York: Norton, 1995), 376–83.

5. Donna Landry and Gerald McLean, *The Spivak Reader—Selected Works of Gayatri Chakravorty Spivak* (New York: Routledge, 1996), 214.

6. Eddy L. Harris, *Mississippi Solo—A River Quest* (New York: Nick Lyons Books, 1988).

7. William Haywood Henderson, *Native* (New York: Dutton, 1993).

8. In "Walking," Thoreau invokes an iconic antelope in the same way in which I am suggesting Henderson does here: "I would have every man so much like a wild antelope, so much a part and parcel of nature, that his very person should thus sweetly advertise our senses in his presence, and remind us of those parts of nature which he most haunts." See Henry David Thoreau, "Walking," in *The Portable Thoreau,* ed. Carl Bode (New York: Penguin, 1982), 610–11.

10

ACTIVISM AS AFFIRMATION

Gender and Environmental Justice in Linda Hogan's *Solar Storms* and Barbara Neely's *Blanche Cleans Up*

Rachel Stein

Solar Storms, by Linda Hogan, and *Blanche Cleans Up,* by Barbara Neely, fictionalize actual instances of environmental injustice. Hogan's novel recounts the grim tale of the massive James Bay hydroelectric project that ravaged Cree and Inuit homelands in the subarctic region of Canada, and chronicles the determined, ongoing, collective efforts of native peoples to block construction of the dams. Neely's novel highlights the insidious problem of lead poisoning of African American children in the Roxbury area of Boston, and portrays family-based community activism that loosely resembles the highly successful Dudley Street Initiative, a grassroots organization that has cleaned up and renewed this neighborhood. Through the use of female narrators and protagonists, Hogan and Neely provide gendered perspectives on these environmental justice issues, emphasizing the particular ways that women of color suffer the effects of environmental racism upon themselves, their families, and their communities, and become radicalized by these experiences. In both novels, environmental injustice violently invades families, threatens the well-being of children, and poisons parent/child relationships. While social scientists often focus upon the physical threats that environmental injustices pose to communities of color, Hogan and Neely also articulate the emotional harm done to intimate, familial relations, and their novels suggest that social ills such as child abuse and youthful violence may result from environmental causes, and should thus be addressed within the context of environmental justice. Furthermore, by portraying the ways in which women are mobilized to concerted political activism by their desires to restore their families and communities to well-being, *Solar Storms* and *Blanche Cleans Up* help us to understand the predominance of women, particularly mothers, in actual grassroots environmental justice organizations.

Solar Storms, by Chickasaw writer Linda Hogan, fictionalizes the history of Cree and Inuit resistance to the massive hydroelectric project that has decimated their homelands in the James Bay region of Canada from the 1970s to the present.[1] The fifty-billion-dollar Hydro-Quebec development built a massive network of 215 dams and dikes along the rivers that empty into James Bay. This project, intended to harness 26,000 megawatts of power from Canada's rivers, dramatically reworked the geography of a subarctic region the size of France, reversing or otherwise altering the course of rivers, emptying existing lakes, and flooding entire regions, with horrific results to native wildlife, and to the native peoples inhabiting these lands, whose traditional way of life depends primarily upon hunting and fishing. Although the Cree and Inuit resisted the project through political and legal avenues, they were unable to halt the initial phase of the development, and even now they continue to fight corporate plans for further development of hydropower (Picard, 10–13).

This struggle of native peoples to protect tribal communities and natural world from wholesale destruction is the overarching subject of Linda Hogan's epic novel, but we approach this issue through the story of Angel, a young mixed-blood Cree and Inuit woman, who had been removed from the tribal community into white foster care as a small child when her deranged mother violently bit away the side of her face. Now an adolescent, Angel returns to her community at Adam's Rib in the remote boundary waters of northern Minnesota, and to the care of four preceding generations of women, in order to piece together the troubled history behind her face, regain her native culture, and finally, make a cross-country canoe journey in the company of her foremothers in order to seek her mother and to join the Cree and Inuit resistance to the James Bay hydroelectric project. The concentric plot, in which Angel's personal story of family violence and reconciliation is framed within the larger context of native resistance to the dam project, emphasizes interconnections between the violation of mother/daughter bonds and the destruction of the northern lands and the northern tribal peoples who inhabit that area. Hogan writes in the essay "Creation" that "the face of land is our face, and that of all its creatures," and her novel makes it clear that the violence done to Angel's face mirrors the scars inflicted upon her land and her people (*Dwellings,* 97). Most importantly, Hogan articulates the curative powers of environmental justice direct action to staunch these wounds.

Hogan emphasizes that contemporary environmental justice issues, such as the James Bay hydroelectric dams, manifest old patterns of white conquest of the North American continent and colonization of its indigenous peoples. *Solar Storms* insists that the story of Angel's scarred face begins long ago with the onset of the European conquest of the Americas. The European mission of capitalist development pushed settlers to consume the continent in what Hogan describes as a cannibalistic frenzy. Angel comments: "It was a story of people eating, as toothy and sharp and hungry as the cannibal clan was said to be—eating land, eating people, eating tomorrow" (302). Imagery and stories of cannibalism recur throughout the novel as a metaphor for the deadly capitalistic mode that deems everything beyond the white male subject, even other humans, as food for profit, to be literally consumed to sate one's greed.

Through Angel's story, Hogan describes the way that white conquest of the land has also invaded Native American familial relations, violating Angel's mother/daughter line. As Angel is gradually told the story of her scarred face, she learns that her mother's violence toward her is one strand of this much larger story of destruction, of the ravages that whites wrought upon the human and animal inhabitants of the region during the fur trade. Angel learns that her maternal grandmother, Loretta, was a survivor of Elk Island, where native people, who were starving because white trappers had overhunted the animals, in desperation ate poisoned meat that the settlers had laced with cyanide to kill the wolves who competed with them for game. Although Loretta survived the poison, she witnessed the rest of her tribe sicken and die, and left on her own, she then became sexual prey for white men, who "fed her, beat her, and forced her" (39). Through this mistreatment, Loretta herself was possessed by their spirit of conquest so that, like her abusers, she became a "cannibal" with a heart of icy destructiveness, a person who could only inflict harm and violence on those whom she should love. Loretta's primary victim was her daughter Hannah, whom she abused and to whom she bequeathed her violent nature. As the land and people have been destroyed, so the relations of mothers and daughters come to reflect the surrounding violence, and instead of nurturing their children, the women in Angel's maternal line do all that they can to destroy them.[2]

When the young Hannah comes to Adam's Rib, her body is a solid mass of scars, a map of the many tortures to which her mother and others have subjected her, and she, too, is now possessed by the cannibal spirit that must destroy whatever it touches. The medicine man concludes that there is no longer any cure in the world for Hannah's sufferings and for the tortures that she inflicts upon others, because her body houses the history of conquest pervading their world: "her life going backward to where time and history and genocide gather and move like a cloud above the spilled oceans of blood. That little girl's body was the place where this all met" (101). While the tribe fears Loretta and Hannah and finds their violence reprehensible, the people understand that the women's physical and psychical scars reflect the plunder of their world by the fur trade, as Angel envisions in her dreams:

> I remembered or dreamed of the animals being taken, marten, beaver, wolverine. I saw their skinless corpses. I heard their cries and felt their pain. . . . We Indian people had always lived from them and in some way we were kin, even now. Behind my eyelids were the high loads of furs on freighter canoes going down a river. . . . The people wore rags by then. There was nothing to warm them. Then the mixed bloods turned against the others, the way dogs will turn against their own ancestors, the wolves, in order to eat, to live. Loretta was sold into sickness and prostitution, and those things followed Hannah into dark, dark places. (118–19)

It is within this history that Hannah's demented act of biting away the side of her daughter Angel's face can be understood as a single instance in a long, braided chain of ecocide and genocide that her tribe has suffered. Through Loretta and Hannah, Hogan suggests that in some extreme cases, intimate, familial relations, particularly those of mother and daughter, have been maimed by the experience of environmental injustice, so that relationships within the native community may reflect the historic ravages that the people have suffered. While Angel's sister is following in Hannah and Loretta's footsteps, cutting and burning herself, and eating glass, Angel chooses to reject such violence and she returns to Adam's Rib in search of answers to the riddle posed by her scars, and in search of some alternative to the deadly legacy she has inherited from her foremothers.

While conquest is shown to take a particular toll on young women and mother/daughter relationships in *Solar Storms,* Hogan also describes Native American women acting as a bulwark against environmental racism, defending and repairing their families and communities in the face of these assaults, as is often the case in actual communities suffering environmental injustices.[3] When Angel returns to Adam's Rib as a scarred and rootless young woman, a strong and loving assortment of her paternal relatives take her under their collective wing and teach her an alternative vision of mutuality and belongingness that challenges the deadly cannibalistic mode. Angel, who has been passed like a valueless object through numerous white foster families and who sees only her own scars and her lovelessness, is cared for, loved, and reintroduced to her cultural heritage by three generations of her father's female relatives: her father's first wife, Bush; his mother, Agnes; and his grandmother, Dora Rouge. From these preceding generations Angel learns indigenous principles of community and interconnection; she gradually understands that she has always belonged to this family and tribe, despite her mother's violence and her own removal, and she comes to know that even though she has been lost for many years, she has always been embraced by their love. In contrast to her mother's destructiveness and the alienation of the white social service system, the women teach Angel the philosophy of mutuality and interdependence at the root of tribal society: Angel comments that "in those days, we were still a tribe. Each of us had one part of the work of living . . . all of us together formed something like a single organism. We needed and helped one another" (262). Furthermore, Angel's female relatives teach her a notion of community that also encompasses the natural world. These foremothers see nature as an inspirited, intelligent, thickly precious "soup" that surrounds and includes humankind: "The people at Adam's Rib believed that everything was alive, that we were surrounded by the faces and lovings of gods. The world . . . was a dense soup of love, creation all around us, full and intelligent" (81–2). Bush, Agnes, and Dora Rouge's view of social/natural community and omnipresent love begins to heal the violations that Angel has suffered, and stands counter to the cannibalistic vision of natural world and native people as objects for consumption that has wrought such destruction upon Angel's maternal line. Hogan's characters illustrate the way that women of color, who often bear the brunt of the effects of environmental racism upon their families and communities, oppose these injustices as an extension of their caretaking roles.

The struggle against environmental injustice takes on new force in the last section of the novel, when Angel, in the company of Bush, Agnes, and Dora Rouge, makes an arduous canoe passage north to find her mother, Hannah, and to join the Cree and Inuit struggle against the James Bay hydroelectric development. It is significant that Angel encounters Hannah within the northern landscape presently under assault, and that her reconciliation with her mother takes place at the moment of Hannah's death, for only then is Hannah released from the torments of the cannibal spirits that have invaded and possessed her body. Angel says: "It was death, finally, that allowed me to know my mother, her body, the house of lament and sacrifice that it was" (250). When Angel claims her infant sister, whom she symbolically names Aurora, and brings her to be raised within the tribal group that has assembled to fight against the construction of the dams, Angel is exorcizing the malevolent spirit that has possessed her motherline, reaffirming the principle of familial nurturance, and reasserting hope for the restoration of her northern tribal community as it fights against the same forces that destroyed her mother and grandmother.

Hogan portrays cannibalism writ large across the face of the northern lands, and she details the wholesale destruction of an entire ecosystem and its inhabitants so that the hydroelectric corporation may produce profitable electricity from the waters of the region. Hogan describes the enormous dikes and man-made channels that violently rework the course of rivers, the huge mudflats caused by the flooding of once dry lands and the draining of former bodies of water, and she poignantly describes the demise of wildlife whose habitats have been irrevocably altered—the loss of healing plants, the drowning of caribou and moose, the mercury poisoning of fish, birds, and of the native peoples who live by fishing and hunting. She also describes the rapid modernization forced upon the native inhabitants in blatant contradiction to their traditional lifeways: the clear-cutting of the forests, the mining for minerals that would be lost under floods, the construction of a network of paved roads, and the installation of electricity.[4] Throughout this section, Hogan uses the cannibal metaphor to describe the hydroelectric corporation, politicians, construction workers, and militia who impose these unnatural and deadly changes on land, creatures, and peoples: "They were the cannibals who consumed human flesh, set fire to worlds the gods had loved and asked humans to care for" (343). Angel sums up their philosophy: "To conquer, to possess, to win, to swallow" (339).

As homelands are lost and villages are drowned in the floods, native communities are forcibly relocated to shanty towns of Quonset huts and shacks at the edges of a ruined world. Having witnessed the wholesale destruction of the natural world with which their culture is interdependent, the displaced native peoples suffer despair and hopeless self-destruction, reminiscent of Loretta's response to the poisoning of her people:

> They were despondent. In some cases, they had to be held back from killing themselves. . . . It was murder of the soul that was taking place there. Murder with no consequence to the killers. . . . The young children drank alcohol and sniffed glue and paint. They staggered about and lay down in the streets. . . . The people wept without end and tried to cut and burn their own bodies. The older people tied their hands with

ropes and held them tight hoping the desire to die would pass. It was a smothering blanket laid down on them. The devastation and ruin that had fallen over the land fell on the people, too. (225–26)[5]

Hogan eloquently portrays the interconnections between ecocide and genocide here, and argues that environmental injustice is not only an external threat, but also a source of deep personal and spiritual anguish, or soul murder, that may poison native families from within.

This novel thus suggests that only resistance and concerted action can preserve the northern communities despite these onslaughts: "Those who protested were the ones who could still believe they might survive as a people" (226). Hogan represents environmental justice activism as a fundamental form of family and community solidarity, based in traditional spirituality, that offers the only hope of preserving native communities and the natural world. Whether or not the actions will stop the dams, resistance reunites the tribal community, restores their hope, and reasserts the people's vision of inspirited mutuality against the cannibal vision of the developers. Tulik and Auntie's house becomes an organizational center for people working to stop the dams, filled day and night with young and old who gather together to comfort each other and to plot their resistance. Angel's extended family and intertribal community come together in this political work, passing Aurora from one person's arms to another's during meetings and mass actions. When negotiations with the hydroelectric company fail, the tribal community organizes a long series of local actions that dramatize their resistance and hinder construction, such as protesting daily at construction sites and barricading the roads and railways used to transport materials in and out of the region. Despite violent intimidation, arrests, and the firebombing of their home, Angel's family stands together with the community against the dam project.

Hogan represents native women fulfilling leadership roles in every phase of this movement, as is often the case in actual grassroots environmental justice actions against threats to home and community: Aunty is the speaker and elder who gives voice to the people and instructs the young men as to proper actions; Dora Rouge, who is willing to die for the cause, parks her wheelchair in front of the barricades, daring the militia to clear the train tracks; Bush documents the destruction of this world and smuggles her writings and photos out to the press; and Angel acts in the spirit of the wolverine by destroying the food stores of the soldiers and builders.

Through this process of resistance, the tribe renews its pact of interdependence with each other and with the land, and recreates a sense of hope, even in the face of the ravages of conquest. Angel comments: "We sat before the fire, thinking . . . how we had come to this through history, how there'd been a prophecy that we would unite and become like an ocean made up of many rivers" (300). Although the direct activism fails to stop the initial phase of the James Bay project, and although the Canadian and Minnesota communities are devastated by the ensuing destruction of lands and waters, by the conclusion of the novel, the tribes have won a legal decree halting further construction. Angel describes the outcome and significance of their environmental justice actions:

> It was too late for the Child River, for the caribou, the fish, even for our own children, but we had to believe, true or not, that our belated victory was the end of something. That one fracture was healed, one crack mended, one piece back in place. Yes, the pieces were infinite and worn as broken pots, and our human pain was deep, but we'd thrown an anchor into the future and followed the rope to the end of it, to where we would dream new dreams, new medicines, and one day, once again, remember the sacredness of every living thing. (344)

Solar Storms illuminates the way that white conquest continues to cannibalize land and native peoples, and to pervert mother/daughter bonds, but more importantly, Hogan articulates the curative effects of indigenous cultural perspectives about human/natural community and grassroots political activism rooted in this vision of collectivity. While this is a novel full of pain and loss, it also offers a difficult and hard-won hope that through resistance, even partially successful resistance, Native American women may restore themselves, their families, their tribal communities, and their interconnection to the natural world. Collective action based in indigenous belief is shown to be one means of undoing the cannibalism and partially healing a ravaged world.

In *Blanche Cleans Up,* African American novelist Barbara Neely uses the popular detective-fiction genre to publicize urban environmental justice struggles affecting the predominantly black Roxbury section of Boston. Due to segregated housing patterns, white flight, and disinvestment, Roxbury is actually one of the poorest and most toxic communities in Boston, marred by more than thirteen hundred blighted lots, illegal trash dumps, and over fifty confirmed hazardous waste sites polluted with lead, chromium, mercury, asbestos, petroleum, and pesticides. Lead poisoning, from paint and

contaminated soil and water, is a major health threat for the children of Roxbury, with confirmed cases located on most streets throughout the neighborhood. To address these environmental ills, a dynamic grassroots community organization named The Dudley Street Initiative, formed in the 1980s,
has worked steadily to revitalize the health of the neighborhood through
trash and brownfield cleanups and antidumping campaigns, a lead-testing
and abatement project, large-scale community gardens, and community redevelopment plans.[6] Neely's protagonist, Blanche White, is a middle-aged
domestic worker and sometime sleuth who utilizes her position within an
elite white household to expose various forms of environmental and ideological toxicity that poison Roxbury. Filling in for Miz Inez, a family friend,
Blanche is temporarily serving as cook and housekeeper for the wealthy
Brindle family. Mr. Brindle, a right-wing bigot, is running for governor of
the state with the assistance of a corrupt black minister, Reverend Samuelson, who acts as Brindle's henchman, doing violence to those who oppose
Brindle, and promising to deliver the votes of the Roxbury community. While
Blanche is in the Brindle household, Miz Inez's son Ray-Ray—who is also the
friend and former lover of Brindle's son, Marc—steals a videotape of Brindle
engaging in sexual acts with animals and children, and threatens to use the
tape to ruin Brindle's political career. This sets in motion a series of murders
and suicides of young gay men, including Ray-Ray and Marc, as well as the
murder of an older Roxbury woman, and Blanche is compelled to expose
Brindle and Samuelson's corruption and bring the killers to justice.

As Blanche cleans up various sorts of "dirt," the novel establishes parallels
between the lead poisoning of black children who live in contaminated
housing and the violent deaths of young gay men. Through these parallel
plots, Neely suggests interconnections between environmental and ideological toxicities. Environmental racism and homophobia poison the community
in different but overlapping ways. Both forms of toxicity destroy parent/
child relationships and put children at risk of engaging in or suffering from
violence, and both forms of toxicity are justified by ideologies about "natural" or "unnatural" racial and sexual behaviors. To restore Roxbury to health,
Blanche and other mothers mobilize a neighborhood network to "clean up"
these poisons, demonstrating that concerted activism is one antidote to
environmental and ideological toxicity.

Blanche becomes involved with lead poisoning of black children when her
adopted son, Malik, is assigned to write about an environmental issue for a
school project. To disprove his teacher's assumption that black people are
uninterested in environmental problems, Malik researches environmental

groups in Roxbury, and discovers the Community Reawakening Project, a fictional organization that loosely resembles some projects undertaken by the actual Dudley Street Initiative. Community Reawakening Project, which works in Neely's novel to educate the community about the hazards of lead, to get children tested for lead poisoning, and to abate lead in housing, was founded by a character named Aminata Dawson, a longtime social activist and resident of Roxbury, whose son suffered from childhood lead poisoning. As an adolescent, this boy became violent and murdered one of his friends, and he is now serving a lengthy prison sentence. Out of grief over the fate of her son, Aminata founded Community Reawakening Project in order, as she says, "to make sure the community knows how our lives and our children's lives are being affected by pollution, toxic waste, and other environmental hazards, especially lead poisoning" (66).[7]

Aminata claims that lead poisoning is responsible for the drastic behavioral changes in her son:

> My boy, who I raised to respect life, to love life, this boy who was so gentle and sweet when he was little. . . . But he changed after he was poisoned by the lead in our apartment. . . . Doctors try to tell me that lead poisoning don't make our kids kill each other. But I know different. I know the medicine wasn't enough to keep my boy from turning into somebody who could kill his best friend, my boy who was so gentle and sweet. . . . A lot of our kids are still getting sick from lead poisoning. How do we know all these kids out here killing each other ain't just like my boy? (66–67)

A concerned and attentive mother, she insists that this environmental toxin, rather than any lack of care or nurturance on her part, is responsible for her son's deterioration, as well as the violence of other black youth in the area. While lead poisoning is known to cause disturbances in physical and mental growth, and to impair intellectual functioning and academic achievement (Kraft and Scheberle, 117), as happens all too often in real cases of lead poisoning, Aminata's concerns for her son's health were dismissed, and his bad behavior blamed on her failure as a mother.[8]

To fight back against society's tendency to blame the victims of lead poisoning, Aminata works to denaturalize the racist idea that violence is endemic to young black men, and she insists instead that violence is an unnatural result of unnatural environmental poisoning, of what she sees as a new form of racist genocide against her people. Aminata argues that lead poisoning destroys the race by damaging the children: "This is genocide. This racist system has found perfect ways to get rid of us. . . . and poison our babies with lead in their own homes. Roxbury is the most lead-polluted community in Boston" (67). U.S. statistics bear out Aminata's claim that lead poisoning primarily affects urban working class communities of color: most lead poisoning occurs in poor people of color communities, and 60 percent of poor, inner-city African American children exhibit blood-lead levels well above the CDC safety guidelines (Kraft and Scheberle, 116). By terming lead poisoning a form of genocide, Aminata historicizes this environmental injustice as a continuation of other assaults upon black lives, such as enslavement and lynching, in the same way that Hogan's novel situated the hydroelectric project within the context of conquest.

Aminata's activism is driven by the loss of her own son. Her maternal pain and suffering over his fate fuel her activism on behalf of the other children of Roxbury. Neely's novel represents black families as the units that suffer from this poison and, therefore, as the target audience of Aminata's mode of activism. Aminata's presentations in the community are addressed toward parents and other caretakers, and she works to mobilize them to political and practical actions that will protect their children from this toxic threat. She teaches parents about getting kids tested for lead, and she organizes to abate lead from housing and to prosecute landlords who knowingly and falsely rent lead-polluted buildings. Aminata's Community Reawakening Project is assisted in this work by the group Ex-Cons for Community Safety, who patrol the neighborhood to prevent trash dumping and to secure abandoned buildings that may be lead-contaminated. Blanche is at first very doubtful about Aminata's movement, because she believes that Aminata's maternal grief has caused her to exaggerate the effects of lead. Through further introduction to Aminata's work, however, Blanche becomes impressed with her commitment to this cause, her use of her own story to motivate the community, and her determination to protect others from her son's fate.

In order to denaturalize the myth of inherent black male violence, and to prove the connections between lead poisoning and antisocial or violent behavior, Aminata and Malik interview the parents of young men in prison, determining that three quarters of the youths had been lead poisoned as children (106). As they gather this information, Blanche comes to understand why an adolescent boy such as Malik would be so drawn to this environmental justice cause, since it denaturalizes black-on-black violence: "He wants a reason for kids killing kids . . . a reason that says it's not something in all black teenage boys' blood, that violence *isn't* natural to them" (157). And at the close of the novel, Aminata's belief that lead poisoning is linked to violence is confirmed when Blanche hears about the actual study conducted by Herbert Needleman at the University of Pittsburgh, which suggests that "childhood exposure to lead increases the chances of juvenile delinquency. Low-level lead has previously been found to lower IQs in children. The latest study suggests that lead's effect on behavior could be even more significant" (304).[9] Neely incorporates references to Needleman's study in order to argue that poor children of color are first poisoned and then incarcerated for the destructive behaviors that result from lead. Neely asserts that youthful violence and self-destruction may well be the result of environmental toxicity, in much the same way that Hogan describes family violence to be a result of conquest.

As *Solar Storms* describes the tribal communities uniting to resist the dams, *Blanche Cleans Up* portrays families and community coming together to protect the children who are the future of the race: Aminata rouses parents, other neighborhood women, and the Ex-Cons for Community Safety to work against lead, and Blanche assists in their campaign by detecting that Reverend Samuelson, the corrupt black minister associated with Mr. Brindle, is knowingly and fraudulently renting out lead-contaminated buildings in Roxbury. With the evidence that Blanche provides, Aminata will be able to bring him to justice. Neely's novel shows that while black families are the primary victims of lead poisoning, mothers and others may become radicalized by this experience, and that by working in concert, they can flush out the hidden poisons harming their community.

The parallel primary plot running throughout this novel concerns toxic ideologies about sexuality, and the ill effects that these views have upon characters' family ties, emotional lives, and even their very existence. While Neely touches on several problematic aspects of sexuality such as teenage pregnancy and sexual violence toward children, the main form of sexual toxicity that she addresses in this novel is homophobia, or heterosexism, which she shows to be prevailing in black and white families alike, causing damage across racial and class boundaries. Because homosexuality is construed as "unnatural," homosexual men and women are put at risk by the ignorance and prejudice of their families and communities. The misunderstanding, isolation, and secrecy surrounding gays and lesbians makes them targets for intrigue and blackmail, and places them in mortal danger: the murder and suicide of two young gay men is one form of "dirt" that Blanche must uncover and redress in this plot. Because of these deaths, Blanche comes to understand that homophobia operates similarly to lead poisoning in its insidious destruction of gay youth and their families. Blanche criticizes the toxic effects of homophobia in Roxbury in particular. While homophobia prevails in most communities within the United States, Blanche finds it painfully ironic that black people who face racist oppression then engage in heterosexist discrimination against fellow blacks. Mick, a black lesbian acquaintance, comments to Blanche, "It just rips my heart out when black people look at me like I'm evil or dirty. Like I don't belong here, or anywhere" (238).

Homophobia has historically been naturalized by condemning homosexuality as a "crime against nature," or as an unnatural form of sexuality,[10] and in the case of African American communities, homophobia has often been further endorsed by the black nationalist belief that homosexuality is a white behavior, not native to people of African descent. Blanche reverses this view and denaturalizes black homophobia by asserting that it is a legacy of enslavement, rather than an essential aspect of black heritage: "She'd once heard a black historian say that hatred of homosexuals was taught to African slaves because slave babies could only be made by female/male couples. Somebody ought to tell gay-hating blacks that slavery was over and loving was about more than baby-making" (239). Much the way Aminata rejected racist naturalization of black male violence, Blanche rejects homophobia by construing it as a form of colonization of black people, a racist means of reinforcing heterosexual reproduction for the profit of the masters, and thus not a legacy for black people to embrace and retain.

Neely's novel emphasizes the cost of this homophobic construction of gays as unnatural, which causes parents to reject gay and lesbian children, thus destroying their own family systems. A friend of Blanche's family, Miz Inez, denies that her son Ray-Ray is gay and blames his lover for corrupting her son and trying to turn him into a homosexual: "'My boy ain't no freak like you! Don't you come around here tryin' to act like my boy's unnatural'" (162). Her equation of homosexuality with unnaturalness leads her to deny her son's identity, which leaves him vulnerable to manipulation and murder at the hands of his money-crazed lover. Even after his murder, Miz Inez continues to evade her son's sexuality. Blanche thinks to herself that this lie "was like killing Ray-Ray a second time" (292). Even though Miz Inez is so deluded by her own homophobia that she cannot see her complicity in Ray-Ray's murder, Blanche asserts the killing force of Miz Inez's denial of her son's orientation.

The wealthy white Brindle family is similarly torn apart by homophobia, through Mr. Brindle's rejection of his gay son, Marc, and his attempt to hide his son's sexuality in order to protect his own campaign for governor. This secrecy and rejection endanger Marc. Due to his alienation from his parents, it is easy for Marc and his mother both to be seduced by the same man who intends to use this love triangle in order to blackmail Mr. Brindle. Marc's outraged murder of this man and his own suicide result from the many homophobic betrayals Marc has suffered: complete rejection by his father, isolation from his mother, and seduction and blackmail by his devious lover. In essence this prominent white family has sacrificed their gay son in order to preserve the father's public image, but the family has been poisoned by this denial, and by the tragedy that ensues.

Through the deaths of these gay youths, Neely argues that homophobia's toxic destruction of children and families functions similarly to the ill effects of lead poisoning.[11] While there is no community organization in this novel to fight against homophobia with the same force that Aminata has roused against lead poisoning, Neely makes it clear that heterosexism must also be addressed for the well-being of the community. Through her sleuthing, Blanche uncovers the links between the murder of Ray-Ray and Marc's suicide and she also exposes the extreme personal and political corruption of Mr. Brindle and his crony Reverend Samuelson, the same minister responsible for lead-contaminated housing in Roxbury. Through Samuelson's involvement in both forms of toxicity, Neely once again calls attention to the parallel damage wrought by lead and homophobia. The fact that Blanche calls upon the Ex-Cons for Community Safety to help her trap Ray-Ray's killer also emphasizes the need for communities to address the dangers posed by homophobia with the same passion that they have fought against lead: both poisons are hazards to the health of families and communities of color.

In *Blanche Cleans Up*, Neely has placed issues of environmental and ideological toxicity at the heart of her detective plot, and through the use of this popular form, Neely gives these issues audience beyond immediately affected communities. As Blanche works to clean up Roxbury, this novel establishes important interconnections between environmental and ideological poisons, calling upon us to consider the interlinking nature of oppressions, and drawing attention to the key roles that local women have played in redressing toxic environments.

These novels from Linda Hogan and Barbara Neely offer us gendered narratives of environmental injustices that present women of color's experiences of these assaults upon themselves, their families, and their communities. The novels urge us to expand our conceptualization of environmental injustice to also encompass resultant personal and social ills, such as maternal violence, youthful violence, and dissolution of family bonds. While examples of environmental injustice have usually been approached as instances of racial oppression, Neely and Hogan also emphasize the gendered aspects of such issues, as well as suggesting their interconnection to sexual oppressions such as homophobia. Most importantly, *Solar Storms* and *Blanche Cleans Up* describe grassroots community activism as a powerful means by which women of color reaffirm and repair themselves, their families, their communities, and the surrounding natural world from the ravages of cannibalistic conquest and various forms of toxicity.

NOTES

1. Jim Tarter's excellent essay, "'Dreams of Earth': Place, Multiethnicity, and Environmental Justice in Linda Hogan's *Solar Storms*," discusses Hogan's incorporation of the history of Cree and Inuit resistance to the James Bay hydroelectric project into this novel. He explains that many earlier reviewers of the novel failed to understand that Hogan was fictionalizing actual issues and events.

2. In an interview with me entitled "An Ecology of Mind," Hogan discussed the way that conquest history has come to inhabit native peoples. She noted:

> It really is true that the history of your people and your land is in the human body. . . . My oldest daughter, whom we adopted when she was ten was tragically abused. One night I was at a pow wow and the woman I thought was her birth mother was drunk and talking into the microphone about all the children that she had lost. I sat there and thought that my daughter was the fallout of the ruin of a nation of people now trying to pull themselves back together. That she is the result of history and it breaks my heart. (115)

Similarly, Hogan's essay, "Silence Is My Mother," in her recent collection *The Woman Who Watches Over the World: A Native Memoir,* describes the historical context for the horrible ongoing abuses that her children had suffered before she adopted them, which led to the daughters' destructive and self-destructive behaviors. Hogan writes of the oldest girl:

> She is the result of a shattered world. She came from the near oblitera-
> tion of a people. . . . We had entered, and taken in, a war that was more
> than child abuse or lack of love. Along with the girls, history came to
> live with us, the undeniable, unforgettable aspect of every American
> Indian life. She was a remnant of American history, and the fires of a
> brutal history had come to bear on her. As a Lakota girl, with her large
> eyes that looked not at anything, she was the result of Custer's dream,
> containing the American violences. (77)

3. Celene Krauss explains that

> working-class women of diverse racial and ethnic backgrounds identify
> the toxic waste movement as a women's movement, composed primarily
> of mothers. . . . By and large, it is women, in their traditional role as
> mothers, who make the link between toxic wastes and their children's ill
> health. . . . This is not surprising, as the gender-based division of labor
> in a capitalist society gives working-class women the responsibility for
> the health of their children. . . . Ideologies of motherhood, traditionally
> relegated to the private sphere, become political sources that working-
> class women use to initiate and justify their resistance. (260–61)

Cynthia Hamilton, writing about LANCER—a group of Los Angeles citizens of color who fought the location of an incinerator in their neighborhood—notes that "women with no political experience, who had no history of organizing, responded first as protectors of their children" (211). Krauss and Hamilton note that African American and Native American women have traditionally acted not only as caretakers of their own families, but also as protectors of the race and the community. Krauss explains that "African American women's private work as mothers has traditionally extended to a more public role in the local community as protectors of the race" (265). Similarly, she notes that Native American women view environmental justice struggles as work against genocide of their entire peoples, and explain that the colonial destruction of lands and peoples is ongoing, and so their environmental justice work is a cultural struggle for life of community, more than just a maternal struggle (266–69). In Hogan and Neely's novels, women act to protect family and community, but the women are not necessarily biological mothers, nor are their families necessarily two-parent nuclear units; instead they may be multigenerational, female-headed households that are partially related by choice rather than blood. While the focus in both novels is on female characters, male characters are also drawn into environmental justice activism through similar concerns for family and community.

4. Hogan's descriptions of the damages wrought by the hydroelectric project accurately portray the effects of the massive Hydro-Quebec development. See Picard, "James Bay II," for further description of the destruction caused by Hydro-Quebec.

5. Andre Picard, "James Bay II," and Winona LaDuke, *All Our Relations*, detail the multiplying rate of suicide attempts, alcoholism, and other chemical addictions among relocated Cree and Inuit villagers, as a result of the Hydro-Quebec projects.

6. For extensive discussion of the economic and environmental problems of the Roxbury neighborhood and the effective programs developed by the Dudley Street Initiative to ameliorate these ills, see Shutkin, *The Land that Could Be;* and Medoff and Sklar, *Streets of Hope.*

7. While Aminata Dawson and Community Reawakening Project are Neely's fictional creations, Aminata's strategies for fighting lead poisoning do resemble the lead abatement programs of the Dudley Street Initiative, as described by William Shutkin, and Peter Medoff and Holly Sklar.

8. A study of the PUEBLO campaign against lead poisoning notes that one of the problems with fighting this toxin is that parents "are told that the problems are caused by poor nutrition, birth defects, or behavioral disability, placing blame on the parent or on the child's heredity" (Calpotura and Sen, 242).

9. Needleman's study of 417 youths in Allegheny County, Pennsylvania, found significantly higher levels of bone-lead in those convicted of delinquency than in the comparison group who had no juvenile convictions. Needleman concluded that lead exposure might be a preventable cause of criminal behavior. For further details on his study, see Tanner, "Millions More Children May Suffer from Lead Exposure."

10. Pauline Christian doctrine distinguished between "unnatural" and "natural" sexual acts by comparing human copulation to planting a field: only heterosexual intercourse that might lead to procreation was deemed "natural" and all other forms of sexual interaction were judged "unnatural." U.S. sodomy laws are still based in such determinations of natural and

unnatural sex. Greta Gaard's "Toward a Queer Ecofeminism" presents compelling historical analysis of the way that conceptions of unnatural sexuality have been used to justify control and conquest of women, queers, and indigenous peoples.

11. In "Fighting Homophobia versus Challenging Heterosexism," Cathy Cohen and Tamara Jones argue that heterosexism threatens the health of black children. They explain:

> Many of those who decry rights for black LGBTs often justify their homophobia and heterosexism in terms of protecting the welfare of black children. Yet it seems to us that it is heterosexism and homophobia which are themselves limiting and threatening the lives of our children. There is the immediate threat to the lives and well-being of young black people who either voluntarily or involuntarily are identified as gay, lesbian, bisexual or transgender . . . (who) are hunted down on city streets, in parks, and even in their own homes and brutalized and murdered because of their sexual identities. (91–92)

WORKS CITED

Calpotura, Francis, and Rinku Sen. "PUEBLO Fights Lead Poisoning." In *Unequal Protection: Environmental Justice and Communities of Color*, edited by Robert Bullard, 234–55. San Francisco: Sierra Club, 1994.

Cohen, Cathy, and Tamara Jones. "Fighting Homophobia versus Challenging Heterosexism: 'The Failure to Transform' Revisited." In *Dangerous Liaisons: Blacks, Gays, and the Struggle for Equality*, edited by Eric Brandt, 80–101. New York: New Press, 1999.

Gaard, Greta. "Toward a Queer Ecofeminism." *Hypatia* 12, no. 1 (Winter 1997): 113–35.

Hamilton, Cynthia. "Concerned Citizens of South Central Los Angeles." In *Unequal Protection: Environmental Justice and Communities of Color*, edited by Robert Bullard, 207–19. San Francisco: Sierra Club, 1994.

Hogan, Linda. *Dwellings: A Spiritual History of the Living World*. New York: Norton, 1995.

———. *Solar Storms*. New York: Simon and Schuster, 1995.

———. *The Woman Who Watches Over the World: A Native Memoir*. New York: Norton, 2001.

Kraft, Michael, and Denise Scheberle. "Environmental Justice and the Allocation of Risk: The Case of Lead and Public Health." *Policy Studies Journal* 23, no. 1 (1995): 113–22.

Krauss, Celine. "Women of Color on the Front Line." In *Unequal Protection: Environmental Justice and Communities of Color,* edited by Robert Bullard, 256–71. San Franciso: Sierra Club, 1994.

LaDuke, Winona. *All Our Relations: Native Struggles for Land and Life.* Boston: South End, 1999.

Medoff, Peter, and Holly Sklar. *Streets of Hope: The Rise and Fall of an Urban Neighborhood.* Boston: South End, 1994.

Neely, Barbara. *Blanche Cleans Up.* New York: Penguin, 1998.

Picard, Andre. "James Bay II." *The Amicus Journal* (Fall 1990): 10–16.

Shutkin, William. *The Land that Could Be: Environmentalism and Democracy in the Twenty-First Century.* Cambridge: MIT Press, 2000.

Stein, Rachel. "An Ecology of Mind: A Conversation with Linda Hogan." *Interdisciplinary Studies in Literature and Environment* 6, no. 1 (Winter 1999): 113–18.

Tanner, Lindsey. "Millions More Children May Suffer from Lead Exposure." Associated Press State and Local Wire, 16 May 2000.

Tarter, Jim. "'Dreams of Earth': Place, Multiethnicity, and Environmental Justice in Linda Hogan's *Solar Storms.*" In *Reading Under the Sign of Nature: New Essays in Ecocritism,* edited by John Tallmadge and Henry Harrington, 128–47. Salt Lake City: University of Utah Press, 2000.

11

SOME LIVE MORE DOWNSTREAM
THAN OTHERS

Cancer, Gender, and Environmental Justice

Jim Tarter

> *I consider myself a daughter of Rachel.*
> —Sandra Steingraber, *Rachel's Daughters:*
> *Searching for the Causes of Breast Cancer*

I come from one of those "cancer families." Fourteen years ago, at twenty-seven, I was diagnosed with Hodgkin's Disease—a cancer of the lymphatic system. The cancer was in an advanced stage, having metastasized, and according to my doctors I would have to do a year of treatment. Fortunately for me, after World War II some American soldiers had been inadvertently cured of Hodgkin's as a result of exposure to mustard gas. So my oncologists were able to prescribe a treatment of nitrogen mustard in chemotherapy, in combination with surgery and radiation, which had achieved good results. They told me I stood an 80 percent chance of surviving five years.

After a year of high-tech medicine and four years of remission, the doctors pronounced me cured. Happy to be one of the lucky few, I tried to just go on with my life and forget about cancer. But a year later, in 1994, a close friend was diagnosed with metastatic breast cancer. Later that year my sister Karen was diagnosed with an advanced stage of the dreaded ovarian cancer. She had a terrible prognosis—a 10 to 15 percent chance of surviving five years.

Then my aunt, who was born and raised in the same town as us—Bay City, Michigan—was diagnosed with breast cancer. At this point the family began to talk about it. We remembered that our mom's father had died of cancer. Some of us would speculate about "the family" and make vague references to genes. But for years after she was diagnosed, Karen and I would privately ask each other if our cancers were really just genetic, or if something else was involved.

We began trying to ask the environmental question about cancer. Our problem was that we could never face the question itself for long. I now see that this problem was not exclusive to us: in my experience, very few people are willing to talk much about the cancer-environment question. In fact, as I see it, our entire culture is in denial about the link between our toxified environment and cancer. In what follows, I hope to interweave my experience of cancer with Sandra Steingraber's work on cancer to show how and why we have to break the silence.

Carson's Children

The silence around cancer retained its grip on me for a decade after I was diagnosed, and I have only recently, with the help of others, begun to break it. For me, the silence was first broken by Audre Lorde, who named the silence as a problem in her great work, *The Cancer Journals*. Lorde, however, does not address in a direct way the environmental question about cancer. This particular silence was broken for me by a "mother-daughter" pair of cancer survivors, Rachel Carson and Sandra Steingraber.

Both Carson's *Silent Spring* (1962) and Sandra Steingraber's *Living Downstream: An Ecologist Looks at Cancer and the Environment* (1997) are essentially environmental justice texts.[1] Environmental justice discourse argues a connection between environmental exploitation and human exploitation or social justice. Carson's and Steingraber's texts are unique in the annals of both environmental literature and the literature of cancer, and for many of the same reasons: featuring an environmental argument about the causes of cancer, they are both written in that rare style of scientific prose that is clear, engaging, and accessible, and yet precise, accurate, and well-documented. There is also a similarity in the political and ethical uses to which Carson and Steingraber apply their science. Both deliberately set out, not to render objectively the "true" scientific facts, but to write from a constructed, political perspective as citizens and environmentalists, as well as scientists, in order to change public and corporate policies. But of all the correlations between Carson's and Steingraber's texts, the most important one involves cancer.

By claiming Rachel Carson as her mother in the film *Rachel's Daughters*, Steingraber is no doubt claiming kinship to Carson's intellectual heritage as environmentalist, scientist, and feminist, and she is acknowledging the influence of Carson's carefully documented, rhetorically moderate style of writing. But their kinship, to my mind, has even more to do with cancer itself. It is now well-established (with the new biographies and the publication of her letters) that Carson knew she had breast cancer as she was writing *Silent Spring*. She died of it in 1964, two years after the book was published, and had carefully kept it a closely guarded secret throughout the debate and publicity that surrounded her after the book appeared. So although there is only one chapter explicitly devoted to cancer in *Silent Spring*, with hindsight it is clear that cancer underlies implicitly the book's whole argument about the dangers of the new chemicals we were releasing into the environment. This same general threat is exactly what Steingraber's book is about—and like Carson, she writes as a cancer victim. Thus, if anyone is Rachel's daughter, it is Sandra Steingraber.

The big difference between the two, however, is that in public and in her writing, Carson kept her cancer a secret, whereas Steingraber foregrounds her own personal experience of cancer. In so doing, Steingraber's book sketches a complex, political interrelationship of cancer, gender and environment, one that I would compare to environmental justice discourse in its connection of social justice issues to the environment. Steingraber does not argue directly on feminist grounds; nor does she use the term "environmental justice," choosing instead to argue on the grounds of human rights in general. Nevertheless, she subtly shows us, if we connect the dots, that gender is a category of environmental justice. As I will argue, cancer, as she represents it, may even help bring together ecofeminism (or gender-conscious environmentalism) and environmental justice discourse and practice.

Facing Living Downstream

Two years ago, after a four-year struggle with ovarian cancer, my sister Karen died. For the last six months of her life, I left my job and moved to Oregon to become her primary, live-in caretaker. Just as I was about to move, a good friend gave me a copy of *Living Downstream*. She had inscribed it, "Here's the book we knew had to be written." It was true; we had been talking about possible environmental connections to cancer for years. But suddenly I couldn't bear to read any further. I almost didn't bring it with me.

At Karen's, my eye fell on a passage in the book's introduction:

There are individuals who claim, as a form of dismissal, that links between cancer and environmental contamination are unproven and unprovable. There are others who believe that placing people in harm's way is wrong—whether the exact mechanisms by which this harm is inflicted can be deciphered or not. At the very least, they argue, we are obliged to investigate, however imperfect our scientific tools: with the right to know comes the duty to inquire.

Happily, the latter perspective is gaining esteem as many leading cancer researchers acknowledge the need for an "upstream" focus. . . . This image comes from a fable about a village along a river. The residents . . . began noticing increasing numbers of drowning people caught in the river's swift current and so went to work inventing ever more elaborate technologies to resuscitate them. So preoccupied were these heroic villagers with rescue and treatment that they never thought to look upstream to see who was pushing the victims in. (xvi)

Suddenly I was confronted with what I had secretly feared most. I couldn't stand to look up that river; I threw the book in a corner. Occasionally, during Karen's naps, I'd pick it up, but I just couldn't stick with it. It was beautifully written, but every time I tried to read it, my heart would race and my head would swim. In shock, I'd gaze across the room at my sister on her deathbed, and put the book down. Too scary—and too close to home.

Of course I couldn't forget anything I'd read of the book, either. As a cancer survivor myself, sometimes Steingraber's basic idea was exhilarating; it showed there was something concrete we could do. So now and then I would mention the book to Karen. "Here is this new book," I'd say, "that synthesizes the new information from toxics right-to-know laws with information from the new cancer registries. It confirms what we've suspected about cancer and the environment."

With a look on her pale, drawn face as though she had just tasted something surprisingly bitter, Karen would gulp and nod knowingly, but we could never discuss it further. Any further comments from me would receive silence from her or an awkward change of subject. One time, after I'd made it through a few pages, I repeated to her some of Steingraber's facts, such as the tripling of the general cancer rate in this country in the last fifty years, and the fact that the worst cancer rates, including lymphomas, breast cancer, and ovarian cancer—all the cancers that had recently struck us as a family—were happening mainly in the industrialized nations. She simply cut me off, and at last I understood. She wasn't denying the truth, but the implications were just too much for her to look at from her position. I didn't have to ask why. About these things we had an intuitive bond.

What Steingraber is saying was usually too hard for me to look at too: it meant that Karen might be a *victim*, not an accident, and not (the politically correct term) simply a patient. Steingraber's book confronted us with the bitter injustice of her premature death. Right then it was too much to take in, as Steingraber does, the injustice involved in the pervasive presence of toxins in the general environment, or our lifetimes of minute, repeated exposures to persistent, organic pollutants. And so we never did talk about these things enough. I was thinking about them all the time, but Karen took a serious turn for the worse before we were able to discuss Steingraber's basic argument in a satisfactory way. Now I am left thinking about why so many of us are getting sick—and why as a society we are still not talking seriously about cancer and its environmental roots.

Looking back, I see it wasn't just our own fear of cancer that blocked us. In contemporary American society there are many layers of silence wrapped around cancer, not only because the disease itself is frightening and we have trouble with issues of death and dying in our culture, but also because it is too frightening to contemplate the huge investment of money, power, and emotional capital in toxifying the environment and ourselves in the way we do now. If we are taking seriously the possibility of environmental contamination's role in the near-epidemic of cancer, we are faced with having to talk scientifically and politically about things like industrial capitalism, petrochemicals, corporate agriculture, environmental racism, or patriarchal science and medicine.

Not that I thought all this while I was sick; I just wanted to get on with my life. But Karen's cancer made me face it—and so does *Living Downstream*. Not that reading this book has gotten any easier. It still makes me cry when I read passages, such as this one about the new cancer maps: "Death from cancer is not randomly distributed in the United States. Shades of red consistently light up the Northeast coast, the Great Lakes area, and the mouth of the Mississippi River. For all cancers combined, these are the areas of highest mortality; they are also the areas of the most intense industrial activity" (63). In other words, although millions are dying, we are not all equally exposed. Some are more at risk, more downstream, than others. Typically, Steingraber doesn't argue this point explicitly, but her information implies it. This map means that cancer is both an environmental issue and an issue that involves social justice. It means, in other words, that cancer is an issue of environmental justice.

Steingraber often suggests environmental injustice with her tone, such as when she tells the story about the moment she knew that she had not and never would accept her friend Jeannie's death from cancer (39). And when she writes, "None of these 10,940 Americans [a conservative estimate of environmentally caused cancer deaths in the United States per year] will die quick, painless deaths. They will be amputated, irradiated, and dosed with chemotherapy. They will expire privately in hospitals and hospices and be buried quietly. Photographs of their bodies will not appear in newspapers. We will not know who most of them are. Their anonymity, however, does not moderate this violence. These deaths are a form of homicide" (269).

Environmental Justice and Cancer

Environmental justice writers and activists have consistently made links between environmental exploitation and human exploitation, attempting to reveal, criticize, and transform relationships between human social practices and environmental issues. The central term in environmental justice discourse and practice has historically been environmental racism. But there are other social categories that are centrally involved in projects of social justice, and Steingraber shows, by example and implication, how to look at gender as a category of environmental justice. Before she does that, however, she first carefully establishes her basic argument that the primary causes of cancer now (i.e., since 1950 or so) are *environmental* in origin.

Federal and state right-to-know laws, established in the past decade, have made available disturbing information about the extent to which our environment has been polluted by known carcinogens (and many others which are probable, suspected, or untested). Meanwhile, newly established cancer registries make it possible to see historical trends in cancer incidence and mortality, and to see some of the ways cancer is distributed geographically and (to a lesser extent) demographically. In *Living Downstream,* Steingraber maps this new toxic release information onto the new cancer registry information, and synthesizes that with other new studies on cancer and toxins. She shows that the case is now clear enough: although the research is not totally conclusive, and much work remains to be done, so much of the information indicates danger now, that we cannot ignore environmental links to cancer just because some uncertainties remain. We must make basic policy changes regarding environmental contamination and public health.

Steingraber is much more clearly a feminist than Carson (as we shall see), but like Carson she prefers to remain basically a scientist, avoiding overtly gendered political rhetoric. Despite the fact that her politics are muted, however, Steingraber makes a powerful environmental argument about cancer. One of her most effective strategies in this regard is to adopt an historical perspective: "If heredity is suspected as the main cause of a certain kind of cancer, we would not expect to see its incidence rise rapidly over the course of a few human generations [as all the worst cancers have done in industrialized nations] because genes cannot increase their frequency in the population that quickly" (32). The new historical perspective available from cancer registries makes clear that the main causes of cancer are environmental, not genetic. Supporting this argument are her skills of synthesis and her knack for the telling fact: "All types combined, the incidence of cancer rose 49.3 percent between 1950 and 1991. This is the longest reliable view we have available. . . . More of the overall upsurge has occurred in the past two decades than in the previous two, and increases in cancer incidence are seen in all age groups" (40). Steingraber's argument is not new. Even the World Health Organization has concluded that "at least 80 percent of all cancer [worldwide] is attributable to environmental influences" (60). (Here they use "environmental," like Steingraber, in the broad sense.) But Steingraber's book is most effective when she speaks on the personal level: "As a woman with cancer . . . I am less concerned about whether the cancer in my community is directly connected to the dump sites, the air emissions, the occupational exposures, or the drinking water. I am more concerned that the uncertainty over details is being used to call into doubt the fact that profound connections do exist between human health and the environment. I am more concerned that uncertainty is too often parlayed into an excuse to do nothing until more research can be conducted" (72–73).

That is, all too often a lack of basic information is taken to mean that there is no real evidence of harm, which chemical industry interests and others then try to spin into the assertion that a chemical in question is harmless. And we continue to wait as the bodies pile up. Most importantly, once Steingraber makes the case that cancer is partly environmental in origin, we are confronted with questions such as who gets cancer, and which groups are more exposed than others to toxics in the environment—that is, we are faced with a range of issues that have come to be called environmental justice.

Looking Upstream from My Hometown

Steingraber also forces each of us to face the question of our own ecological roots. My sister and I grew up in Bay City, Michigan, a Rust Belt city of sixty thousand. Bay City lies at the mouth of the Saginaw River, on Lake Huron, about a hundred miles north of Detroit. Founded as a sawmill town at the hub of the clear-cutting of the state in the nineteenth century, its basic identity as a city is built upon early- and mid-twentieth-century heavy industry. It was World War II that made our town socioeconomically what it remains to this day, with its focus on automotive, petrochemical, and transportation industries.

We grew up very near where the Saginaw River dumps into Saginaw Bay. That river always looked bad, and so did the beaches on the bay. Riding our bikes along the river, peering into the thick, gray-black soup, imagining what sorts of creatures survived in there, we didn't wonder much about why it looked so nasty. It always smelled like metal, oil, and dead fish. The few fish we ever saw were dead suckers and carp. Only now do I realize how many species of plants and animals were endangered or extinct there. The only living things we saw were rats, gulls, and flies. Across the river were the storage tanks and slag piles, and upriver were docks, rail yards, and the General Motors factory, just visible to the west. To the north, the cement factory smokestack kept watch.

As teenagers we would often take off to the water in the summer. A couple of our more well-to-do friends would take us waterskiing, and if the bay was choppy (which was more often than not) we'd ski up the river right past the holding ponds, brownfields, storage tanks, dumps, and factories. Neither my sister nor I had ever seen the river from that perspective before: mile after mile of industrial wasteland. It didn't stop us. We weren't very good, but we tried hard, making sharp turns on the slalom ski and wiping out a lot. Afterwards we would party on the beach at the mouth of the river, swimming and making out with our dates in the gray waters of Saginaw Bay.

Nobody said a thing to us. In those days, nobody seemed to think much about dioxin, or even about the tap water, which was from up the bay, or the fish from the Great Lakes. No one talked about mercury, lead, polychlorinated biphenyls, or persistent organic pollutants. No one seemed to know about the tremendous increases in deformities, cancers, and extinctions of wildlife in the Great Lakes.

Even though I worked one summer in the Chevy factory just upriver, it wasn't until I had left for college that I began to realize how much was upstream from where we had lived. There was Dow Chemical's home base in Midland, on the Tittabawassee River just to the west, which empties into the Saginaw; it had been making napalm and Agent Orange for the Vietnam War and handling millions of tons of chlorinated hydrocarbons the whole time.

There were power plants, Defoe Shipbuilding (the biggest Great Lakes ship-building factory of World War II), power plants, waste dumps, and many of the Big Three's factories, from the Bay City parts plant just upstream to the massive industrial complexes of Saginaw farther upriver. Only later did we realize that the awesome General Motors factory city we went through along the freeway in Flint, not quite an hour's drive to the south, was also up-stream: the Flint River flows into the Saginaw. Later yet, in the mid-1980s, we heard that in Bay City, just a mile upstream from where we grew up, right where we used to water-ski, there was a big industrial waste dump that had just become a Superfund site.

What happened to the Saginaw is not at all exceptional. That is the scary thing; something like it has happened to nearly every major waterway in the industrial Midwest.[2]

Karen and I will never know with any degree of precision why we got cancer. Cancer usually has multiple causes, and many carcinogens take de-cades to reveal their effects. But all that last summer, as my sister was dying, we had each begun to think that perhaps many of the thousands of people like Karen, who were dying, *didn't* have to. Maybe their deaths were not genetically programmed. We heard that most cancers were not determined by genetics, but that some people who get cancer are, genetically speaking, more sensitive to carcinogens; but that, we reasoned, still involves envi-ronmental causes. So we began to wonder if the causes of cancer were not only genetics and lifestyle, as the hospital booklets told us, but environmen-tal carcinogens. Without knowing it, we had become two more of Rachel's many children.

Cancer and Gender

The last six months of Karen's life, during which I lived in her house as her primary caretaker, taught me a lot about gender politics in cancer. We had always compared notes on our experiences, but at that time we went into much more depth—about her hysterectomy, her sense of physical unat-tractiveness, her loss of fertility, her issues with past boyfriends and present prospects, her courses of treatment, and her problems with male doctors. At the same time, we had to work through some delicate gender issues on intimate terms, such as how I could help her bathe or change her colos-tomy bag and bladder catheter. It became clear to me then that my expe-riences with cancer were differently gendered than my sister's. And now I can understand better what Steingraber is talking about when, in *Rachel's Daughters,* she says something that she never says in *Living Downstream;* that cancer is a feminist issue.

Steingraber has actually been arguing this point for some time. In her 1991 essay, "We All Live Downwind," Steingraber wrote, "I know as a woman that having cancer alters one's physical and sexual self and is thus a gendered experience which requires a feminist analysis" (38). Six years later in the 1997 documentary film *Rachel's Daughters,* Steingraber makes other kinds of feminist arguments: "Every time we [women cancer patients] go into the doctor's office and sit down we bring our gender with us, which means we also bring the fact that we have less money, we are more poorly insured, and we are more likely to be deferential to authority, perhaps because we've been socialized that way." Here Steingraber concentrates on issues surrounding treatment. But in that same documentary she also handles other issues in feminist terms:

Interviewer: Why is cancer a feminist issue?

Steingraber: It is a feminist issue because the parts of women's bodies that have been affected—our ovaries, our uterus, our breasts—are the parts of the body that have been despised, objectified, fetishized; so what it means to cut off a woman's breast in our society . . . says a lot about our culture, and the way we might value a breast over a woman's mind, or a woman's life, even.

Steingraber, following Audre Lorde here, is arguing that cancer is a feminist issue because it involves the way our society attempts to ideologically code women's bodies.

Given Steingraber's history as a feminist cancer activist, then, it is interesting to me that she never overtly makes such a claim in *Living Downstream.* However, although Steingraber never makes the argument explicitly, there is a complex, detailed gender-related subtext in *Living Downstream.* This subtext takes various forms. One form it takes is the pattern of evidence the book presents on breast cancer, which is by far the most frequently mentioned cancer in the book and the only cancer mentioned in every chapter. The facts she cites about it are among the most suggestive of environmental causes in the entire book. And then there are the issues of persistent organic pollutants concentrating in breast milk and being passed down to infants: clearly women and children are at greater risk than men.

Aside from this accumulation of evidence about breast cancer, there are a number of other lines of suggestion that help make the implicit case about gender and cancer for Steingraber. One is the pattern Steingraber repeatedly points out concerning the way women's cancers are seriously under-researched. To be sure, lack of research into environmental connections to cancer in general is one of the central motifs in Steingraber's book, but very often these are women's cancers she is talking about. So although she never says explicitly that this is a gender issue, the pattern is there.

Another gender issue in cancer is adipose tissue (fat). Again, although she never says it is a feminist issue, she repeatedly shows that some of the most dangerous carcinogens—those that are most persistent in the environment and the most persistent in our bodies—are stored in fatty tissues. Obviously this affects women in a different way than men.

The most complicated and subtle aspect of Steingraber's implicit feminism, however, is the way in which these specific issues (breast cancer, under-research, and fat) relate to her more general levels of analysis, particularly her analysis of the war machine and its relation to the post–World War II "petrochemical economy," as she calls it. She never spells it out, but she does tip her hand: "Seek. Strike. Destroy. Of all the unexpected consequences of World War II, perhaps the most ironic is the discovery that a remarkable number of the new chemicals it ushered in were estrogenic—that is, at low levels inside the human body, they mimic the female hormone estrogen. Many of the *hypermasculine* weapons of conquest and progress are, biologically speaking, emasculating" (109; emphasis mine). This passage suggests nothing less than an association between the patriarchal war machine and cancer, because it was World War II, as her whole chapter shows, that led to the invention of most of the dangerous new chemicals we use routinely now. Steingraber has been talking at length about the petrochemical economy and the chemicalization of our environment since World War II, but this is the only time she reveals that she might consider the whole War machine—from which the chemicals and the attitudes toward their use derive—to be patriarchal as well as carcinogenic.

In these ways Steingraber implies, with complexity and detail, that women are unfairly exposed to cancer risks. However, she never spells out this point explicitly. Why not? For one thing, her Carsonian rhetorical form involves a subtle masking at the political level, which includes gender (Carson, after all, had to hide her cancer in order to protect herself from personal attacks—she was labeled a hysterical woman and a spinster—by her male enemies in the chemical industry). For another, perhaps she felt that to argue explicitly as a feminist would take away from her status as a scientist or from the book's broad appeal. Most importantly, however, I would argue that she wished to avoid the appearance of bias, limitation, or compromise in her larger argument on behalf of human rights.

Conclusion: Human Rights and Environmental Justice

In the conclusion of her book, Steingraber goes back to Carson in order to construct her book's basic conclusion around human rights. By claiming explicitly that cancer is a human rights issue, she suggests a linkage between environmental issues and issues of social justice. What pushes Steingraber's conclusion further than Carson—and implicitly suggests that cancer is an environmental justice issue—is the phrase "the right to protection." For Steingraber this is a basic human right. It is the key link in moving toward an environmental justice argument, though, because once she makes it, we are faced with the fact that some people's rights to protection are more well-enforced than others. Another way of saying this is that there is a pattern, at least in this country, of unequal protection from environmental hazards. The pattern largely breaks down along racial and ethnic lines, although class is also involved. This concept is captured well by the title of Robert Bullard's best-known, book-length collection of essays, *Unequal Protection*. Bullard's title displays the essential connection between established environmental justice discourse and Steingraber's book: the issue is one of the right to protection. The human rights argument, as Steingraber articulates it, is thus an issue of social justice—of equal protection—and as such, her argument may be a different way of articulating cancer as an environmental justice issue: "Such an approach recognizes that the current system of regulating the use, release, and disposal of known and suspected carcinogens—rather than preventing their generation in the first place—is intolerable. So is the decision to allow untested chemicals free access to our bodies, until which time they are finally assessed for carcinogenic properties. Both practices show reckless disregard for human life" (268). Passages like this are the reason why I am arguing that Steingraber is close to making an explicit environmental justice argument, and that, as in this case, she may be already doing so—because her book establishes clearly that we have here a question of unjust and intolerable social practices at the environmental level. However, as much as she stresses human rights in general, she doesn't directly confront the fact that some human lives are more recklessly "disregarded" than others, with clear patterns of discrimination along racial and class lines as well as the gender lines she has indicated. Steingraber shows she is aware of the issue when she goes on to say, "we do not all bear equal risks when carcinogens are allowed to circulate within our environment" (268).

In itself, this conclusion and the rhetorical structure of human rights that supports it is plausible, but in the process of making this general case she has lost sight of race and class issues that may have been raised by her original point that "we do not all bear equal risks." Instead, she adopts the political line of Carson on human rights. This is the same line Steingraber sketched out in "We All Live Downwind." The tone has thus shifted; with this formulation she makes an important general point, but by saying no more, she precludes any further exploration of the argument that *some people live more downwind than others.*

In this manner, Steingraber generally avoids dealing with race as an issue in cancer. By way of contrast to this subtle sidestepping of racial issues, Steingraber develops (as we have seen) a complex and detailed structure of argumentation on gender issues in cancer. In fact, this is one of her book's greatest achievements—but it also tells us something about the way she omits considerations of race. I am simply saying that, given some of the information she presents, she could make a clearer connection than she does to race as an issue in cancer. (She could also do more with class, but as the above example about workers suggests, she does work a little with issues of class and labor.) She consistently prefers, like Carson, to pull back and argue at the more general level of human rights.

I find this move somewhat troubling in its similarity to the long history in this country of blindness to racial issues, and to different people's ways of seeing the environment, in mainstream (i.e., white, middle-class) American environmentalism. To be sure, Steingraber does imply that cancer is an issue that involves race and class as well as gender—she just deals with the latter issue in a more complete way. In the end, then, although this book remains a powerful, effective toolkit, it is one which is still incomplete.

My experience with cancer—and some of Steingraber's own information— shows that we can't separate issues of race, gender, and class from environmental issues of toxicity and public health. In this light, Steingraber's work does suggest a potentially productive convergence of these issues. And if her work suggests that the environmental justice writers and activists haven't done as much with gender as they might, it also shows us how ecofeminists, indeed all environmentalists, need to deal much more with race and ethnicity as environmental issues. Historically, ecofeminists have been overwhelmingly white in terms of basic demographic composition and in their ways of defining and working on their environmental issues. One of the most original contributions of Steingraber, in this context, is the way she shows how cancer may function as a bridge issue between different kinds of environmentalists; she shows that cancer as an environmental issue may function as a principle of alliance between ecofeminists (or gender-conscious environmentalists) and environmental justice activists, artists, and scholars. It may even be a link between environmentalists and multi-cultural, social justice movements.

At the personal level, Steingraber, like Carson, remains one of my heroes. She is a cancer survivor who has become active, taking responsibility for having survived and for the knowledge she has gained. I see Steingraber's book not only as an heroic achievement in itself, like *Silent Spring,* but as a powerful toolkit for community activists. Not only does it help me understand better what happened to my sister, it helps me to be more effective as an environmental activist. In fact, it compels me to do so, because now that I have this information—this set of tools—I am responsible for the resolution of the problem it exposes.

This year, my x-ray is clear. I am relieved, at least for the moment, unlike too many others who are getting bad news. And I realize that following Steingraber's act is not going to be easy. Steingraber wrote in 1991, "For me, dealing with the social implications of cancer can feel like being forced to look at my own body lying in the street" (47). For me, dealing with those implications—thanks in large part to Steingraber—is more like being forced to look at my sister's body. And to look at the millions of dead, dying, and soon to be cancer-ridden bodies all around us. *And* to look at the socio-economic patterns: who is getting sick? Who benefits?

NOTES

This essay is dedicated to the memory of my sister, Karen Tarter. Thanks to the "Ecological Conversations" Program in Association with the University of Oregon's Center for the Study of Women in Society for their financial support in the form of a research grant. Thanks also to my parents, James and Mary Tarter, and to Rachel Stein, Mei Mei Evans, Ellen Cantor, Rich Stevenson, Molly Westling, Mary O'Brien, Suzanne Clark, Linda Rose, and Eldon Haines for their guidance and support.

1. Historically, environmental justice as a term emerged from the practice of community activists protesting environmental racism. It can be traced back at least to the 1982 protests in Warren County, North Carolina, against the dumping of toxic soil near black neighborhoods. Ever since then, the key term in the movement has been environmental racism, a basic fact of life in this country, which was demonstrated clearly by the now-classic 1987 landmark study *Toxic Wastes and Race in the United States*. This study established race as the most important single factor nationwide in determining the distribution of environmental hazards, more so even than class. In the late 1980s, environmental justice as a term began to be used in some regions of the South and Southwest by activists in networks such as the Southern Organizing Council, and the Southwest Network for Economic and Environmental Justice. The term was widely accepted after the first National People of Color Environmental Leadership Summit of 1991, with their adoption of the now famous "Principles of Environmental Justice" (see Bullard, *Unequal Protection*). Since that time a small industry of activists, artists, and academics has developed a discourse of environmental justice (see, for example, Bullard, Di Chiro, Hofrichter, LaDuke, Peña, Hamilton, Shiva, and Pulido).

2. The first chapter of Winona LaDuke's recent *All Our Relations* shows how Mohawk people in the Great Lakes region (near Lake Ontario) have been affected disastrously by very similar kinds of industrialization. LaDuke's book shows how many native people in North America are facing environmental racism, health threats, and clear environmental injustices from the same socioeconomic system.

WORKS CITED

Bullard, Robert, D., ed. *Confronting Environmental Racism: Voices From the Grassroots*. Boston: South End, 1993.

——. *Unequal Protection: Environmental Justice and Communities of Color*. San Francisco: Sierra Club Books, 1994.

Carson, Rachel. *Silent Spring*. Boston: Houghton Mifflin, 1962.

Di Chiro, Giovanna. "Nature as Community: The Convergence of Environment and Social Justice." In *Uncommon Ground: Toward Reinventing Nature*, edited by William Cronon, 298–320. New York: Norton, 1995.

Hamilton, Cynthia. "Women, Home and Community: The Struggle in an Urban Environment." In *A Forest of Voices: Reading and Writing the Environment*, by Chris Anderson and Lex Runciman, 673–80. Mountain View, Calif.: Mayfield, 1995.

Hofrichter, Richard, ed. *Toxic Struggles: The Theory and Practice of Environmental Justice.* Philadelphia: New Society, 1993.

LaDuke, Winona. *All Our Relations: Native Struggles for Land and Life.* Cambridge, Mass.: South End, 1999.

Lorde, Audre. *The Cancer Journals.* 1st ed. Argyle, N.Y.: Spinsters, Ink, 1980.

Peña, Devon, ed. *Chicano Culture, Ecology, Politics: Subversive Kin.* Tucson: University of Arizona, 1998.

Pulido, Laura. *Environmentalism and Economic Justice: Two Chicano Struggles in the Southwest.* Tucson: University of Arizona, 1996.

Rachel's Daughters: Searching for the Causes of Breast Cancer. Directed and produced by Allie Light and Irving Saraf. Women Make Movies. New York, 1997. Film/videocassette.

Shiva, Vandana. "Development as a New Project of Western Patriarchy." In *Reweaving the World: The Emergence of Ecofeminism,* edited by Irene Diamond and Gloria Feman Orenstein, 189–200. San Francisco: Sierra Club Books, 1990.

Steingraber, Sandra. *Living Downstream: An Ecologist Looks at Cancer and the Environment.* Reading, Mass.: Addison-Wesley, 1997.

———. "We All Live Downwind." In *1 in 3: Women with Cancer Confront an Epidemic,* edited by Judith Brady. Pittsburgh: Cleis, 1991.

United Church of Christ Commission for Racial Justice. *Toxic Wastes and Race in the United States: A National Report on the Racial and Socio-Economic Characteristics of Communities with Hazardous Waste Sites.* New York: Public Data Access, 1987.

12

STRUGGLE IN OGONILAND

Ken Saro-Wiwa and the Cultural Politics of Environmental Justice

Susan Comfort

> *I am recreating the Ogoni people, first and foremost, to come to the realisation of what they have always been which British colonisation tried to take away from them. So my effort is very intellectual. It is backed by theories, thoughts and ideas which will, in fact, matter to the rest of Africa in the course of time.*
>
> —Ken Saro-Wiwa, *The News,* May 17, 1993

From struggles by rubber tappers to protect the Amazonian rain forest, to the Chipko movement of the Himalayas fighting deforestation, to the more recent events in Ogoniland, Nigeria, to stop environmental degradation from large-scale oil drilling, the last few decades have witnessed the emergence of vital environmental movements in the Third World. Images of women hugging trees in the Himalayas to stave off clear-cutting (*chipko* means "to hug") and the faces of Ogoni dissidents detained by the military government in Nigeria have inspired activists and scholars to link the struggle for the environment to issues of basic human rights and social justice. As struggles for "environmental justice," these movements are as much struggles for environmental conservation as they are battles against poverty and racism.[1] Indeed, they constitute a profound challenge to global patterns of development that have precipitated growing inequality, pollution, and land closures.

As part of a broad effort to develop a critical method for understanding the cultural politics of environmental justice, this article examines the cultural production of one writer who was deeply involved in a struggle for environmental justice—Ken Saro-Wiwa. Tried and executed on unsubstantiated murder charges by a military tribunal during the repressive days of Sani Abacha's regime, Saro-Wiwa is mostly remembered as a tireless advocate of the Ogoni people and the environment of the Niger Delta. Also a prolific writer, he produced a considerable range of autobiographical testimony, political journalism, and fiction.

As I examine the cultural politics of Ken Saro-Wiwa, I argue that he is engaged in an attempt to resist the hegemony of state-sponsored maldevelopment and neocolonial capital by building an alternative consensus that transforms conventional political categories and expectations. Through an analysis of selected works by Saro-Wiwa, I explore his varied efforts to construct new narratives of social change that draw together environmental struggle with challenges to racial, ethnic, and class oppression. I pay special attention to the Nigerian context, one often neglected by critics and activists in the United States, where political discourse conflates racism and minority discrimination into a single oppression. Thus, there has been little recognition that the Ogoni were subject to *both* racism by global corporations *and* discrimination by an elite faction of dominant ethnic groups in Nigeria. Given the complexity of the political terrain that Saro-Wiwa negotiated, I argue that his political practice was multivalent and pragmatic. This article will analyze his cultural politics in-depth, specifically his explicitly polemical work, and I will argue that his attempt to construct an oppositional Ogoni identity is carried out through an appeal to the epic conventions of an embattled moral community. Even as his environmental claims for the Ogoni are premised on the assertion of their rights to self-determination and cultural sovereignty, an analysis of his work also reveals an accompanying critique of global capitalism and a broader collective vision of environmental justice.

Ken Saro-Wiwa, the Ogoni and Environmental Justice

Before his involvement in the Ogoni movement, Ken Saro-Wiwa led a varied and active life as a writer, journalist, publisher, businessman, and civil servant. Contrary to the popular image of Saro-Wiwa as a political outsider, he was a consummate politician, though he would use his "insider" knowledge to advance environmental justice and new pathways to social change. Born in 1941 in the area of the Niger Delta then designated the Rivers State, Saro-Wiwa obtained an undergraduate degree from the University of Ibadan, where he studied theater and literature. After graduation, he taught at Government College at Umuahia and at Stella Marris College in Port Harcourt. During the Nigerian Civil War from 1966 to 1970, Saro-Wiwa allied himself with the Federal side against the Igbo secessionists, whom he believed would dominate the Ogonis and other Delta minorities if they seceded. When the secessionists were defeated, the Federal side appointed him Administrator of Bonny Province in the Rivers State, and he was active in the Rivers State government as a commissioner and a member of the Executive Council. He was later appointed as Executive Director of the National Directorate for Social Mobilization in 1987, though he resigned one year later in protest over the corruptions of the Babangida government. While not serving in government, he built a business in trading to finance his activism and writing. Saro-Wiwa was keenly aware that his ambitions to advocate for Ogoni rights required a financial basis, and he consciously sought financial security for this purpose.

While he built a business in trading and continued to be involved in politics, Saro-Wiwa maintained a prolific output as a writer. Frustrated by the lack of publishers, he began his own publishing company, Saros International in 1973, which enabled him to publish and distribute many of his books. He produced a considerable range of work and journalism, including poetry, children's literature, plays, short stories, and novels, as well as newspaper columns and satirical pieces. Beginning with the teleplay "The Transistor Radio," which won a BBC competition in 1972, he wrote and produced radio and television pieces, of which his most famous is the popular television sitcom *Basi and Company*. He also wrote two satirical, dystopian novels, *The Prisoners of Jeb* and *Pita Dumbrok's Prison,* both of which originated as weekly newspaper serials. Probably his best-known work is *Sozaboy*, a trenchant antiwar novel critical of the Nigerian Civil War. In addition, Saro-Wiwa's oeuvre includes forays into narrative realism: his two short story collections, *A Forest of Flowers* and *Adaku and Other Stories,* both of which focus on a fictional community modeled after Ogoni villages in the Niger Delta, experiment with a dynamic interplay of parable and folktale with social realism. In addition to his satirical work and fiction, he has written a wide range of polemical work and nonfiction, notably his treatise on Nigerian ethnic politics, *Nigeria: The Brink of Disaster;* his historical research of the Civil War, *On a Darkling Plain: An Account of the Nigerian Civil War;* his passionate account of the Ogoni struggle, *Genocide in Nigeria: The Ogoni Tragedy;* and his prison diary, *A Month and A Day: A Detention Diary,* which is as much a report on his detention as it is an argument for the cultural rights of the Ogoni.

Saro-Wiwa's experience as a writer, television producer, and especially his work with a government public relations service, were profoundly influential in shaping his strategies for organizing and advocating the Ogoni cause. He observes that it is as a producer of popular culture that he gained some of his most valuable skills as an organizer: "Television production sharpened my writing skills and the flying success of the series, *Basi & Co.,* established my reputation as a creative writer. But above all, I learnt how to deal with the press and how to promote an idea, publicity being very central to the success of a television series. That was the importance of my television work to the Ogoni question" (*A Month and a Day,* 58–59). As critics have observed, in his role as television producer, Saro-Wiwa was a participant in the creation of a popular culture for the urban middle class that in Abiola Irele's words, "rejects the revaluation of traditional culture . . . which has become a dominant feature of African literature" (266). A major contradiction that runs through Saro-Wiwa's work is the conflict between his refusal to romanticize the folk and his commitment to a profoundly populist role as an advocate for Ogoni rights. He also cannot be described as a socialist (and thus he cannot be easily identified with the socialist intellectual tradition in Africa associated with writers such as Ngugi wa Thiong'o or Wole Soyinka) even though his writing contains powerful critiques of global capital.[2] As the analysis that follows demonstrates, his politics were transitional, pragmatic, and sometimes contradictory, and they were shaped in large part by his advocacy of the Ogoni cause within both national and international contexts.

Before examining his political practice in depth, let me first provide some background on the Ogoni and oil in Nigeria. Located in the eastern region of the Niger Delta, Ogoniland has a population of approximately five hundred thousand, and it consists of six kingdoms, where four closely related languages are spoken. During the colonial era and the subsequent First Republic, Ogoniland was included in the Eastern Region, where the Igbo formed the majority ethnic group. After the Civil War and the attempted secession of the Igbo, the Eastern region was broken up into smaller states including the present day Rivers State that administers Ogoniland and several other minority ethnic areas.

Oil production in the Rivers State, including Ogoniland, began in 1958 shortly after petroleum was discovered by Shell Oil.[3] Today, Nigeria draws 80 percent of its revenue from oil production and earns 90 percent of its foreign exchange from oil exports (Sachs, 14). In the early twentieth century, the colonial government granted concessions to foreign companies to conduct exploration for oil, and in 1938, Shell D'Arcy Petroleum Development Company was granted an exclusive exploration license, and has dominated oil production in the country ever since. A subsidiary of Shell Oil Company, Shell Petroleum Development Company, currently produces 50 percent of Nigeria's crude oil, and maintains control over 60 percent of commercially viable oil-bearing land (Ihonvbere and Shaw, 237). Despite a program of indigenization initiated by the military government in the late 1960s, which instituted joint ventures and the establishment of the Nigerian National Petroleum Corporation (NNPC), oil production remains an enclave industry in which the technology, management, and profits are mostly controlled by transnational corporations. Since the worldwide oil bust of the early 1980s, and the subsequent debt crisis and structural adjustment prescribed by the International Monetary Fund, the Nigerian government has relinquished even more control, and it has offered even greater incentives to foreign companies, in order to stave off economic hardship and an escalating foreign exchange crisis. Since oil production began in 1958, Shell has drilled over one hundred wells and established two refineries and a fertilizer complex in Ogoniland. According to Julius O. Ihonvbere and Timothy Shaw, "Shell estimates that about 624 million barrels of oil have been extracted from Ogoniland since it commenced operations," and an estimated $30 billion worth of oil has been produced (226–27).

The environment of the Niger Delta has suffered as a result. Agricultural lands that produce cassava, yam, and other essential staples have been devastated by oil spills and toxic leakage from waste pits, and lands have been polluted or expropriated with little compensation to local communities. The United Nations has declared the Niger Delta one of the most endangered river deltas in the world. Between 1976 and 1991, there were nearly three thousand oil spills totaling over two million barrels of oil spilled (238). Indeed, 40 percent of Shell's oil spills worldwide have occurred in Nigeria, suggesting that Shell maintains a lower environmental standard there than elsewhere. Shell practices environmental racism by waiving, as one critic points out, "onshore drilling standards that it routinely upholds elsewhere" (Nixon, 116). In one notorious spill on farmland near Ebubu in 1970, the spilled oil was burned rather than cleaned up, resulting in the significant degradation of the land. Gas flaring is another serious pollution problem. According to a World Bank study, "76 percent of the natural gas produced in the process of petroleum production is simply flared. . . . The emission of CO_2 [carbon dioxide] from gas flaring in Nigeria releases 35 million tons of CO_2 a year and 12 million tons of methane, which means that Nigeria's oil fields contribute more to global warming than the rest of the world together" (qtd. in Ihonvbere and Shaw, 237). In addition, the oil pipelines, which crisscross Ogoni lands and villages, frequently leak and do not receive regular maintenance.

The Ogoni movement emerged in protest of this environmental devastation as well as the closure of communal lands decreed by the 1979 Constitution. Environmental devastation and closure have hit women and poorer peasants particularly hard, given that these groups derive their subsistence and economic security from communal lands. Another significant factor influencing the emergence of the Ogoni struggle, particularly the participation of Ogoni elites, is the state's reduction of revenue allocated to state and local authorities (from 50 percent in 1960 to 2 percent in the 1980s). The publication of the Ogoni Bill of Rights in October 1990 is typically regarded as a significant starting point in the mass mobilization of the Ogoni movement, and Saro-Wiwa is said to have drafted it. The 1990 Bill of Rights calls for "political autonomy" for the Ogonis as "a distinct and separate unit"; the preservation of Ogoni languages and culture; as well as environmental reparations and a more equitable distribution of oil revenues. Ignored by the government, the Bill of Rights was followed by a 1991 Addendum reiterating the basic demands, and subsequent mass mobilization of the Ogoni signaled by the founding of the Movement for the Survival of the Ogoni People (MOSOP), the National Youth Council of Ogoni People, the Conference of Ogoni Traditional Rulers, and the Council for Ogoni Rights. In a pivotal moment, on December 3, 1992, MOSOP sent a letter to the oil companies and the NNPC demanding reparations for environmental degradation; payment of royalties on oil sales since 1959; and an end to environmentally damaging practices.

The next few months witnessed several significant mass actions, during one of which, on January 4, 1993, an estimated three hundred thousand people gathered to celebrate Ogoni Day in recognition of the United Nations Year of Indigenous Peoples. Mass rallies continued for the next few months and at the end of April, government troops fired on protesters attempting to stop the bulldozing of cropland by an American contractor, Wilbros. One person was killed and twenty others were wounded. In June 1993, though some of the Ogoni leadership disagreed with the decision, MOSOP boycotted the national elections to protest the constitution's failure to recognize minority rights. Charged with treasonous activities, Ken Saro-Wiwa was detained by the government for over a month that summer. During the summer and fall of 1993, amid increased government surveillance and repression, ethnic clashes broke out in the Rivers State. In fact, in fighting between the Ogoni and a neighboring ethnic group, the Andoni, which left over one thousand dead and at least thirty thousand homeless, there is evidence that government soldiers orchestrated the hostilities.[4] In addition, military involvement has also been documented in the violence between the Ogonis and Okrikas in December 1993, and state security agents are said to have aided the Ndokis in their raids on Ogoni villages the following spring. As a result of the violence, Shell temporarily ceased all operations in Ogoniland, and government repression was stepped up with the establishment of the Rivers State Internal Security Task Force in January 1994. In the summer of 1994, this mobile police force engaged in ongoing raids on Ogoni villages, which, according to Human Rights Watch/Africa, involved shooting and beating people indiscriminately; looting and destroying property; as well as arresting and detaining hundreds of Ogoni.[5] On May 21, 1994, four progovernment Ogoni chiefs were killed in a mob attack, the crime for which Ken Saro-Wiwa and eight other Ogoni activists were tried before a military tribunal. The trial itself was riddled with irregularities and violated basic tenets of fair, independent, and impartial judicial procedures: the tribunal was appointed by the illegitimate government of Sani Abacha; the defense lawyers were denied access to their clients; and prosecution witnesses are said to have been bribed by state agents to provide false information. Moreover, the undisputed fact that Saro-Wiwa was nowhere near the scene of the four murders did not have any bearing on the final guilty verdict.

Saro-Wiwa's documentary research, essays, speeches, and polemical journalism were instrumental in articulating and calling attention to the Ogoni cause. His advocacy started during the Civil War when he wrote the 1968 pamphlet, *The Ogoni Nationality: Today and Tomorrow,* which recounts the repression of the Ogoni during the war and criticizes the government for not sharing the wealth generated by oil production in the region. He went on to develop this critique in documentary work published during his involvement in MOSOP. In *Genocide in Nigeria* (1991), for example, he cites original letters and memos in their entirety to construct a historical record of exploitation and destruction. It is a text designed to present evidence to support his case that Ogoniland has been subjected to repression because of the oil production in the region. Saro-Wiwa's argument draws its power from its evocative presentation of the plight of the Ogoni people and a narrative of their repression by the British and by the Nigerian government after independence. Under the British, according to Saro-Wiwa, the Ogoni were able to assert some measure of autonomy, organizing the Ogoni Central Union (1930) and the Ogoni State Representative Assembly (1950). They were also granted a Native Authority in 1947, with the legendary T. N. Paul

Birabi as the chief administrator. After independence, and during the Civil War, the Ogoni suffered massive repression by the Igbo, who sought to control the oil resources of the region. Saro-Wiwa argues here, and elsewhere, that the Civil War was a resource war, and that the environmental devastation of the war was matched by the human one: according to Saro-Wiwa, as many as thirty thousand Ogoni were killed during the war, and many more were driven into detention camps by the Igbo, who suspected them of collaboration with the Federal side. After the war, the Ogoni did not fare much better due to the oil exploitation that has devastated the region.

In his analysis of maldevelopment in Ogoniland, Ken Saro-Wiwa relates a familiar story, one of ethnic politics and elite collaboration with foreign power. As many commentators have observed, Saro-Wiwa emphasizes "internal colonialism" or ethnic domination by the northern Hausa-Fulani rulers as the primary explanation for the exploitation of Ogoni lands. Ethnic politics in the country is arguably one of the legacies of colonial style rule: the British applied the principle of "divide and rule," administering the country regionally through Native Authorities, and thus creating ethnic and regional rivalries that have become more competitive and entrenched in the post-colonial era. As Sam C. Nolutshungu has observed, decolonization was a hierarchical affair in which the formation of regional political parties "from the top down, to respond to an opportunity created by the imminent departure of colonial rule . . . necessitated an aggressive definition and bounding by each prospective leadership of its own territory upon the received template of the region which could be given a cultural and ethnic significance as well" (89). In other words, as Nolutshungu argues, and as Mahmood Mamdani has also recently outlined in his book *Citizen and Subject: Contemporary Africa and the Legacy of Late Colonialism,* "British colonialism contained no concept of citizenship for natives" (Nolutshungu, 89). The colonial policy of indirect rule emphasized "the distinctness of peoples, their cultures and needs," and thus required that the colonized be ruled through Native Authorities, which the British created for the purposes of colonial administration (89). Decolonization has resulted in the consolidation of ethnic distinction as the basis of power for competing regional elites. Furthermore, state power means access not only to political power, but also to the means of capital accumulation and patronage. Thus, the postcolonial state in Nigeria is dominated by patron-client relationships defined by ethnic allegiances and alliances among elites. Any semblance of democracy that the Second Republic claimed to have inaugurated was constituted from above. As Nolutshungu argues, "the colonial transfer of power set the precedent, and subsequently encouraged the expectation that democracy could be created from above by the enactment of constitutions that struck bargains among political elites—not classes—poised to succeed the preceding (undemocratic) regime" (103).

Saro-Wiwa's advocacy on behalf of the Ogoni is markedly different from conventional political practice in Nigeria, and it is his articulation of environmental injustice that complicates the typical logic of Nigerian politics. His political practice may be said to demonstrate the residual features of ethnic politics, but also the emergent characteristics of a new social formation constituted by movements for environmental justice. His argument for environmental justice draws its power and legitimacy from his assertion of Ogoni nationhood, and his narration of the Ogoni as a moral community of environmental stewards draws on the epic tropes associated with nationalist narratives. In other words, Saro-Wiwa's depiction of the political ecology of the Ogoni inscribes their collective culture, history, and geography in epic terms.

Let us take a closer look at one specific text wherein Saro-Wiwa makes a case for the cultural sovereignty of the Ogoni. *Genocide in Nigeria: The Ogoni Tragedy* begins with a remarkable chapter that outlines Ogoni history and culture. Its first line reads, "The Ogoni are a distinct ethnic group within the Federal Republic of Nigeria." This is followed by a descriptive ethnography that establishes the boundaries of Ogoni territory, identifies a time in the past of their settlement and names the specific kingdoms which make up the Ogoni group: "the Ogoni are said to have settled in the area well before the fifteenth century and established themselves in the six kingdoms of Babbe, Eleme, Gokana, Nyo-Khana, Ken-Khana and Tai" (11). The chapter continues by describing the Ogoni attachment to the land and their sustainable agricultural practices: "The Ogoni had inherited a precious part of God's earth and did everything to preserve it. The rich plateau soil provided agricultural plenty and the rivers which wash the borders of the entire area brimmed with fishes and sea food. The Ogoni seized the opportunity to become competent farmers and fishermen and to transform their territory into the food basket of the eastern Niger delta" (12). Implied here is a prelapsarian, reciprocal and nonexploitative relationship to the land. The biblical overtones of this passage also suggest that the Ogoni attachment to this territory is sanctioned by a higher power. This enchanted relationship is further elaborated in language of holistic ecology: "To the Ogoni, rivers and streams do not only provide water for life—for bathing and drinking etc.; they do not only provide fish for food, they are also sacred and are bound up intricately with the life of the community of the entire Ogoni nation" (12–13).

The narration of the Ogoni past stresses their territorial isolation and also the remoteness of their past. M. M. Bakhtin has suggested that the epic conjures up an "absolute past" that is "inaccessible" and marked off from the present.[6] By rendering Ogoni history and culture an "immutable fact" and by attributing a sacred sanction to their ecological values, Saro-Wiwa renders the claims of the Ogoni unassailable and inviolable. Scholars and activists have noticed that movements for environmental justice have appealed to what has been called a "medieval" notion of justice, which is: "at one and the same time a moral and cosmic principle, to which all human activity must be subordinated. Any departure from this principle is equivalent to trans-gression of the divine order of things and of natural law" (Harvey, 388). Like so many groups that have challenged dispossession and environmental de-struction, Saro-Wiwa inscribes the contours of a moral community that holds out noncommodified, "enchanted," equitable social relations and a sustain-able relationship to the land against systemic maldevelopment and neo-colonial exploitation. The epic narrative of cultural rights constitutes what David Harvey describes as "a medium of social protest . . . [that] articulates ideas about a moral economy of collective provision and collective respon-sibility as opposed to a set of distributive relations within the political economy of profit" (Harvey, 389). Furthermore, this epic narrative holds out the ideal of the nation, which, according to Benedict Anderson, is a "deep, horizontal comradeship," an imagined political community, whose magic "turn[s] chance into destiny" and thus renders history purposeful (16, 19). Those values are a powerful challenge to the machine of "development" that also claims historical necessity and inevitability.

Saro-Wiwa's argument for environmental rights is thus intricately inter-woven with his calls for Ogoni cultural autonomy, and the multivalence of his cultural intervention is further complicated by his claims that the Ogoni share a history of environmental injustice with other groups around the world. In doing so, he rewrites the Ogoni past within a larger transnational context of colonial history and contemporary globalization. For example, on the first Ogoni Day, January 4, 1993, timed to celebrate the United Nations Year of Indigenous Peoples, Saro-Wiwa gave a speech comparing the plight of the Ogoni with "the Maori of New Zealand, the Aborigines of Australia and the Indians of North and South America" (*A Month and A Day,* 131). In another speech later that day, Saro-Wiwa elaborated on that comparison, drawing together the pasts of divergent groups into a collective history of oppression and exploitation:

> Contrary to the belief that there are no indigenous people in black Africa, our research has shown that the fate of such groups as the Zangon Kataf and Ogoni in Nigeria is, in essence, no different from those of the Aborigines of Australia, the Maori of New Zealand and the Indians of North and South America. Their common history is of the usurpation of their land and resources, the destruction of their culture and the eventual decimation of the people. Indigenous people often do not realize what is happening to them until it is too late. More often than not, they are the victims of the actions of greedy outsiders. EMIROAF [Ethnic Minority Rights Organization of Africa] will continue to mobilize and represent the interest of all indigenous people on the African continent. It is in this regard that we have undertaken to publicize the fate of the Ogoni people in Nigeria. (131)

By claiming an "indigenous" identity for the Ogoni, Saro-Wiwa indicates that MOSOP seeks broader political goals that include resistance to systemic global maldevelopment. Indeed, the Ogoni are now regularly featured as antiglobalization icons by the left popular media in the West.

By engaging in cultural activism that fosters an identification as an environmental justice movement, Saro-Wiwa developed a critical analysis and oppositional identity that challenged the politics of patronage and elite corruption in Nigeria. In his reflections on other elites who abandoned MOSOP to return to the state machinery of patronage and party politics, he remarked: "Mainstream politicians work for immediate reward. A movement like MOSOP is involved in alternative politics with a more long-term perspective" (*A Month and A Day,* 101). That "long-term perspective" included a strategy of mass mobilization to build a movement from below. In mass meetings held throughout Ogoniland in November and December 1992, MOSOP formulated a list of demands to Shell and the NNPC, demands that Saro-Wiwa would present in a formal letter in mid-December. His organizing strategy also included an emphasis on land closures and environmental degradation that appealed directly to the women and small farmers who had depended on expropriated land for subsistence. His critical analysis also appealed to Ogoni youth who were not party to the brokered land deals or small compensations made by the oil companies to traditional chiefs and state agents. Saro-Wiwa referred repeatedly to the many women and young people involved in the ranks of the movement. The April 1993 protest against Wilbros contracting company, who were bulldozing croplands in Biara, consisted mostly of women. Furthermore, peasant women were the main organizers and participants in earlier revolts documented by political economist Terisa E. Turner, including the 1984 Ogharefe and 1986 Epan uprisings in what is now Delta state in the oil center of Warri, which is about one hundred miles east of the Niger Delta. In those struggles, peasant women whose land had been despoiled confronted elite men aligned with foreign capital.

As the political base of MOSOP broadened, and as Ken Saro-Wiwa's environmentalism became more critical of the collusion between the Nigerian state and global capital, the divisions within MOSOP reached a crisis point, and political violence was the result. It is significant that Shell would exploit this rift in order to identify a more moderate voice of MOSOP that would discredit Saro-Wiwa. By appealing to environmental justice as a basis for broadening the Ogoni movement, it is arguable that Ken Saro-Wiwa attempted to foster a political identity that combined a desire for cultural autonomy with a struggle to democratize the local sphere of political power and economic patronage that is the legacy of colonial capitalism and indirect rule. In *Citizen and Subject,* Mahmood Mamdani has argued that the colonial state was a "double-sided affair" divided between urban civil power and rural tribal authority. Urban civil power, a form of direct rule typically administered by Europeans, denied Africans their civil rights by an appeal to racism, whereas rural tribal authority subjected Africans to state-enforced customary orders. In short, indirect rule essentially reshaped native governing institutions into authoritarian, despotic Native Authorities designed primarily to extract taxes and labor (Mamdani, 18–19). In the postcolonial era in Africa, various attempts to institute political reforms in the sphere of civil power have partially dismantled the racist civil structures of the colonial era, but not the authoritarian character of Native Authorities. One might interpret Saro-Wiwa's activism as an attempt to challenge politics-as-usual in the Ogoni Native Authority. Indeed, in his detention diary Saro-Wiwa explains that several Ogoni leaders betrayed the movement because they had a material interest in maintaining the status quo. The day after the first Ogoni Day in 1993, Saro-Wiwa reflects on the collaboration of some Ogoni leaders with Rivers State Governor Ada George: "If I thought that there would be no answer to the march by those we had challenged, I was greatly mistaken. And, as usual, the first persons to be used were the Ogoni people themselves. A few of them were very close to Governor Ada George and were benefiting by his being in power. And it was to them he turned for assistance to wreak his revenge on the Ogoni people" (142).

The broader significance of the Ogoni movement for the struggle for democracy and human rights during the recent dictatorship of Sani Abacha has also been the subject of recent scholarly debate. One critic has suggested that the pollution in Ogoniland became a figure for the corruptions of the "vampire state" of Nigeria.[7] I would suggest it was the Ogonis' persistent drive to democratize local as well as national and global spheres of socio-economic power that appealed to so many Nigerians. During the pro-democracy struggles in the Abacha era, their protest of the massive exploitations of the state found resonance with many Nigerians who had grown increasingly impoverished, as cronies of the state appropriated the vast majority of the wealth. For example, in *The Open Sore of a Continent: A Personal Narrative of the Nigerian Crisis,* Wole Soyinka features the Ogoni in his rallying cry against state repression and exploitation under Abacha: "Ogoni people are, alas, only the guinea pigs for a morbid resolution of this smouldering inequity that was instituted by the British as they planned for their departure. The beneficiaries remain, till today, a minority made up of a carefully nurtured feudal oligarchy and their pampered, indolent, and unproductive scions" (6). Political ecologist James O'Connor argues that social movements such as the Ogoni struggle are erroneously dismissed as simply espousing parochial agendas, when, in fact, the agendas of these movements resonate with broader goals of economic equality and democratic accountability. The Ogoni call for democratic values is one example of a "site specific" movement, which became a model for human rights struggle against a repressive state in collaboration with global capitalism:

> In the well thought out versions of post-Marxist thought, the "site specificity" which new social movements base themselves on are considered to make any universal demands impossible. . . . This is contrasted with the bourgeois revolution which universalized the demand for rights against privilege and the old working-class struggle which universalized the demand for public property. . . . However, [an analysis] . . . of production conditions and the contradictions therein reveals clearly that there is a universal demand to democratize the state (which regulates the provision of production conditions), as well as the family and local community. (35)

In an era of globalization and structural adjustment, movements to democratize the state and its power to regulate global capital's access to nature and labor—the production conditions that capitalism requires—have become one of the most significant arenas of struggle. The Ogoni movement is one among many movements, including protests against the Narmada Dam Project in India and the Green Belt Movement in Kenya, which are struggling to reassert a public sphere of accountability against neoliberal schemes of privatization and debt-driven economic imperatives.

By linking environmental destruction, economic exploitation and oppressions of ethnicity and race, these movements attempt to build a broad oppositional consensus. In other words, they redefine poverty and cultural oppression as environmental issues, and thus build bridges among forces of resistance previously segregated into separate spheres of struggle. These movements engage, in the language of Gramscian analysis, in strategically coordinating diverse and often contradictory interests, beliefs, and values in order to construct a counterhegemonic formation. The cultures of these movements are thus shot through with contradictions: as movements that often strive for cultural autonomy and local power, they may develop parochial agendas, but their appeal to the values of environmental justice, such as equitable development, and Enlightenment principles of equal rights and democracy, implies a broader collective identity. Similarly, these groups may advocate for separatist goals, but at the same time their identification as indigenous or ethnic minorities under assault from destructive development implies a broader identity with other groups similarly under siege elsewhere. The 1992 Rio Conference and the more recent protests in Seattle make it clear that a new "Non-Aligned Movement" is emerging from the movements for alternative development and environmental justice.

Conclusion

Retired General Olusegun Obasanjo, the newly elected president of Nigeria, has recently established a commission to investigate human rights violations during the Abacha dictatorship. Among the abuses being investigated is the execution of Ken Saro-Wiwa in 1995. Despite this attempt to rectify the abuses of the past regime, according to scholars and activists, the current government is not doing enough to alter the pattern of underdevelopment in the country and especially in the Niger Delta. Still denied meaningful democratic access to the central government, ethnic groups in the Delta—including the Ogoni, the Ijaw, and the Itsekiri—continue to mobilize protests against government collaboration with foreign oil. Also, labor unions have been staging strikes and walkouts to protest economic exploitation by oil companies and government cronies. In addition, the press, an important voice during the pro-democracy struggles, has continued to push for more state accountability and equitable development in the Delta as well. Indeed, *Tempo*, one of the major Nigerian weeklies, has attributed recent ethnic violence between the Ijaw and the Itsekiri in the Delta to maldevelopment: "The animosity, actually, is not among feuding communities. Rather it is a sort of resentment against the state which exploits the oil—yielding billions of dollars—and leaves the area underdeveloped. And when such animosity lasts too long, the concerned people start suspecting one another of collaborating with the enemy or of being too passive with him. Hence the inter-communal clashes, which only justice in the sharing of oil revenue can solve in the long run" (qtd. in Fleshman, para. 7).

As struggles to democratize the state continue in Nigeria and elsewhere, I have argued that what is needed is an analysis that highlights the material connections among different sites of environmental degradation and economic exploitation but that also emphasizes the particular cultural idioms and local complexities of these struggles. It is hoped that attempts such as this one to theorize environmental struggle will facilitate not only alliances across race, ethnicity, and gender in specific sites but also coalitions across the borders of the First and Third World. At a recent conference at Ohio University on Global Human Rights, Owens Wiwa, a MOSOP organizer and Ken's brother, represented the Ogoni on a panel that included activists speaking about environmental devastation and Appalachian coal mining. The audience learned about mining subsidence experienced by poor, rural homeowners in southeastern Ohio in the same hour that they learned about Ogoni women struggling to grow yam and cassava on farmland despoiled by oil spills. In this instance, an analysis of environment injustice is generating a recognition of the similarities between two disparate sites, and thus contributing to a new international community of resistance.

NOTES

1. I use the term "environmental justice movement" in a broad sense to refer not just to the toxic struggles that emerged in the United States in the

early 1980s, but also to environmental movements in the Third World. I do so advisedly. As some have argued, the environmental justice movement is not a singular movement. Specific struggles are differently mediated by class, race, gender, and ethnicity. For example, in Appalachia, environmental justice features corporate power and class, whereas in African American communities in the South, race is a prominent feature of environmental justice. In Nigeria, I will argue, *both ethnicity and race* are significant to the analysis of environmental justice, yet class is also an integral part of the critique of corporate exploitation. I gained clarification on this point from the work of Rob Nixon. See Nixon, "Pipe Dreams"; and Harvey, *Justice, Nature and the Geography of Difference.* Also see Krauss, "Women of Color in the Front Line."

2. For a comparative analysis of Saro-Wiwa's writing and cultural activism in an African context, see Irele, "Ken Saro-Wiwa"; McLuckie, "Literary Memoirs and Diaries"; and Nixon, "Pipe Dreams."

3. I have relied on the following sources for background on oil production and environmental conditions in Ogoniland: Cayford, "The Ogoni Uprising"; Hammer, "Nigeria Crude"; Kretzmann, "Nigeria's Drilling Fields"; Sachs, "Dying for Oil"; Ihonvbere and Shaw, *Illusions of Power;* and Osaghae, "The Ogoni Uprising."

4. See Human Rights Watch/Africa, "Nigeria," 12.

5. Human Rights Watch/Africa, "Nigeria." Not only was the government involved, but there is also evidence that Shell funded the operations of the Rivers State Internal Security Task Force. The commander of the Task Force, Major Paul Okuntimo, reportedly wrote a memo to the Governor of the Rivers State requesting that he put "pressure on oil companies for prompt regular inputs as discussed." See also Ihonvbere and Shaw, *Illusions of Power,* 239.

6. According to Bakhtin in *The Dialogic Imagination,* "The epic world is an utterly finished thing, not only as an authentic event of the distant past but also on its own terms and by its own standards; it is impossible to change, to rethink, to re-evaluate anything in it. It is completed, conclusive and immutable, as a fact, an idea and a value" (17).

7. See Apter, "Death and the King's Henchmen."

WORKS CITED

Anderson, Benedict. *Imaginary Communities: Reflections on the Origin and Spread of Nationalism.* New York: Verso, 1983.

Apter, Andrew. "Death and the King's Henchmen: Ken Saro-Wiwa and the

Political Ecology of Citizenship in Nigeria." In *Ogoni's Agonies: Ken Saro-Wiwa and the Crisis in Nigeria,* edited by Abdul Rasheed Na'Allah (Trenton, N.J.: Africa World Press, 1998).

Bakhtin, M. M. *The Dialogic Imagination.* Edited by Michael Holquist. Translated by Caryl Emerson and Michael Holquist. Austin: University of Texas Press, 1981.

Cayford, Steven. "The Ogoni Uprising: Oil, Human Rights, and a Democratic Alternative in Nigeria." *Africa Today* 43, no. 2 (1996): 183–98.

Escobar, Arturo. "Imagining a Post-Development Era? Critical Thought, Development and Social Movements." *Social Text* 31/32 (1992): 20–56.

Fleshman, Michael. "Report on the Crisis in the Niger Delta." *Nigeria Transition Watch Number 9, Report from Nigeria 1.* New York: Africa Fund, 17 June 1999 [www.prairienet.org/acas/nigeria1.html].

Hammer, Joshua. "Nigeria Crude." *Harper's Magazine* (June 1996): 58–68.

Harvey, David. *Justice, Nature and the Geography of Difference.* London: Blackwell, 1996.

Human Rights Watch/Africa. "Nigeria: The Ogoni Crisis." *Human Rights Watch/Africa Report 7, Number 5.* July 1995.

Ihonvbere, Julius O., and Timothy Shaw. *Illusions of Power: Nigeria in Transition.* Trenton, N.J.: Africa World Press, 1998.

Irele, Abiola. "Ken Saro-Wiwa." In *Ogoni's Agonies: Ken Saro-Wiwa and the Crisis in Nigeria,* edited by Abdul Rasheed Na'Allah, 255–67. Trenton, N.J.: Africa World Press, 1998.

Krauss, C. "Women of Color in the Front Line." In *Unequal Protection: Environmental Justice and Communities of Color,* edited by Robert D. Bullard (San Francisco, 1994).

Kretzmann, Steven. "Nigeria's Drilling Fields." *Multinational Monitor* (January/February 1995): 8–25.

Mamdani, Mahmood. *Citizen and Subject: Contemporary Africa and the Legacy of Late Colonialism.* Princeton, N.J.: Princeton University Press, 1996.

McLuckie, Craig W. "Literary Memoirs and Diaries: Soyinka, Amadi, and Saro-Wiwa." In *Ken Saro-Wiwa: Writer and Political Activist,* edited by Craig W. McLuckie and Abrey McPhail, 29–52. Boulder: Lynne Rienner, 2000.

McLuckie, Craig W., and Abrey McPhail, eds. *Ken Saro-Wiwa: Writer and Political Activist.* Boulder: Lynne Rienner, 2000.

Nixon, Rob. "Pipe Dreams: Ken Saro-Wiwa, Environmental Justice, and Micro-minority Rights." In *Ken Saro-Wiwa: Writer and Political Activist,* edited by Craig W. McLuckie and Abrey McPhail, 109–25. Boulder: Lynne Rienner, 2000.

Nolutshungu, Sam C. "Fragments of a Democracy: Reflections on Class and Politics in Nigeria." *Third World Quarterly* 12, no. 1 (January 1990): 86–115.

O'Connor, James. "Capitalism, Nature, Socialism: A Theoretical Introduction." *Capitalism, Nature, Socialism* 1 (November 1988): 11–38.

Osaghae, Eghosa E. "The Ogoni Uprising: Oil Politics, Minority Agitation and the Future of the Nigerian State." *African Affairs* 94 (1995): 325–44.

Sachs, Aaron. "Dying for Oil." *World Watch* (May/June 1996): 10–21.

Saro-Wiwa, Ken. *Adaku and Other Stories*. Lagos, Nigeria: Saros International, 1989.

———. *Basi and Company: A Modern African Folktale*. Lagos, Nigeria: Saros International, 1987.

———. *A Forest of Flowers*. Lagos, Nigeria: Saros International, 1986.

———. *Genocide in Nigeria: The Ogoni Tragedy*. Lagos, Nigeria: Saros International, 1991.

———. *A Month and a Day: A Detention Diary*. London: Penguin, 1995.

———. *Nigeria: The Brink of Disaster*. Lagos, Nigeria: Saros International, 1991.

———. *The Ogoni Nationality: Today and Tomorrow*. Lagos, Nigeria: Saros International, 1968.

———. *On a Darkling Plain: An Account of the Nigerian Civil War*. Lagos, Nigeria: Saros International, 1989.

———. *Pita Dumbrock's Prison*. Lagos, Nigeria: Saros International, 1991.

———. *The Prisoners of Jeb*. Lagos, Nigeria: Saros International, 1988.

———. *Sozaboy*. Lagos, Nigeria: Saros International, 1986.

Soyinka, Wole. *The Open Sore of a Continent: A Personal Narrative of the Nigerian Crisis*. New York: Oxford University Press, 1996.

Turner, Terisa A., ed. *Arise Ye Mighty People: Gender, Class and Race in Popular Struggles*. Trenton, N.J.: Africa World Press, 1994.

13

TOWARD A SYMBIOSIS OF ECOLOGY AND JUSTICE

Water and Land Conflicts in Frank Waters, John Nichols, and Jimmy Santiago Baca

Tom Lynch

The upper Rio Grande watershed of southern Colorado and northern New Mexico consists of arid and semiarid plateaus and valleys surrounded by high mountains. The Sangre de Cristo Mountains rise to the east, the San Juan and Jemez Mountains to the west. Much of the area is steeply sloped. All waters falling within this basin drain quickly towards the Rio Grande that slices through a faulted rift zone splitting down the heart of the landscape.

This bioregion, often referred to as the Rio Arriba or "upper river," is unique. Environmental historian William deBuys asserts that "no other region in all of North America so richly combines both ecological and cultural diversity" (6). During the past four hundred years a distinctive Chicano agropastoral culture has evolved here, characterized by a riparian long-lot settlement pattern, subsistence agriculture, communally owned grazing lands, and an acequia irrigation system. (For further details on this cultural pattern, see chapter 3 in this volume.)

Since the United States took control of the area through military conquest in 1846, however, these bioregionally integrated communities have undergone a series of assaults: The transfer of the land grant commons, often through nefarious means, to private Anglo ownership or to the U.S. Forest Service; the replacement of communal acequia irrigation districts by market-oriented conservancy districts that impose taxes that traditional water users are unable to pay; the replacement of a subsistence economy by both a market economy and by a reliance on industrial tourism; the enforcement of government regulations—including well-meaning environmental regulations—that conflict with vernacular behavior; and the arrival of a large number of Anglo "amenity migrants" whose culture is supplanting that of the Hispano community.

In many cases, these changes have had negative consequences not just for the Hispano villagers, but also for the natural environment. Gary Paul Nabhan asserts a direct linkage between colonial conquest and ecological degradation. "Wherever empires have spread to suppress other cultures' languages and land-tenure traditions," he claims, "the loss of biodiversity has been dramatic" ("Missing the Boat," 37). In regard to the Río Arriba, recent scholarship, most notably by Devon Peña and Rubén Martínez, explores the local details of Nabhan's theme, arguing that the Chicano agropastoral system represents a sustainable, socially just, bioregionally adapted, and ecologically viable pattern of land use in the arid mountains of New Mexico and Colorado and that its displacement by colonial conquest and Anglo incursion damages not just the area's cultural but also its natural integrity (see Peña, "Los Animalitos" and Martínez, "Social Action Research, Bioregionalism, and the Upper Rio Grande).

While Nabhan warns us of the ecological degradation that accompanies colonial conquest, he also suggests ways to halt and reverse this process, emphasizing the role of storytelling and ritual: "To restore any place," he says, "we must also begin to re-story it, to make it the lesson of our legends, festivals, and seasonal rites. Story is the way we encode deep-seated values within our culture" ("Epilogue," 319). Drawing from such a premise, this essay considers literary works by three authors from the Upper Rio Grande bioregion in terms of their portrayal of the various assaults on the Chicano agropastoral culture; in particular it considers the degree to which the maintenance of social justice through the preservation of the traditional Chicano land and water-use patterns is symbiotic with sustainable ecological health.

In the early decades of the twentieth century, numerous writers settled in northern New Mexico. Among those whose works have been most enduring is Frank Waters. A native of Colorado Springs, Colorado, Waters was more attuned than were most of his fellow writers, who largely came from the East, to the cultural importance of land and water in the Southwest, and he has specifically addressed social justice issues regarding land and water control throughout his writings.

However the predominant literary criticism on Waters seeks to rescue him from the "regional writer" pigeon-hole by emphasizing the "universal" aspects of his work. "We should object to the fact that Frank Waters is constantly referred to as a 'western' writer,'" William Eastlake has complained, suggesting instead that "writing of any value is universal" (4). While it's true enough that some of Waters' own tendencies encourage a universal interpretation, I would suggest that insistence on the "universal" significance at the expense of local relevance whitewashes over the very details that render a work amenable to a bioregional reading, and trivializes the specific issues of social justice and ecological concern that, in our present context, make a work meaningful.

In 1936 Frank Waters lived in the small village of Mora, New Mexico, on the eastern slopes of the Sangre de Cristo Mountains. Out of this experience he crafted his novel *People of the Valley*, which regards an Hispano community in the Mora Valley and its response to the construction of a dam by Anglo interlopers. The novel opens with a description of the valley, situating itself as a tale concerning a watershed-specific agropastoral ecology. Waters then brings us down the drainage with the flood waters in a grand gesture of watershed consciousness: "A thunder cloud snags on the western cliffs of the Sangre de Cristo, and from the converging box cañons of Luna and Lujan the water foams down along the ridge rock of Los Alamitos" (3). He follows the course of the growing flood waters down the watershed until the flood "rips through the willows, uproots cottonwoods, tears out old acequias so patiently banked by hand" (4).

These floods with which he introduces us to the locale, which in a sense define the place, and which the Hispano residents accept as God's will, lead the Yankee newcomers to propose damming the river. To such a proposal, the community voice collectively asks: "why do they build this dam? There has never been one before; it is not the custom. The floods will come, like sunshine and the drought. They are all God's will" (5). This comment encapsulates the tension in the book, to live in accordance with custom, following the will of God and nature, even if that means suffering an occasional flood, or to accept innovations, the "Máquina of progress," that will reduce flooding but that also seem to deny faith and hinder the will of God.

This dichotomy symbolizes some of the themes Waters is seeking to illustrate, an archetypal clash between primal faith and modern faithlessness, or, if one prefers a Jungian formulation, between the anima and the animus, but it also has the unfortunate outcome of reinforcing the cliché that the Hispano community is fatalistic, trapped in passive customs before the onslaught of energetic Anglo power. As a means of justifying the colonial process, many writers have labelled the Hispanos of northern New Mexico as "indolent." And a reductive universal approach to *People of the Valley*, unfortunately, plays into this formulation. On the other hand, the novel's main character mounts an energetic and shrewd resistance to the dam. Maria del Valle, as her name suggests, personifies the valley as well as the in-placed wisdom and endurance of her people. She makes her living from the land and collects its produce for sale in the markets. She gathers and knows the uses of herbs and plants for medicine and dyes.

Waters is familiar with the natural and cultural history of the valley. He effusively catalogues the biological treasures of the landscape, with long passages lovingly listing plants and their uses. In this way, he signals his delight in the richness of nature and suggests the abundance of the natural world and its more-than-sufficiency for the people who reside in the valley. Their tenancy, it would seem, has not diminished the wealth of nature. Waters also incorporates into his narrative the history of the valley, describing its indigenous inhabitants, the incursion of French fur trappers, the arrival of Spanish settlers and their endowment with land grants, the transfer of control to the new Yankee government following the conquest of 1846, and the subsequent difficulties and injustices involved with measuring and confirming the land grants. Finally, he itemizes the gradual incursion of Anglo-style industrialism, epitomized by the dam. This is all useful knowledge for enhancing a sense of storied residence in the region and it further serves to highlight the elements of injustice that provide a historical context for the struggle over the dam.

Maria understands that the dam means that people will lose their land, both from submergence beneath the reservoir and from their inability to pay the new taxes levied for the water district, so she rallies her neighbors against it. Her strategy is indirect, "not opposing it with any reason, but calling forth the feeling for the land it would supplant" (141). For example, Maria revives the custom of blessing the fields on San Isidro day. San Isidro is the patron saint of farmers, and it is a common custom in the Hispano Southwest for his image to be carried in a procession through the community's fields on May 15. As portrayed in *People of the Valley,* this custom has not been followed for some time, but Maria revives it as an act of cultural resistance. One old farmer tells Maria that "it has not been a good thing to forget this old custom of late, and that it is a good thing to continue it again. . . . Madre!" he exclaims, "I had forgotten how beautiful the fresh black earth looks from here on high" [ellipsis in original] (140). This scene nicely illustrates Nabhan's suggestion that seasonal rites can enhance people's "storied residence" in their place, an awareness that will lead them to defend and restore it.

Maria battles the dam on many fronts. However as construction begins and people are evicted from their homes, Maria relents, admitting oracularly that "I see now that nothing will stop this Máquina. So this I know, it is for each man and all peoples to become one with their defeat, and so rise above it.

This dam has defeated me. I give in to it wholly. Thus I am free of it; it cannot touch me" (184). She has, perhaps, expressed a wise paradox to live by, a transcendent philosophy that engages the world (she did resist the dam, after all) but that seeks to rise above circumstances. Yet to readers concerned with social injustice or environmental degradation, her response is ungratifying. It suggests that a retreat from social and political engagement is sometimes the course of wisdom. To the considerable degree that the novel portrays Anglo-style "progress" as inevitable, to the degree that it makes the forces of domestic colonization seem unstoppable, it figures resistance, however heroic, as futile.

And yet one doesn't wish to overstate the case. For reading against the grain of most of the criticism of Waters, and against the grain of some of his own inclinations, one still hears the plea, however muted, that Anglo-style progress is not always a good thing, that people have a right to the integrity of their culture and that our loss of faith in the natural processes of the land deprives us of a fulfilling relationship to our place.

No novelist has engaged the issues of social justice and environmentalism in northern New Mexico more directly, more sympathetically, or with more surprising twists, than has John Nichols. Like Waters, Nichols eschews being labeled as a "regional" writer, but his reasons differ. Where Waters and his critics often aspire to universal significance through the explication of abstract meaning (often Jungian archetypes of the collective unconscious), Nichols aspires to universal significance through his Marxist portrayal of the global class struggle. Nichols explains that when he published *The Milagro Beanfield War* in 1974 he "was disappointed when critics called it a 'regional novel.' I thought my characters and my community were as universal as anything written by Faulkner or Carson McCullers or Émile Zola." And, he concludes, "local Taoseños asked me how I could know so much about their culture after living in New Mexico only a short while. I replied that ninety percent of it was universal" ("Everything I Always Wanted to Know about the West," 244).

Perhaps, but the claim that his portrayal of Chicano villages is mostly universal is also a tad evasive. For when his neighbors ask him how he manages to know so much about them, they politely hint at a complaint stated decades earlier by Cleofas Jaramillo, a native of nearby Arroyo Hondo. Jaramillo expressed annoyance at "these smart Americans" who make money portraying Hispanic culture, while members of that culture "sit back and listen" (*Romance of a Little Village Girl,* 173). Paula Gunn Allen, who grew up in Cubero, New Mexico, has more overtly complained about Nichols, asking, "how come it's the writer with the New England literary perspective who gets to define northern New Mexico rather than the northern New Mexico writer?" (qtd. in Dunaway).

Allen raises a reasonable question, one that signals distress at the process by which colonialism is played out in the publishing world. In choosing to write about the largely Chicano towns of New Mexico, Nichols has taken on an ethical burden that cannot be evaded simply by claiming to have written a work that is "ninety percent universal." Viewed skeptically, Nichols' works of social protest on behalf of Chicano agropastoral culture can be interpreted as themselves appropriations of voice, as further incursions of the very colonialism they seek to decry (see Dasenbrock).

Several scholars of Chicano literature, however, have considered and sought to allay such concerns. Francisco A. Lomelí and Donaldo W. Urioste, for example, suggest that Nichols' portrayal of Chicano culture is just. Lomelí and Urioste use the term *literatura chicanesca* to distinguish Chicano literature—that is, literature by and about Chicanos—from literature that is about Chicanos but is written by Anglos. In their consideration, Nichols fares well. Lomelí and Urioste conclude that *Milagro Beanfield War* is "perhaps the most convincing chicanesca novel. Written after Nichols studied his subject matter extensively, thus capturing local color, customs, legends, beliefs and geographical particularities with the insight of a keen eye." It is, they conclude "a good example for non-Chicanos to follow" (qtd. in Bus, 215).

John Nichols settled in Taos in 1969. He headed for New Mexico, he says, not as an escape to a bucolic land of enchantment, but, on the contrary, because "New Mexico seemed to resemble a colonial country where political struggle could be as clearly focused as it was in four-fifths of the rest of the world" (*Fragile Beauty*, 5). Nichols soon immersed himself in reading about the history and culture of the area and became involved with the Tres Rios Association, a coalition of acequias organized to prevent the construction of the Indian Camp Dam, a project that would trigger socioeconomic changes threatening the local Chicano farmers. Nichols also wrote for a leftist publication, *The New Mexico Review*, covering the political conflicts in the region. Further, he conducted research for Legal Aid lawyers in the process of which, he says, he "learned more about land and water rights history than I could ever have dreamed possible" (*Fragile Beauty*, 11). All of this, combined with his friendships and conversation with local Chicano farmers and activists, and his outings to fish the rivers and hike the mesas, added up to an outstanding bioregional education.

With the information he gained from his research and activism, and influenced by the "raucous, comic style" of the Teatro Campesino (*Fragile Beauty*, 8), Nichols composed *The Milagro Beanfield War* in a burst of manic energy. *The Milagro Beanfield War*, along with the subsequent volumes of his New Mexico Trilogy, *The Magic Journey* and *The Nirvana Blues*, explores the various nuances of the struggle for social justice in northern New Mexico. In *The Milagro Beanfield War*, Joe Mondragón decides to let irrigation water into a field that he has inherited from his late father even though he has lost the water rights for the field to Ladd Devine III, a local development mogul. Describing the basis of Joe's decision, Nichols educates us on the historical background necessary to appreciate the social justice dimension of Joe's defiant gesture. Nichols details a litany of abuses Mondragón and his community have suffered at the hands of the Forest Service, the state government and, most recently, "the local malevolent despot, Ladd Devine the Third" (20). Specifically relating to water matters, Nichols further explains that "Milagro itself was half a ghost town, and all the old west side bean-fields were barren, because over thirty-five years ago, during some complicated legal and political maneuverings known as the 1935 Interstate Water Compact, much of Milagro's Indian Creek water had been reallocated to big-time farmers down in the southeast portion of the state or in Texas, leaving folks like Joe Mondragón high and much too dry" (21). Nichols makes it clear, then, that Joe Mondragón's simple gesture of defiance—opening a small headgate so water could flow into his father's muddy field—is motivated by a long history of oppression and rich with complex political implications.

While underscoring the social justice dimension of Joe Mondragón's act of resistance, Nichols delights to undermine our simple notions of what is good for the environment, challenging what he sees as a superficial middle-class environmentalism. Nowhere does he do this better than with the character of Kyril Montana, the undercover cop who's assigned to derail Joe Mondragón's revolt. Montana is an environmentalist and an ethical hunter who belongs to all the right groups. He "thoroughly enjoyed the outdoors with or without a gun. He was a member of the Isaac Walton League, the Sierra Club, and Ducks Unlimited" (95). Nichols makes it clear that Montana is not a cliched, brutal, thuggish cop. He and his wife, we're told "were a clean-cut couple with clean-cut kids, a suburban house with a water sprinkler on the manicured front lawn and a small pool in back" (41). Here, though, we begin to sense Nichols' critique of middle-class environmentalism, for the water sprinkler and the family pool suggest a squandering of water, a misguided desire for class status and respectability at the expense of the environment. Immediately upon returning from a meeting on how to sabotage Joe

Mondragón's efforts, Montana goes for a swim. In the pool, he and his wife "kissed once more and flicked a little water at each other and rubbed noses, chuckling together, standing in about five feet of softly lapping water, enjoying the peaceful evening" (103). This seemingly innocent and endearing scene shimmers in a more sinister light when we contrast it with Joe Mondragón's plight and with Montana's participation in the efforts to deprive him of his historically sanctioned water. Indeed throughout *The Milagro Beanfield War* and the other works in the New Mexico Trilogy swimming pools symbolize and serve as scenes of bourgeois corruption, seduction, and decadence.

Another scene dramatizes even more overtly just how complicated matters of environmental protection can be. Toward the novel's end, Montana is leading a posse of reluctant local Chicanos up into the mountains in search of Joe Mondragón. They pause for lunch, then Montana sends the inept posse home and plans to continue the search alone: "Suddenly the agent noticed all the refuse that had been left behind, pieces of waxed paper and tinfoil, discarded Baggies, a few aluminum bean dip cans, empty cigarette packages, and some crushed coffee cups. And it angered him, the way people mistreated wilderness. So before shoving off, cursing softly under his breath, he canvassed the area, collecting the garbage, which he crushed and buried in his pack" (379). Montana is self-righteous in his indignation at the way people mistreat wilderness, but he's oblivious to the fact that his own green yard and swimming pool, by depleting a scarce life-giving resource, are more harmful to the environment than superficial litter. The irony is further compounded by the fact that Montana is working as an agent for those who seek to injure the land in a far more egregious manner than littering. Nichols' point is not to condone littering, but to grant us a sense of proportion.

Devon Peña laments that "in Taos . . . environmentally correct members of the white middle class are now among the forces displacing natives" ("Los Animalitos," 32). Nichols illustrates the details of this process throughout the New Mexico Trilogy. For example, in *The Magic Journey* he explains how "pressured by a well-meaning but politically naïve ecology-oriented group of middle-class Anglo citizens known as the Amigos of Chamisa Valley, the town council had recently passed an ordinance barring outhouses within Chamisaville limits" (355). The consequence of this ordinance is that "approximately one hundred impoverished families, unable to afford indoor toilets and a sewer hookup, would either have to sell out or mortgage their homes in order to make improvements, incurring debts impossible to meet and only forestalling for a year or two the ultimate loss of their homes" (355). A similar issue arises regarding junked cars in yards, affronts to middle-class aesthetics, bad for a tourist industry marketing the "Land of Enchantment," but not really harmful to the environment. "Then the well-meaning Amigos of Chamisa Valley," Nichols writes, "had decided all junk cars desecrating every indigenous family's front and backyards were a tremendous aesthetic eyesore necessitating immediate correction" (356). An ordinance is passed; poor people are fined; the junked cars, a valuable source of spare parts, are hauled away; and the net result is to transfer more land away from Chicano agropastoralists and into the hands of Anglo real estate developers. In these cases, what seem like gains for the environment at the perhaps lamentable but justifiable expense of social justice, are, in the end, revealed to be injurious both to social justice and to the environment on whose behalf they are implemented.

The Magic Journey follows the machinations of a local cabal, the Committee for the Betterment of Chamisaville, tracing the rise of industrial tourism in Chamisaville and its displacement of the local people. Rodey McQueen, a local developer, explains the long-term scheme to his cohorts: "with the industry and people we've already brought in . . . property taxes are going to zoom." The local farmers, living on subsistence agriculture, will be forced to sell out, and, he exalts, "half the county [will be] on the auction block inside ten years." In twenty years, he brags, he'll "have all land out of agricultural production and onto the market" (28).

In The Milagro Beanfield War and The Magic Journey, both Anglo and Chicano members of the local community organize to resist the forces that assault them. Political struggle, however comic, disorganized, and confused, still seems a viable response. In the third novel of the trilogy, The Nirvana Blues, however, evil has triumphed. The plot of this novel, a jocose satire of the "hippie era" in Taos, is launched by the main character, Joe Miniver, and his desire to purchase the last remaining farm in Chicano hands in the valley. By the end of the 1970s, we're told, "Only Eloy Irribarren, a stubborn old man, hung on to his tiny farm, which everybody but everybody wished to wrest from his grasp" (19). Miniver, a character a lot like Nichols, and perhaps a self parody, decides he'll buy Eloy's farm, transferring it to Anglo hands but at least protecting it from development. But to do so, he needs to raise cash and so decides to engage in just one big cocaine deal. The travails of trying to pull this off, and the response of others in town who want the land for themselves, initiate the crazy shenanigans of most of the novel.

Nichols understands the importance of the acequia system to the vitality of the traditional communities. In a very real sense the irrigation ditches both embody and enable the culture's survival. Near the end of *Nirvana Blues*, Eloy Irribarren has been shot in a bank heist gone wrong and goes home to die. Bleeding, he and Joe go to clear out the irrigation ditch one last time. In this scene, Nichols illustrates the destruction of acequia agriculture and its replacement by a middle-class suburban culture indifferent to its significance: "The acequia wandered through backyards, it almost touched the foundations of newly built homes." And, he continues, "some newcomers occasionally used the acequia water for their lawns and gardens. But basically, the agricultural area the ditch had once served was extinct" (508). The newcomers are using the ditch as a dumping ground, and Joe and Eloy remove "smashed tricycles, overturned doghouses, and bald car-tires"; ironically, they also move aside "a dozen fifty-five-gallon oil drums, the refuse of a home builder who was into solar collectors" (508). As Eloy and Joe finish cleaning out the ditch and coax water through it, we see that nature, too, is restored: "Birds gathered in nearby trees, their sharp eyes hunting worms and bugs carried to the surface. A sparrow hawk landed on a dead cottonwood branch: head cocked, it searched the field for fleeing mice. Magpies swooped from the sky and waddled through inch-deep puddles, spearing tidbits. Redwing blackbirds, grackles, and starlings alighted in the water and began to gobble" (514).

As the old and bleeding Eloy nears death, his last act is to splash ditch water on his face, a sacramental gesture, a last rite of sorts. This scene illustrates both the literal and symbolic importance of the acequias and, especially, of *la limpia*, the spring ditch cleaning. This cleansing becomes the archetypal symbol of belonging, a ritual of renewal that binds a person, a family, and a community to each other and to the land. Though he is dying, Eloy Irribarren must clean the ditch one last time, engaging in a gesture of faith that hardly seems warranted by circumstances.

A defender of the natural world as well as a proponent of social justice, Nichols has been dismayed by the conflicts between environmentalists and the small Chicano communities of northern New Mexico. After the Sierra Club opposed efforts of Ganados del Valle, a sheep raising and weaving cooperative in Rio Arriba County, to open up land for sheep grazing, Nichols lectured the Santa Fe Sierra Club chapter. He explained how much of the old-time Chicano culture in the area "has been working class and economically deprived," but, he continued, "it has had a strong sense of community and a tradition of responsible land management." By contrast, he explained, "environmentalists tend to be relative newcomers and middle class." In conclusion, he warned that "a critical class struggle is taking place and the environmental movement is in danger of being on the wrong side" ("Case for Social Ecology," 92–93).

Nichols supports a strong environmentalism, but he recognizes that it must be informed by a well-developed class consciousness and an appreciation for how ethnic diversity alters perceptions of ecological integrity. He is aware that environmentalism and movements for social justice could be, but are not always, symbiotic, especially when environmentalism is overly dependent on middle-class Anglo perceptions and fails to accommodate the perspectives of working-class people and Chicanos.

Jimmy Santiago Baca, from Albuquerque, lives at the southern fringe of the Upper Rio Grande bioregion. Best known as a poet who discovered his art while in prison, Baca's work extends far beyond those confines. In his celebration of natural cycles, in his use of rich metaphors derived from local imagery, and in his awareness of how personal identity emerges from a sense of place, Baca is one of North America's great bioregional poets.

Baca's semiautobiographical epic poem "Martín" shows how closely his identity is derived from his homeland and how his mythic consciousness emerges from the history of his place. When Baca/Martín (the author and his character are almost, but not quite, equivalent) is only two years old, his destitute and dissolute parents abandon him, first to his grandmother and then to an orphanage. With this abandonment, he says, "the corn seedling of my heart / withered—like an earth worm out of earth" (5). He repeatedly portrays this abandonment as an uprooting: "Your departure uprooted me mother," he exclaims at one point (13). In this imagery we sense that land and family are synonymous.

Later, in young adulthood, Baca/Martín departs for the West Coast, but feels that in doing so he has betrayed his homeland, his personal Mother Earth. He declares his remorse in a sequence abundant with imagery blending language, self, and land.

I have been lost from you Mother Earth
No longer
does your language of rain wear away my thoughts,
nor your language of fresh morning air
wear away my face,
nor your language of roots and blossoms
wear away my bones.
But when I return, I will become your child again,
let your green alfalfa hands take me,

let your maiz roots plunge into me
and give myself to you again,
with the crane, the elm tree and the sun.
$$(7-8)$$

A psychological need for a sense of home, for a mother, and for stability leads him to claim the Mother Earth of his New Mexico landscape as his homeland. He will give to it the allegiance due a mother.

His geo-mythic wanderings take Baca/Martín to the Quarai Ruins in the Manzano Mountains south of Albuquerque. Abandoned in the 1670s, these ruins are from a Pueblo community appropriated by the Spanish, a place where Pueblos and captured Apaches lived for several decades with their Spanish conquerors before Apache raids caused the settlers to flee. It is a site of intense *mestizaje*—a crucible where cultural blending created a proto-Chicano identity. Here, Baca/Martín has an epiphany, a powerful mythic and literal identification with the soil of his Chicano homeland. After riding his motorcycle up to the ruins, he says;

I step into the open rock-pit
hollowed in earth
with flat rock door facing east,
pinch red clay and chew
my teeth black with earth prayer,
                    then speak with QUARAÍ—
O QUARAÍ! Shape
the grit and sediment I am,
mineral de Nuevo Mejico.

$$(39)$$

Here, Baca/Martín establishes a literal communion with the land. He consumes it, he speaks through teeth black with soil, and arises from the pit at Quarai reborn as a son of the Mother Earth, offspring of the land, recognizing that he is quite literally composed of the "mineral de Nuevo Mejico."

Baca has numerous poems that celebrate the acequia culture and suggest its importance in his community and to the natural world. In "Spring" he notes how the beginning of irrigation season marks the start of that season. We see how both the human and natural communities are enriched by the irrigation ditches. Each spring, headgates are opened and snowmelt waters "gush, lunge, and hurl down Río Abajo to community fields, / fill the dry ditches and canals" (*Black Mesa Poems*, 38). The water, he demonstrates, nurtures "Plants, bushes, weeds," and the poet witnesses tadpoles and catfish in the murky flow (38). He describes blue-grey doves, geese, crawdads, spiders, snakes, frogs, lilac leaves, and sandhill cranes—a rich biodiversity brought to life by the swell of ditch water. In "Too Much of a Good Thing" he worries that an early spring is causing the high mountain snow to melt too soon and too quickly—an effect that can be exacerbated by clear-cut logging. "What happens / when I need to irrigate pastures / in summer / and there is no water?" he worries. He contrasts this concern with "two suntanned ladies" he overhears in a shopping mall who, disconnected from the bioregion's rhythms, praise "our wonderful weather." These recent arrivals, divorced from the land, don't realize the consequences of the weather they praise. He wonders what "a farmer's wife would tell them" (*Black Mesa Poems*, 27).

In addition to sustaining natural biodiversity, the ditches also nurture and connect the community. In many of his poems we see how the paths along the ditchbanks serve as an informal network where neighbors meet. For example in "Custom," Baca jogs along the ditchbanks and meets an old neighbor, Juan, astride his horse. Baca admires the man's ease on horseback, a true caballero. Juan, he realizes, isn't just on a "relaxing ride on the *acequia*," rather, he is responding to "an ancient custom ingrained in his blood" (*Black Mesa Poems*, 87). The ditchbank paths bind the community together in a more intimate way than the busy roads and highways can.

These celebrations of the acequia culture, however, are tempered by his awareness that he lives in a conquered homeland and that, in spite of their storied identity with it, his people's hold on the place is tenuous and constantly threatened. His poem "Invasions" succinctly captures both the historical and contemporary conflicts. The poem begins as the narrator leaves early in the morning for a fishing trip to the Jemez River. Along the way, he imagines that "Coronado rode / through this light, dark / green brush" (*Black Mesa Poems*, 70). His excursion calls to mind the history of the area, of Esteban and mythic Cíbola, of Jemez and Pecos Pueblos, and the revolt of 1690. While standing in the very waters of time, tossing his baited hook for trout and contemplating a history as rich as that anywhere in the United States, the narrator links himself with the complex tales of this place and realizes that

I am the end result
of Conquistadores,
Black Moors,

American Indians,
and Europeans,
bloods rainbowing
and scintillating
in me

         (71)

Later, he climbs a hill and peers out "as my ancestors did," but now he sees not advancing conquistadors or cavalry troops but "vacation houses" and "sun decks and travel trailers," all of which constitute, he declares, a "new invasion" (72). The vacation homes and trailers suggest the arrival of amenity migrants, a seemingly innocuous contingent compared with armed and armored conquistadors, but one with as much if not more potential to alter and injure the prevailing land and cultures. To a great extent, the children of the conquistadors have assimilated to the contingencies of the bioregion; whether the owners of vacation houses and travel trailers will likewise assimilate remains much in doubt.

This invasion becomes more personal, and the connection between social justice and environmental harm becomes clearer, in his poem "Roots." Baca begins this poem, as so many, by connecting the narrator to his place. After describing a battered old cottonwood tree, apt symbol of his Chicano culture's endurance, he then says, "I come back to myself / near this tree, and think of my roots / in this land" (*Black Mesa Poems,* 11). The narrator then recounts working with his grandfather in the fields when an agent of the government arrives to tell his grandfather he must move, the land is no longer his. This poem takes our abstract awareness of land grant injustice and rivets our attention on its tragic particulars in the lives of real people. The narrator's grandfather responds by lifting "a handful of earth," and replying to the agent in Spanish that this dust "carries the way of his life." The grandfather underscores his bond to the place by asserting that "family blood ran through this land" and "My heart is a root in this earth!" (12). The government agent, of course, does not understand Spanish, further signaling the invasive and alien character of his power over the grandfather. Even if the agent did speak Spanish, however, they would not understand each other, for, both literally and figuratively, they speak a different language.

In their resistance to this sort of displacement, some Chicano activists have lost their lives. Baca memorializes his uncle, Antonio Ce De Baca, in the poem "Mi Tío Baca El Poeta de Socorro." This "Poet de Socorro," Baca tells us, "whose poems roused *la gente* / to demand their land rights back," was murdered in the dark of night by masked intruders (*Black Mesa Poems,* 73).

In "Black Mesa" Baca recalls the destruction when Interstate 25 was built through the area in 1968. Like the dam in Waters' *People of the Valley,* the highway is an apt symbol for the intrusion of an alien, mechanistic culture that lacks respect for the land and for the traditional people who live on it. The highway cuts through Black Mesa, near Baca's farmstead in Albuquerque's South Valley. On a hike through the area, Baca recalls how Rito, a "brown beret Chicano activist" who "tried to stop / them blasting Black Mesa" was "murdered here / by sheriffs." During his hike across the mesa many years later, Baca muses that "under my hiking boots his blood / crossbeds minerals / and forms into red crystals" (*Black Mesa Poems,* 119). As Baca/Martín is reborn with the discovery that he is "mineral de Nuevo Mejico," so the red crystals of Rito's mineralizing blood return reciprocally to the earth. We sense that, while title to the land may be wrested from the Chicano community, the blood they've spilled to defend it grants a more enduring bond than that conferred by mere title of ownership.

As Baca hikes across the Mesa, he recalls the destruction the highway project caused:

Sky showered stones
at children playing
on ditchbanks,
dynamite blasts cracked porches,
foundations and walls
with shuddering volts.

                    (118–19)

This literal and immediate damage to homes and irrigation ditches suggests an attack on the community, but the highway, with its indifference to place, suggestively implies a much more ominous assault, an assault on the very idea of community itself.

Baca's dismay at the destruction, violation, and death, however, is tempered when he encounters a series of petroglyphs: "Etched on slabs, / wolf and coyote wear / skins of stone" (119). Admiring them, touching them, he senses their meaning; they are, he declares, "a narrative of love / for animals and earth" (120). And, in spite of dynamite blasts and highways, they endure. Later, he remarks, how "the old man who lives / in stone / offers me a different view / of life and death" (120). Renewed by his glimpse of the petroglyphs, gratified by the deep historical perspective they provide, and inspired by those ancestors who inscribed "a narrative of love / for animals and earth" into the very rocks, Baca pledges "to speak the heart's language. / To write the story of my soul / I trace in the silence and stone / of Black Mesa" (120–21).

Whether hiking across Black Mesa, strolling an acequia ditchbank, or rising from the ruins at Quaraí, Jimmy Santiago Baca calls us to witness the injustice he and his people have suffered, but also to share his delight in the natural and cultural richness of the land they continue to inhabit and defend.

In his talk to the Santa Fe Sierra Club chapter, John Nichols argued for the urgent need to merge concern for social justice with environmental organizing. "If the environmental movement," he told them, "can develop an understanding of and a sympathy with social, economic, and cultural issues, wildness—and community—stand a much better chance. I hope," he concluded, that "we can learn to base our future struggles on this social ecology, where conservation and human equality go hand in hand" ("Case for Social Ecology," 95). Gary Nabhan suggests that this effort to synthesize justice and environmentalism is not simply good politics, but good ecology as well. "Ultimately," he explains, "the most potent way of conserving biological diversity may be to protect the diversity of the cultures that have stewarded the plant and animal communities on which our agriculture is based" ("Let Us Now Praise Native Crops," 223). Literary works such as those considered here by Waters, Nichols, and Baca simultaneously expand our notions of justice, enrich our sense of belonging in the more-than-human world, and, not insignificantly, alter our ideas of the function and the power of literature.

For far too long the appreciation and assessment of literary works has followed a path of growing abstraction. The virtues of a literary work, and the merits of a literary scholar, have grown to depend upon the ability of the scholar to subject the work to increasingly abstract and abstruse levels of analysis. One ought to ask whose interests are served by such a process. Not, I think, the interests of poor, minority, and working-class peoples, nor, I dare say, the interests of the increasingly debilitated natural communities with which we share our world. I hope that these bioregionally informed considerations of the ecological and social justice dimensions of selected literary works from the upper Rio Grande watershed suggest the potential for literature and scholarship to move in a different, more fruitful direction, towards an engagement with the real work to be done to promote both justice in our social relations and generosity and restraint in our relations with the natural matrix that surrounds and sustains us.

WORKS CITED

Baca, Jimmy Santiago. *Black Mesa Poems.* New York: New Directions, 1989.

———. *Martín, & Meditations on the South Valley.* New York: New Directions, 1987.

Bus, Heiner. "John Nichols' *The Milagro Beanfield War* (1974): The View from Within and/or the View from Without?" In *Missions in Conflict: Essays on U.S.–Mexican Relations and Chicano Culture,* edited by Renate von Bardeleben, Dietrich Briesemeister, and Juan Bruce-Novoa, 215–24. Tübingen: Gunter Narr Verlag, 1986.

Dasenbrock, Reed Way. "Southwest of What? Southwestern Literature as a Form of Frontier Literature." In *Desert, Garden, Margin, Range: Literature on the American Frontier,* edited by Eric Heyne, 123–32. New York: Twayne, 1992.

deBuys, William. *Enchantment and Exploitation: The Life and Hard Times of a New Mexico Mountain Range.* Albuquerque: University of New Mexico Press, 1985.

Dunaway, David. "John Nichols." On *Writing the Southwest.* Audiocassette. Albuquerque: KUNM-FM, 1995.

Eastlake, William. "The Word Trader." In *Frank Waters: Man and Mystic,* edited by Vine Deloria Jr., 3–5. Athens, OH: Swallow, 1993.

Jaramillo, Cleofas. *Romance of a Little Village Girl.* San Antonio: Naylor, 1955.

Martínez, Rubén O. "Social Action Research, Bioregionalism, and the Upper Rio Grande." In *Chicano Culture, Ecology, Politics: Subversive Kin,* edited by Devon G. Peña, 58–78. Tucson: University of Arizona Press, 1998.

Nabhan, Gary Paul. "Epilogue: Restorying the Sonorous Landscape." In *Cultures of Habitat: On Nature, Culture, and Story,* 311–19. Washington, D.C.: Counterpoint, 1997.

———. "Let Us Now Praise Native Crops: An American Cornucopia." In *Cultures of Habitat: On Nature, Culture, and Story,* 209–23. Washington, D.C.: Counterpoint, 1997.

———. "Missing the Boat: Why Cultural Diversity Didn't Make It onto the Ark." In *Cultures of Habitat: On Nature, Culture, and Story,* 30–42. Washington, D.C.: Counterpoint, 1997.

Nichols, John. "The Case for Social Ecology." In *Dancing on the Stones: Selected Essays,* 92–95. Albuquerque: University of New Mexico Press, 2000.

———. "Everything I Always Wanted to Know about the West, I Learned in New York City." In *Dancing on the Stones: Selected Essays,* 237–47. Albuquerque: University of New Mexico Press, 2000.

———. *A Fragile Beauty: John Nichols' Milagro Country.* Salt Lake City: Gibbs Smith, 1987.

———. *The Magic Journey.* New York: Holt, 1978.

———. *The Milagro Beanfield War.* New York: Holt, Rinehart and Winston, 1974; New York: Ballantine, 1994.

———. *The Nirvana Blues.* New York: Holt, 1981.

Peña, Devon G. "Los Animalitos: Culture, Ecology, and the Politics of Place in the Upper Rio Grande." In *Chicano Culture, Ecology, Politics: Subversive Kin,* edited by Devon G. Peña, 25–57. Tucson: University of Arizona Press, 1998.

———, ed. *Chicano Culture, Ecology, Politics: Subversive Kin.* Tucson: University of Arizona Press, 1998.

Waters, Frank. *People of the Valley.* New York: Farrar & Rinehart, 1941; Athens, OH: Swallow, 1969.

14

SAVING THE SALMON, SAVING THE PEOPLE

Environmental Justice and Columbia River Tribal Literatures

Janis Johnson

For many American Indians in the Northwest, salmon is a treasured resource and numinous being. It has provided essential nutrition, spiritual meaning, education, entertainment, and economic livelihoods for generations of Umatilla, Warm Springs, Yakama, and Nez Perce families. Before the reservation period, these Columbia River tribes organized their lives around the life cycle and mythical personality of the salmon, which is present in the rivers only at certain times of the year. By the 1990s, the millions of salmon that once teemed in the Columbia and Snake River Basins for centuries had dwindled to fewer than ten thousand on the Snake (Monks, 22). In 1999 the Nez Perce Indians counted only seven Snake River sockeye salmon. Today, several species of Northwest salmon appear on the Endangered Species List (Monks, 22). To the Umatilla, Warm Springs, Yakama, and Nez Perce Tribes, the impending extinction of the salmon signals a threat to their own salmon-based cultures.

Salmon are "anadromous," meaning they hatch in freshwater upriver streams, swim hundreds of miles downstream to the ocean where they mature, then swim back upstream, returning to the place of their birth in order to spawn and die. But every season, fewer fish complete this cycle due to human-caused degradation of salmon habitat and decreased water quality. Over one hundred federal hydroelectric dams on the Columbia River System have contributed to this degradation, impairing the salmon's ability to reach the ocean and return. For the Columbia River tribes this is a tragedy of immense proportion. They see the future of human existence in the area tied directly to the survival of the salmon, since the habitat that supports the fish also supports the plants, animals, and humans (Landeen and Pinkham, 1).

As a unifying and integral element of Northwest indigenous cultures, the salmon may soon provoke a test of the United States' commitment to environmental justice and to its treaty obligations to these Indian nations. In this essay I detail connections between the Columbia River tribes' struggles to save the salmon and the environmental justice movement, particularly indigenous environmental justice actions. I then discuss the history of the Columbia River dams and their effects on Northwest tribes, and the current movement to remove four dams from the Columbia River hydrosystem. From there I analyze salmon as a character in Northwest indigenous literature—specifically, Nez Perce tribal mythology and contemporary poetry—and as a symbol in several ads put out by mainstream environmentalist organizations protesting the extinction of the fish. Reading Northwest tribal literature is particularly important to an understanding of Indian responses to the salmon crisis because it elucidates the worldview and values of these indigenous peoples and can inform our understanding of activist responses to the extinction of the salmon. This literature presents a system of relations between beings that can encourage right relations between human and nonhuman species to provide for environmental sustainability and social justice. Nez Perce storytellers refer to this system of relations as "pity." I look at the notion of "pity" as something very similar to the principles of environmental justice which emerged from the First National People of Color Environmental Leadership Summit in 1991. I argue that these environmental justice principles are an articulation of ancient concepts like that of "pity," but in modern environmental terms.

American Indian peoples are land-oriented. Specific places are enormously important because they are sacred to Indian communities. Indigenous peoples feel great affection for these places and believe they have a responsibility to care for them (Whalen, 30). Colonialist development and expansion, however, has been a long assault upon Indian lands and environments, and laws and policies of the mainstream culture have never provided justice for the tribes and their lands. Treaties have been broken or violated, and Indian nations' sovereignty—their right to self-determination and self-rule—has often been ignored. This is why Indians feel that they have never been treated justly. For example, the original treaty the Nez Perce Tribe negotiated with the U.S. government in 1855 was superseded by the Treaty of 1863, despite the leaders of the adversely affected bands of the tribe not having signed it. The 1863 Nez Perce Treaty radically reduced the size of the Nez Perce Reservation, caused the eviction of Chief Joseph's band from its homeland, and resulted in the so-called Nez Perce War of 1877, the bloodiest and most devastating event in tribal history. In addition, although both treaties recognize the Nez Perces' right to fish in off-reservation "usual and accustomed places," the Indians have at times been forcefully denied access to some of these spots by state fish and game agents. Not only have indigenous concepts of justice been violated, but the United States has violated its own legal system and therefore has violated even its own articulated concepts of justice. Because of Indian peoples' "long experience dealing with colonial oppression, they recognize that justice is dependent on the individuals, groups, and places involved," and that "justice has no universal meaning" (Adamson, 73). Thus, Indians must define justice for themselves; they "need once again to enforce their own environmental values, unfettered by regulations and environmental practices of the industrial state" (Weaver, *Defending Mother Earth*, 18).

American Indians and other peoples of color and low-income groups define what they see as environmental justice issues, conceiving of the environment as encompassing both humans and nonhumans, consistent with most tribal worldviews.[1] This suggests an idea of the environment and nature as "community," of seeing place as "geographic, cultural, and emotional—where humans and environments converge" (Di Chiro, 318). Giovanna Di Chiro in "Nature as Community: The Convergence of Environment and Social Justice" suggests that "this idea of community presupposes connection to and interconnectedness with other groups, other species, and the natural environment through everyday experiences with family, comradeship, and work" (318). For many Indians, the natural world is a significant part of not only tribal identity but also daily life, and its degradation poses an intimate threat. American Indian environmental justice actions include efforts to reintroduce buffalo to the Plains, prevent the destruction of the Everglades, and keep nuclear waste from being dumped on Indian lands. These actions are occurring precisely where Indian families live and work; their physical, emotional and spiritual health exists in direct relation to the health of these places.

The Columbia River tribes' efforts to save the salmon exemplify indigenous environmental justice actions. These tribes dispute definitions of justice which support political actions, development plans, and court decisions that are leading to the extinction of the salmon. The western system of "justice," founded on private property and individual rights, values the human over the nonhuman, the individual over the communal, and sometimes—despite its claim of colorblindness—the white person over the person or community of color. This system supports a parallel assault on the Northwest tribes' salmon-based cultures by threatening their ability to survive.

The history of the Columbia River dams and of fisheries management is a long story of broken promises and denials of justice to the Northwest tribes and their lands. In 1855, the Warm Springs, Yakama, Umatilla, and Nez Perce Tribes signed a treaty with the U.S. government. In return for enormous cessions of land these tribes were guaranteed their own reservations and the right to fish, hunt, and gather traditional foods outside of reservation boundaries in their "usual and accustomed places" (Landeen and Pinkham, 59). These tribes have lived for centuries along the Columbia River and its tributaries with fish and fishing occupying a central focus in tribal life. For decades the tribes warned state and federal agencies of decreasing salmon populations, and shouldered a disproportionate burden of conservation efforts through reduced fishing, despite poverty, illness, and unemployment rates many times greater than those of non-Indians (Sonner, 2D; Berg, "Endangered Species Act Update," 18). This disproportionate burden is unfair by mainstream standards, and results in injustice for the Indians.

For most Columbia River tribal members, salmon contributes directly to the quality of daily life, through ceremonial, subsistence, and/or commercial means. These tribes hold "First Salmon" ceremonies to honor the fish each spring when they make their appearance in the rivers and streams. With its heart-healthy oils, salmon has been a staple of these Indians' diet for thousands of years. Tribal members have observed a decline in their health and life span along with the decline in salmon as they are forced to eat less fish (Smith and Berg, 14). Generations of Columbia Basin Indian families made a livelihood catching and trading, and, later, selling salmon. In fact the destruction of salmon runs caused many Northwest natives to enter a money economy, when salmon could no longer be used as a reliable trade commodity (Smith and Berg, 10). Many Indians who previously would have made a living fishing now are employed in tribal fish restoration facilities (Smith and Berg, 12). Reduced numbers of fish, reduced fishing, and failures by the U.S. government to protect the fish and the treaty fishing rights of the tribes deprives the tribes of resources necessary for their meaningful survival. Because salmon is a pillar of Columbia River tribal culture, its loss contributes to the adverse circumstances of the tribes. These circumstances include poverty rates between 27 and 44 percent; unemployment rates between 19 and 26 percent, and up to 80 percent in the winter; and death rates between 20 percent and 2.3 times higher than nontribal neighbors. The tribes are currently harvesting salmon at rates between 1 and 10 percent of traditional levels, and 78 percent of the tribes' treaty-protected lands are in nontribal hands (Meyer Resources).

In 1977, the four Columbia River 1855 Treaty Tribes, as they are often called, combined their fish committees to form the Columbia River Inter-tribal Fish Commission (CRITFC), which represents the four tribes' fishing interests (Ulrich, 154–56). In 1999, in an effort to prevent total extinction of wild Snake River salmon, CRITFC called for the breaching of Ice Harbor, Lower Monumental, Little Goose, and Lower Granite Dams on the lower Snake River in southeastern Washington State near the Idaho border (Monks, 30). Breaching means to remove the earthen portion from a dam's concrete structure, allowing the river to return to a free flowing state—a 140-mile stretch in this case. The four Snake River dams have been identified by scientists as particularly harmful to Snake River salmon runs, and many scientists believe breaching dams is the single most effective way to restore salmon populations (Monks, 30; Stevens, F1). With one hundred two dams on the Snake and Columbia Rivers, these four dams provide less than 5 percent of the region's hydropower and supply irrigation water to only thirteen farms (Monks, 31).

However, powerful political and business lobbies and most citizens of the region fiercely oppose breaching the dams. Some politicians downplay the seriousness of the salmon crisis. In 1994, Idaho's U.S. Representative Helen Chenoweth announced that she didn't take the salmon's endangered species status seriously because she could buy canned salmon in a grocery store (*Lewiston Morning Tribune,* 5C). But surely a consumer's current ability to purchase salmon should not be a criterion for setting environmental policy. Environmental justice would consider the inherent right of the salmon to exist, the health of the entire ecosystem, and the needs of local tribal cultures and others that depend upon the fish. Opponents of dam breaching predict the devastation of the economy of the Northwest due to the costs and effects of breaching, including loss of jobs and increased utility rates. Furthermore, they argue, breaching cannot guarantee the restoration of the salmon. They urge a search for alternatives to breaching and improvements to current salmon restoration policies. Yet, decades of strategies to mitigate the harm done to salmon by the dams have been unsuccessful. These include fish ladders and bypass chutes at the dams, trucking or barging juvenile salmon hundreds of miles around the dams, supplementation of salmon runs through fish hatcheries, and moratoriums on fishing, at a cost of over 3 billion over two decades (Stevens, F1, F4).

Many Northwest tribal leaders see these technological mitigation efforts as "human arrogance," (Monks, 27; Landeen and Pinkham, 109), and as attempts to preserve the hydrosystem, not the ecosystem needed by the salmon (Berg, "Endangered Species Act Update," 9). According to Ted Strong, a Yakama Indian and ex-director of the Columbia River Intertribal Fish Commission,

> While the species themselves—the fish, fowl, game, plants—and the habitat they live in have given us unparalleled wealth, they live crippled in their ability to persist and in conditions of captive squalor. . . . Perhaps what saddens me most is that salmon restoration is mostly illusion. It is a tangled morass of processes that, in the final analysis, protect the groups who have a vested interest in keeping things the way they are. . . . What passes as salmon science, conducted by or on behalf of the federal government, is little more than an effort to provide a rationale for perpetuating the very conditions that have brought salmon to the edge of extinction. (3)

Instead of removing the hydrosystem, state and federal agencies favor improving the other "H's"—habitat, hatcheries, and harvest—even though the dams appear to be the major cause of salmon mortality.

The construction of hydroelectric dams and fishing management policies in the Northwest have contributed directly to tribal loss of resources necessary for material and spiritual survival. The dams created a source of cheap energy and provided water to irrigate normally arid land for farming. They transformed Lewiston, Idaho, into a seaport able to barge grain to the coast, though Lewiston lies over three hundred miles inland from the Pacific Ocean. These transformations have all come at the expense of the salmon and the area's Indians. In 1999, the CRITFC submitted a report to the Army Corps of Engineers stating that "from treaty times to the present, non-Indians have taken most treaty-protected assets of value from the tribes, particularly their lands, waters, and salmon" (Barker, 6A). The report finds that "by decreasing the salmon productivity of the Snake River system," the dams "have effectively transferred wealth from the tribes to non-Indians" (Barker, 6A). This is a breach of environmental justice as defined by the Environmental Protection Agency (EPA).

More specifically, the EPA states that communities experiencing environmental injustices are often minority or low income; excluded from the environmental policy setting and/or decision-making process; subject to a disproportionate impact from one or more environmental hazards; and expe-

riencing disparate implementation of environmental regulations, requirements, practices, and activities ("FAQ"). The Columbia River tribes are minority and low income, excluded from the setting of environmental policy,
and they are shouldering a disproportionate impact of an environmental
hazard in the potential extinction of the salmon on which their cultures
depend. Thus, according to the EPA's own definition of environmental injustice, the government's failure to protect the salmon may result in a form
of cultural genocide perpetrated on these Northwest tribes.

Potentially genocidal fishing policies have a history in the Northwest. For
thousands of years the Columbia River's Celilo Falls was the center of subsistence and commercial fishing for Northwest Indians. It was the largest
remaining Indian fishery on the continent when it was flooded by the construction of The Dalles Dam in 1957. This devastating loss to the tribes was a
blatant violation of their sovereign treaty fishing rights (Berg, "Where Have
All the Fishes Gone?" 18). In 1941, nearly two decades before the inundation
of Celilo, Richard Neuberger, a Northwest journalist and later U.S. Senator
from Oregon, wrote in an article for *Saturday Evening Post* that "a number
of wild-life experts hope to forbid Indians from spearing and netting the
homeward-bound salmon at Celilo Falls, but others ask if we take away even
this from the country's original owners, what are we accusing Hitler of,
anyway?" (Cone and Ridlington, 198). Sixty years ago Neuberger correctly
recognized attempts to deny the Indians fish as potentially genocidal.

Furthermore, the U.S. government's failure to preserve the salmon is a
breach of treaty fishing rights guaranteed the four Columbia River tribes in
return for vast areas of ceded land. It is also an assault on tribal sovereignty
because the loss of salmon prevents the tribes from determining their own
futures. When making treaties, the tribes were careful to protect fishing
rights, and would not have agreed to the treaties had they known that
salmon populations would plummet (Barker, 6A). The Columbia River Treaty
Tribes believe that breaching the four Snake River dams to restore salmon
runs would partially fulfill 1855 treaty obligations ("Report: Breaching,"
5C). Tribes cannot determine their own affairs and futures if they are deprived of the basic resources needed for cultural perpetuation. Therefore,
their inherent right to self-government is threatened by the impending
extinction of salmon.

Combined with a cavalier disregard of treaty rights by non-Indians, racism
has played an undeniable role in the history of the Northwest dams and
Indian fishing. Damming of the Columbia River System by the federal government for cheap power began in the 1930s and continued into the 1970s.

Transcripts of Congressional hearings in the 1930s reveal that Congress knew the dams would damage or eliminate Indian fisheries, and it planned for mitigation, primarily through fish hatcheries. But the hatcheries were set up almost exclusively downstream from traditional Indian fishing areas where nonnative sport and commercial fishers, not Indians, would benefit from them (Taylor, 13–15). A 1947 statement from the Department of the Interior claimed that "the overall benefits to the Pacific Northwest from a thorough going development of the Snake and the Columbia are such that the present salmon run must, if necessary, be sacrificed" (Taylor 15). In "The Role of Race in Salmon Policy," Douglas W. Dompier writes that "the elimination of tribal fisheries has, arguably, always been a primary objective of the fishery agencies. . . . had the hatcheries been constructed in the upper river, rather than below the dams, and a supplementation program carried out, the natural runs would have been maintained and tribal fisheries that had flourished for thousands of years would have continued" (215). The targeting of Indian fisheries for elimination clearly fits the EPA's definition of environmental injustice.

In the late twentieth century, as fish populations continue to decline, Indians have been harassed and threatened with violence by non-Indians while fishing. "I take a lot of verbal abuse out there," reports Alfred McConnville, a Nez Perce/Yakama man who has fished the Columbia River for thirty-five years. "They will often curse me with my son in the boat when they pass by on the river. They will yell things like 'You — — — —-ing Indians. Get the hell off the river'" (Middleton, 14). Indian fishers have been disproportionately targeted by state fish and game agencies for fishing violations despite U.S. District Court rulings that uphold Indians' treaty rights to fish in their "usual and accustomed places." In 1982, the National Marine Fisheries Service set up a sting to catch Indian fishers on the Columbia River they believed were responsible for forty thousand missing salmon. Dubbed "Salmonscam" by the press, this sting netted several Indian fishers who were given five-year prison sentences. Meanwhile, nonnatives who were illegally catching and selling large numbers of salmon to Seattle and California restaurants were either ignored by the agents or given minor sentences. The forty thousand missing fish were ultimately accounted for: an aluminum plant had discharged fluoride into the river, discouraging the fish from migrating upstream where they would have been counted (Taylor, 16–17). In "A Century of Loss," Rick Taylor writes that "the whole [Salmonscam] operation appears to have been calculated to cast Indian fishing in the worst possible light, to arouse antagonism toward Indian fishers, and to insinuate that they may be to blame for the fish runs rapid decline in the early 80s" (17). This racial profiling clearly fits the EPA's definition of environmental discrimination based on race.

The cultural importance of salmon has united the Columbia River tribes in an effort to prevent its extinction. In 1994, the Columbia River Inter-Tribal Fish Commission created an intertribal salmon recovery and preservation plan called *Wy-Kan-Ush-Mi-Wa-Kish-Wit*, or "Spirit of the Salmon."[2] This plan utilizes centuries of tribal knowledge gained through close interaction with the fish, treaty fishing rights, and modern science. Traditional tribal knowledge of the salmon and the peoples' relationship to the fish and its habitat is the foundation of this comprehensive plan. The tribes' expression of its relationship to the salmon in *Wy-Kan-Ush-Mi-Wa-Kish-Wit* makes this plan a part of Columbia River tribal literature, with salmon an important part of this literature. American Indian literatures play a powerful role in creating Indian identity and community; tribal stories keep Indian peoples connected to their land, their ancestors, and to their traditions, values, and communities. Geary Hobson writes that "Literature, in all its forms, oral as well as written, is our most durable way of carrying on this continuance [of the People]" (Weaver, *That the People Might Live,* 43). For example, in Leslie Silko's novel *Ceremony,* Tayo is a young man from the Laguna Pueblo who returns from wartime combat alienated, isolated, and ill due to his "separation from the ancient unity of person, ceremony, and land" (Allen, 128). Riven with anger and grief, Tayo is finally healed by tribal stories and rituals and by the land itself, and is able to take his place in the life and continuity of Laguna.

Wy-Kan-Ush-Mi-Wa-Kish-Wit is concerned with the continuance of the salmon and of the people. It is quintessentially political in that it seeks to address and ameliorate the effects of colonial policies on tribal life; it is active on its own behalf in seeking justice for the salmon and the tribes. This is a tribally defined justice based largely upon natural laws that the Northwest tribes have practiced for hundreds of years. The Principles of Environmental Justice formulated in 1991 at the First National People of Color Environmental Leadership Summit reflect the declarations of *Wy-Kan-Ush-Mi-Wa-Kish-Wit,* and are an instance where specific groups working for specific environmental goals reformulate the ancient concepts found in texts such as the Columbia River tribes' *Wy-Kan-Ush-Mi-Wa-Kish-Wit*. These environmental justice principles affirm "the sacredness of Mother Earth, ecological unity and the interdependence of all species, and the right to be free from ecological destruction"; they recognize a "special legal and natural relationship of Native Peoples to the U.S. Government through treaties . . . which impose upon the U.S. Government a paramount obligation and responsibility to affirm the sovereignty and self-determination of the indigenous peoples whose land it occupies and holds in trust."[3]

The significance of salmon to the Columbia River tribes and the salmon crisis' connection to the environmental justice movement is made clear in this brief summary of the tribes' *Wy-Kan-Ush-Mi-Wa-Kish-Wit,* "Spirit of the Salmon" preservation plan:

> Salmon are part of our spiritual and cultural identity.
> The annual salmon return and its celebration by our peoples assure the renewal and continuation of human and all other life.
> Salmon and the rivers they use are part of our sense of place.
> The Creator put us here where the salmon return.
> We are obliged to remain and protect this place.
> The annual return of the salmon allows the transfer of traditional values from generation to generation.
> Without salmon returning to our rivers and streams, we would cease to be Indian people. (Landeen and Pinkham, 110)

The Indians would cease to be "Indians" because with salmon extinct, an integral element of their cultural identity—from spiritual practices to economic livelihood—is lost. They would still be Indians racially, but they would not be Indians as they define themselves, and as they have a right to define themselves. Thus, as the Principles of Environmental Justice declare, political justice for the tribes must mean self-determination. We can begin to understand how the Columbia River Indians without the salmon would no longer be Indians when we read tribal literature such as *Wy-Kan-Ush-Mi-Wa-Kish-Wit,* which reveals how integrally salmon is a part of tribal identity. Other tribal literatures, such as myths and contemporary poetry, also illuminate this relationship.

Salmon is a prominent figure in Columbia River tribal mythology. According to Nez Perce stories, before the arrival of human beings, animals and plants with humanlike qualities populated the world. This is the narrative world, where mythological beings and the spiritual guides of traditional Nez Perce religion reside (Aoki and Walker, 6–7). In one story, Coyote, the Nez Perce trickster hero, discovers that the salmon are trapped behind a high ridge of mountains. If they can only get through the mountains they will be able to travel upstream to spawn and to feed other animal-people. So Coyote digs a hole through the mountains, creating the Columbia River and allowing the salmon to migrate upriver to the tributaries (Landeen and Pinkham, 13–14). The freeing of the salmon is one of Coyote's greatest accomplishments because so many other beings in the narrative world depend upon the fish. Coyote could have kept all the salmon for himself, but if he had, other animal-people would have suffered and the salmon would eventually have disappeared. Coyote takes into account all those who will be affected by the salmon's fate. This story demonstrates indigenous justice because it allows for all beings in the narrative world to be sustained. It's hard to miss the parallel in this story to the breaching of the Snake River dams: it would likely have the same effect as Coyote digging through the mountains to free the salmon.

In another story, a short time after Coyote has freed the salmon he becomes hungry and beseeches the fish, "Take pity on me, because I gave you freedom. One of you, come to the shore for me." Then, Nez Perce storytellers say, "a huge chinook salmon came swimming right up there," which Coyote roasts and eats (Aoki and Walker, 498). "Taking pity" or having "pity" is an important element of Nez Perce culture and identity. "Pity" in this story illustrates the concept of reciprocity and the natural law of the interdependence of species articulated in the Principles of Environmental Justice composed by the First National People of Color Leadership Summit. Many Columbia River tribal stories illustrate the cultural concept of "pity."

Salmon, like other members of the Nez Perce narrative world, prepared for the coming of human beings. In "A Meeting Between Creator and the Animals," the Creator calls all the animals together on a hillside above a tributary of the Snake River and asks how each would like to help the human beings that will soon be coming. After several kinds of deer, birds, and insects describe how they would like to look and how they will help the humans, the Creator transforms them accordingly because they have "qualified" to help the humans. Then,

> Salmon and Steelhead came forward and said, "We can help the human beings with our flesh." Salmon said, "When we come up the river we will die, so the human beings will have to catch us before that happens. I'll come up only on certain times of the year, and that's when they'll have to catch me." Then Steelhead said, "I want to come in the wintertime, but I'll give them something special. That will be the glue from my skin. This glue can be used to make bows and spears. I'll be in the water all winter long." So Creator let Steelhead become qualified. Sockeye Salmon came forward and he said, "I don't want to be big like Chinook

Salmon and Steelhead, and my flesh will be red because I'll eat different foods." . . . So this is how the fish became qualified. (Landeen and Pinkham, 4–8)

In Nez Perce literature and tradition, the salmon perform an essential service for humans, and in return, the people are responsible for the well-being of the fish.

These stories illustrate the concept of "pity," a reciprocal relation of compassion and responsibility that ensures appropriate behavior within the mythic world. Coyote shows pity when he frees the salmon, and the salmon show pity by providing Coyote with dinner. "Pity" can also be recognized as "reciprocity," which—for American Indian peoples—"begins with an understanding that anything and everything that humans do has an effect on the rest of the world around us. Even when we cannot clearly know what that effect is in any particular action we know that there is an effect. Thus Indian peoples, in different places and in different cultural configurations, have always struggled to know how to act appropriately in the world" (Tinker, 160). Like reciprocity, "pity" can be read as an indigenous conception of justice and as a type of justice based on the natural law of the interdependence of species. Ideally, people who grow up hearing these tribal stories express "pity" in their own communities by caring for others and for tribal resources. For example, if you kill an elk in the winter you might share the meat with elders who are unable to hunt. Taking "pity" might also mean a tribal council regulating the number of elk that community members may kill each season, in an effort to control and preserve elk populations. The ethic of "pity" stands in marked contrast to the ethic that socializes people to exploit natural resources with limited concern for the complex consequences of that exploitation, an ethic largely responsible for the destruction of salmon habitats.

Nez Perce poet Phil George also demonstrates the importance of salmon to contemporary Northwest native people, particularly in his poem "Salmon Return":

Like many Grandfathers before me,
I spear Salmon, splashing, flapping.

These echoing waters no longer your home.
Up Celilo Falls you will dance no more.

Cleansed, Grandmother will weave
Willows into your needle-boned flesh.

Beside night fires you will roast—
Fat oozing, dripping, sizzling.

My people will not go hungry.
We fast. We sing. We feast.

May your spirit always live, my friend,
If even in the Moon of High Waters.

From saltwaters you swim upstream to die.
We remember: "Return home to die."

"Return[ing] home to die" evokes the idea of "homing," the scientific name
for the ability of a fish to correctly identify and return to the stream of its
birth after maturing at sea, and reveals a close relationship between the
people and the fish (Landeen and Pinkham, 229). Critic William Bevis identifies a pattern in American Indian literature he calls "homing in," suggesting that "'identity' for a Native American is not a matter of finding
'one's self,' but of finding a 'self' that is trans-personal and includes a society, a past, and a place" (585). Bevis' communal, synchronic self also
sounds like the identity created through the Nez Perce cultural value of
"pity"—compassion and action taken for others to ensure the larger community's balance, health, and survival. The impending extinction of salmon in
the Northwest and the debate over breaching dams to save the fish makes
clear the importance for Columbia River tribal Indians of "pity" and the
justice it creates: their world depends upon it, and fundamentally, the non-
Indian world does too.

Recognizing the threat presented by species extinction, several non-
Indian regional and national consumer and outdoor organizations have
joined the tribes to support the removal of the four Snake River dams. These
groups include Save Our Wild Salmon, Idaho Rivers United, the Sierra Club,
the National Wildlife Federation, American Rivers, Patagonia, Taxpayers for
Common Sense, and U.S. PIRG, (the Public Interest Research Groups). At this
point these mainstream groups have not defined the salmon crisis specifically as an environmental justice issue, but they share with the Columbia

River tribes the goal of saving the salmon from extinction. The four Columbia River Treaty Tribes see the impending extinction of the salmon as an environmental justice violation and are considering litigation on that basis, in addition to treaty and trust violations.[4] Together these groups lobby for the breaching of the Snake River dams, and work to inform the public of the benefits that can result from breaching, including hundreds of millions of saved taxpayer dollars now spent on unsuccessful mitigation efforts and a $500 million fishing and recreation industry.

The ad campaign created by this coalition utilizes several themes in an attempt to appeal to a broad audience. One ad presents a large "Timeline to Extinction," revealing that scientists believe the Snake River salmon will be extinct by the year 2017 if the four dams are not breached. A gruesome photograph of a dead salmon dominates another ad with text reading, "Your Tax Dollars at Work," in reference to the millions spent on failed mitigation. A third ad compares the impending extinction of the salmon to the decimation of the buffalo in the nineteenth century. To the Columbia River tribes, the salmon is every bit as essential and sacred as the buffalo was and is to the Plains Indians. The salmon coalition's final ad, in bold type forcefully implores readers to "Give a Dam. Well, actually four" (see figure 14.1). Beneath a drawing of a large, leaping salmon the ad states: "If we don't act now Snake River salmon will go extinct." Below small photographs of the four dams the ad lists ramifications of the loss of the fish: the disappearance of a "magnificent species and symbol of the Pacific Northwest, and a resource and heritage that belongs to all Americans"; "a $500-million-a-year salmon-based economy and the jobs that go with it." Finally, the ad claims, "if we lose the salmon, we also expose U.S. taxpayers to a potential liability of billions of dollars for violation of court-tested treaties with Columbia River Basin Indian tribes." This ad makes clear the inextricable connection between the survival of the salmon and justice for the tribes. The devastating decline of the salmon due to the dams results in an injustice to the tribes whether based on notions of "pity," U.S. law, grassroots environmental justice actions or environmental justice as defined by the EPA. Justice for the Columbia River tribes requires the restoration and preservation of the salmon.

In this final ad, the salmon is larger in relation to all other images. It is larger than the four dams it leaps over, larger than the ten environmental and consumer groups pictured at the bottom of the page, and larger than the Nez Perce Tribe—larger even than Chief Joseph, who is depicted in the Tribe's official seal. The salmon symbolizes "pity" and justice, and the

Fig. 14.1. Salmon coalition ad supporting removal of four Snake River dams. (Courtesy of Idaho Rivers United and Patagonia)

alliance of Indians and non-Indians working to preserve the conditions necessary for the survival of all forms of life in the Columbia River ecosystem. Indeed, as a symbol it promotes the concept of "pity," becoming an activist for environmental justice for both humans and nonhumans.

In July of 2000, the National Marine Fisheries Service announced its recommendation to delay removal of the dams for at least the next eight to ten years in favor of renewing efforts to mitigate salmon mortality. This long-awaited decision was a bitter and infuriating disappointment to the Columbia River tribes who arguably have more to lose than any other group should the salmon continue to decline. The costs to taxpayers of keeping the dams should make this decision one of concern to all citizens: approximately $7 billion to keep the dams operating for the next fourteen years—the length of time before they would conceivably be removed—opposed to $1 billion to take them out immediately, according to tribal estimates.[5]

It is certain that the Columbia River tribes will never give up the fight for the survival of the salmon. Through decades of court battles and activist actions along the rivers both to exercise their rights to fish and to save the fish from extinction, these Northwest tribes have been extraordinarily tenacious as well as patient (Ulrich, 229). Explains ex-CRITFC director, Ted Strong, "We are not willing to give up on these magnificent, innocent, and spiritual creatures. We have a responsibility to them. . . . This is a testament to the faith of the Indian peoples: no matter how badly the salmon have been mistreated, no matter how serious the decline, it has only made native people deeper in their resolve. It has doubled their commitment. It has rekindled the hope that today is beginning to grow in many of the younger people" (Smith and Berg, 15). The Yakama, Umatilla, Warm Springs, and Nez Perce Tribes believe that the Indian nations, the states and the federal government should work together to restore the salmon runs. The tribes' restoration plan with its emphasis on ecosystem restoration rather than hydrosystem preservation can provide invaluable guidance. Not allowing the tribes to have a voice in the decision-making process on this issue is a blatant violation of environmental justice as defined by the EPA itself. But we all have a role to play in the salmon crisis. Citizens must demand justice, and not a justice defined by a self-interested U.S. government that historically has not taken the rights and views of Indian tribes into account.[6] The justice inherent in "pity"—compassion and action taken to ensure the entire community's balance, health, and survival—offers an important ethic for addressing this crisis. The survival of Columbia River tribal cultures may depend upon the survival of the salmon; the survival of the salmon may depend upon us.

NOTES

1. See Winona LaDuke, *All Our Relations* and Weaver, *Defending Mother Earth.*

2. See the tribes' salmon restoration plan at www.critfc.org/text/trp.htm.

3. Di Chiro 307–09. I am quoting from the "Principles of Environmental Justice," which can be found in their entirety in Di Chiro's "Nature as Community."

4. From telephone interview with David J. Cummings, Deputy Counsel for the Nez Perce Tribal Executive Committee, 14 November 2000.

5. From telephone interview with Charles Hudson, Public Information Manager for CRITFC, 13 November 2000.

6. To learn more about these issues and to get involved in them, see www.critfc.org and www.removedams.org.

WORKS CITED

Adamson, Joni. *American Indian Literatures, Environmental Justice, and Ecocriticism: The Middle Place.* Tucson: University of Arizona Press, 2001.

Allen, Paula Gunn, ed. *Studies in American Indian Literature: Critical Essays and Course Designs.* New York: MLA, 1983.

Aoki, Haruo, and Deward E. Walker Jr. *Nez Perce Oral Narratives.* Berkeley: University of California Press, 1989.

Barker, Eric. "New Study Says Breaching Best for Tribes." *Lewiston Morning Tribune* 26 May 1999: 6A.

Berg, Laura. "Endangered Species Act Update." *Wana Chinook Tymoo* 1–2 (1993): 8–9.

———. "Where Have All the Fishes Gone?: A Short History of Fish Mitigation on the Columbia River." *Wana Chinook Tymoo* 1–2 (1993): 16–19.

Bevis, William. "Native American Novels: Homing In." In *Recovering the Word: Essays on Native American Literature,* edited by Brian Swann and Arnold Krupat, 580–620. Berkeley: University of California Press, 1987.

Cone, Joseph, and Sandy Ridlington. *The Northwest Salmon Crisis: A Documentary History.* Corvallis: Oregon State University Press, 1996.

Di Chiro, Giovanna. "Nature as Community: The Convergence of Environment And Social Justice." In *Uncommon Ground: Rethinking the Human Place in Nature,* edited by William Cronon, 298–320. New York: Norton, 1996.

Dompier, Douglas W. "The Role of Race in Salmon Policy." In *The Northwest*

Salmon Crisis: A Documentary History, by Joseph Cone and Sandy Ridlington, 206–15. Corvallis: Oregon State University Press, 1996.

"FAQ (Frequently Asked Questions)." Environmental Protection Agency Office of Enforcement and Compliance Assistance. 12 June 2000. 5 November 2000 [http://es.epa.gov/oeca/main/ej/faq.html].

George, Phil. "Salmon Return." In *Kautsa (Grandmother)*. Lewiston, Idaho: Confluence, 1984.

LaDuke, Winona. *All Our Relations: Native Struggles for Land and Life.* Cambridge, Mass.: South End, 1999.

Landeen, Dan, and Allen Pinkham. *Salmon And His People: Fish and Fishing in Nez Perce Culture.* Lewiston, Idaho: Confluence, 1999.

Lewiston Morning Tribune 28 August 1994, 5C.

Meyer Resources, Inc. "Tribal Circumstances and Impacts of the Lower Snake River Project on the Nez Perce, Yakama, Umatilla, Warm Springs and Shoshone Bannock Tribes." Columbia River Inter-Tribal Fish Commission. April 1999. 14 November 2000 [www.critfc.org/legal/circum__summ.htm].

Middleton, Rusty. "View from the River." *Wana Chinook Tymoo* 1–2 (1993): 10–15.

Monks, Vicki. "When A Fish Is More Than A Fish." *National Wildlife* 38, no. 2 (2000): 22–31.

"Report: Breaching Needed To Honor Treaty." *Lewiston Morning Tribune* 28 May 1999: 5C.

Smith, Yvonne and Laura Berg. "Ancient Tradition, Modern Reality: Is There a Future for a Salmon-Based Culture?" *Wana Chinook Tymoo* 1 (1998): 10–15.

Sonner, Scott. "Is Too Much of the Burden on Indians?" *Lewiston Morning Tribune* 10 May 1994: 2D.

Stevens, William K. "Will Dam Busting Save Salmon? Maybe Not." *New York Times* 5 Oct. 1999: F1, F4.

Strong, Ted. "Director's Message." *Wana Chinook Tymoo* (Winter 1999): 2–3.

Taylor, Rick. "A Century of Loss." *Wana Chinook Tymoo* (Winter 1999): 12–17, 22.

Tinker, George E. "An American Indian Theological Response to Ecojustice." In *Defending Mother Earth: Native American Perspectives on Environmental Justice,* edited by Jace Weaver, 153–76. Maryknoll, N.Y.: Orbis Books, 1996.

Ulrich, Roberta. *Empty Nets: Indians, Dams, and the Columbia River.* Corvallis: Oregon State University Press, 1999.

Weaver, Jace, ed. *Defending Mother Earth: Native American Perspectives on Environmental Justice.* Maryknoll, N.Y.: Orbis Books, 1996.

——. *That the People Might Live: Native American Literatures and Native American Community.* New York: Oxford University Press, 1997.

Whalen, Sue. "The Nez Perces' Relationship to their Land." *Indian Historian* 4 (Fall 1971): 30–33.

15

SUSTAINING THE "URBAN FOREST" AND CREATING LANDSCAPES OF HOPE

An Interview with Cinder Hypki and Bryant "Spoon" Smith

Giovanna Di Chiro

> Art is not a mirror
> held up to reality
> but a hammer with which to shape it.
>
> —Bertolt Brecht

The urban environmental art projects of Baltimore-based community activists Cinder Hypki and Bryant "Spoon" Smith embody the bold spirit expressed in Brecht's hammer with which to shape the world.[1] The world-making potentialities of art are clearly exhibited in the community-based, public artwork produced by residents of Baltimore's most impoverished urban environments. Art and greening projects, crafted by people struggling to make ends meet and who are unsure about the possibility of a future "beyond the hood," raise questions about whose concerns are embedded in popular imaginings of the "green city" or the "sustainable community." These commonplace terms that have emerged in the last decade within government, NGO, and academic discourses, while gesturing to the indisputable good of "public participation," often fall short of creating the conditions for most inner-city communities to be involved in "sustaining" their environments in meaningful ways.[2] The community-based environmental art projects that Hypki and Smith organize confront the fundamental assumptions behind these contemporary environmental rhetorics and ask: What counts as "green"? Where is the "environment" located, and what does it contain? What are we trying to "sustain" and for whom?

Environmental art, situated in urban spaces and produced by marginalized communities, challenges the boundaries and hierarchies traditionally defining the culture as represented by those in power.[3] Both Hypki and Smith describe their environmental art projects in inner-city neighborhoods as vehicles for social change—strategies that powerfully give voice and visibility to community members to represent their life experiences and their visions for the future. More important, they argue, environmental art is transformative; it engages the aesthetic dimensions of the imagination, those places in the mind that resist colonization, are potently regenerative, and can "experience freedom."[4] With its process orientation, community-based environmental art provides people with experiences and media of self-expression, which sometimes transforms their sense of identity. Participating in greening and art projects also enables community residents to make a difference in their local places: a foul-smelling pile of construction backfill, or an ad hoc dumpsite located in one of the many abandoned lots in inner-city neighborhoods, can become a flourishing, vital community park. Likewise, a brick wall along an alleyway that dead-ends in a heap of rubble consisting of rusted-out car parts and garbage becomes the visionary palette for a group of inner-city teens of color. Hypki's account of linking art and greening with children and teens demonstrates how this process helps them see through "artist's eyes" and, in the words of one young boy, "brings what's beautiful inside, out for everyone to see."

Although the ability of community-based environmental art to nurture the spirit by transforming one's neighborhood from an "industrial sacrifice zone" into a place of beauty and vitality is in itself worthwhile, this is not where Hypki's and Smith's vision ends. Their projects articulate with the broader goals of environmental justice—artmaking and greening help build community, they meld hand, heart, and brain and generate skills, experience, and economic options, they engender political efficacy and commitment by starting from inside the person and working out. Hypki and Smith discuss the changes they witness when people have opportunities to participate in reconstructing the polluted, neglected landscapes they inhabit everyday into those that are filled with flowering bushes, shade trees, and exuberant, colorful murals. Changing the physical landscape sometimes alters the political one—both activists recount stories of community residents, after being involved in art or greening activities, organizing together to address other issues, such as housing, drugs, education, unemployment, and campaigns for a living wage. For Hypki and Smith, Baltimore's inner-city neighborhoods, largely populated by poor and low-income African Americans, Latinos, and working-class whites, are skewed landscapes overflowing with the excesses of industrial society—too much pollution, too much poverty, too much unemployment, too much disheartenment. Moreover, they are landscapes starved by a scarcity of other elements—too few trees and green spaces, too little artwork, too few good jobs, too little hope. According to environmental justice advocates like Hypki and Smith, challenging these excesses and scarcities is how we start to create an authentically sustainable city where all residents benefit.

Baltimore, Maryland, one of the nation's oldest industrial cities, is characterized by its residents as a "city of neighborhoods." The friendly descriptor "neighborhood" invokes the notion of commitment, connection, belonging, and investment; the positive side of "community." However, "neighborhood" also signifies the potent racial divisions—sometimes degenerating into communalism—that characterize the city's social climate. Baltimore's neighborhoods are primarily delineated by race and income, and residents of each neighborhood clearly recognize the unofficial boundaries that demarcate the separate sections of the city. Of the three quarters of a million people living in Baltimore, approximately 63 percent are African Americans. Those black residents who are living at or below the poverty line reside primarily in the East and West Baltimore neighborhoods, such as Madison East End, Clifton-Berea, and Greater Rosemount. They know not to wander into the primarily white, upper-class neighborhoods of North Baltimore's Hampden and Woodberry. Southeast Baltimore's neighborhoods of Fells Point, Highland Town, and Canton are witnessing a blurring of the racial divide, with the historically working-class Eastern European immigrant population mingling with an influx of African American families, Latinos, Asians, and the largest population of Lumbi Indians in the city.

Consider the following statistics as indicators of the socioeconomic and environmental conditions of the city: there are approximately forty thousand vacant and abandoned houses in the city, which has a housing stock of about three hundred thousand units within the city limits. The number of soup kitchens has risen statewide from sixty to nine hundred since 1980.[5] The city schools are two and a half years behind the national average in reading and math skills, and 70 percent of them have no programs for art, music, and physical education.[6] Life expectancy is among the lowest in the nation (63 for men and 73 for women) and the inner city has an infant mortality rate of 11–17.5 deaths per 1000 births—one of the highest rates recorded in the United States, and comparable to many developing countries.[7] The rate of HIV infection and AIDS is among the highest in the country, and according to the Environmental Protection Agency, asthma has increased at an astonishing rate from around 8 to nearly 170 per 10,000 inhabitants—this is especially evident in children living in the housing projects in the inner-city neighborhoods.[8] These public health statistics are particularly appalling considering that one of the best medical centers in the world sits right in the middle of one of the poorest neighborhoods in Baltimore (and in the United States), and whose residents have some of the worst health problems.

From this backdrop of Baltimore's inner-city neighborhoods, in the following interview Hypki and Smith talk about the community-based greening and art projects they are organizing, as "insurgent architects,"[9] to remake the deteriorating urban landscapes of East and Southeast Baltimore and to "hammer out" a more environmentally just and sustainable city.

Giovanna Di Chiro: To get us started, would you please describe the work you do linking art and environmental justice in your community in Baltimore, and also tell us something about the influences and experiences that brought you to this work.

Bryant Smith: Alright, I'll start. Currently, I am the executive director of the Urban Arts Institute, a nonprofit organization I started that aims to bring art into the lives of people in Baltimore's inner-city communities. Through the Urban Arts Institute—located in East Baltimore in the low-income and *no*-income neighborhood of Madison East End—I use art as a tool to help strengthen communities, to provide skills that may open up new sources of income, and to provide opportunities for self-development. The different art projects and art media that we focus on in the organization include photography, stained glass, welding, mosaic art, the development of "art parks," music, and woodcarving. The plan is, you as an individual can sign on for one of these programs just for fun or for a hobby, and if you wanted to take it a step further, we would continue your training and then find you some possible employment.

I have also worked for the Parks and People Foundation for about six years. What I did there was to work with communities to improve the environment through street tree plantings, stream restoration projects, and projects to develop vacant lots into community-managed open spaces. The plan at Parks and People was to use these environmental projects to address *social* issues as well as environmental ones.

Before I started working for Parks and People, I was strictly in the community development field and not working on the environment per se. I knew, in order for me to take my community development activities to a different level, I had to get trained, and Parks and People provided that for me. Parks and People did a great thing by coming into the hood and training someone like me, and it's something that environmental organizations today need to do more of. I'm tired of showing up at forestry meetings with five hundred people and there are only twenty people of color there.

Giovanna Di Chiro: Could you explain more about the kind of training you obtained at Parks and People—which is more of what we might consider a traditional environmental organization—and how it helped you to achieve your social change and community development goals?

Bryant Smith: I had no skills at all regarding the environment—none. I got a year's training program where they taught me some tree biology, how to identify and plant trees, how to protect watersheds, and how to organize stream restoration projects. Parks and People really provided me with the education and awareness of my environment. From there, applying it to my community development background, I was able to move into community forestry projects.

Giovanna Di Chiro: You are a native of Baltimore and have decided to stay and work to help improve the social and environmental conditions of the city, and your community in East Baltimore in particular—can you talk about what motivates you to do this?

Bryant Smith: All my life I have worked in the nonprofit sector in communities in Baltimore. I grew up in the Broadway Homes Housing Project here in Baltimore City. From living and growing up in that neighborhood, I had the chance to witness the needs of the inner city. These experiences are what really pushed me to become more involved in community-based programs and actually to start my own nonprofit.

I was first introduced to a local community organization called "The Door" when I was thirteen. At that time, I was into a little bit of everything—I was selling drugs, I was getting paid to steal cars for some of the big hustlers in the hood. I was in gangs, I've been shot at, I've been beaten up, I've carried guns myself, and it was all because that was what I knew in my environment. The Door provided programs where I could get computer skills, I could work on art projects; I could leave Baltimore City and go out of town on field trips to youth conferences and that kind of thing.

The Door rounded up lots of young people from the hood, took them to Delaware, or Ocean City for three-day youth development conferences. They took us camping, exposing me to the wilderness—that's something I only saw on television. I was fascinated with the college students who were volunteering at The Door. I wanted to talk like them; I wanted to hear stories of how they had traveled all around the world, or how they would hang out in D.C. and other cities. I never thought anybody my color would have had that type of experience and would have been to those places. That was the beginning, the thirst to want something different. I was able to see that sometimes you actually have an opportunity to get out.

That desire to want to know more about that other world and to become a part of that world is what pulled me away from the hood. I hung around The Door constantly. I want to read something to you: "He who walks with wise men will be wise, for the companion of fools will be destroyed." Proverbs 13:20. I wanted to walk with these people who could introduce me to the world that I was curious about. So many of my friends are gone. If I hadn't hooked up with the people at The Door, I would have been dead by now—I look back sometimes and I think, "whoa, I'm surprised I didn't die that night." All I knew was the Projects—sell a little bit of rock here on the corner, steal cars for the hustlers, or defend myself and win respect. I was able to see that in the real world, what makes you important is how you give back to the community, your educational level, the jobs you've had. And, that's what I wanted. The Door opened my mind to what was beyond the Projects, beyond the hood. And, it was The Door that really got me into the environmental movement.

Giovanna Di Chiro: I want to get more details on the art and greening projects you both are involved in but, first, Spoon, I'd like to hear your thoughts on the concept of "environment" that you have been using in this discussion so far. The idea of environment, as it's most commonly understood in this country, conjures up something like the "wilderness," or the wild, open spaces that are devoid of people. For many, the environment is certainly far away from the urban core, in fact, many people would say the city space is precisely where the environment is *not*. But, you talk about lots of different urban problems as *part* of the environment. So, tell me about your conception of the "environment," given that that word is used very differently in popular terminology.

Bryant Smith: Yeah, it really is. You know, as a member of the National Forest Congress Committee, I serve with a lot of folks who are part of national environmental organizations like the Audubon Society, the American Forests Institute, the Pinchot Institute, and the North American Association of Environmental Education, and I've been to a lot of conferences that deal with the "environment." I find myself defending the position that the hood *is* part of the environment. For example, at the Seventh American Forest Congress you're put at one of these huge round tables with other participants. I sat at a table where I was the only person representing urban forestry issues—everybody else was from Weyerhaeuser, or they were owners of tree farms, or reps from the timber industry. For three days, I had to fight to get these people to respect where I was coming from. So, I have to say, "Ok, the forest you're talking about is made up of trees, streams, and wildlife. My forest, which I call the "urban forest," is made up of some trees, some green space, and the majority of the space is taken up by people and buildings and all the issues we have to deal with." That's a major thing that I often find myself having to fight at the national level, or with the "true" environmentalists—that is, to try to get people to recognize and respect the urban forest and the problems that we are dealing with in the cities.

In the hood, on the other hand, there is that piece where people don't know the definition of the environment. Many folks in the hood don't know that the idea of the environment exists. I mean, I never knew what the benefit of the tree out front of our house was. I just knew Grandma broke a switch off of it when she wanted to "correct" me.

So, the education piece is something that has been very successful in the city—just showing folks the benefit of the tree, why you shouldn't break the branches off the tree or carve your name into it. And, it works—people grab onto that knowledge, they stick with it and they use it. I've done a lot of tree plantings with elementary school kids in East Baltimore. We start out with tree identification. So, I say, "Look at the Ginkgos across the street versus the Bright Red Maple we're about to plant." We look at the differences in the bark, the differences in the shape of the leaves. I then talk to them about how trees help to clean the air and to clean the soil. Depending on the kids' age, I talk about how trees in the city can raise the property value by 30 percent, how they provide shade in the summer, and that they provide benefits to wildlife in the hood.

I then talk about what happens when you break a branch off the tree, what happens when you carve into the bark. Then I go into how to plant the tree properly, how to maintain it, water it, use wood chips, and how to prune it correctly. And, then we'd go into using the right species for the right space. You don't want to plant an elm in front of a row home. Usually there's not enough space in a street tree pit in front of a row home to plant an elm so that the wide crown won't be growing into the house. If the space is small, I would talk about using a Bright Red Maple, which has a more upright and narrow crown—the right tree for the right space. Those things help them if they are fortunate enough to plant a tree again in the future. A couple of years ago, I was in the local market here, and this little kid came up to me and he said, "Hey, you're the tree man! We planted a Red Maple, and we know how to prune it, and this is how we maintain it." And, I thought to myself, "Whoa, this thing works." You know, he's going to pass that along, and every time he sees a tree, he knows about its benefits and he's going to stop his friends from busting it up. That's one of the big things about traditional environmentalists—they feel as though folks in the city don't respect the environment. But, they do respect the environment once we can help educate them that, in fact, the environment really exists.

Giovanna Di Chiro: How common is it for people to have gardens, or to plant flower beds, or to participate in community gardens in the city? I would imagine that there are people in these urban neighborhoods who *do* have an awareness of the environment and its importance to their community.

Bryant Smith: Yes, I'm glad you brought that up. A lot of black people in Baltimore are originally from the south and are gardeners from way back. They've been gardening all their lives and then they come to Baltimore and don't have access to any green space. Some of them have the opportunity to use a vacant lot and they're able to apply their gardening skills. So, there *are* a lot of people who are knowledgeable about the environment and who know if you dump the oil in the gutter, it's going to go into the Chesapeake Bay, or if they dump it out in the backyard, it will poison the soil. They respect and understand the land.

Giovanna Di Chiro: I like your idea of the urban forest because foresters or forest ecologists will often talk about the complexity of the forest, but it rarely has people in it. I like the point that you insist on—that although the urban forest certainly has trees, and streams, and various kinds of animals, it also has humans and their relationships and what they do and what they create, and that these things are also part of the forest. So, I'm sure you bring a lot of provocative ideas to the table at these national environmental organization meetings.

I'd like to shift at this juncture to Cinder. Please tell us what you think are some of the important parts of your origin story. Unlike Spoon, you are not a native of Baltimore. Would you talk about how you came to your chosen work in what has now become your chosen community?

Cinder Hypki: Both Spoon and I have come to similar conclusions about what art can do in inner-city neighborhoods, and we've come at it from totally different life experiences and perspectives. I was born and raised on a dairy farm in Wisconsin with parents who had a deep love and respect for the environment, for nature. That was just part of my growing up—looking at and exploring bugs, trees, and fairy shrimp in the water. The farm I grew up on was my world completely; it's been a long road that has brought me here to Baltimore.

I took a more traditional route of studying environmental science. I have a Master's degree in international natural resources conservation. For me, it was being outside of my own country, working for the National Park Service in Costa Rica, that made me come to the same conclusions that Spoon was just talking about—his idea that the notion of environment has to include people. I learned this in Costa Rica when campesinos who I met would come up to me and say, "You work for the National Park Service, they're protecting this piece of ground, and we're not allowed to hunt there, or cut trees down, but if it were between feeding your kids or protecting this piece of land—what would you do?"

It suddenly became very clear to me that the real purist notion of environment—that it is just the natural world—just can't work in today's world. It doesn't work for peasants in Costa Rica, and it sure doesn't work for people living in inner-city Baltimore. After I left Costa Rica, I came here to Baltimore to work in the field of community development and I've spent the last twelve years in the nonprofit world. During that time, I began to develop myself as an artist and, like Spoon, realized that art could be a way for me personally to express a lot of things in my own life, but art could also have a big role to play in community development work.

In the last year and a half, I've been working with teenagers all over East Baltimore and I have come to believe that art, as a means of expression, is a fundamental right—one facet of our freedom of speech. And, just like we need food to sustain our bodies, we also need "soul food" to nourish our spirit. So, the access to art and the ability to experiment with art as a way to express who we are, should be fundamentally egalitarian, but it is not. We do not have equal access to the arts, beginning with the lack of good—or any—arts programs in many public schools. The state of the Baltimore City public schools is shameful, in fact, it's been on the national news that most of the city schools provide substandard education in many ways. One of the ways it's robbing kids in the neighborhood of their future is that it does not provide them with arts education—in Baltimore, about 70 percent of our public schools have no arts program. Until the new mayor puts art back in the public schools, it's going to be organizations like the Urban Arts Institute or the Southeast Youth Academy that will give kids these kinds of opportunities.

Eventually, I decided to explore ways to work with communities, kids, and adults, and to really make art a part of people's lives; to be part of what they see when they walk down the street—and this includes beautiful green spaces in the city. It's through art that I came back to environmental education and to define urban areas as being part of the environment. While creating gardens and planting street trees with kids, we'd talk about the reasons you don't want to break branches off this tree. I'd ask them, "Did you know our city has the fifth worst air pollution in the country and every time you damage a tree it's like you're slashing your own lungs?"

Giovanna Di Chiro: I would like us eventually to get back to an issue that both of you have raised, that is, the relationship between art as individual, personal development, or as Cinder put it, "soul food," and also the role of art in terms of broader, economic, or structural change in support of social justice concerns in a city like Baltimore. But before we do that, I would like you Cinder, to comment on your being a relatively new immigrant to Baltimore. What kinds of issues are raised for you as somewhat of an outsider, a white woman doing broadly defined environmental justice work in an urban community that is primarily populated by people of color?

Cinder Hypki: I've lived in Baltimore for twelve years now, and I've lived in my current neighborhood for ten years. Unlike Spoon, I am not a native to the city, but I have made Baltimore my home. My feeling as both an insider and an outsider in Baltimore comes together in this notion of what it means to have a sense of community. The degree to which we're involved in our community—on our immediate block, in the local park nearby, in the region of town where we do our shopping—those kinds of ever-widening circles in which we live our lives, these are important layers of a sense of community that I need to feel at home in a place. So, I'm not an outsider at all to my neighborhood, to my immediate block, to my local park. I think I feel that way because I've invested in my neighborhood. I know the children who live on my block. I've organized with my neighbors to close down drug houses, to plant street trees, to fundraise for a library, to create a friends group for the local park. I've organized a literacy program in my neighborhood. And now, as I do these art and greening projects with children, this becomes more and more my community because of my ties to more and more people.

The question of race for me is a very important one, and a very deep issue. Baltimore is a very racially divided city, unbelievably so, but I think our country is too, overall. I think the issue of race, like the issue of class, is something we don't want to talk about. It especially makes white people uncomfortable. It rocks the boat. There are a lot of people who make their way here in Baltimore living in separate worlds, really. There aren't a lot of social events that truly have very mixed crowds in Baltimore.

For me personally, as a white person, I will always be struggling with issues of race. I think we all do in this country, whether we want to admit it or not. It's part of how we were raised, it's part of what the wider culture has pressed upon us. My years of working in neighborhoods primarily with children of color is a learning experience—I have as much, if not more, to learn before I have anything to teach. I've learned the enormous challenges kids face growing up. I've learned a lot about the effects of institutionalized racism on young people. What I mean by that is the consistent decisions made in corporate board rooms, public bureaucracies, and state legislatures to disinvest in poor neighborhoods and the refusal to allocate equitable funding across counties for education. So, to interact daily and meaningfully with young people in tough neighborhoods is to see the visible ways in which those kinds of decisions affect people's lives every day. These kids also give me a lot of hope. Seeing their friendships that cut across racial boundaries and their alliances with each other that are a lot more up front than their parents' ever could be—that's incredibly hopeful.

Now, as a working community artist in a city like Baltimore that has a majority of folks of color, I've found it important to look at who I partner with and how I go about my artmaking. I don't think people in communities, whether young or old, see enough interracial friendships, partnerships, marriages—real relationships where people from different cultures and ethnicities are really working on their connections with each other. And so, I partner with other artists of color when I do work in communities. I personally feel it's important to put my energies into building alliances with artists who are different from me. I think it's important for the children and teens I work with to see that white people and people of color can work side by side and can have similar goals. I've watched children at the Teen Center watch me, as a white person, interacting with people of color, and I know they don't miss a beat. It's important to them to see adults crossing those harsh lines. I'm trying to make a commitment to that in my own work.

Giovanna Di Chiro: I know that both of you have collaborated together, and I was wondering, Spoon, if you could talk about your reflections on the ways that art and environmental projects may address interracial communication or collaboration. Do you see these kinds of projects being able to challenge the racial divide in Baltimore?

Bryant Smith: It's hard, because, just like Cinder said, Baltimore is so racially segregated. You know, you have your areas where African Americans live, you have your areas where white folks live, and there are not a lot of areas where they mingle. In so many ways it's hard for communities that are racially diverse to mix together. But the great thing about art and environmental projects is that they can be used as tools where race doesn't make a difference. If you're in a community where you're planting trees together, you start not to see the white person, or the black person, but you see this other person who's a neighbor who's helping to dig the hole to put the tree in the ground. And, you see the tree as something that both you and your neighbor will benefit from. It's the same with art projects in the community. You see this piece of art as something that you and your neighbor are creating and not simply me as a black person or as a white person.

Giovanna Di Chiro: There are a lot of people who do not believe that "color-blindness" actually occurs in this country—in other words, they believe race is so powerful that it cannot simply disappear in our daily experiences. Can you talk more about why you think race becomes invisible during these art and greening projects you have been involved in and not when you are working with, for example, the national environmental organizations or with traditional environmentalists?

Bryant Smith: Art and greening projects do not make us colorblind. There are times when working on these projects can bring people together and times when it can't. For example, Paul, my old supervisor, who is white, and I went into Canton to plant trees with the primarily white community there. They wouldn't listen to me. They completely ignored me, and it was to the point that they basically planted the trees wrong. Paul had to come down and talk to them, and they listened to him. So, in that case, color still stood out. On the flip side of it, if I'm a white person and walk in cold to an all black neighborhood, I will be seen as this white person coming to save the world and to tell us what to do. It's once you're in the community and have built up the trust, and you're working hand in hand with this person—that's when you do forget that this person is a different color and from a different world. And, you focus on the fact that it's two people working together making a change and creating something beautiful, whether it's art or planting trees.

Giovanna Di Chiro: When you worked with community forestry projects in Baltimore, were you working primarily with white people or was it a diverse staff getting out into the neighborhoods planting trees and restoring streams?

Bryant Smith: Well, for a period of time I was the only person of color in the organization I worked with, and now in the program that really works on environmental programs in the hood, there's only one person of color onboard. You know, organizations like that really frustrate me. For one, the folks on staff who are not from Baltimore and who would try to work in areas where they were the only whites, would have a lot of problems trying to get people to participate. Then, they would blame the people for these problems. They couldn't understand why the people in the community wouldn't open their arms to them. They'd come to do their programs, and see the conditions in which people are living in some of the neighborhoods, and they'd say they couldn't understand why people would want to live like that. They would constantly blame the people, and it would kill me. I would tell the leaders of the organizations, "You need to hire more people from the hoods that you're working in to get onboard."

It's also about giving back to the community. The most successful environmental project is not just coming in to plant the trees, but to teach the people how to plant them, to educate them on how to obtain trees and planting materials from the city agencies, to help them learn about what the best trees are to plant in which areas. We're forgetting the part of leaving something behind, giving the people in the community the skills and the opportunities to improve their own neighborhoods and environment. Instead, some of these projects look at it as though, "We gotta go in and save the people—we're here to help them fix their environment." We should be here to help them obtain the skills that they need to do it themselves.

Giovanna Di Chiro: One of the things that I have heard over and over again is when environmental organizations go to a community as "outsiders" and get frustrated when people are not comfortable about participating, the most common explanation is, "Oh, these inner-city people are not interested in environmental issues."

Bryant Smith: Right, totally. You know, some organizations have shut down entire programs that served the community in West Baltimore because the one staff person they sent in to start up a program had a hard time getting it together. You don't do that. You don't pull back the resources when you run into problems. You send somebody else in there who's better equipped.

Cinder Hypki: Or, you send somebody in who is humble enough to think that maybe they didn't do it right the first time. You have to ask yourself some tough questions about how you might do it better. There's nothing wrong with making mistakes, but if you don't learn from that, or you don't feel that you have something to learn, that's a problem.

Giovanna Di Chiro: Both of you use the metaphors of art and environment as "tools" to enhance personal development and to enrich the spirit. I'm wondering if you could also speak to the role of art and the environment as addressing broader issues of environmental justice and social change. How does that happen in your view?

Cinder Hypki: I don't think that there can be any broader structural change unless you have individual people in a country, in a city, in a neighborhood, who are able to have opportunities for, as Spoon called it, "self-development." You can't have any kind of substantive change, you can't have a real democracy, unless you work at the level of the individual, unless individuals are self-confident enough, unless they are literate in many different ways, unless they have their basic needs met of a roof over their head, and clothes that they won't be ashamed of, and food on the table. Unless you have all of those things—things that many middle-class people tend to take for granted—you can't participate in your world in any but the most limited ways. If there's anything that goes to the heart of why I'm motivated to work with kids on art in the neighborhood, it's because I see kids having so few opportunities to explore what's inside themselves and all their possible talents, hopes, and dreams.

To address your question of the relationship between individual change and broader social transformation—most of the teens I have worked with, in general, have a really low threshold for failure and frustration. It goes back to not having a lot of experiences that enable you to try things out, fail, then try something else. If you can get kids really focused and hooked on art, it's a perfect means to allow them to experiment. It teaches important skills: focus, concentration, discipline. Art isn't just a pretty picture of flowers on the wall; it's hard work. Art is about patience and slowly growing confidence in yourself. I think people need those basic tools if they're ever going to have the confidence to change major systems of discrimination and inequality. People have to have some prior experiences that lead them up to the ability to productively change their world.

I remember an anecdote that bears this out. Two years ago I worked with a group of teenagers—we called ourselves the "Green Team"—to plan and create a garden in a pretty tough neighborhood that's adjacent to a senior apartment building. These teens met with the seniors to find out what they wanted. We got planting material and trees donated, and we organized a huge greening event one Saturday. We transformed this quite large vacant space, which was mostly construction backfill with some sod on top, into a beautiful garden, now known as the St. Elizabeth Garden. The kids worked really hard, it was a long day, and at the very end, we took one last look at the garden before going home. I remember standing very close to Shawn, who was fourteen years old at the time. He just shook his head and in a whisper, he said, "Man, I can't believe we did this." I'll never forget that because when I heard that whisper with so much awe in his voice, I realized that what was left with Shawn of that experience was the realization for him that he could be a part of something that could transform his neighborhood—something that made his neighborhood look better, that made people proud of him. I don't think we can transform broad political systems until we know we can transform a little bit of our own neighborhood. That's where art and greening are so powerful. They're tangible, you can get your hands dirty, you can be out there interacting with people, bringing people together. Art and

Fig. 15.1. "Green Team" members, *left to right,* Shawn Stevenson, Ernest Brown, Patrice Kruger, and Winston Burke, plant a flowering perennial during the creation of the St. Elizabeth's Community Garden, Baltimore, Maryland. (Photograph by Paul Flinton)

greening are about transforming a neighborhood as you yourself are being transformed, as people around you are being transformed. Sometimes "transformation" is this big twenty-five-dollar word, but I don't think it's too big a word to use.

Giovanna Di Chiro: I wanted to direct this question to you, Spoon. Cinder raised the issue that both art and greening are activities that transform—they transform an actual physical space, they transform a community space, and they transform the people who live there. I know that you have been involved in community development projects, such as the Rose Street Community Garden, in which physical spaces such as run-down abandoned lots, or, what some people have called "geographies of sacrifice," are turned into beautiful community parks and flourishing gardens. Can you talk about your sense of this idea of transformation, and how art and greening can bring this about in the urban spaces of Baltimore?

Bryant Smith: Well, I'll talk about the Rose Street Community as an example. When I first started working in Rose Street, that area was a complete dump site. There were some plans for urban renewal, to improve the area by

Fig. 15.2. Community members join teens from the Southeast Youth Academy to prepare the soil and sow the seeds for the St. Elizabeth's Community Garden, Baltimore, Maryland. (Photograph by Paul Flinton)

building new row homes, but no new development ever happened. So, over time, the abandoned lot on the street became a fenced-in dump site. It made folks lose respect for the community because you have this huge, rotting piece of land there in the middle of the neighborhood. They didn't know what to do with it, how to clean it up, how to change it into a positive space. What I did was to work with a community group headed up by Elroy Christopher and Mr. Clayton Guyton. We all talked about what could be the possibilities for that space and how that space would best benefit the community.

Elroy Christopher and Clayton Guyton are two community leaders who just got fed up and took an active role in trying to make change in the neighborhood. There was a crack house on Rose Street, and they went in and physically threw out all the junkies and drug dealers and told them if they came back in they would get their heads busted. Then they took this abandoned building, fixed it up with their own money, and that became the Rose Street Community Center. They raised funds for computer equipment and they started running a community-based program out of this old crack house. The drug war in that neighborhood thickened and the dealers burned them out; they set the Center on fire. And, that's when all hell broke loose—Elroy and Mr. Guyton became vigilantes. They went out on the corner with bats, they threatened the drug dealers, they slept out on the drug strip in a tent for six months.

Because of this visible commitment to the neighborhood, other people in the community then got the confidence to start organizing to do other things, like getting rid of the trash in the area. For a long time, the local residents had begged the Department of Sanitation to come pick up trash on a regular basis in that community. So, what happened was they organized every community resident within a square block to bring all of their trash out to Madison Avenue, which is one of the busiest strips in this city, and they blocked traffic with their trash. The Rose Street community locked up part of the city to get the message across that, "We need our trash picked up." It's those kinds of actions that really helped change the neighborhood.

The first project I did with the community was tree planting—we started off planting five trees on Mr. Christopher's block. Immediately afterwards, we got a request for one hundred trees to be planted in the neighborhood, and we began to see how people started working together to put these trees in the ground. One man told me that that was the first time he ever heard birds singing in the morning. It began with the tree planting—we showed people that when we get organized, these are the things we can do.

The next step was dealing with the vacant lot, which people thought would never change. So, I talked with the community residents about what their goals were, and what they identified was that they would love to turn the dump site into a community park where folks could come and hang out, or have cookouts, or family reunions. For months, what we did was to work with community groups and residents in the area to clean it up. We got the city involved to help haul away the trash. We got Parks and People involved to help provide plant materials, grills, and gazebos. We developed that area, this once trashed vacant lot that was an eyesore in the community for years, into a productive, open space. The residents now have a yearly Christmas ceremony, they have community cookouts there every summer, they do these huge youth events out on that lot. Creating that community park was a tool to help the community residents to gain respect for that neighborhood. It also showed them this is what we can do when we organize and work together—we can make change in our neighborhood. It helped them to use those skills of community organizing to address the drug problem in that neighborhood, to address the trash problems. Now the trash is collected every day—the Department of Sanitation sends a huge dump truck and a crew to Rose Street to clean up trash. The skills people learned from transforming the vacant lot were now being used to address other issues. People in the community know that "We did this, we put this together, based on our coming together as a community."

Giovanna Di Chiro: One thing that's interesting in this story that you didn't touch upon, but you did in your interview in the *Baltimore City Paper,* was that the Rose Street Community Garden still is fenced off; it's not an "open space," so to speak, because it's still enclosed by a fence and a lock.[10]

Bryant Smith: One of the big problems we have in Baltimore is illegal dumping on vacant lots. There is a lot of renovation going on in the city, and companies need to haul trash away. Light haulers will get three hundred bucks to help haul all the trash out of somebody's back yard, and instead of paying a percentage of that money to dump it at the city landfill, they'll just pull up to these vacant lots in the middle of the night and dump all the trash there. The fence is up at Rose Street, therefore, to help defend the space. Unfortunately, in order to have successful open space projects, you've got to defend them.

Cinder Hypki: I would like to add to the discussion about the potential impact of art on society. While, yes, I agree that art can change the world, it cannot do it in a vacuum. Art cannot bring about change as icing on the cake in the midst of this bombed-out neighborhood. I think art can change the world if it's intimately linked to other community development efforts going on in a place. That's when painting murals, planting trees, and making gardens matter. I couldn't have gone into the Rose Street community and made a mosaic mural with kids if the two local community activists, Mr. Guyton and Mr. Christopher, hadn't slept on the corner in a tent armed to the teeth to reclaim it from the drug trade. To make a wall beautiful is practically like an act of guerilla warfare. People do give up, they're afraid to go outside, afraid to let their kids play in the street. Art can change the world, but it's got to be really smart about it; it's got to be street smart. And, by that I mean it's got to be integrated into efforts in which people are working together to bring about change.

During the many months of creating a mosaic mural that I worked on with elementary school kids and teens—a mural that adorned the entrance to their school—local community members wandered by as we were diligently working, and they talked to us about their lives and the history of the neighborhood. Many would say, "There's never been a beautiful mural like this, it would just be vandalized." After we were finished with the mural

Fig. 15.3. Esmerelda Castro and Unique Bullock identify their clay tiles mounted on the mosaic mural adorning the front walls of General Wolfe Elementary School, Baltimore, Maryland. (Photograph by Cinder Hypki)

Fig. 15.4. Young artists learn the intricacies of mosaic craftsmanship in Baltimore, Maryland. *From left to right:* Cinder Hypki, John Johnson, Tukoria Bette, Dorethea Sanford, and Darrion Spears. (Photograph by Rebecca Yenawine)

project, some residents, like Miss Brooks, came to the school and volunteered to help tutor kids after school because she saw our mosaic art crew volunteering to beautify the school.

Bryant Smith: People in communities need an example. We can talk until we're blue in the face, but it's not until they see it working that they are willing to get on board. I want to bring up a point that Cinder made about working on her community mural projects. You described how people would wander by and shake their heads and say, "It won't last, people will vandalize it." I think that point is the beginning of change, because when they come back and see that the mural has not been destroyed, they will become more interested, like Miss Brooks did, in participating in projects that make a difference in their community.

Cinder Hypki: You can't talk about this theoretically without seeing tangible results. Not a single teen I worked with to plant the St. Elizabeth's Community Garden thought that garden would last, that those flowers would still be growing. A few months ago, Shawn, one of the original planners of the garden, said to me, "You know, Miss Cinder, maybe we could stick a mural on the wall." That comment bears out what Spoon is saying—you do one thing and people get some confidence and skills and they realize that they can do that, and it won't necessarily get destroyed, then they're on to the next thing, and then you can get some momentum going.

So, if I think about what art can do, in concert with other change efforts, I think it can begin a cycle of hope and renewed energy to work for a better community. The reason that Shawn said, "I can't believe we did this," is because it was the first time he had the opportunity to see the results of his toil and labor, he had an opportunity to actively take part in something that made his neighborhood more beautiful, and you don't often have that chance. Shawn could see plainly, the way teens need tangible things to be able to see, that he has made a difference.

Giovanna Di Chiro: What's the next step in the "cycle of hope" that you referred to? In your view, how does the momentum build from nurturing Shawn's sense of empowerment in his own community, to challenging his future prospects in a discriminatory society?

Cinder Hypki: People will not do what they don't think is possible. No one-shot deal ever turns a neighborhood around—lots of organizations and lots of people need to come together. I see momentum building when six months to a year down the road, having done a project with kids, I find out that the kids are still involved in something in their community. Last Saturday, we held a street tree planting training in Patterson Park, our local park. Much to my delight, when the Southeast Youth Academy brought five kids along, one of those kids was Amber, who has gotten a summer job helping to care for street trees in the neighborhood. I also saw Winston, who was one of the Green Team's faithful members. Well, it's been a year since we completed the garden, and the Green Team has now metamorphosed into the "Community Action Group." This "Action Group" is not only involved in greening things, but in all sorts of community cleanup and other neighborhood actions. Now, Winston is showing up on a Saturday morning at 9 A.M.—which is not the most popular time for teens—to be involved in an effort where he will be trained as a leader in the community. This to me demonstrates some momentum, and the possibility of movement into other arenas of change.

Giovanna Di Chiro: Are there any final comments you would like to share concerning the future directions of your work?

Bryant Smith: One project I'm really excited about is working with 150 inmates at the Maryland Penitentiary in downtown Baltimore. The project is a skill-building program, giving inmates a chance to create garden spaces and artwork to change the physical environment of the prison. It's hard to develop your creativity and sense of your future when you're locked up in this cage for years. Right now we're working in partnership with several landscaping companies and nurseries throughout the city who have promised to have jobs available for skilled gardeners and landscapers when they are released from prison. I'm hoping to encourage 150 artists and help create 150 green thumbs.

Cinder Hypki: I would have to say that I'm excited about this work; there's a lot of joy in art. When people get their hands dirty with it, it's amazing what happens. It's even more amazing when it's about folks who haven't had the opportunity to experiment with and to taste so many different possibilities. I would like to propose a term—you know how you referred to neglected and abandoned urban areas as "geographies of sacrifice"? As a poet, that term really catches at my heart. I think of all these wastelands that we've polluted, from the mountains of West Virginia to Fairfield Wagner's Point here in Baltimore. Those are places that have been sacrificed to the industrial growth of Baltimore, together with the people who live there and their children's futures. I would like to say that art and greening can help create "geographies of possibility," and "geographies of hope." I think they do that by bringing the best out in us—all the things Spoon and I have been talking about today. But, I hope we've been clear that geographies of hope need some wider political will to be created. They will require a larger community all pulling together and clearly investing in the future of its children.

NOTES

1. Cinder Hypki is an artist, environmental educator, and community development consultant; and Bryant "Spoon" Smith is the Executive Director of the Urban Arts Institute and a community forestry consultant with the United States Forest Service. They both live in Baltimore, Maryland.

2. See Mary O'Brien, *Making Better Environmental Decisions* (Cambridge: MIT Press, 2000); and Lizette Hernandez, *Building Upon Our Strengths: A Community Guide to Brownfields Redevelopment* (San Francisco: Urban Habitat Program, 1999).

3. See Nina Felshin, *But is it Art? The Spirit of Art as Activism* (Seattle: Bay, 1995).

4. Carol Becker, "Herbert Marcuse and the Subversive Potential of Art," in *The Subversive Imagination: Artists, Society and Social Responsibility,* ed. Carol Becker (New York: Routledge, 1994), 113–29.

5. David Harvey, *Spaces of Hope* (Berkeley: University of California Press, 2000), 133–36.

6. Statistics taken from the Annie E. Cayce Foundation (www.aecf.org); and the Enoch Pratt Free Library Regional Information Center, 2700 Lighthouse Point East, Suite 310, Baltimore, MD 21224.

7. Information from Baltimore City Healthy Start, Inc., 210 Guilford Avenue, 2nd floor, Baltimore, Maryland 21202.

8. Statistics taken from the Annie E. Cayce Foundation (www.aecf.org); and Community Resources, 4900 Wetheredsville Road, Baltimore, MD 21207.

9. For David Harvey, the insurgent architect is the political subject who creates the ability to design his or her individual and collective fates. Insurgent architects/artists work within heterogeneous communities of action to demonstrate the ways that personal experiences and socioecological predicaments can be hammered into political visions and actions for environmental change.

10. In Michael Anft, "Green in the City," *Baltimore City Paper,* 12 April 2000, 17–25.

PEDAGOGY

16

TEACHING FOR TRANSFORMATION

Lessons from Environmental Justice

Robert Figueroa

Introduction

Struggles for environmental justice have produced a correspondent scholarship, complete with conferences, articles, books, and curricula. Some
schools now have concentrations in environmental justice, many environmental studies programs teach environmental justice explicitly or implicitly,
and the production of academic material in environmental justice grows at
an impressive rate. Though growing academically, the study of environmental justice should not stray from its roots and status as a social movement.
This fact of the field, that it is a study of a social movement, brings the
teacher to a critical position in the social process of education: the classroom, too, must be placed within the context of the social movement. The
classroom becomes a space where citizens can generate and discuss their
visions for transforming our social and political world in ways that ameliorate environmental injustices.

In this essay, I consider three aspects of teaching environmental justice
from within the politicized classroom. First, I offer a skeletal discussion of
my course and its literature to share a sense of my interpretation and goals
for the scholarship of the issues. Since my academic training is largely
philosophical, my approach to the relevant literature will display this bias.
Second, I give consideration to the relationship between theory and practice, which includes my endeavor to explain the benefits of teaching environmental justice as an interdisciplinary philosophy course. Theory and
practice are described through classroom projects and service learning experiences. Lastly, I consider the transformative aspects for pedagogy and moral

imagination. My intention is to describe one kind of course, not necessarily the best kind of course, but a philosophically oriented course that enhances the application of environmental justice in the curriculum.

Part I: A Philosophical Take on Environmental Justice

In many respects, the study of environmental justice comes upon a renaissance of interdisciplinary discourse, which has led to the unique opportunity to engage the subject matter while the origin of many terms, concepts, and the meaning of associated action is in its earliest developmental stages. In philosophy, there is a plethora of training techniques to acquire the skills for developing, designing, and operating terms and concepts. This feature of philosophy allows a rich interaction with a field of study offering a berth (birth) of new ideas. Thus, one of the main emphases of my course is to encourage students to feel that they are part of the community of scholars and activists working to clarify these issues by developing ways of articulating the problems and solutions.

Since 1994, I have introduced environmental justice courses into the curriculum of three universities. The debut course at the University of Colorado at Boulder may very well be the first course in the nation with the official course title of "Environmental Justice." In this essay, I dedicate my discussion to the courses at CU-Boulder and more recently, courses at Colgate University. These courses are "freestanding," not fly-by-night special topics courses; they typically cross-list between philosophy, environmental studies, and ethnic studies.

The courses encompass three general sections. The first section is primarily philosophical, setting down background concepts. The second section wrestles with domestic environmental justice, recognizing that all countries have their own version of domestic struggles. Issues of citizen responsibility, the role of the government and social institutions, and domestic policies and cases are applied to the theoretical base from the first section of the course. The third section deals with global environmental justice: the study of international relationships between sovereign states, transnational agencies and corporations, and the global implications of domestic cases around the world. This section allows students to explore North/South global environmental conflicts, indigenous environmental struggles, development issues, traditional environmental knowledge, and the politics of global ecology, to name a few. Again, the implications of human activities upon the world's environments are set in practice with the background of theory.

TENDENCIES TOWARD THE DISTRIBUTIVE PARADIGM   Suppose the first question we ask in the study of environmental justice is as primordial as "what do we mean by justice?" In the history of philosophy, this question has been approached from a variety of intellectual angles. Indeed, we have a history of theories of justice from the philosophical canon as well as renowned contenders in critical theory, race theory, feminist theory, and identity politics. From the canonical arena, theories build a liberal distributive paradigm, and nondistributive responses construct a second paradigm. I tend to survey the philosophy of environmental justice across these paradigms.

I ritually begin course readings with Book Five of Aristotle's *Nichomachean Ethics*. This certainly gives away that I enjoy teaching the applications and insights of philosophy, and it is probably unnecessary for educators from other disciplines. At the end of the semester, students always agree to keep Aristotle even though they initially wondered how this difficult work would be relevant to environmental justice. I use his interpretation as an ancient description of distributive justice, which is then used with contemporary scholars to show the continued proliferation of distributive accounts of environmental justice.

I then use Peter Wenz's book *Environmental Justice,* because it provides a distributive definition of environmental justice, which he expands through the liberal tradition from libertarian theory to Rawlsian theory. The best principles from the distributive theories are then compiled into a pluralistic convergence with Wenz's method of biocentric individualism ecocentric holism, which he then applies to his concentric circle theory of obligation. In many respects Wenz's project is an expected and somewhat appropriate account of the dominant distributive paradigm. Unfortunately, it leaves out many other theories of justice, specifically those accounts like critical theory, feminist theory, and other views that make use of (but are not to be reduced to) the politics of recognition. This oversight in Wenz's approach presents an incomplete picture for students to understand vital concerns, such as environmental racism, ecofeminism, indigenous struggles, and other nondistributive accounts of justice. My impression is that he may have written the book without much regard or knowledge of the growing literature on environmental justice during the 1980s, particularly the meaning of environmentalism for people of color. He has a digestible and clear description of theories of justice analyzed by the measure of environmental equity. Nonetheless, one simply cannot use this book to give an accurate picture of the movement.

I also use Wenz's book in comparison to the grassroots literature and anthologies written explicitly on cases and theories from the environmental justice movement. My favorite alternatives have been *Toxic Struggles,* edited by Richard Hofrichter, and *At Issue: Environmental Justice,* edited by Jonathan Petrikin. Some years I have relied heavily upon Robert Bullard's edited work *Confronting Environmental Racism,* which includes critical cases and literature. Other semesters I add *Faces of Environmental Racism,* edited by Laura Westra and Bill Lawson, to explore other cases and excellent philosophical analyses. Complementing these texts, I use a hefty reading packet and reserve texts like Bunyan Bryant and Paul Mohai's, *Race and the Incidence of Environmental Hazards,* Bryant's sequel *Environmental Justice,* and Laura Pulido's *Environmentalism and Economic Justice.*

These texts and supplemental works provide the critical basis of the environmental racism debate, as well as the consideration of paradigms of justice. Indeed, each of the edited texts (mentioned above and below) contains a variety of theoretical approaches, case studies, and accounts of social policy. Instead of describing all in detail, I would emphasize that each text offers a spectrum of diverse voices, supporting the rally cry of environmental justice: "We Speak For Ourselves." The local emphasis in the literature is crucial, and we cannot understate that the theories of environmental justice must address grassroots dynamics. The most appropriate arrangement of texts would simultaneously present students with voices from the grassroots (to quote Bullard's subtitle), the theoretical and critical tools for interpreting the literature, and an ability to analyze the peculiar position of the scholar and student of environmental justice. The peculiar position involves the obligation to hear these local voices in the most thoughtful and sympathetic process available to us.

ENVIRONMENTAL RACISM AND THE ARGUMENT FOR BIVALENT ENVIRON-MENTAL JUSTICE   It is good to avoid equating the environmental justice movement with the important history and literature of environmental racism, but educating about the movement still fundamentally means educating about environmental racism. And, there is still much to gain by the scholarship and concern for what sometimes seems the ever-presence of environmental racism.

The initial definitions of "environmental racism," from Benjamin Chavis and Robert Bullard in particular, describe the injustice in terms of the distribution of burdens *and* the political representation and moral considerations of racial discrimination.[1] Furthermore, environmental racism has regularly included a general extension beyond a black-white distinction by including other ethnic minorities. This approach to environmental racism is insightful and problematic in ways that must be studied. What do we mean by "race"? What do we want the environmental considerations to actually say about people of color and the poor communities? The most common problematic is the debate that contrasts the role of race and racism against class and classism. The debate stems over which one better substantiates causation and correlation, even though just about every scholar agrees that race and class have interpenetrating features.

On the one side, we have the scholars and activists who declare race as both the major indicator and causal factor for the location of environmental burdens in the United States. The counter-arguments challenge the environmental racism charge with descriptions of economic inequities by two main strategies. Either the locations of environmental burdens are dependent solely on market forces, which are presumably morally neutral, or the locations are guided by market decisions that are immorally biased to exploit the poor and politically powerless. Thus, the latter version pits environmental classism against environmental racism. The allegedly neutral position of economic efficiency is the most dangerous in the literature, and I work diligently for students to come to their own realizations of the logic and moral implications of that position. In the field of environmental justice there appears to be no morally neutral activity, and what often gets described as economically efficient later turns out to be evidence supporting the environmental racism charge.

In Petrikin's edited *At Issue,* we find reprinted some of the initial studies on environmental racism and counter studies contending that market forces and socioeconomic conditions determine the location of environmental burdens. For example, Bryant and Mohai's, "Environmental Injustice: Weighing Race and Class as Factor in the Distribution of Environmental Hazards," which confirms environmental racism in Detroit, is followed by the study by Doug Anderton. He argues that industrial districts are impacted most by the environmental burdens, concluding that earlier studies inaccurately base environmental inequities on race. Also, we can find Vicki Been's challenge to the founding studies on environmental racism. Been argues that the early studies do not distinguish between a community coming to the nuisance of an environmental burden and the burden being distributed to the community.

I supplement Petrikin's volume with my reading packet. For example, Bullard responds to Been's important challenge in his article, "A New 'Chicken-or-Egg' Debate." Other readings allow students to expand the theoretical discourse on the relationship between race and class. For instance, some of my writings provide the link between the environmental racism debate and race theory, including discussions on Latino/a theory.[2] These writings emphasize the earlier cases of the environmental justice movement, the work of philosophers in race theory, and my own categories of institutional racism to help students make sense of the critical distinction between intentional and unintentional racism. The socioeconomic challenges noted above are juxtaposed with readings that decipher the moral content of efficiency theory and negotiated compensation. We read Mark Sagoff's, "Economics and Environmental Ethics," in order to show the logical problems of efficiency theory; particularly the tendencies of cost-benefit analysis, the asymmetry between the personal ownership and distributive market forces, and the failures of fully assessing the differences between consumers and citizens.

The philosophical approach to the environmental racism debate discloses nuances to lead us beyond the race versus class platitude. Embedded within the environmental racism debate are underlying presumptions about the very nature of social and environmental justice. A nagging question arises: Is distribution the best paradigm for understanding justice? If the political institution is designed to habitually discriminate against particular groups, then the notion of merit and distributive fairness is already undermined by the terms of political participation and recognition. Rather than simply look at the social goods and provide a calculus for distribution by an impartial rational method, environmental justice requires an approach in which moral actors are politically bound by their social location that is simultaneously cultural and environmental. Distributive theories tend to focus on the goods and fairness, rarely questioning the connection between the value of the goods and harms that are culturally and environmentally informed. Critical theory and the politics of recognition contextualize participatory parity by placing the moral agent in an environment that is interpreted by virtue of real cultural social location. Placing environmental burdens in the social spaces of the poor and people of color communities is an expression of the ways in which the inhabitants are valued by the more powerful decision-makers in our society. When the decision-makers are set in participatory power, they value their social location enough to consciously avoid locating harms upon themselves and in their environments. The regularity with which environmental burdens are concentrated in the spaces of poverty and color announces who is the most institutionally powerful and who is represented in environmental decision-making. Environmentalists have only recently recognized that their social location serves to determine the environmental struggles they choose, and that their environmental interests will be similar to those similarly situated. Thus, affluent lobbyists battle over affluent interpretations of environmental concerns. The politics of recognition and critical theory presents a way for analyzing the political dynamics and implications of these factors of social location.

The arguments for recognition and participation, especially regarding the empowerment and involvement of local voices, become more crucial as we get into the specific cases of environmental racism and global environmental justice. To what extent is distributive justice able to address the claims of Kettleman City residents who speak Spanish and receive reports in English? Clearly, the democratic participation by the citizens is denied by this habitual language prejudice, and that produces a major injustice of the siting process, among other suspiciously discriminatory procedures. In addition, we find that even the most skeptical voices against environmental racism charges often admit that the policy of least resistance is determined according to the lack of political voice from the community. The utilized assumption is that institutional procedures and political background conditions are structured so that these communities historically and reliably lack political voice. To decide the siting of environmental burdens according to this assumption is clearly a process of reifying and perpetuating the institutional structures that disempower the voices of citizens from specific social locations. Critical analysis, the politics of recognition, and other strands of nondistributive theories of justice directly challenge these assumptions that perpetuate the institutional status quo.

Hofrichter's *Toxic Struggles* is a seminal volume that enriches the study of environmental justice by extending discourses into the cultural dimensions of the issues. He includes authors who analyze the politics of environmentalism by deciphering the different cultural interpretations of environmental concerns in domestic and global environmental justice. His text also presents the connections between ecofeminism, indigenous struggles, global politics, and workers' struggles. The tone of the text is an overarching set of critiques of capitalist market assumptions interpreted from the perspective of ecological social justice. By teaming the Petrikin and Hoftrichter volumes, the class is able to question whether or not the current social institutions and distributive assumptions are suited to address environmental justice.

In 1983, Iris Marion Young published, "Justice and Hazardous Waste," to analyze the case of Warren County, Massachusetts (not to be mistaken for the landmark case of Warren County, North Carolina). She questioned possible distributive theories and argued that none could satisfy what the residents considered to be just. Instead, she interpreted their call for justice as a need for self-determination and political recognition in the siting process. The injustice was not merely the distribution of the burden, but more critically, the ways in which the political process failed to include the concerns and voice of the citizens most affected by the siting. According to Young, participatory self-determination sets the conditions for the latter distribution of goods and harms. This precondition of distributive politics is where we should be focusing our basis of justice. In 1998, Young revisits this argument with Christian Hunold, in "Justice, Democracy, and Hazardous Siting." They outline a communicative democratic model for negotiated compensation, which allows students to observe the incomplete considerations of other authors. For instance, Boerner and Lambert argue for negotiated compensation as a means for circumventing the environmental racism debate; however, they fail to present ways to avoid institutional hegemony within the negotiation process. Another good comparison is Wenz's article "Just Garbage." It is a truncated version of his theoretical survey that relies upon the principle of commensuration between benefits and burdens, which requires that communities benefiting the most from the environmental burdens are morally obligated to take the most burdens ("other things being equal," as Wenz is fond to saying). His notion of fairness is commendable and his distributive solution is provocative: achieve commensuration by redistributing environmental burdens to the spaces of the most privileged members of society. But, Wenz fails to take into account the mobility of the rich and the institutional processes that render the victims of environmental discrimination unable to experience the justice of commensuration, not to mention the all-important question regarding who has the voice in the distributive political structure.

These philosophical contrasts enable me to develop a *bivalent* approach to environmental justice.[3] On the one hand there is the ever-popular distributive paradigm, and then there is a paradigm determined by social and political recognition. This is not to say these are the *only* two paradigms, but that these two have distinguishable characteristics for useful study. The most important aspect of the bivalent interpretation is that it moves the debates in environmental justice to another level of analysis. Instead of getting stuck in a holding pattern of dueling experts arguing between race and class, the bivalent interpretation requires that students attempt to find ways in which these two paradigms can be simultaneously operationalized.

FROM DOMESTIC TO GLOBAL ENVIRONMENTAL JUSTICE   Global environmental justice requires a whole section of the course. Like that of domestic environmental justice, this section is steered by theoretical applications to cases. Among the many issues are development, indigenous rights, environmental regimes, global policymaking, the politics of space, paradigms of justice, and a myriad of concerns regarding global markets and technologies. The transition from U.S. domestic environmental justice to global issues, in my class, often launches from Native American struggles for environmental justice. Issues of sovereignty and the ability of corporate agencies to exploit the power relations between the United States and Indian nations, as well as the historical appropriation and exploitation of resources with cultural destruction, raises the philosophical importance of environmental justice to global dimensions. Useful texts have been Peter Eichstaedt's *If You Poison Us* and Jace Weaver's *Defending Mother Earth*.

For global problems, I have relied upon Wolfgang Sachs' *Global Ecology* and Fen Osler Hampson and Judith Reppy's *Earthly Goods*. The former is a series of articles that attend to the philosophy of development and the implications of the 1992 Rio "Earth Summit." The latter is a series of articles mapping directly onto the bivalent analysis of paradigms of justice in global environmental contexts. Issues of international obligations to environmental and economic compensation between North and South nations arise in both of these texts, which I supplement with Dale Jamieson's, "Global Environmental Justice." In addition to this literature, I use United Nations documents to explore the politics of sustainable development and articles on the human rights approach to the environment. The human right to a safe environment serves a useful discussion of the kinds of rights, including considerations of minority rights for indigenous peoples, associated with environmental justice. I use James Nickel's "The Human Right to a Safe Environment"; William Aiken's "Human Rights in an Ecological Era"; and Will Kymlicka's "Concepts of Community and Social Justice."

The section devoted to global environmental justice extends the moral considerations and involvement of students. The social ontology of the United States, as the ultimate consumer of global resources, the hilt of global capitalism's nation-states, and a dominant military power, leads students to realize that critical aspects of the domestic issues, like waste sitings, cannot be extinguished by shipping out the problem. Our consumption practices already set the background injustices that reveal our self-image as morally superior to those in far greater need, which goes to prove that our domestic problems of environmental justice are intricately linked to global prejudices. While this insight turns out to be an overwhelming lesson to weigh on the shoulders of our students, I find they become empowered by the raised consciousness.

REGARDING OTHER MEDIA   The use of film, popular media, and video documentation often exists at the center of conveying information about environmental justice. What sense does a philosophical discussion of the paradigms of justice really make if we cannot *see* what we are talking about being played out and tested in the struggles of peoples? It seems unquestionably better to see real cases working with these ideas than the thought experiments traditionally applied as a tool of the trade.

A good example of how valuable the video medium is in portraying struggles of environmental justice comes out of my first environmental justice course. Two students from this first course went on to produce a professional-quality documentary *(Sin Agua No Hay Vida [Without Water There Is No Life])* of a Chicano community in San Luis, Colorado, protecting its cultural landscape against the destruction of their common watershed and alpine forest.[4] In addition to displaying the inseparability of the cultural heritage with its environment, the video-work etches concerns and resolutions of discriminatory environmentalism between the Chicano community and Ancient Forest Rescue. Students are inspired by the show of unity between the subaltern and mainstream forms of environmentalism. And, the class itself gains a sense of transformative heritage from the knowledge that former students have set the caliber of active participation as a legacy for future students.

Other documentaries on the issues of environmental justice abound and sources are rich once we begin to search them out. There is the award-winning news documentary *Town Under Siege,* about a Cajun community in Grand Bois, Louisiana, and its struggle with major oil corporations dumping oil waste products like benzene into a local pit. *Laid to Waste* offers a video account of environmental racism in Chester, Pennsylvania—a case which can also be found in recent literature like Luke Cole and Sheila Foster's *From the Ground Up.* Another documentary, *Building Bombs,* reveals the environmental injustices and ecological impacts of the Savannah River Plant, a high-level nuclear complex known as one of the biggest construction projects in human history. In the global arena, *Delta Force* depicts the tragic drama of Nigerian operations of Shell Oil on Ogoniland. The film documents the environmental injustices and events leading to the state execution of Ken Saro-Wiwa (see chapter 12 of this volume). Also for indigenous rights, I use an episode of *Rights and Wrongs*, a human rights education program of the Corporation for Public Broadcasting, which excerpts James O'Connor's Academy Award–nominated documentary *At the Edge of Conquest*. This work exemplifies the problems of social location and political recognition that emerge when assessing the implications of background justices for distributive justice agreements, a dilemma that is explored impressively throughout the text of Hampson and Reppy's *Earthly Goods*. The documentary *Rachel Carson's "Silent Spring,"* discussing her life and the impact of *Silent Spring*, can be used to reflect upon the media manipulation so common in environmental justice struggles, as well as to set an historical backdrop for the struggles against the political triumvirate of chemical corporations, agribusiness, and government favoritism. Since class periods are short compared to the vast resource of documentaries, I collaborated on an Environment Justice Film Series with my student Joyce Tseng. She organized a coalition of the students of color organizations with the "green" student groups to sponsor the series. Documentaries were shown about every week for the greater campus audience, and professors from a variety of disciplines would facilitate discussion following the screenings.

From Hollywood cinema, cover-ups and paper trails earmark films depicting environmental justice. Undisclosed risks to toxic waste and the violation of rights to information about industrial activities are ripe material for conspiratory mysteries. Think of *A Civil Action, Erin Brokovich, Silkwood,* and even Stephen Seagal movies like *On Deadly Ground* and *Fire Down Below*. Comparative studies of popular media reveal important themes like the role and treatment of gender and race. The films with leading women depict their leadership in the movement, as well as the value of grassroots organizing. These characters are often working mothers who must juggle activism, household and family responsibilities, public scrutiny, and interpersonal relationships. In comparison, Seagal-like cinema unfortunately overshadows its own accuracies of community disempowerment, environmental burdens, and discrimination (racial and economic) by the high-action, super-violent solutions of the elusive military hero. In these latter films, the women, though expressive of admirable integrity, are depicted as distressed damsels. Their characters amplify the wretched environmental villains who are cold-blooded killers, destroyers of local cultures, and sex offenders. While these comments provide mere surface analysis of Hollywood and environmental justice, they begin to show the types of discussions that follow classroom screenings.

In television programs we can also find environmental justice. The public health component makes for an exciting mystery in *Quincy* reruns devoted to environmental discrimination and hazardous waste. If one looks hard enough, s/he can find racism and hazardous working conditions poignantly paired together even in unexpected places, like an episode of *Little House on the Prairie*. With these few exceptions, the more independent and localized the film producer, the more likely the case involves minority struggles for environmental justice; while the more Hollywood, the whiter the cases.

Part II: Exploration of Social Location through Voices, Cases, and Action

Each semester is devoted to group presentations of particular case studies. The case list in my class includes a wide range of global and domestic cases, cases of women in grassroots leadership, cases of environmental and cultural catastrophe, and policy debates relevant to understanding the scope and dimensions of environmental justice. The groups consist of four to five students, each of whom is responsible for delivering some aspect of the case to the class. I often provide some springboard research for the groups to get a sense of the issues. They take it from there and their presentation must involve some critical analysis and theoretical consideration, typically from the philosophical approaches of the class.

The value of each case study offers enormous practice for students to understand the breadth of issues and interpretative ranges of environmental justice. Students become intimate with the cases and retain the information remarkably better by presenting the information rather than reading and studying the cases for an exam. They come to know about the places and peoples involved, the strategies of grassroots action, and the environmental values and concepts of justice being forged by the local voices. In the end, each student knows at least one case extremely well and s/he develops a means for articulating the transformations necessary to remedy and/or ameliorate the injustices of the case.

TRANSFORMATIVE TEACHING AND SERVICE LEARNING   Service learning is a pedagogical tool that inherently links theory and practice, education and society, student identity with citizen responsibility, and the classroom with social action. Carried out correctly, service learning blurs these distinctions to the point of actually moving the classroom spaces beyond the campus. Distinct from internships or volunteer projects, which may be admittedly steeped in social transformation and the expansion of an individual's repertoire of moral experience, service learning requires that students bring their experiences back into the regular classroom to share what they have learned. The service is contextual to the course content and ought to be incorporated into the lessons. Public reflection of the experiences in the classroom should indicate our ability to embrace the experiences of others who are differently situated. Students realize themselves as political entities whose experiences help to inform, generate, and conduct the political meanings of the education process. The interaction with other members of the community who are working in dimensions of environmental justice helps students to see which social epistemologies are dominant because of institutional habits and personalities, and which epistemologies are made silent and subversive because of oppressive social mechanisms.

Though a fan of service learning, I didn't feel confident enough to take on the project until some time had passed. I was intimidated by the amount of work I believed it would require. I was nervous that the community would not be open to receiving a student participant who would also need special scheduling and have different interests from an ordinary employee or volunteer. Organizations were initially apprehensive, but by the end of our conversations they were enthusiastic. I undid my fears. The students were openly welcomed. The more the students participated in setting up their placements, the better for all involved. There are aspects of the placement process that could go awry: placement can take too long and cause delays in the student project; students could be (but weren't) exploited to do grunt work rather than be involved in the action; and, the students could (but didn't) fail to satisfy the needs of the organization. A greater obstacle may come when the college is so remote that students cannot reach the location of the needed service. My students in Boulder did not experience this, but vicinity became an obstacle with Colgate University students willing to do service learning—this is changing with a new campus center for community service.

Student projects included: direct activism in an environmental justice mobilization; working with Habitat for Humanity; working with the Rocky Mountain Justice and Peace Center; assisting attorneys in toxic law cases; and, environmental justice education in primary schools. Students were required to fulfill three to ten hours a week of service, give a class presentation of their work, and write a final paper on their project.

Environmental justice service learning sometimes involves a level of activism that requires a distinction of responsibilities between citizen and student. One student's accounts of her own service involved activism in the San Luis case. She devoted her time to working with the Chicano community members and Ancient Forest Rescue. Acting according to her own political conscience, she was dragged into a jail cell for participating in a lockdown (locking oneself to machinery or vehicles) to stop logging trucks from hauling the lumber from La Sierra, the community's alpine watershed. This student related her experiences of direct action that reinterpreted the course content through the firsthand experience of an environmental justice activist. That was enough to convince me that service learning would have transformative ramifications if used to its full extent. An echo of this experience occurred when recent students participated in the Quebec demonstrations protesting the Free Trade of the Americas Agreement. They returned to class with a video presentation and sophisticated insights on the issues. Class discussion lasted a lively full session. These are obviously unusual descriptions of service learning and quite unintended effects. However, they are notable because of their student-as-citizen resonance.

Though differing in detail and dimensions, each of the projects offered opportunities for students to develop their repertoire of moral experiences. My student working with a toxics lawyer was brought into cases that involved visiting poor Latino and African American communities in Denver. She met the residents in their neighborhoods and in their conferences with the lawyer. In effect, she came to know a people with whom she had little prior experience. She learned their struggles and realized the sacrifices that real social problems require. Speaking to her peers, the students of similar backgrounds and material expectations, she related to them the conditions that they are often shielded from and the implications of affluence most of them share. The contradiction of her service learning project, coming in as a white, affluent student, expecting to learn the ropes of a perceived luxurious career from a lawyer practicing social change with poor Latino and African Americans, is extremely helpful for conveying the social contradictions that are constantly raised during the course. The realities of these contradictions suggest further reflection for transformative teaching.

Part III: Closing Thoughts—Moral Imagination, Despair, and Transformative Teaching

Moral imagination, as I use the concept, refers to our cognitive capacity as moral agents to sympathetically apprehend the moral experience, feelings, and judgments of others. This includes the ability to imagine ways of transforming social relations and political situations in order to conceptualize how things ought to be. Mark Johnson's view of the moral imagination exemplifies the inherently public and situated character of this sympathetic response. Johnson remarks: "Moral imagination is public and shared. It has the same public character as do our social relations, practices, and institutions, for all these are defined by metaphors and other imaginative structures. Imagination . . . is the primary means by which social relations are constituted."[5]

We may question our ability to actually feel what others feel, but we are quite able to stretch our imagination to wonder what we would feel like if we projected our self-image into the place of the other. Again, this does not entail the claim that we are feeling exactly like the other, or feigning impartiality, but that we can imagine ourselves into similar circumstances. Indeed, the social location of the other is a critical sphere of knowing and feeling that we may not be anywhere near. We should not use the moral imagination to speak for others. My point instead is that we work through our process of understanding environmental justice by stretching our moral imagination to personally grasp a notion of the injustices involved, as well as the potentialities for alleviating and ameliorating the injustices. The latter part of this process often involves stretching the moral imagination to envision political changes. If people are environmentally burdened as a result of underlying social conditions, then we often imagine a different political process, or a shift in social conditions. This transformative process opens the political imagination, where more than a sympathetic response is apprehended as we actively consider different social arrangements by which we should live.

When a person is trapped in an unjust situation with no clear vision of escape, and when we imagine ourselves in that position, I think we share despair. Likewise, when my students use their moral imagination in the process of studying environmental justice they initially experience a weight upon their political imagination and despair begins to turn over in the classroom. Helplessness looms in many cases of environmental justice. The remedies of the injustices are often arguably lame compromises of human life and socioenvironmental values against political and economic agendas. Even victories can appear Pyrrhic at best, given the constant uphill struggle against related injustices.

Despair is not an objective of this course, although it is unfortunately one part of the subject matter. Likewise, the student is not in the classroom to despair, but the classroom should not deny the student this experience of moral imagination. In fact, the classroom, as I understand it, should strive to stretch the moral imagination whenever there is a relevant opportunity for this process. And even when I do not always see or seize the opportunity, I certainly have little power in restraining a student from engaging this cognitive process. It is most imperative though, that the classroom transform despair into a proactive lesson rather than one of paralyzing helplessness. The excitement of the course is getting students to face the despair and develop tools for understanding and transforming this state into intellectual, personal, and hopefully, social, action. As students come to this process, the ethos of the classroom begins to shift into a closer involvement with the material and the issues at hand.

Radical pedagogy may be understood as teaching with attitudes and approaches that politicize the classroom and the curriculum. By identifying the classroom as a place of reproducing institutional processes in a political economy, which in turn generates political actors, we can enliven the student's political imagination. The academic's pursuit of environmental justice carries political baggage and obligation that many subjects lack. The study of a contemporary social movement lends itself to the use of pedagogy as a form of activism. The social activism is a consciousness raising that utilizes the moral and political imagination of the student to seriously consider the options for transforming current social conditions. Students feel compelled to ask, "What can we do?" and "What is our responsibility?" By asking these questions, the classroom is transformed into a place where citizens can think these matters through without losing sight that the matters are upon us.

NOTES

For a sample syllabus from my Environmental Justice course (PHIL232/ENST232), email me (rfigueroa@mail.colgate.edu) or Joni Adamson (jadamson@u.arizona.edu).

1. For definitions of "environmental racism" from Chavis and Bullard, see United Church of Christ Commission for Racial Justice, *Toxic Wastes and Race*

in the United States: A National Report on the Racial and Socio-Economic Characteristics of Communities with Hazardous Waste Sites; and U.S. House Committee on the Judiciary. Environmental Justice: Hearings before the Subcommittee on Civil and Constitutional Rights.

2. See Figueroa in works cited.

3. I use the term "bivalent" respectful of its use in Nancy Fraser's theories, see Justice Interruptus: Critical Reflections on the Postsocialist Condition.

4. The importance of the video activism/documentary is made apparent by recognizing that although several authors in this volume have discussed this case (e.g., Devon Peña and Tom Lynch), there may be no other specifically environmental justice documentaries on the case.

5. Johnson, Moral Imagination: Implications of Cognitive Science for Ethics.

WORKS CITED

Aiken, William. "Human Rights in an Ecological Era," Environmental Values 1, no. 2 (Summer 1992): 191.

Anderton, Doug. "Studies Used to Prove Charges of Environmental Racism Are Flawed." In At Issue: Environmental Justice, edited by Jonathan Petrikin, 24–37. San Diego: Greenhaven, 1995.

Aristotle. Nichomachean Ethics, translated by Richard McKeon. New York: Random House, 1941.

Bryant, Bunyan, ed. Environmental Justice: Issues, Policies, and Solutions. Washington, D.C.: Island, 1995.

Bryant, Bunyan, and Paul Mohai. "Environmental Injustice: Weighing Race and Class as Factor in the Distribution of Environmental Hazards," University of Colorado Law Review 63, no. 4 (1992): 921.

———, eds. Race and the Incidence of Environmental Hazards: A Time for Discourse. Boulder: Westview, 1992.

Bullard, Robert D. Dumping in Dixie: Race, Class, and Environmental Quality. Boulder: Westview, 1999.

———. "A New 'Chicken-or-Egg' Debate: Which Came First—The Neighborhood, or the Toxic Dump?" The Workbook 19, no. 2 (Summer 1994): 60.

———, ed. Confronting Environmental Racism: Voices from the Grassroots. Boston: South End, 1993.

Cole, Luke W., and Sheila R. Foster. From the Ground Up: Environmental Racism and the Rise of the Environmental Justice Movement. New York: New York University Press, 2001.

Eichstaedt, Peter H. *If You Poison Us: Uranium and Native Americans.* Santa Fe: Red Crane Books, 1994.

Figueroa, Robert. *Debating the Paradigms of Justice: The Bivalence of Environmental Justice.* Ann Arbor: University Microfilms International, 1999.

———. "Other Faces: Latinos and Environmental Justice." In *Faces of Environmental Racism: Confronting Issues of Global Justice,* edited by Laura Westra and Bill E. Lawson, 167–84. Lanham, Md.: Rowman & Littlefield, 2001.

Figueroa, Robert, and Claudia Mills. "Environmental Justice." In *A Companion to Environmental Philosophy,* ed. D. Jamieson, 426–38. Oxford: Blackwell Publishers, 2000.

Fraser, Nancy. *Justice Interruptus: Critical Reflections on the "Postsocialist Condition."* New York: Routledge, 1997.

Hampson, Fen Osler, and Judith Reppy, eds. *Earthly Goods: Environmental Change and Social Justice.* Ithaca: Cornell University Press, 1996.

Hofrichter, Richard, ed. *Toxic Struggles: The Theory and Practice of Environmental Justice.* Philadelphia: New Society Publishers, 1993.

Hunold, Christian, and Iris Marion Young. "Justice, Democracy, and Hazardous Siting," *Political Studies* 46 (1998): 82.

Jamieson, Dale. "Global Environmental Justice." In *Philosophy and the Natural Environment,* edited by R. Atfield and H. Belsey, 201. Cambridge: Cambridge University Press, 1994.

Johnson, Mark. *Moral Imagination: Implications of Cognitive Science for Ethics.* Chicago: University of Chicago Press, 1993.

Kymlicka, Will. "Concepts of Community and Social Justice." In *Earthly Goods: Environmental Change and Social Justice,* edited by Fen Osler Hampson and Judith Reppy. Ithaca: Cornell University Press, 1996.

Nickel, James. "The Human Right to a Safe Environment: Philosophical Perspectives on Its Scope and Justification," *The Yale Journal of International Law* 18, no. 1 (Winter 1993): 281–95.

Petrikin, Jonathan, ed. *At Issue: Environmental Justice.* San Diego: Greenhaven, 1995.

Pulido, Laura. *Environmentalism and Economic Justice: Two Chicano Struggles in the Southwest.* Tucson: University of Arizona Press, 1996.

Rawls, John. *A Theory of Justice.* Cambridge, Mass.: Belknap of Harvard University Press, 1971.

Sachs, Wolfgang, ed. *Global Ecology: A New Arena of Political Conflict.* Atlantic Heights: Humanity, 1993.

Sagoff, Mark. "Economics and Environmental Ethics." In *Earthbound: New*

Introductory Essays in Environmental Ethics, edited by Tom Regan, 147–78. Philadelphia: Temple University Press, 1984.

United Church of Christ Commission for Racial Justice. *Toxic Wastes and Race in the United States: A National Report on the Racial and Socio-Economic Characteristics of Communities with Hazardous Waste Sites.* New York: Public Data Access, 1987.

U.S. House Committee on the Judiciary. *Environmental Justice: Hearings before the Subcommittee on Civil and Constitutional Rights* 103rd Cong., 1st sess., 3–4 March 1994.

Weaver, Jace, ed. *Defending Mother Earth: Native American Perspectives on Environmental Justice.* Maryknoll, N.Y.: Orbis Books, 1996.

Wenz, Peter S. *Environmental Justice.* Albany: State University of New York Press, 1988.

———. "Just Garbage." In *Faces of Environmental Racism: Confronting Issues of Global Justice,* edited by Laura Westra and Bill E. Lawson, 57–73. Lanham, Md.: Rowman & Littlefield, 2001).

Westra, Laura, and Bill E. Lawson, eds. *Faces of Environmental Racism: Confronting Issues of Global Justice,* 2nd ed. Lanham, Md.: Rowman & Littlefield, 2001.

Young, Iris Marion. "Justice and Hazardous Waste." *The Applied Turn in Contemporary Philosophy: Bowling Green Studies in Applied Philosophy* 5 (1983): 171.

Films

A Civil Action. Directed by Steven Zaillian. Touchstone Pictures, 1998.

Building Bombs: The Legacy. Produced by Mark Mori and Susan Robinson. 1990.

Delta Force. Directed by Glen Ellis. U.K., 1995.

Erin Brokovich. Directed by Steven Soderbergh. Universal, 2000.

Fire Down Below. Directed by Felix Enrique-Alcala. Warner Home Video, 1997.

Laid to Waste: A Chester Neighborhood Fights for Its Future. Produced by Robert Bahar and George McCollough. 1996.

Little House on the Prairie. "To Live With Fear: Part II." 21 February 1977.

On Deadly Ground, Directed by Steven Seagal. Warner Home Video, 1994.

Rachel Carson's "Silent Spring." Produced for *The American Experience.* PBS Video, 1992.

Rights and Wrongs. "Brazil #303." International Center for Global Communications Foundation, 1995.

Silkwood. Directed by Mike Nichols. Anchor Bay Entertainment, 1984.

Sin Agua No Hay Vida (Without Water There is No Life). Produced by Jay Bowman and Dana Wilson. Wet Mountain Productions, 1998.

Town Under Siege. Aired on CBS, 23 December 1997.

17

NOTES ON CROSS-BORDER ENVIRONMENTAL JUSTICE EDUCATION

Soenke Zehle

Across the United States, multiracial organizations are battling pollution as well as the cultural, economic, and political marginalization that has resulted in the environmental degradation of their communities in the first place. A multitude of organizations have coalesced into an environmental justice movement whose tremendous (and virtually irreconcilable) heterogeneity has already provoked critiques of its viability as a collective effort.

In one of the few attempts to assess the political effectiveness of the environmental justice movement, Christopher Foreman argues that environmental justice activists who avoid the prioritization of ecological costs and risks in order to maintain organizational coherence and commitment of movement actors, ultimately do so at their own expense: people with few economic and political resources are less likely to focus on major problems as long as an ecopopulism suggests that all struggles are equally important and communities deserve no less than the (unrealistic) elimination of pollution altogether. Honest discussion of possible (and painful) tradeoffs rarely occurs—the experience of native communities that followed the expulsion of waste management industries from other communities is a case in point. Federal agencies like the Environmental Protection Agency, already operating without mandated priorities, are weakened when yet another item (environmental justice and the pursuit of "distributional equity" in the allocation of ecological costs and risks) is added.[1]

Foreman suggests instead that minority communities might benefit more if an analysis of various ecological risks identified the largest and most easily reduced hazards, and federal as well as local resources were directed accordingly. He also argues that an exclusive focus on race and environmental racism is itself symptomatic of an attachment to the civil rights heritage rather than the consequence of consistent analytical differentiation among relevant factors.

But activists respond that the environmental mainstream, long characterized by suburban chauvinism in its attitude toward the rural and urban poor, simply ignores too many of the sites and fault lines of ecopolitical conflict. Laura Pulido contends that within the environmental justice movement (which includes whites), organization by people of color continues as an increasingly autonomous effort. She interprets environmental justice organization as a counterhegemonic dynamic of resistance, "subaltern" in that it marks a complex social location affected by structured and institutionalized inequality not easily reducible to either class or race. She conceptualizes a "subaltern environmentalism" in part to draw parallels between livelihood struggles of minority communities in the First World and the Third World, and to offer an alternative to the dominant "new social movement" paradigm that attributed the emergence of mainstream environmentalism to the importance of "post-materialist values" and often integrated race and ethnicity as a mere cultural attribute no longer connected to legal and economic challenges.[2]

Rather than subsuming this ecopolitical and theoretical dynamic under a single "environmental justice" perspective, environmental justice education can explore and maintain the contradictory heterogeneity of such a subaltern environmentalism. In my own courses, I have found the following to be among the major "fault lines" of ecopolitical conflict. They are not easily arranged in a narrative of the all-too-popular "problem-solving" variety of environmentalism-as-management but emerge as simultaneous sites of experimentation, exploration, and intervention.

Subaltern vs. Suburban Environmentalism

The economic and cultural location of environmentalisms affects their scope and agenda. To come to terms with the antiurban naturalism of an environmental mainstream whose collective subject is white and suburban, it makes sense to situate the conflict between different ecopolitical agendas within a much larger process: the increasing cultural and economic divergence between urban communities of color and an ethnocultural majority at home in suburbia.

Until recently, research on racial and class differences in support of environmental issues focused on the identification of nature with a wilderness understood as antithesis of urban life, civilization, and industrialization, as well as other traditional indicators of environmental awareness (magazine subscriptions, participation in mainstream organizations, events, and education programs). Such studies not only reproduced the cliché that the urban and rural poor cannot be considered "environmentally conscious," but reaffirmed the role of a (white) suburban middle class as proper custodian of environmental integrity and legitimized subsequent marginalization of "minority" concerns in environmental education and organization.

The concept of nature-as-wilderness is tied to the cliché of the city as center of disease, pollution, and social instability.[3] This archetypal city, endlessly reproduced in more or less apocalyptic literary and cinematic narratives, was in part created by the very process that constructed suburban communities as mythological manifestations of social mobility and ethnocultural homogeneity. New expressways, freeways, and highways not only accelerated the move to suburbia, but cut cohesive ethnic communities into isolated urban ghettos. As the decline in manufacturing hit the cities, civil service jobs, traditional buffer for minority employees, disappeared into suburbia, where large communities incorporated themselves to siphon off additional federal urban aid and used their political visibility to block the siting of dirty industries and waste disposal sites, putting additional pressure on urban communities to accept such development.[4]

Because such policies aggravate the structural consequences of discrimination, and because main beneficiaries continue to be suburban whites who have little to gain from a shift back to the city, George Lipsitz speaks of suburbanization in terms of a "possessive investment in whiteness." In his analysis of the vast array of policies that support suburbanization, Lipsitz illustrates the relationship between multiple aspects of suburban existence and general social mobility. Families that own real estate, for instance, and thereby build equity, have access to college loans (where wealth is often more important than actual income) and maintain standards of living through a significant intergenerational transfer of wealth. The situation of families who rent and already have less access to credit, on the other hand, is often aggravated by (illegal) federal and commercial practices of redlining, the denial of loans and credit to people who live in particular areas.[5]

Environmental justice activists argue that you cannot be both environmentally conscious and support the marginalization of poor and minority communities, yet millions of white suburbanites think of themselves as passionate environmentalists. Suburban ecopolitics often separates ecological and social justice issues and continues to be compatible with economic and cultural conservatism. This is especially apparent in debates on crime and punishment. Not surprisingly, the latest growth-industry, an immense prison-industrial complex, follows the trend of shifting power and mobility to the suburbs. The 2000 census counts prison inmates in the populations of the towns and counties in which they are incarcerated and not in their home neighborhoods. Whenever the census count is used to redraw legislative districts, prisoners will be reapportioned to the largely rural (and Republican) areas hosting their prisons. In communities populated by the (white) poor and "working poor," a new prison can easily drive down the median income on the census and make them eligible for additional funding from the federal Department of Housing and Urban Development. Since half of all U.S. prisoners are African American and one-sixth are Latino, with the vast majority coming from places like East New York and South Central Los Angeles, this constitutes a substantial transfer of economic and political power from urban communities of color to (white) rural and suburban America.[6]

Once you add the spread of "Three Strikes and Out" provisions which guarantee a steady flow of inmates to underwrite the profitability of private prisons, and consider the increasing reluctance to rein in police brutality as long as urban crime rates appear to decrease, you arrive at a "possessive investment in whiteness" that quite literally has a stake in (maintaining) the marginalization of urban communities of color. The question of a naturalist aesthetic that is essentially suburban is, then, not really an issue for anyone other than the communities affected (and marginalized) by it. Much of mainstream environmentalism goes hand in hand with an uncritical acceptance of the ongoing cultural, economic, and political shift toward suburbia: many environmentalists have yet to embrace the city as an ecologically sound alternative to the sprawl at the heart of ongoing suburbanization and are, it seems, quite unlikely to do so anytime soon.[7]

Even though the history of ecology is closely intertwined with the history of empire, environmentalism as a social and political concern is often given an exclusively "metropolitan" genealogy, omitting experiences of colonial (settler) states and histories of popular resistance.[8] This parochialism contributes in turn to what many consider to be a problematic eco-colonialism, the assumption that international ecopolitics amount to nothing less than the spread of an environmentalism "proper" across the globe—already evident in the language of many international agreements and conventions.[9]

Indigenous Environmentalism

Although environmentalists are beginning to employ the term, "subaltern" is most often associated with postcolonial (and, of course, subaltern) studies and might offer a conceptual vehicle for an "internationalization" of environmental justice education as well as resistance to the NIMBY (Not In My Backyard) tendencies inherent in grassroots efforts. To address suburban environmentalisms of the "wilderness" variety beyond a national context, the colonial provenance of much environmental thought has to come back into view, and with it the exoticisms at its origin. Any ecopolitical encounter with postcolonial studies will demand such investigation not least because the latter exists within the context of a now well-established "alterity industry" which perpetuates multiple exoticisms of its own.[10] Many ecopolitical arguments, on the other hand, are articulated in the problematic vocabularies of organicity and authenticity, often in contrast to rather ambiguous alternatives of ecological integrity—the image of the "ecological Indian" is a case in point.[11]

Common academic treatment of indigenous peoples suggests that they appear primarily as repository of ecospiritual alternatives.[12] The commercialization and exploitation of indigenous spiritual traditions á la Castañeda continues as native peoples remain central to (new age) constructions of ecological alternatives. The latter continue a long tradition of primitivist projections designed to relieve unease over the ecological cost of industrialization and the problematic legacies of colonization and white paternalism. Occasionally, such clichés turn out to be (strategically) useful, when images of sustainability and ecospiritual integrity are appropriated and mobilized by indigenous peoples themselves, precisely because they resonate with supporters in the environmental mainstream and can contribute to the affirmation and protection of native communities along with their own ecological traditions.[13] More often, they lock native peoples in immutable identities: when communities open their land to commercial development, resource extraction, or waste disposal in the pursuit of economic autonomy and self-determination only to be confronted by others who consider such acts a betrayal of their ostensible identity as spiritual ecologists, without acknowledgement of their desperate need for jobs and income.[14]

Course segments on indigenous environmentalism risk simplifications of the "indigenous experience" and sometimes offer little more than uncritical affirmations of eco-mythological superiority. In addition to examples of contemporary indigenous politics, theories, and philosophies that would place important yet reductive eco-mythological images in context, courses might nonetheless introduce material to trace the origin of many "ethnic" conflicts in ecological struggles over access to arable land, water, and raw materials.[15]

Eco-Internationalism

Attention to the heterogeneous terrain of the larger nation states that surround indigenous communities soon exposes the complexity of any attempt to "internationalize" the scope of environmental justice. The exploration of structural locations within transnational flows leads to the multiple elements of the international system that create, assign, and maintain these locations.[16] The real price of oil, for example, quickly turns out to link individual and collective mobility, urban and ocean pollution, trade and development regimes, transnational corporate activity, massive human rights violations, and local demands for self-determination.[17] The localism of environmental justice organization inevitably opens into multiple international dimensions, and environmental justice education can follow.

The ecopolitical scope of subaltern environmentalism might be impossibly broad and might diffuse its political impact: corporate accountability, cultural and media criticism, worker organization, human rights, indigenous self-determination, social justice, international solidarity, sustainable development, worker health and safety. This is an ambitious wish list, but also a necessary consequence of the heterogeneity at the grassroots, a heterogeneity which constantly moves toward transnational spheres of interaction and cooperation.

One of the most surprising features of recent discussions of the ecological effects of globalization is the poverty of its spatial imagery: few authors venture beyond some version of the tension between locality and globality. Both local and global are often assumed at the outset of the discussion, which then proceeds to lament the parochialism of the local and celebrate the radicalizing hybridization associated with globalization, or alternatively laments the loss of autonomy and integrity associated with globalization and celebrate a (natural) difference of the local as inherently adversarial or communal.[18]

This can only occur because the question of how ecopolitical terrains and territories are produced and articulated is itself neglected.[19] The spectrum between the local and the global is vast and needs to be differentiated to identify levels of impact and possible intervention: neither a toxic waste dump nor the ozone layer exists on local or global levels alone, a false dichotomy which isolates problems as well as actors. Greater spatial differentiation expands the sense of agency, when the local is no longer understood as an isolated political unit but as a node in networks of production, distribution, and consumption, which contain multiple sites of ecopolitical cooperation and intervention.

Theoretical and organizational internationalism is not only a question of transnational activity, but also a question of how multiple local actors and agendas are incorporated into ecopolitical efforts. The legacy of community orientation, characteristic of previous minority social movements, exists in some tension with internationalism. Observers emphasize that many organizational efforts are not all that different from the NIMBYs (Not In My Backyard) of an earlier era: they remain local, they remain reactive, and participation is temporary. But maybe the most useful examples are not so much the ones that can be considered "representative" but those that creatively explore the potential of the environmental justice agenda, moving across borders, not only between (indigenous) nations, but between social movements, movement cultures, and different constituencies.[20]

Ecopolitics across the Curriculum

The problem that cultural, ecological, economic, and political marginalization support each other, is, of course, not new, and environmental justice education taps the intellectual and organizational resources of previous (minority) social movements.[21] Environmental education, on the other hand, is an heir to the traditional environmental movement, and a subaltern environmentalism, or the productive tension of its heterogeneity, could easily disappear in a mere multicultural extension of environmental studies. To succeed, environmental justice education may have to remain at a critical distance from the multicultural mainstream, which has done much to divorce an often celebratory exploration of difference and diversity from material struggles for social justice.

This does not mean that environmental justice advocates should shy away from the articulation of a transdisciplinary agenda that can be mobilized across the curriculum. The list of academic sites where a radical ecologization of the curriculum can be explored includes the natural sciences, extending the traditional scope of cross-cultural education. The grassroots toxicology practiced by many activists, for instance, contains a transformative challenge to science education and encourages the democratization of the production of scientific expertise and authority. Access to reliable scientific information and subsequent interpretation of its ecopolitical implications is mediated by institutions whose role and authority is in turn legitimated by the natural sciences. Ostensibly "apolitical" education in math and the sciences are important sites of ecopolitical engagement, even though they are sometimes overlooked in the general (and more immediate) demand for accountability, democracy, and transparency in the "traditional" political process.[22]

Ecological Democracy

One of the core challenges of environmental justice education is to translate the mantra of ecology (all is connected) into a web of concrete relations that includes not only ecological but cultural, economic, and political processes. Different concepts of nature correspond to actual contradictions between different and competing notions of environmental politics. The exploration and expansion of individual and collective agency has much to do with the identification of potential sites of activist intervention: beyond mobilization for participation in traditional political processes, environmental justice efforts stress the need for a lively politics of culture to challenge dominant concepts of nature and the cultural marginalization of poor and minority concerns.[23]

Environmental justice activists often stress the need for ecological democracy, grassroots participation, and community involvement whenever decisions about natural resource use, industrial policy, or waste disposal are made.[24] To support the movement for ecological democracy and explore the democratization of educational processes, environmental justice courses can emphasize autonomy and collective self-organization through cooperative learning, role plays, or strategy games. In one strategy game, students are to jump into an organizing process in which four groups (Sierra Club, NAACP, a local of the Oil, Chemical, and Atomic Workers, and management representatives) consider their options and positions in a local environmental conflict: a government report reveals that the International Chemical

Company has been releasing toxins in excess of Environmental Protection Agency guidelines. Danger to local fish, wildlife, and water as well as workplace and community health are the main issues, especially for sections of the black population, many of whom have found employment with the company through its progressive affirmative action program and who have lived near the plant for decades. Local media, churches, and government are more or less in the hands of the company. In a first round, group members identify their own position, resources, interests, potential partners, and obstacles to future alliances; a second round provides the opportunity to enter into coalitions and work on action plans, tactics, media strategies, and alternatives.[25]

Such arrangements can be adapted to introduce the contradictory agendas of individual, collective, and institutional actors, encourage the articulation of interests in multiple registers to enter into coalitions, and confront students with the limits of consensus and negotiation that assume an ultimate reconcilability of concerns. Above all, they demonstrate that the structure of a (political or educational) process is intimately related to the legitimacy and credibility of its outcomes. Positions and assignments are easily tailored to a given issue or conflict, assumptions about individual and collective agency, potential lines of conflict and cooperation, and the authority and legitimacy of positions mobilized in argument and negotiation can become the basis for subsequent theoretical work.

Worker Organization and Corporate Accountability

While not all environmental justice activists have adopted an ecosocialist perspective, most agree that environmentalists and workers need to cooperate in their demand for corporate accountability, a "just transition" to jobs that are ecologically sustainable and pay living wages, and democratic control of processes of transnational economic integration.[26] So-called "blue-green" alliances have already (if temporarily) been organized within the antiglobalization movement ("Teamsters & Turtles").[27]

Worker organization and environmentalism are often assumed to represent incompatible, if not antagonistic agendas. The common interpretation of environmental conflict in terms of the "jobs vs. nature" cliché suggests that most accept it as a truism, even though study after study shows that corporations both routinely exaggerate the cost of regulatory compliance and use it quite effectively in public relations campaigns to legitimate downsizing or closures and transfer the blame to "environmental extremists."[28]

One of the reasons lies in the assumption that ecological concerns are nothing but elitist preoccupations, a mere luxury of (white) affluence divorced from struggles of livelihood and survival. Few are aware of the extent to which worker organization has revolved around ecological concerns, especially workplace health and safety or community health.[29] A strict separation of movements according to increasingly narrow agendas deprives them of common histories and traditions of radicalism. This weakens new efforts and alliances because it isolates them historically as well as strategically, and retrieval and incorporation of these histories is an important task of environmental justice education.[30]

The isolation of movements is in turn based on the isolation of different aspects of individual and collective identity: workers are also mothers, immigrants, churchgoers, consumers, residents, voters, etc. Unions have long assumed that immigrant workers, for example, are "unorganizable" yet overlooked that many of them are active members of neighborhood or religious networks, all of which can become the basis for further organization and radicalization.[31] Although immigrant workers are concentrated in particularly toxic workplaces, they have been neglected by environmentalists interested in consumer mobilization rather than worker rights. Campaigns around occupational hazards are often a first form of collective organization, and immigrant unions are among the most democratic, militant, and progressive organizations within the labor movement. Fear of job loss and low-wage competition, intensified by media coverage sympathetic to nativist arguments, nevertheless present environmental justice activists and educators with serious challenges. Cross-racial and cross-border worker organization will require also some discussion of whiteness in the context of organized labor both in the United States and abroad, where cold war AFL-CIO activity often supported what Victor Reuther (United Automobile Workers) has termed a "trade union colonialism."[32]

To expand beyond their traditional boundaries, courses can move into labor education centers and other institutions open to workers (continuing education programs, night school, community and worker centers), adopt teaching techniques from the tradition of popular education, include ongoing labor-community campaigns, efforts around workplace health and safety issues as well as sustainable production, and support reform movements within official labor organizations committed to the creation of blue-green alliances.[33]

Colonial Commodities

Consumer concern over the safety or toxicity of products does not always extend to the well-being of its producers. Because environmental justice demands for fair trade and sustainable development depend on solidarity between consumers and producers, linking conscientious consumption here with support for worker organization there, entire commodity cycles— extraction, production, distribution, consumption, disposal—need to come into view so existing (inter) dependencies can be articulated. Most commodities turn out to be "colonial commodities"—their stories map and remember vast geographies of colonization and empire—Martin Luther King once observed that each cup of coffee contains the history of slavery. Be it coffee, tea, sugar, spices, fish, beef, textiles, oil—students are often unaware of how even inconspicuous consumption integrates them into processes that are also narratives of complex ecopolitical interdependencies. These narratives link a multitude of individual and collective structural locations within a transnational horizon. This, of course, is a central environmental justice concern: to follow the flow of commodities, toxins, and populations and connect communities in a cross-border cartography of struggle and solidarity.[34]

Media Ecology and Literacy

Controversy over the cultural implications of different concepts of nature and ecology already place issues of representation at the center of environmental justice education. The rift between an environmental mainstream and the environmental agendas of low-income and minority communities widens when nature and environmentalism are defined through more or less canonical U.S. writers and events which locate environmental awareness within a white, middle-class experience, when an uncritical focus on wilderness transmits the ethnic chauvinism of the transcendentalist and romantic traditions, or when an unhistorical emphasis on the "natural" integrity of endangered ecosystems encourages the latent nativism of a bioregional vision.

Since the 1980s, the national media landscape has seen profound transformation, concentration, and corporatization.[35] Tax reforms shifted an enormous amount of taxable wealth to public interest organizations, which have supported a cultural and political turn to the right. A wide array of conservative think tanks and academic institutes now feeds studies and experts into the mainstream media circuit as well as the legislative process.[36] Corporations have launched numerous "astroturf" organizations which appropriate and employ direct action tactics and media strategies pioneered by radical social movements.[37]

As a result, grassroots organization and direct action have lost much of their influence and credibility as more "professional" forms of political organization and mobilization emerged. This is one of the challenges of environmental justice organizations: the attempt to revive an extra-parliamentary culture that expands a political process increasingly reduced to meaningless instances of political expression and participation.

The problem of environmental racism cannot be solved on the community level, as long as a cultural context provides rationale and legitimacy for the ecological, economic, and political marginalization of low-income and minority populations. Challenges to environmental destruction must also be challenges to the organization of the cultural environment. Ironically, many environmental justice campaigns affirm the association of poverty and pollution with urban communities of color that is at the heart of an antiurban naturalism. The wilderness aesthetic remains too overwhelming and spectacular to be easily challenged by the aesthetic banality of campaigns around toxic waste or leaded paint in public housing, which articulate environmental concerns in an entirely different register and cannot easily tap such imagery to mobilize concern and support.

Between sensationalist celebrity news and aesthetically overwhelming marketing blitzes, skillful exploitations of romantic imagery confer ecological credibility on corporate actors, brands, and products, and dispel second thoughts on the reconcilability of consumerism and sustainability. As "all natural" injunctions to consume go hand in hand with campaigns to marginalize ecocritical alternatives, the politicization of consumer identities, a time-tested method of traditional environmental mobilization, now affirms reductive notions of individual and collective agency.

Ecological and human rights demand ongoing (cultural) contestation over their material implications, beyond the passive enjoyment of a radicalized consumerism. Classical media literacy includes the analysis of individual texts and images as well as the assumptions that inform and sustain their commonsensical intelligibility, legitimacy, and authority. An active media ecology situates cultural production in its social, economic, and political context and stresses the exploration of multiple means of media eco-activism, creative expression, and cultural communication to challenge the continued separation of ecology and social justice. Support for alternative grassroots media like video and public access TV, internet, community papers, and microradio stations is central to the ability of environmental justice organizations to communicate with each other, create alternative public spheres, and challenge formulaic representations of collective agency, ecological conflict, and "natural" desires for unsustainable forms of consumption and production.[38]

Cross-Border Environmental Justice Education

I have worked primarily with white students, and there is no doubt that whiteness continues to be a major factor in the allocation of social risks and resources. The subaltern environmentalism activists describe is still, after all, primarily a movement by people of color. I do not think, however, that ecological destruction is the consequence of a single antagonism that could then inform and organize resistant practices.

These notes follow my own sense of both the weak spots of traditional environmental education and the implications of a heterogeneous subaltern environmentalism. While it is a truism that specific ecological concerns appear (differently) when one explores different economic, cultural, and political locations, it is not always easy to remember this in the educational process. While international solidarity cannot be taught, cross-border environmental justice courses that stress the whirl of material relations that connect each and every one can do much to encourage it.

That is also where cross-border environmental justice education begins its movement into an internationalist horizon and back into one's own sphere of reference and experience. The ability to articulate concerns within a local-global dynamic comes more or less "naturally" out of such a structure, especially when the analysis of ecological issues is accompanied by ongoing self-situation that identifies the multiple processes and institutions that affect and inform one's own position, identity, and sense of agency.

Part of the task of environmental justice education is to create its own historical and academic horizon, to resist the homogenization of historical predecessor movements and retrieve their radical heterogeneity. The absence of a "coherent" movement philosophy and policy orientation lamented by observers is also a sign that many older movements continue to be alive and well, in contradictory and subterranean ways. Theoretical contradictions within the environmental justice agenda may never be resolved, but imaginative coalitions already confront them in practice: new organizing models emerge around blue-green alliances, cross-border cooperation, immigrant worker organization, transnational indigenous networks.

NOTES

I want to thank the students in my course (Race, Nature, and the Transborder Struggle for Environmental Justice) at BOCES (a program for continuing education in Broome County, New York State), whose intellectual curiosity and increasing enthusiasm for the project of environmental justice inspired me to write these notes.

1. See Christoper H. Foreman Jr., *The Promise and Peril of Environmental Justice* (Washington, D.C.: Brookings Institution, 1998).

2. See Laura Pulido, "Subaltern Environmental Struggles," *Environmentalism and Environmental Justice* (Tucson: University of Arizona Press, 1996), 3–30.

On the link between subaltern environmental struggles in the Global North and the Global South (as well as a similar critique of the new social movement paradigm and its "post-materialist thesis"), also see Joan Martinez-Alier, "Environmental Justice (Local and Global)," in *The Cultures of Globalization,* ed. Fredric Jameson and Masao Miyoshi (Durham: Duke University Press, 1998), 312–26; and Ramachandra Guha and Juan Martinez-Alier, *Varieties of Environmentalism: Essays North and South* (London: Earthscan, 1997).

3. For an overview of movies that feature Los Angeles in this archetypal role, see Mike Davis, *Ecology of Fear* (New York: Vintage, 1998).

4. See Kenneth T. Jackson, *Crabgrass Frontier: The Suburbanization of the United States* (New York: Oxford University Press, 1985); and Jane Holtz Kay, *Asphalt Nation: How the Automobile Took Over America, And How We Can Take it Back* (Berkeley: University of California Press, 1998).

5. See George Lipsitz, *The Possessive Investment in Whiteness: How White People Benefit from Identity Politics* (Philadelphia: Temple University Press, 1998). Comparisons like this can easily be translated into course activities to address housing as an environmental justice concern (students fill out different mortgage applications, discuss them with bank representatives, report back on standards or minimal requirements, and analyze who may or may not be eligible).

6. See Tracy Huling, "Prisoners of the Census," *Mother Jones,* 10 May 2000.

7. See Andrew Ross, *The Chicago Gangster Theory of Life: Nature's Debt to Society* (New York: Verso, 1995). In part because its depoliticized concepts of nature have successfully marginalized issues of social justice, suburban environmentalism is also troubled by nativist appropriations of its ostensibly "neutral" environmental rhetoric and imagery—see David Helvarg, *The War Against the Greens: The "Wise-Use" Movement, the New Right, and Anti-Environmental Violence* (San Francisco: Sierra Club, 1997).

Supported by the infamous Pioneer Fund, the "Federation for American Immigration Reform" is the largest anti-immigrant organization in the United States and publishes *The Environmentalist's Guide to a Sensible Immigration Policy* (www.fairus.org). Along with "Sierrans for U.S. Populations Stabilization" (www.susps.org) and "Population-Environment Balance" (www.balance.org), it has exerted significant influence on major environmental organizations and encourages them to take strong positions against immigration, often as part of campaigns against "urban sprawl."

8. See various publications by Richard Grove, esp. *Green Imperialism: Colonial Expansion, Tropical Island Eden, and the Origins of Environmentalism, 1600–1860* (Cambridge: Cambridge University Press, 1996), and the later *Ecology, Climate and Empire: Colonialism and Global Environmental History, 1400–1940* (Cambridge: White Horse, 1997); as well as Tom Griffiths and Libby Robin, eds., *Ecology and Empire: Environmental History of Settler Societies* (Seattle: University of Washington Press, 1997).

9. See Wolfgang Sachs, ed., *Global Ecology: A New Arena of Political Conflict* (London: Zed, 1993), as well as essays in Fredric Jameson and Masao Miyoshi, eds., *The Cultures of Globalization* (Durham: Duke University Press, 1998).

10. See Gerald Huggan, *The Postcolonial Exotic* (New York: Routledge, 2001),

11. See Shepard Krech III, *The Ecological Indian: Myth and History* (New York: Penguin, 1999).

12. On the academic and commercial appropriation of indigenous traditions as well as the "hucksterism" of native purveyors of an ersatz spirituality (pow wow, sweat lodge, and vision quest included), see Ward Churchill, *Fantasies of the Master Race* (San Francisco: City Lights, 1998) and *Indians Are Us? Culture and Genocide in Native North America* (San Francisco: City Lights, 2000).

13. One of the few international arenas in which indigenous concerns have achieved some acknowledgment is the controversy over biodiversity. Even though various exoticisms continue to flourish in the discourse of

nongovernmental organizations, states, and corporations alike, the process has attracted attention to the close link between biological, cultural, and linguistic diversity and survival. See Luisa Maffi, ed., *On Biocultural Diversity: Linking Language, Knowledge, and the Environment* (Washington, D.C.: Smithsonian, 2001).

14. For a survey of contemporary politics of sovereignty in the context of the general cultural renaissance of native U.S. peoples, see Fergus M. Bordewich, *Killing the White Man's Indian: Reinventing Native Americans at the End of the Twentieth Century* (New York: Anchor/Doubleday, 1996).

15. The international beef, nuclear, oil, and mining economies have turned out to be particularly devastating for native peoples. The literature is vast; here are a few texts that seem to be popular with students: on the beef economy, see Jeremy Rifkin, *Beyond Beef: The Rise and Fall of the Cattle Culture* (New York: Plume, 1993). On the (cold war) nuclear economy, see Ward Churchill, "Cold War Impacts on Native North America: The Political Economy of Radioactive Colonization," in *A Little Matter of Genocide: Holocaust and Denial in the Americas 1492 to the Present* (San Francisco: City Lights, 1997), 289–362; and William Thomas, *Scorched Earth: The Military's Assault on the Environment* (Philadelphia: New Society Publishers, 1995). On oil and mining economies, see materials produced by Project Underground (www.moles.org).

16. In part as a response to current grassroots mobilization around issues of global commerce, multiple organizations produce (instructional) materials that offer "a basic literacy of globalization"—information about major intergovernmental and nongovernmental organizations, agreements on trade and investment, etc. See Corporate Watch (www.corpwatch.org), Third World Network (www.twnside.org.sg), and Tradewatch (www.tradewatch.org).

17. See Project Underground for materials (www.moles.org).

18. See Bruce Robbins, *Feeling Global: Internationalism in Distress* (New York: New York University Press, 1999).

19. See David Harvey, *Justice, Nature, and the Geography of Difference* (Cambridge: Blackwell, 1996).

20. Organization along the U.S.-Mexico border (South-West Organization Project, SouthWest Network for Economic and Environmental Justice, Coalition for Justice in the Maquiladoras) serves as an encouraging example of (future) cross-border environmental justice efforts. See Devon G. Peña, *The Terror of the Machine: Technology, Work, Gender, and Ecology on the U.S.-Mexico Border* (Austin: Center for Mexican American Studies/University of Texas, 1997); and "The Border," *Race, Poverty, and the Environment,* special

issue (Summer/Fall 1996). Much work done under the new rubric of "Border Studies" (necessarily) addresses ecopolitical themes.

21. See Elizabeth Martínez, *De Colores Means All Of Us: Latina Views for a Multi-Colored Century* (Cambridge, Mass.: South End, 1998); "Multicultural Environmental Education," *Race, Poverty, and the Environment*, special issue (Winter/Spring 1996); Devon G. Peña, ed., *Chicano Culture, Ecology, Politics: Subversive Kin* (Tucson: University of Arizona Press, 1998).

22. Much of the literature of the new "science studies" that deals with the role concepts of agency, certainty, objectivity, standardization, etc., has come to play in the natural sciences. Because complex historical processes have linked not only freedom, technological or religious transcendence, and civilization, but also standards of juridical and scientific objectivity to whiteness, historical and theoretical critiques of scientific racism definitely have their place in environmental justice courses. See, for instance, Sandra Harding, ed., *The Racial Economy of Science: Toward a Democratic Future* (Bloomington: Indiana University Press, 1993); and Stephen Jay Gould, *Mismeasure of Man*, Rev/Expanded ed. (New York: Norton, 1996).

23. Richard Hofrichter, ed., *Toxic Struggles: The Theory and Practice of Environmental Justice* (Philadelphia: New Society, 1993).

24. Daniel J. Faber, ed., *The Struggle for Ecological Democracy: Environmental Justice Movements in the United States* (New York: Guilford, 1998).

25. See the special issue of *Race, Poverty, and the Environment* on "Multicultural Environmental Education" (Winter/Spring 1996) as well as "Classroom Simulation of Environmental Conflicts" (syllabus available through the Center for Political Ecology at http://gate.cruzio.com/~cns/index.html).

26. David Moberg, "For Unions, Green's Not Easy," *The Nation*, 21 February 2000.

27. Also see landmark efforts by the late Judi Bari (Earth First!) and the late David Brower (Earth Island Institute). Earlier campaigns around the North American Free Trade Agreement have shown that the split between the environmental mainstream and environmental justice remains, while worker organizations and environmental justice groups agree on common agendas. After the integration of major environmental groups into the orbit of legal and parliamentary activism, as well as the increasing presence of corporate representatives on the boards of environmental groups, this is not surprising.

28. Eban Goodstein, *The Trade-Off Myth: Fact and Fiction about Jobs and the Environment* (Washington, D.C.: Island, 1999); Richard Kazis and Richard Grossmann, *Fear at Work: Job Blackmail, Labor, and the Environment*, rev. ed. (Philadelphia: New Society, 1991).

29. Robert Gottlieb, *Forcing the Spring: The Transformation of the American Environmental Movement* (Washington D.C.: Island, 1995).

30. See Lois Gibbs, *Love Canal: The Story Continues* (Philadelphia: New Society Publishers, 1998); James Schwab and Lois Gibbs, *Deeper Shades of Green: The Rise of Blue-Collar and Minority Environmentalism in America* (San Francisco: Sierra Club, 1994).

31. Robin D. Kelly, "Building Bridges: The Challenges for Organized Labor in Communities of Color," *New Labor Forum* 5 (Fall/Winter 1999): 42–58. Asian Immigrant Women Advocates, one of the best-known immigrant worker centers, is often referred to as an environmental justice rather than a labor organization. See Sonya Shah, ed., *Dragon Ladies: Asian American Feminists Breathe Fire* (Boston: South End, 1997); and Lisa Lowe, *Immigrant Acts: On Asian American Cultural Politics* (Durham: Duke University Press, 1996). Also see Jennifer Gordon, "Immigrants Fight the Power: Workers Centers are one Path to Labor Organizing and Political Participation," *The Nation* (3 January 2000).

32. See Paul Buhle, *Taking Care of Business: Samuel Gompers, George Meaney, Lane Kirkland, and the Tragedy of American Labor* (New York: Monthly Review, 2000); Daniel Cantor and Juliet Schor, *Tunnel Vision: Labor, the World Economy, and Central America* (Boston: South End, 1987); David Roediger, *The Wages of Whiteness,* 2nd ed. (New York: Verso, 1999); and Beth Sims, *Workers of the World Undermined: American Labor's Role in U.S. Foreign Policy* (Cambridge, Mass.: South End, 1992).

33. See John Anner, ed., *Beyond Identity Politics: Emerging Social Justice Movements in Communities of Color* (Boston: South End, 1996); and Jeremy Brecher and Tim Costello, *Global Village or Global Pillage: Economic Reconstruction from the Bottom Up,* 2nd ed. (Cambridge, Mass.: South End, 1998). For labor videos, see Labor Beat (www.wwa.com/~bgfolder/lb) or Working TV (www.workingtv.com).

34. See Sidney Mintz, *Sweetness and Power: the Place of Sugar in Modern History* (New York: Virgin, 1995); and Wolfgang Schivelbusch, *Tastes of Paradise: A Social History of Spices, Stimulants, and Intoxicants* (New York: Vintage, 1993). Also explore texts listed under beef, nuclear, and oil economies (below) as well as social histories of objects and tastes or ongoing campaigns on college campuses (anticorporate: www.corporations.org/democracy, anti-sweatshop: www.usas.org, general campus organizing: www.cco.org, www.seac.org).

35. See various publications by Noam Chomsky, Robert W. McChesney, Edward S. Herman, or Herbert Schilling.

36. See Russ Bellant, *The Coors Connection: How Coors Family Philanthropy Undermines Democratic Pluralism* (Boston, Mass.: South End, 1991); *Buying a Movement: Right-Wing Foundations and American Politics* (Washington, D.C.: People for the American Way [see www.pfaw.org]); Sally Covington, "How Conservative Philanthropies and Think Tanks Transform U.S. Policy," *CAQ* 63 (Spring 1998); and Jean Stefanich and Richard Delgado, *No Mercy: How Conservative Think Tanks and Foundations Changed America's Social Agenda* (Philadelphia: Temple University Press, 1996). Media watchdogs Fairness and Accuracy in Reporting (www.fair.org) and the Institute for Public Accuracy (www.accuracy.org) maintain a joint "Think Tank Monitor."

37. John C. Stauber and Sheldon Rampton, *Toxic Sludge is Good for You: Lies, Damn Lies, and the Public Relations Industry* (Monroe, Maine: Common Courage, 1995).

38. There is no reason to resort to corporate productions or pious PBS documentaries, grassroots video activism accompanies environmental justice efforts all over the world. Distributors include: Big Noise Films (www.big noisefilms.com), Bullfrog Videos (www.bullfrogfilms.com), California Newsreel (www.newsreel.org), Earth Visions (www.earthvisions.org), EnviroVideo (home.earthlink.net/~envirovideo/), First Run/Icarus Films (www.frif .com), Third World Newsreel (www.twn.org), Turning Tide Productions (www .turningtide.com), Video Activist Network (www.videoactivism.org), Videoproject (www.videoproject.org). Also see productions by grassroots television networks: Deep Dish TV (www.igc.org/deepdish) and Paper Tiger TV (www.papertiger.org). Some grassroots organizations produce their own videos (Labor/ Community Strategy Center, www.thestrategycenter.org) or provide annotated resource lists (Environmental Justice Resource Center, www.ejrc.cau.edu).

18

CHANGING THE NATURE OF ENVIRONMENTAL STUDIES

Teaching Environmental Justice to "Mainstream" Students

Steve Chase

> *Properly speaking, there is no "crisis of biological diversity" or even an "ecological crisis." But there is a large and growing political crisis that has ecological and other consequences . . . [To date,] we have focused on the symptoms, not the causes of biotic impoverishment. The former have to do with the vital signs of the planet. The latter have to do with the distribution of wealth, land ownership, greed, the organization of power, and the conduct of public business.*
>
> —David Orr

Earth in Mind: On Education, Environment, and the Human Prospect

The students in my environmental studies classes at the Antioch New England Graduate School are all unique and cannot be easily classified. Yet, they do have several things in common. Almost all of them are white and the majority are from middle-class to upper-middle-class backgrounds. They are all passionate about preserving wild nature, improving public health, and creating a sustainable way of life. Many of them are also very sophisticated in their scientific understanding of ecology and resource management. Few, however, are savvy about social oppression, political economy, or the history of people's movements in this country. As David Orr laments, little in their education has helped them develop insight into our society's underlying political ecology.

This should probably not come as a surprise. A lack of political literacy is common among environmental professionals—including even most environmental studies professors. As feminist geographer Joni Seager notes: "The physical manifestations of environmental problems are often presented as both the beginning and end of the story. . . . Questions about agency—that is, the social and economic processes that create a state of scorched trees and dead otters—are placed a distant second, if they are raised at all" (2). The problem here, though, is that environmental studies programs are doing a disservice to their students if they do not educate for critical social consciousness. Indeed, to ignore the "political" side of the environmental story is to miss the heart of the matter and render oneself largely ineffective. This is particularly true in an era of growing corporate globalization.

This concern first emerged for me in the early 1990s when I was a master's student at Antioch. I had chosen Antioch's environmental studies program because the graduate school was openly political. Antioch New England's mission statement proudly declares that "by linking the worlds of scholarship and activism . . . we promote social justice, ecological literacy, organizational integrity, common economic good, and respect for the whole person." Historically, the Environmental Studies Department had also embraced a strong commitment to environmentalism, which long-time Antioch professor Mitchell Thomashow describes as "a social and intellectual movement" that is "dynamic, diverse, and radical" (5). Yet, even at Antioch, I discovered some significant blind spots in the department's political focus.

I remember, in particular, a course I took on the "Patterns of Environmentalism." In it, the professor suggested that the environmental movement is best understood as a continuing argument between the ghosts of John Muir and Gifford Pinchot, the two competing icons of the Progressive Era conservation movement. To illustrate his point, he drew a line across the chalk board and asked the students to imagine that the left side of the board represented the romantic wilderness preservationism championed by Muir and the right side, the pragmatic, professional approach to natural resource management supported by Pinchot. He then asked the students to name contemporary environmental groups and place them somewhere along this continuum.

Several groups were mentioned by my class members during this brainstorm—the Sierra Club, the Environmental Defense Fund, Earth First!, The Nature Conservancy, and Greenpeace—and each was placed somewhere on the continuum. I mentioned Mothers of East Los Angeles, a grassroots Chicana group that had successfully blocked the construction of a giant incinerator project in their already polluted neighborhood. Interestingly, the professor said, "That's not an environmental group," and would not write it on the board. He seemed to instinctively know that this group did not "fit" his conceptual map of environmentalism and, in the pressure of the moment, he did not choose to open up his interpretive framework for critical discussion. Instead, he inadvertently dismissed the legitimacy of the environmental justice movement in front of his students, most of whom did not have the background or context to question his assumptions.

A few of us did, however. After class, four of us got together and discussed our frustrations with the neglect of the environmental justice movement at Antioch and how, as Carl Anthony puts it, environmental problems were all too often discussed "as if the human community were uniform, without great differences in culture and experience, without differences in power or access to material influence" (17). By the end of that bull session, we had founded the Antioch Environmental Justice Workgroup. It was the efforts of this student organization that eventually led to my own experiments in teaching environmental justice at Antioch.

From Student Organizing to Critical Teaching

The goal of our workgroup was to render the invisible visible: to educate ourselves and the Antioch community about the grassroots movement for environmental justice that had emerged in barrios, urban ghettos, rural poverty pockets, and native lands across North America and the rest of the world. In particular, we wanted all Environmental Studies students to explore how the power dynamics of race, class, and gender shaped how environmental issues are experienced, framed, and addressed by various communities and organizations. It was our belief that Antioch would not have a sufficiently positive impact on the environmental movement if its graduates were not challenged to grapple with the issues raised by the National People of Color Environmental Leadership Summit and the Citizen's Clearinghouse on Hazardous Waste. In particular, we wanted the Department of Environmental Studies to build the capacity of its graduates to be politically savvy allies, coalition builders, and supporters of such efforts—both as environmental professionals and as citizen activists.

Our assumption was that any faculty resistance to this new approach was due more to a lack of familiarity with the environmental justice movement than with any entrenched objection. We thus chose a collaborative and educational approach to our work rather than a conflictual model of organizing. We donated books on environmental justice to the library and gave the librarian several bibliographies to guide future acquisitions. We started writing articles on environmental justice for student publications. We also supported each other to speak up about the issue in our classes and in out-of-class dialogues with core faculty members. Next, we started bringing environmental justice speakers to campus and sponsored a public performance of the Underground Railway Theater's production *Intoxicating: An Environmental Justice Cabaret*. Finally, we petitioned the department to offer two new courses on "Environmental Justice" and "Diversifying Environmental Organizations."

Our efforts were successful. The Environmental Justice Workgroup soon grew to be one of the largest student organizations at the school, an anonymous alum who had been inspired by reading about our work in the alumni newsletter donated $10 thousand to the department to help support our efforts at changing the curriculum, and we soon found many allies on the faculty. Indeed, the faculty member who had initially sparked our organizing was extremely sympathetic to our efforts and led the charge to have the faculty issue a public statement that the Environmental Studies Department "supports and affirms the Principles of Environmental Justice which were adopted at the First National People of Color Environmental Leadership Summit." The department also agreed to offer the two courses we requested and gave our group a strong hand in planning the syllabi and selecting the adjunct faculty members to teach the courses.

It was in the midst of taking the newly created "Environmental Justice" course in the fall of 1994 that I began to seriously consider moving into a new role at Antioch. I felt a pull to join the ranks of the many activists who have struggled "to find more effective ways to challenge oppressive systems and promote social justice through education" (Adams et al., 1). Happily, the professor who taught the first environmental justice class agreed to my proposal for serving as his co-teacher when the course was offered again in the fall of 1995.

Making a Mess of It

My new experiment in teaching was anything but smooth, however. The second Environmental Justice course was very different from the first. In the first course, twelve of the fifteen students were members of the Environmental Justice Workgroup and everyone was highly motivated, reasonably well-informed of the main issues, and committed to some sort of action on behalf of environmental justice. The vast majority of the first group had also spent a year working together in a student organization and was familiar with democratic group process. People also knew our teacher socially through our pre-course organizing, and all of us liked to hang out informally after class at a town pub. This was an ideal teaching situation. The class was energetic, engaged, cooperative, and, in many ways, taught itself. This was not true with the new class.

None of the new students were participants in the Environmental Justice Workgroup. Indeed, most of the new students were only mildly curious about the environmental justice movement, and a sizable minority reported that the course was just a way to fulfill the credit requirements for their degree. Motivation was not particularly high, background political knowledge was spotty at best, and commitment to the principles of environmental justice could not be assumed. Nor was there a preexisting sense of community among the students or in relation to us as teachers.

This second course—which I was now jointly responsible for designing and facilitating—was also perceived by most of the students as didactic and more than a bit too "politically correct" for their comfort. Early in the course, three of the students complained to the cochairs of the Environmental Studies Department about their dissatisfactions with our class. They argued that the course's content was not relevant to them professionally and that the class dynamics did not reflect the cooperative, experiential learning approach they were used to at Antioch.

At first, I tried to deflect this criticism—and the increasing boredom and restlessness evidenced in class—as little more than a case of our having bad luck in drawing a resistant group of students. Yet, we did not really have "bad" or "difficult" students. The reality was simply that we were just reaching a different, but important, sector of the student body and we had not adapted our approach appropriately. In bell hooks' words, we had violated the central insight "that engaged pedagogy recognizes each classroom as different, that strategies must constantly be changed, invented, reconceptualized to address each new teaching experience" (10).

If anything, we unconsciously adopted a very conventional pedagogy in the face of a resistant class—the "banking" approach to education so powerfully critiqued by Freire (57–74). I remember, in particular, a long, detailed lecture that my co-teacher gave early on about the relative validity of the different research designs and statistical analysis used in the nearly sixty studies looking at the disproportionate correlation of race and the siting of polluting industrial facilities (see Goldman). During the lecture, the students' eyes glazed over, faces went slack, and the response voiced by the only vocal students was that statistics can always be twisted to say whatever a researcher wants and that none of these studies could really be relied on as useful indicators of what is actually going on in the world. Our teaching approach had backfired and fostered confusion and indifference. We thus missed an opportunity to make the reality of environmental racism come alive for our students and foster a "hot cognition" that would inspire empathetic indignation at such injustice.

Even worse, I squandered a teachable moment during the same session by being too quick to "correct" an "incorrect" idea espoused by a student. After viewing a videotape of the proceedings of the People of Color Environmental Leadership Summit, the student spoke up in class and challenged the claim made by one of the summit speakers that the "Big Ten" national environmental groups had not done enough to diversify their staffs. The student asserted that he felt this particular criticism was "unfair" and "there are just not enough black people interested in or qualified for these environmental jobs." As he put it, "It has nothing to do with racism." Instead of welcoming his critical comment and asking some key questions that would help the class explore the validity of this student's assertion, I sharply disagreed with him and quickly jumped into explaining how racism shapes not only who becomes "qualified" in this society, but also how many organizations' personnel practices unconsciously reproduce a predominantly white workforce and do not reach out meaningfully to qualified applicants of color. The student got very quiet and deflected further discussion of the topic. I had pushed him into resentful silence.

It was with a pained sense of irony that I finally read bell hooks' book *Teaching to Transgress*. In it, she explains how she has always found it "particularly disappointing to encounter white male professors who claimed to follow Freire's model even as their pedagogical practices were mired in structures of domination, mirroring the styles of conservative professors even as they approached subjects from a more progressive standpoint" (17). I would have to plead guilty on all counts. This was not the radical and empowering class I had hoped to create. My co-teacher and I had unwittingly reproduced the dynamics of a conventional, teacher-dominated classroom.

Digging My Way Out

In my effort to find a way out of this mess, I conducted a crash self-education course in educational theory by reading and rereading several books by the heavyweights of critical pedagogy, including Paulo Freire, Ira Shor, bell hooks, Bunyan Bryant, and Myles Horton. This renewed my conviction that empowering political education is not "just about liberatory knowledge," but also "about a liberatory practice in the classroom" (147). The basic educational approach I was (re)learning is probably best summarized today by the seven key educational principles articulated by the Peruvian Institute for Education in Human Rights and Peace (Flowers, *Human Rights Education Handbook,* 16):

Principle 1: Start from Reality—All learning must be based on the needs, interests, experiences, and problems of the participants.

Principle 2: Activity—Learning must be active, through a combination of individual and group activity.

Principle 3: Horizontal Communication—Learning takes place through dialogue in which people share their thoughts, feelings, and emotions in an atmosphere of mutual respect.

Principle 4: Developing the Ability to be Critical—One must develop the capacity to be critical and to evaluate ideas, people, and acts in a serious fashion.

Principle 5: Promoting the Development and Expression of Feelings—It is only possible to learn values if the training methodologies take into account participant's feelings.

Principle 6: Promoting Participation—The best way to learn is by participating, being consulted, and taking part in making decisions.

Principle 7: Integration—Learning is most effective when the head, the body, and the heart are integrated in the learning process.

Still, I was having trouble making the leap from these general principles to actual curriculum design and classroom practice. One of the core faculty members in the department suggested I read a book written for elementary school teachers, but which he found applicable to teaching at the graduate level. The book, *In Search of Understanding: The Case for Constructivist Classrooms* by Jacqueline and Martin Brooks, proved to be a huge help. While devoid of any of the political insight common in the literature on critical pedagogy, this little book focused directly on the *how* of teaching well and offered a clear vision of the kind of class experience my partner and I wanted to create. As the authors note: "When the classroom environment in which students spend so much of their day is organized so that student-to-student interaction is encouraged, cooperation is valued, assignments and materials are interdisciplinary, and students' freedom to chase their own ideas is abundant, students are more likely to take risks and approach assignments with a willingness to accept challenges to their current understandings" (10).

My first foray into a self-consciously "constructivist" pedagogy was our two sessions on "class and capitalism." For these sessions, I decided to develop activities that encouraged students to reflect on their own experience, discuss questions thoroughly with each other, and have them generate their own theories on the topics at hand, and then, and only then, would I lead a group discussion interspersed with a mini-lecture or two offering missing information or ideas that had not come up yet.

I started the first evening by asking whether anyone thought that the United States was a classless society. No one did. I then pointed out that while this point is not particularly controversial, what constitutes different social classes in America has historically been a hotly debated topic. I then asked the students to brainstorm all the different classes that they thought existed in the United States. I said the goal here was not to come up with a consensus position about the issue, but to get everybody's ideas on the board so we could see where people agreed or disagreed about class stratification. The brainstorm yielded about twelve different names of classes from "dirt poor" to "filthy rich." We then discussed if any of the class names that people had mentioned were about the same group and could be combined into single categories. This brought us to about five distinct classes that people thought existed.

I then asked people to estimate what percentage of the population fell into each category. Here there was much less agreement and I wrote up the range of estimates by each category. The differences in population estimates prompted some students to ask others why they chose their particular guesses. These students' answers quickly revealed different assumptions about what distinguished a particular class from others. For example, some students put highly paid skilled laborers into the middle-class category along with public school teachers who sometimes made less than these skilled tradespeople. Others felt that the nature of the work needed to be taken into account, not just income, and that people like plumbers belonged in the blue-collar, working-class category.

To make these different assumptions clear, I had the class brainstorm all the factors they could think of that might distinguish classes from each other, and I wrote their ideas up on the board. The class came up with such things as property ownership, income level, source of income, nature of work life, and educational levels. On seeing all the different ways people distinguished class position, they started to see why there had been so many different percentage guesstimates. This led to a debate about the validity of various people's assumptions. I served as a facilitator for this discussion to make sure everybody got to have their say, and to encourage good listening, yet I did not offer my own view at this point.

Only after this discussion did I hand out a one-page flyer on class stratification that I adapted from Dennis Gilbert's and Joseph Kahl's *The American Class Structure: A New Synthesis.* At this point, the students seemed very interested in considering the thinking of other folks who had specifically researched this question, and to compare these ideas to their own theories. I stressed that the handout, while reflecting my own view of the topic, was not the "right" answer, but just one potentially useful way to look at the question. My goal here was—in the words of Jacqueline and Martin Brooks—to underline for the students "that the world is a complex place in which multiple perspectives exist and truth is often a matter of interpretation" (22).

As we discussed the handout, most students found themselves agreeing with the basic framework outlined by Gilbert and Kahl. One woman, however, raised the point that the framework gave no insight into the class position of married women who did not work at paid jobs in the formal economy. Did that experience define their class position, or did the class position of their husbands define their class position? We discussed this critical question without coming to a consensus, but concluded that people are stratified, and often marginalized, along several different gradients, such as class, race, and gender. I then posed the idea to the class that looking at social stratification from multiple lenses might yield a more accurate picture than only looking at society through the lens of race, or class, or gender, or age, and so on.

At this point, I wanted to take the discussion to a more personal level and explore the class diversity that might exist in our small group of twelve Antioch students. I told the class that I was about to read a series of questions about different people's lives growing up and wanted them to stand up briefly after each question if their personal answer to the question was yes. In this way, people would not only get to reflect on their own class backgrounds as they considered whether the questions applied to them, they also got to see who else stood up for which questions, and thus get a glimpse of the classmates' class backgrounds. I worried about this exercise feeling too threatening, but in the midst of the silence between the slowly read questions, and the interested gaze of students as they looked through this window into the life experience of their classmates, I sensed that the students were engaging the issue of class stratification in a highly personal way.

I then broke the class into four small groups and asked them to discuss their personal reflections on their location in the class system with the other students in their groups. As an aid to these "go-arounds" and discussions, I suggested some possible questions to explore and posted them on the wall: What class do you belong to? Have you had much intimate contact with people from class backgrounds different than your own or do you rely mostly on cultural stereotypes for your information about the life chances, worldviews, and concerns of folks from other class backgrounds? How might the quality of your information and knowledge about other class backgrounds affect your work as an environmentalist? As a coalition builder? The discussions in the small groups took off and were searching and animated. There was nothing dry or didactic sounding in the energetic buzz of conversation. In contrast to my relying on teacher talk, students were constructing their own views, eagerly internalizing and assessing outside input, and working cooperatively with each other to understand the social world around them.

To finish off this class, I brought the whole group back together for a debriefing of the small group discussions. People were struck by the range of diversity in the student body's class backgrounds. Almost everyone had assumed that Antioch students came from middle-class backgrounds. Yet, this was not the case in our class. Indeed, while no one in this group came from either the "capitalist" class or from an "underclass" background, the students were fairly evenly divided between the upper middle class, the middle class, the working class, and the working poor. Even the people from working-class or working-poor backgrounds were surprised at the diversity of experience in the group. They had often assumed they were the only ones who were not from middle-class backgrounds at Antioch and were excited to see the actual diversity of experience that did exist at Antioch.

The group then spent some time discussing how a middle-class bias does seem prevalent in many environmental organizations and how this inhibits the process of building coalitions with labor and civil rights groups, as well as building a diverse, broad-based environmental movement itself. As we explored this topic, I occasionally offered up some relevant information. However, I most often said things such as "Good question. What's your guess about that?" "What do other people think?" When students made very strong assertions, I often turned to the rest of the group and asked if other people held different views on the question at hand. By the time we finished class that night, the group energy was high and many informal discussions of class stratification continued long after class was officially over. The tone was clearly different from our class session on racism. I was thus excited at the possibilities of teaching in this new way.

In the follow-up class I chose to continue my experiments with integrating challenging political material with a "constructivist" approach to teaching. My goal was to look at how the capitalist system distributes social and environmental benefits and costs along class (and racial and gender) lines. In particular, I wanted to focus on the concept of "externalities," where the price of a commodity does not reflect all of the social and environmental costs involved in its production, costs which are usually paid for by the society as a whole, but most particularly by the less powerful. My hope was to spark a discussion of corporate globalization as a generator of social and environmental injustice on an international scale. The readings for this week provided a good background on all these issues. My challenge was to make this material come alive.

Instead of a lecture, or even a class discussion on the readings, I decided to build the next class around a thirty-minute video tape on labor conditions in the "free trade zones" of Honduras. The video, produced by the National Labor Committee, focused on the exploitation of the teenage women who make up over 90 percent of the Honduran labor force for U.S. textile and apparel companies like the GAP, OshKosh, and Gitano. The interviews with these teenage girls, who often must work over twelve hours a day under abusive supervisors for less than a few dollars a day, are both vivid and emotionally stirring. I felt this video tape would not only raise important issues, but that it could not easily be reduced to something distant and abstract.

Prodded by the book on constructivist pedagogy, however, I did not want the students just sitting and passively taking in information, even if it was emotionally compelling. As noted by the Brookses:

Constructivist teachers inquire about students' understandings of concepts before sharing their own understandings of those concepts. (107)

[Constructivist teachers realize that] the facts that accompany topics become more relevant for students once the students become engaged in reflection on the big concepts. (48)

Constructivist teachers encourage student inquiry by asking thoughtful, open-ended questions, and encouraging students to ask questions
of each other. (110)

Constructivist teachers engage students in experiences that might engender contradictions to their initial hypotheses and then encourage
discussion. (112)

I thus devised a class exercise to serve as a prelude to the video. I divided
the class into two groups and gave each one a cotton shirt produced in
Honduras and purchased from the GAP. I left all the labels on the shirts so
the students could see the price and any other information that would be
available to them as consumers. I then asked the groups to come up with a
group statement of what they knew for sure about the social and environmental costs involved in the shirts' production; what they guessed, and what
they did not have any idea or information about. Passing the shirt around so
each person could hold it and inspect it, each group began a spirited discussion of what they knew, or could guess, about the production of their shirt.

Both groups quickly agreed that the tags on their shirts offered little
information about production-related costs, and that the price probably did
not fully reflect them. Students then started making educated guesses about
the "externalized" production costs missing from the price: soil depletion
and pesticide poisoning involved in the growing of cotton; pollution and
resource depletion related to moving the cotton to the manufacturing plant
in Honduras and the finished goods to North America; and the social costs of
low-wage factory work. The groups also discovered that, beyond these few
guesses, they didn't really know many things about the exact impacts of the
production process—from the dyes used, the amount and type of energy
consumed, where the plant waste was dumped, or who the workers were and
how they were treated. After about fifteen minutes in small groups, each
group reported their theories and questions to the other group and discovered that they had come up with similar "GAPs" in their knowledge.

At this point, I introduced the video and explained that it would offer some
information on the questions and hypotheses they had generated among
themselves. The video opened with shots of company labels on shirts, including the GAP's, and then dissolved into a picture of the faces of young Honduran girls locked behind factory gates and watched over by armed guards. By
the end of the video, many of the students' questions about the social costs

that are obscured and unreflected in the price of the shirts they had examined had been answered. The reality of child labor, low wages, union-busting, and the lack of meaningful social and environmental regulation in these U.S.–supported free trade zones were now vivid for them. They now had a beginning picture of how economic globalization and the power of multinational corporations threatens many social and ecological communities.

Most of the class was in tears when the lights came up, and we discussed both their feelings and what they had learned from the experience. I facilitated this discussion and increasingly asked questions about what in their readings offered them clues as to what economic structures engender such conditions and made a few points of my own. By the end of the night, the students were asking if we were going to spend time in later sessions exploring how people could change these kinds of conditions. When I answered yes, and talked about some of the class topics coming up during the last few sessions of the course, they expressed an urgency to explore these topics and get a handle on how the environmental justice movement could achieve its goals. This session felt like a turning point in the class, and several students in conversations with me outside of class, and in their student journals, said that it was after these last two class sessions that the course really came alive and engaged them.

Getting into the Field

Building on the new energy in our class, my co-teacher and I organized a field trip so that our students could have a direct experience of the disproportionate environmental degradation impacting poor communities of color and how such communities have organized effectively to meet these challenges. As Jacqueline and Martin Brooks note, constructivist teachers use the "raw data and primary sources" of direct experience in their teaching whenever possible (104).

I could see the impact of this approach on our students when we first walked into the cluttered one-story storefront of the Dudley Street Neighborhood Initiative (DSNI) in the center of one of Boston's poorest and most run-down neighborhoods. The walls inside the DSNI headquarters were covered with seemingly haphazard notices of welfare eligibility procedures, lead-paint abatement programs, affordable housing possibilities, and crime watch alerts. The staff at DSNI's headquarters also reflected the demographics of the neighborhood as a whole, and was made up of a patchwork quilt of African Americans, Cape Verdeans, Hispanics, and a smattering of white folks.

Looking around, I could read in my students' faces the underlying question: "This is an environmental group?" Yet, when DSNI's organizing director began talking, the pieces started to fall into place in their minds. DSNI seeks to improve the built, social, and natural environment where the neighborhood's twelve thousand residents live, work, and play. This view of what the word "environment" means is different from what most conservation groups talk about, but our students began to see this definition is legitimate too.

During a guided tour of the neighborhood in our rented van, it also became quite clear that environmental hazards are a pressing concern for this community. Over fifty-four toxic waste sites are located in this 1.5-square-mile neighborhood. While Dudley Street residents make up only 4 percent of Boston's population, they live amidst 10 percent of the city's known waste sites listed with the Environmental Protection Agency (EPA). Adding further to their pollution problems, the neighborhood is also home to a number of poorly regulated industrial enterprises, and it has been declared a Lead Emergency Zone by the state of Massachusetts. The neighborhood had also been the site of illegal dumping from solid waste haulers from all over the city. Its many abandoned lots and poorly lit streets had acted like a magnet for illegal dumping.

What captured the students' imaginations was not the community's victimization, however, but its response. For over ten years, the organization has worked on an aggressive "Don't Dump On Us" campaign that has challenged and sought alternatives to the economic and political forces that have trashed their community (see Sklar and Medoff). With a combination of citizen lobbying, public relations savvy, militant civil disobedience, and other political pressure tactics, the community has also shut down three illegal trash transfer stations, changed EPA policy in the neighborhood, improved city services, and forced the city to remove the many abandoned cars that used to blight the streets. The community has also reclaimed several parcels of abandoned land and created lead-free community gardens, small parks, and newly built affordable housing.

In response to student questions about how more "conventional" environmentalists can aid efforts like DSNI, the organization's organizing director explained how DSNI has begun setting up partnerships with environmental groups who are seeking to work in concert with urban-based environmental justice groups. The plus side of such a relationship for DSNI is that an infusion of volunteers, financial support, and legal and technical assistance can go a long way toward helping achieve their goals. However, such partnerships are difficult if the environmental groups do not develop an understanding of the environmental justice perspective or move beyond a paternalistic approach to joint work. Overcoming these problems within environmental groups was held out as one of the major contributions emerging environmental professionals like our students could make to environmental justice organizing. Having more partners prepared to work together effectively would be a huge help, according to the DSNI staffer.

The van ride home took two hours and provided students with an opportunity to discuss what they had experienced and learned during the day. One thing stood out to me, they were afire with a sense of hope for the future that had often eluded them in our class. In particular, they felt that they could actually play a role in furthering the environmental justice agenda. In that moment, I felt our class had been a success.

Conclusion: From Critical Teaching to Activist Training

My co-teacher and I were able to rescue this course and create a learning environment that sparked intense dialog, had students examining their previous assumptions, provided them with new experiences, and encouraged them to read deeply and think critically about previously neglected political issues. We were also able to engage students emotionally and explore value questions about what kind of contributions they wanted to make in the world as environmental professionals and citizen activists. Interestingly, the student evaluations of the course were among the strongest for a course taught at Antioch that year. They talked of how the course was eye-opening as well as profoundly moving on a personal level. Several students said that the course had significantly changed how they looked at their work as environmental professionals and as citizens.

In *Greening the College Curriculum,* Collett and Karakashian argue that the kind of pedagogical approach we developed in this course is particularly useful for racially diverse, "nontraditional" students within higher education. As they put it:

> We know, for example, from numerous recent studies that the kind of academic experience that worked for most faculty when they were students (90 percent of all full-time faculty are white and 72 percent

are male!) goes against the learning styles of an increasing number of students today. The competitive, analytic, disciplined, orderly approach that most faculty learned to master is at direct odds with a more participatory, spontaneous, holistic approach characteristic of African-American, Latino, and Native American cultures, and indeed of working class white students as well. (311)

My experience, however, suggests that this approach to education also has enormous value for a so-called "mainstream" student population that is white and includes many upper-class and middle-class students. The conventional "banking" approach to education simply does not appear well-suited to teaching environmental justice to "mainstream" environmental studies students who may not yet be aware of the social and personal importance of the issues. Indeed, our stumbled-on approach—which encouraged participation, personal engagement, empathy, critical thinking, and searching dialog—seems especially congruent with teaching a course focused on human dignity, social justice, and democratic practice. As noted by human rights educator Nancy Flowers, "How you teach is what you teach" (*Human Rights Here and Now*, 32).

The "good buzz" from this course inspired the department to offer even more courses in political ecology and has led to other spin-offs. Most recently, in response to a proposal I drafted in September 1999, Antioch's Environmental Studies Department has decided to develop a new master's program in Environmental Advocacy and Organizing by September 2002. The goal of this new effort is two-fold: 1) serving the advanced training needs of professional activists working on issues of environmental protection, corporate accountability, and social and environmental justice, and 2) creating a sustainable ripple effect throughout the entire department, deepening all students' understanding of the cross currents of social change they face as environmental educators, conservation biologists, and environmental resource managers.

Our hope is that the new students and faculty attracted to the Environmental Advocacy and Organizing program will become a dynamic force within the department and help foster a more holistic perspective among all of our students—one that integrates human rights and environmental protection. Teaching environmental justice has been, and will remain, vital to this on-going effort to deepen the political sophistication of our environmental studies program.

WORKS CITED

Adams, Maurianne, Lee Anne Bell, and Pat Griffin. *Teaching for Diversity and Social Justice.* New York: Routledge, 1997.

Anthony, Carl. "Understanding Culture, Humanities and Environmental Justice." *Race, Poverty & the Environment* 6, no. 2–3 (1996): 17–18.

Brooks, Jacqueline Grennon, and Martin G. Brooks. *In Search of Understanding: The Case For Constructivist Classrooms.* Alexandria, Va.: Association for Supervision and Curriculum Development, 1993.

Bryant, Bunyan. *Environmental Advocacy: Concepts, Issues and Dilemmas.* Ann Arbor, Mich.: Caddo Gap, 1990.

Collett, Jonathan, and Stephen Karakashian, eds. *Greening the College Curriculum: A Guide to Environmental Teaching in the Liberal Arts.* Washington D.C.: Island, 1996.

Flowers, Nancy, ed. *The Human Rights Education Handbook: Effective Practices for Learning, Action, and Change.* Minneapolis: Human Rights Resource Center and Stanley Foundation, 2000.

———. *Human Rights Here and Now: Celebrating the Universal Declaration of Human Rights.* Minneapolis: Human Rights Educators' Network of Amnesty International USA, Human Rights USA Resource Center, and Stanley Foundation, 1998.

Freire, Paulo. *Pedagogy of the Oppressed.* New York: Seabury, 1974.

Gilbert, Dennis, and Joseph Kahl. *The American Class Structure: A New Synthesis.* Belmont, Calif.: Wadsworth Publishing, 1993.

Goldman, Benjamin. *Not Just Prosperity: Achieving Sustainability with Environmental Justice.* Washington, D.C.: National Wildlife Federation, 1993.

hooks, bell. *Teaching to Transgress: Education as the Practice of Freedom.* New York: Routledge, 1994.

Horton, Myles, and Paulo Freire. *We Make the Road By Walking: Conversations on Education and Social Change.* Philadelphia: Temple University Press, 1990.

Horton, Myles, with Judith Kohl, and Herbert Kohl. *The Long Haul: An Autobiography.* New York: Teachers College Press, 1998.

National Labor Committee. *Zoned for Slavery: The Child Behind the Label.* 23 minutes running time. New York: Crowing Rooster Arts, 1995.

Orr, David. *Earth in Mind: On Education, Environment, and the Human Prospect.* Washington, D.C.: Island, 1994.

Seager, Joni. *Earth Follies: Coming To Feminist Terms With The Global Environmental Crisis.* New York: Routledge, 1993.

Shor, Ira. *Empowering Education: Critical Teaching for Social Change*. Chicago: University of Chicago Press, 1992.

Shor, Ira, and Paulo Freire. 1987. *A Pedagogy For Liberation: Dialogues on Transforming Education*. South Hadley, Mass.: Bergin & Garvey, 1987.

Sklar, Holly, and Peter Medoff. *Streets of Hope: The Fall and Rise of an Urban Neighborhood*. Boston: South End, 1994.

Thomashow, Mitchell. *Ecological Identity: Becoming a Reflective Environmentalist*. Cambridge: MIT Press, 1995.

19

TEACHING LITERATURE OF ENVIRONMENTAL JUSTICE IN AN ADVANCED GENDER STUDIES COURSE

Jia-Yi Cheng-Levine

Teaching is more than transmitting knowledge or modes of thinking; it helps form political subjects who will determine the future of this planet we call home. My goal for teaching literature of environmental justice was to foster a literacy of the environment in my students' everyday lives, to call their attention to the power structures of society and the political struggles of the impoverished, as well as to encourage them to examine configurations of knowledge and the dispensation of power. By addressing the interrelated issues of race, gender, class, and the environment, I wanted to bring environmental and social justice education into the class. The neglect of the interrelatedness of these issues would most likely reinforce the patriarchal, compartmentalized ways of learning that devalue women, nonwhites, less privileged, and the environment; it may also reduce these subjects into objects of discussion and studies, and therefore further perpetuate oppressive social injustice and relationships that contribute to the destruction of the environment.

As environmental educator Joy A. Palmer asserts, environmental education, although not new, is a relatively young and immensely complex field.[1] In acknowledging ecological conditions facing the world today, few of us would doubt the urgency of "greening" our literary studies. These conditions, as Greta Gaard puts it, "offer sufficient motivation for academics to become activists and to bring an awareness of the need for social and ecological justice to every class we teach" (224). Environmental education at the level of higher education, however, will not empower our students as critical and responsible world citizens if we do not ask students to study, question, and challenge the history and ideological frameworks that have contributed to the environmental devastation we experience today. The human/nature, culture/nature, and male/female hierarchical dichotomies that have contributed to the world's ecological imbalance need to be addressed in a classroom where environmental education takes place.

The western patriarchal colonial mindset segregates culture from nature, man from woman, white from nonwhite, self from the other, with white male culture remaining at the center of power and the feminine side of nature at the margin. Patriarchy, as Carol J. Adams states, "simultaneously feminize[s] nature and naturalize[s] women" (1). In the Eurocentric model of society in which women are devalued, the feminization of nature legitimatizes the detrimental exploitation of both women and nature. Similarly, minority peoples are also categorized into the same group with women and nature, and therefore, suffer greatly from the injustices imposed by local, national, and international policies about which they usually have little say in the process of decision making. Furthermore, many environmental policies are made under the influence of multinational corporations whose main interest lies in maximizing profits not human benefits and which possess the capitalistic power to determine or alter a Third World country's mode of production, and often further exploit people, especially women and children, of poorer countries. Multinational corporations have extended environmental injustice beyond national geopolitical borders and justified a market system that allows the rich of the North to exploit people of the South, to extract the South's raw materials, and to dump the North's toxic waste on the South.

The Course

In the fall of 2000, I taught literature of environmental justice in an advanced gender studies course (ENG4350 Advanced Gender Studies: Women and the Environment). This was a senior-level class offered through the Department of English at the University of Houston-Downtown.[2] The concept and development of ecofeminism were introduced, followed by the historical background of the economic and social subjugation of women and people of color. We studied the interrelationship between the degradation of women's lives, especially those of color and economically less privileged, and the devastation of the environment due to the expansion of multinational corporate culture, a mutual concern shared by both ecofeminists and environmental justice advocates. Ecofeminism's critique of the twin domination of women and nature as well as its attempts to bring justice back to the environment and the lives of women correspond to the environmental justice movement's demand for the restructuring of the social order and its requirement for incorporating ecological issues into a larger social and political agenda. Reading literature of environmental justice in a gender studies course, then, would only reinforce the interconnectedness among the issues of gender, justice, and the environment.

Despite the fact that this course was offered through the Department of English, I saw the necessity of including writings by international scholars and writers, since the issue of environmental justice cannot be limited locally or nationally without considering the interdependence and inter-relatedness of the environment at the global scale.[3] Writings from other disciplines and activities groups, such as the "Principles of Environmental Justice" put out by the First National People of Color Environmental Leadership Summit[4] and selections from *Toward Environmental Justice*, a study conducted by Committee on Environmental Justice from the Institute of Medicine, therefore, were incorporated onto our reading list as well.

The reading list included writings from activists, historians, scholars, and scientists, to offer students background knowledge on the concepts and principles of environmental justice and to help them detect and interpret literature of environmental justice. The novels read were Ana Castillo's *So Far from God*, Mahasweta Devi's *Imaginary Maps*, Buchi Emecheta's *The Rape of Shiva*, and Linda Hogan's *Solar Storms*. Carolyn Merchant's *Earthcare* and Richard Hofrichter's *Toxic Struggles* provided us with key concepts such as ecofeminism and environmental justice, as well as helped establish the link between these two. Vandana Shiva's *Staying Alive* gave the class a better understanding of colonial history and the impact of postcolonial ecology. We concluded the course by reading the book of essays *Dangerous Intersections*, edited by Jael Silliman and Ynestra King, and Christopher Foreman's *The Promise and Peril of Environmental Justice*.

The objective of this course was to motivate students to question history and authority, to expand their view of women, literature, and the environment to a global scale and perspective, as well as to be aware of the environmental history of their local communities—communities in which they themselves might be victims of institutionalized environmental racism/ injustice. Major concepts/issues examined were: race and gender, violence, cultural practices that encourage violence against women and the environment, history of colonization and decolonization, and neocolonial/post-colonial ecology.

Pedagogy and Assignments

The generative power of critical consciousness plays an essential role in helping our students to be responsible and responsive world citizens. A more comprehensive understanding of social and political issues, therefore, should accompany their study of literature. As a strong advocate of ecofeminism and social justice, my intention was to nurture and empower. I conducted a dialogic classroom that embodied feminist theories and practices challenging the traditional, hierarchical structure of the dispensation of power. Also influenced by the concept of "liberatory learning," as advocated by Ira Shor and Paulo Freire, I encouraged students to be involved in generating ideas and discussing topics through oral participation and collaborative journals.[5]

Ultimately, what I tried to achieve in this course was for students to foster their rhetorical capacities and further develop their critical analysis skills so that after the course ended, they would, hopefully, still actively decode the power structures that invade their daily lives. In order to develop their rhetorical skills, assignments that encourage dialogue within oneself and with others, such as a collaborative journal, would be more effective than, let's say, exams, which usually are a one-way demonstration of knowledge effective in testing students' ability in memorization—the banking method of teaching. As knowledge is situated and culturally, socially, and politically determined, the audience of students' journals, in this class, would not be necessarily the instructor, but the people they choose to dialogue with in their entries.[6] When they dialogue with each other, students gradually become aware that they should be held accountable for their beliefs and be able to defend or modify their thoughts as necessary.

In their journals, in addition to their reaction to the reading and class discussion, students were asked to record any findings on environmental injustice performed by institutions that affected their community's life (for instance, the zoning in Houston and the designation of landfills that surround mainly Black and Mexican American communities) and to examine cultural practices that are hostile to women's development and to the environment (how the excessive consumerism encouraged by the media/advertisements, for instance, directly impacts the health of our environment). From their responses to, and analysis of, the texts, I encouraged students to exercise critical thinking on the processes and results of public policy making; in researching local environmental policies, they charted changes in their modes of thinking and reasoning regarding their immediate environment.

As for their final research paper, although a literature-oriented one was encouraged, students had also proposed to research other issues related to environmental justice, especially findings that were directly related to their immediate environment. Some of them found their own stories of environmental injustice and critiqued instances of institutionalized racism that affected their daily lives.

The Course Plan

I divided the semester into three parts. First, we read about the interrelated exploitations regarding women, people of color, and the environment. Since this is a gender studies course, at the beginning of the semester, we discussed how the role of gender was conceptualized and its association with the feminization of nature. We then sought the connection between ecofeminism and the environmental justice movement by comparing issues raised in Shiva's *Staying Alive* and essays from Hofrichter's *Toxic Struggles*. The second part of the semester directly addressed the causes of social and environmental injustices, the need for and the principles and practices of the environmental justice movement, in both our lives and in literature read. The last part of the semester brought in a broader scale of problems caused by instances of environmental injustice around the world and the solutions offered by activities and scholars.

We started the course with Carolyn Merchant's *Earthcare* to examine how a gender role is culturally and politically constructed, to investigate how, when, and why the feminist movement and the ecological movement intertwine, and to discuss how the devastation of the environment and the subjugation of women and people of color are closely related.[7] In *Earthcare,* Merchant documents "the many aspects of the association of women with nature in Western culture and their roles in the contemporary environmental movement," and looks at the "connections between women and nature, symbols of nature as female, and women's practices and daily interactions with the earth" (xv). With this book as an introduction to the subject of the course, we questioned the epistemologies of gender and race as well as the gendering of nature and the construction of gender and race before and in the wake of modern science. With the historical background provided by Merchant, we brought the history of colonization, the expansion of imperialism, and the rise of capitalism into discussion, since it is hard to ignore the fact that the environment underwent dramatic alteration with the rise of imperialism.

The readings, at this point, focused on providing historical backgrounds of colonial expansion and its relationship to the exploitation of the land and people of the South. We discussed extensively the second part of Merchant's book, "History," in which the author explains the history of human understanding of nature and the progressive human domination over nature through justified social needs (colonial expansion) and ideological constructions (antagonistic dualism: men vs. women, culture vs. nature, white vs. nonwhite, etc.). In this part of the semester, I asked students to begin their journal by asking themselves what they thought their relationship with the environment was, how they defined such words as "environment," "justice," "nature," "culture," "history," as well as "civilization." Many students commented that they never associated nature and the environment with the concept of "justice" and most of them regarded the word "environment" as interchangeable with nature.[8]

Following Merchant's work, we read Mahasweta Devi's *Imaginary Maps* and Buchi Emecheta's *The Rape of Shiva*. Both novels deal indirectly with the impact of colonial expansion, and directly with the detrimental effects of the dehumanizing colonial ideology on a postcolonial country. Devi's three stories expose the impact of imperialist exploitation, especially on women's lives in India and Pakistan. Both novelists examine the impact of colonial legacies that negate local cultural diversity and encourage monocultural production that constitutes economic dependence on the North, subordination of local people, especially women, and discrimination against their own traditions. It alters the country's modes of production to an economic system that heavily relies on outsiders. In Emecheta's novel, the bareness of the land is embodied in the female protagonist's infertility. We asked questions such as: Why does the author use a woman's body to symbolize the bareness of the environment? What effects have resulted from colonialism imposed on women, people of the South, and the environment? How are women portrayed in both novels? Where in the novel are the environmental justice issues dealt with? And, what is missing in these texts? Students were quick to see how injustice was present in all stories; however, they were still struggling with the concept of environmental justice.

Then Vandana Shiva's *Staying Alive* provided a detailed historical account and explanation of how colonial expansion and postcolonial capitalistic concepts of development have subjugated nature and women for (white) men's disposal in the name of progress. She discusses how colonized countries often suffer from environmental injustice due to racial discrimination and economic status of the country. She discusses how a newly independent

India, with the "help" of her own national elite who were educated under the colonial education system, continued to exploit women and extract natural resources in order to "catch up" with the global capitalistic system that supports the wasteful habits of the North. Shiva exposes how women of color have been victims of modern technological development and the scientific revolution, which marginalizes them economically and politically. She also challenges "the western concept of economics as production of profits and capital accumulation" and offers the alternative ecological concept of "economics as production of sustenance and needs satisfaction" (xvii). While we read Shiva's *Staying Alive,* we again picked up the discussion of production and reproduction, questioned the controversial paradigm involved with production—the economic wealth it brings for the privileged as well as the poverty and dispossession it deepens for the poor—and discussed how the concept of development in the age of post–World War II has evolved into the excessive consumerism that many of us practice today. Shiva's work, therefore, served as a good transition to gradually move our discussion on eco-feminism to the issues of environmental justice.

Having read two novels from two different continents, we discussed whether the exploitation of women, people of color, and nature is universal; what problems are specific to some locales due to the historical, cultural, and geographical differences; what women's role is in policy making; and what kind of danger we ran into by reading a few select novels as representative of a culture and people. At this point, some students began to articulate what they thought environmental injustice meant: racist and sexist implications in the unequal distribution of economic wealth and in the neglect for people of color's health and well-being.

The second part of the semester addressed principles and practices of the environmental justice movement. While both Devi and Emecheta portray women and people of the South as victims of development and colonial ideology, Linda Hogan's *Solar Storms* presents these people as agencies of their own fate, taking action in fighting against environmental injustice. This narrative, like the previous two novels, examines the impact of "development" in the lives of ethnic minorities in the United States, in this case, Native Americans. *Solar Storms* exposes students to the world of Native Americans who suffer culturecide and genocide due to the destruction of the land. It beautifully chronicles the struggle of a community of women in search of their roots and connection to the water that sustains their culture and community, the same water that is later cut off by a dam. The community's few survivors, most of whom are women who do not or can not leave the land, fight against the corporate invasion of their sole survival space. What the novel also presents is a young woman who, in search of her subjectivity, realizes that her sense of being is intimately connected to the changes of the seasons and the environment. Accompanying Hogan's novel was Leslie Marmon Silko's article "Landscape, History, and the Pueblo Imagination." This piece provided students with a cultural background that challenges the Euro-concept of time and space to which most students are accustomed. Hogan's novel and Silko's article prompted students to define their own "subjectivity"—is it logical, social, political, and/or ecological? With the help of Hogan's protagonist, I asked students again how they saw themselves in the contexts of nature and the environment, and we discussed such questions as: Are women really closer to nature than men? How do we connect the issues of race and gender to environmental justice? Students at this point made a stronger connection between racism and the issue of justice in environmental health.

Reading about Hogan's characters fighting against environmental racism led us to examine the principles of environmental justice in Richard Hofrichter's book, *Toxic Struggles*. Hofrichter and his contributors clearly define the central principle of environmental justice, which "stresses equal access to natural resources and the right to clean air and water, adequate health care, affordable shelter, and a safe workplace"; it points out that the failure to fulfill these basic needs is the result of "institutional decisions, marketing practices, discrimination, and an endless quest for economic growth." It further emphasizes that environmental problems are "inseparable from other social injustices such as poverty, racism, sexism, unemployment, urban deterioration, and the diminishing quality of life resulting from corporate activity" (4). With these articulated definitions, students questioned the lack of consideration of gender issues in the principles and practices of the movement as presented by these essays. We also revisited three previous novels to find incidents of environmental injustice, with special attention to the issue of race and gender.

In order to further examine the principles of environmental justice, we also discussed the recent boycotts of companies such as the GAP and Nike, whose overseas production sites have violated environmental justice principles as advocated by contributors' to Hofrichter's book. Hence, in their four-page papers, students were asked to investigate how corporate culture, through media, advertisements, and internet convenience, have dictated our consumption habits; how, or if, they see that excessive consumption might have contributed to cultural violence against people of color, women, and nature; or what the reasons are for the lack of exposure of environmental injustice incidents in the mainstream media.

Ana Castillo's *So Far from God*, a novel portraying a Chicana mother raising four rather eccentric daughters in a world invaded by large corporations, also corresponded well with Hofrichter's book. Documenting the issues of race and gender in the age of high-tech industry, Castillo questions the harmful effects of industry on the environmental health of a Southwest community predominantly occupied by Mexican Americans. This novel chronicles how women of Tome, New Mexico, empower themselves with their love for their family, community, and the land, and, in the face of losing everything they own, decide to stand united and use their local resources to battle against these corporations.[9] With this novel, students were finally able to make the connection between environmental justice and gender issues because, as demonstrated in the novel, they saw how, when environmental health is under attack, women's bodies are first to react to the toxic elements in the water and the air by developing cancer or having spontaneous abortions.[10]

The last part of the semester directed our discussion to other problems caused by environmental injustices not yet mentioned in novels read. Jael Silliman and Ynestra King's *Dangerous Intersections* provides grounds for debating the complex issues of population, development, and the environment; with the debate on population comes gender issues, and with development, race issues. Addressing the "dangerous intersections" of racism, sexism, and classism, this book seeks to dismantle the ideological framework that blames women of color for "over-population" problems that "supposedly" further diminish natural resources, and "elides other structural and historical causes that may explain the situation" (viii). It also offers multicultural perspectives and localized alternative solutions that encourage women, especially women of color, to be not only agents of their own lives, but a changing force that sustains an environmentally just world. Many contributors of the book—such as Asoka Bandarage (on population and development), Joni Seager (on militaries and the environment), H. Patricia Hynes (on consumption), and Marsha J. Tyson Darling (on African American women)—in their critique of colonial mentality, neocolonial ecological destruction, and patriarchal domination, expose the interrelated issues of colonial history, corporate control in extracting natural and human resources of the South, and economic inequalities between the South and the North. These are core issues that may have contributed more to the global environmental problems than "the over-population problem." This collection also reminds the reader of the leading role women play in environmental justice movements, such as the Green Belt Movement in Africa and the Chipko movement in India. Both Hofrichter's and Silliman's books helped the class investigate further the environmental justice movement, especially as led by women of color in the literature read.

Christopher Foreman's *The Promise and Peril of Environmental Justice* concluded our class.[11] Identifying environmental hazards and the risk they place on populations of different ethnic and economic backgrounds, Foreman emphasizes that the environmental justice movement does not aim at decreasing health risks, but at community empowerment. The class discussed the role of literature of environmental justice plays in community empowerment. We also revisited students' earlier journals, comparing how their previous definitions of "environment," "justice," "culture," and "nature" differed from what we had learned throughout the semester from the readings.

Conclusion

Let me conclude the essay by sharing with you a story of one of my students in this class, K. In the Spring of 2000, I offered two upper-division humanities classes at a remote satellite campus in the southwest outskirts of Houston, where the fastest growing city in the area, Sugar Land, is located. In one of the classes, three out of ten students either had cancer, had just finished cancer treatment, or were still undergoing treatment with the same kind of cancer. The comparison of their treatments in their casual conversational exchange immediately caught my attention: they were all in their early twenties. One of the three students, K, was in this Advanced Gender Studies class in the fall of 2000. Reading Carolyn Merchant's *Earthcare* prompted K to recontextualize her own history of cancer. In some parts of the book, Merchant documents women's struggle against devastating environmental pollutions, such as the ones caused by radioactive and chemical waste. K began to make connections between her own cancerous history and many people she knew of who lived in the same area (a relatively poor neighborhood surrounded by many sugar and other chemical plants), shopped in the same stores, drank the same water, and had the same kind of cancer she had—Hodgkin's disease. Inspired by Lois Gibbs and other stories as reported by Merchant and Gibbs herself in Hofrichter's book, K began a research project examining materials from the Health Department, hospital records, personal interviews, and the sugar plants neighboring her home and schools. Although K did not have enough time or resources to draw conclusive findings regarding the cause of her cancer, I know that the environmental justice movement is no longer just a concept or mere words for her.

Discourse of environmental justice and an environmental education are desperately needed everywhere because environmental devastation and injustice affects our daily lives. This issue crosses the racial, economic, gender, and political divides that we humans so foolishly use to compartmentalize each other. By introducing literature of environmental justice to our students, we help form political subjects who would seek to dismantle racism, sexism, classism, and unbridled capitalism, which wreak havoc on our planet and people. Only when this faulty foundation is replaced with its counterparts—unity, equality, and compassion—can policies that promote real justice and democracy be implemented.

NOTES

1. According to Palmer, the term "environmental education" first appeared in 1948 in an International Union for the Conservation of Nature and Natural Resources Conference in Paris. In 1970, this group formulated an influential definition of "environmental education": "Environmental education is the process of recognizing values and clarifying concepts in order to develop skills and attitudes necessary to understand and appreciate the interrelatedness among man [sic], his culture, and his biophysical surroundings. Environmental education also entails practice in decision-making and self-formulation of a code of behavior about issues concerning environmental quality" (qtd. in Palmer, 7). Environmental education was further consolidated in the 1980s when its importance was recognized globally. With the Earth Summit in 1992, environmental education has evolved from "nature study" in the 1960s through "outdoor/adventure" "environmental education" in the 1970s and global level of awareness in the 1980s, to "empowerment" and "peace education" in the 1990s (3–31).

2. A junior-level course, ENG3350 Gender Studies, covers basic principles and concepts in this field. ENG4350 is an advanced course that focuses on special topics depending on the instructor's specialty. For a sample syllabus, email me (jiayi@dt.uh.edu) or Joni Adamson (jadamson@u.arizona.edu).

3. This was also an attempt to show my students my critique regarding compartmentalized disciplinary studies so prevalent in U.S. higher education.

4. Available on the web through a link from the Political Ecology Group

website (www.igc.org/saepej/principles.html) or in Hofrichter's *Toxic Struggles*.

5. I attribute many of these ideas to Greta Gaard's article on teaching ecofeminist literature and Patrick Murphy's graduate-level courses of which I was fortunate to be a part.

6. I have personally benefited tremendously from a collaborative journal assignment from a course offered by Patrick D. Murphy a few years back. In that assignment, we had four people writing to each other about our analysis of the texts and class discussion. Although the first few entries were more therapeutic (such as complaining about some male classmates' underlying chauvinistic comments) than literary or "graduate-level work," we gradually entered into dialogue with each other. Our personal findings and thoughts were either much encouraged or challenged by our peers, whose comments or questions were always easier to accept than from the "authoritative" figure, the professor who held our grades in his hand.

7. For the sake of length, I only briefly introduce each text and what discussion it produced in class.

8. I have taken information from both my own teaching notes/journals and students' journals to present what we discussed in class about the texts and the issues of environmental justice.

9. A novel that is comparable to Castillo's portrayal of women's role in organizing their people for the sake of the community and the land is Kingsolver's *Animal Dreams*.

10. For an in-depth analysis of *So Far from God* and the inseparability of race, gender, class, and environmental issues in this novel, see Platt's "Ecocritical Chicana Literature."

11. A few other books on the subject of environmental justice, such as *Invisible Houston* and *Unequal Protection* by Robert D. Bullard, *Environmental Injustices, Political Struggles* by David E. Camacho, and *Woven Stone* by Simon Ortiz, were placed on reserve to help students on their final research papers.

WORKS CITED

Adams, Carol J, ed. *Ecofeminism and the Sacred*. New York: Continuum, 1993.

Bullard, Robert D. *Invisible Houston: The Black Experience in Boom and Bust*. College Station: Texas A&M University Press, 1987.

——, ed. *Unequal Protection: Environmental Justice and Communities of Color*. San Francisco: Sierra Club Books, 1997.

Camacho, David E., ed. *Environmental Injustices, Political Struggles: Race, Class, and the Environment.* Durham: Duke University Press, 1998.

Castillo, Ana. *So Far from God.* New York: Plume, 1994.

Committee on Environmental Justice. *Toward Environmental Justice: Research, Education, and Health Policy Needs.* Washington, D.C.: National Academy, 1999.

Devi, Mahasweta. *Imaginary Maps.* Trans. Gayatri Chakravorty Spivak. New York: Routledge, 1995.

Emecheta, Buchi. *The Rape of Shiva.* New York: George Braziller, 1985.

Foreman, Christopher H., Jr. *The Promise and Peril of Environmental Justice.* Washington, D.C.: Brookings Institution Press, 1998.

Gaard, Greta. "Hiking Without a Map: Reflections on Teaching Ecofeminist Literary Criticism." In *Ecofeminist Literary Criticism: Theory, Interpretation, Pedagogy,* edited by Greta Gaard and Patrick D. Murphy, 224–47. Chicago: University of Illinois Press, 1998.

Hofrichter, Richard. *Toxic Struggles: The Theory and Practice of Environmental Justice.* Philadelphia: New Society Publishers, 1993.

Hogan, Linda. *Solar Storms.* New York: Scribner, 1997.

Kingsolver, Barbara. *Animal Dreams.* New York: HarperCollins, 1991.

Merchant, Carolyn. *Earthcare: Women and the Environment.* New York: Routledge, 1995.

Ortiz, Simon. *Woven Stone.* Tucson: University of Arizona Press, 1992.

Palmer, Joy A. *Environmental Education in the 21st Century: Theory, Practice, Progress and Promise.* New York: Routledge, 1998.

Platt, Kamala. "Ecocritical Chicana Literature: Ana Castillo's 'Virtual Realism.'" In *Ecofeminist Literary Criticism: Theory, Interpretation, Pedagogy,* edited by Greta Gaard and Patrick D. Murphy, 139–57. Chicago: University of Illinois Press, 1998.

Shiva, Vandana. *Staying Alive: Women, Ecology, and Development.* London: Zed Books, 1989.

Shor, Ira, and Paulo Freire. *A Pedagogy of Liberation: Dialogues on Transforming Education.* South Hadley, Mass.: Bergin and Garvey, 1987.

Silko, Leslie Marmon. "Language, History, and the Pueblo Imagination." In *Writing Nature: An Ecological Reader for Writers,* edited by Carolyn Ross, 381–93. New York: St. Martin's, 1995.

Silliman, Jael, and Ynestra King, eds. *Dangerous Intersections: Feminist Perspectives on Population, Environment, and Development.* Cambridge, Mass.: South End, 1999.

SOURCE ACKNOWLEDGMENTS

"Environmental Justice: A Roundtable Discussion" originally appeared in *ISLE: Interdisciplinary Studies in Literature and Environment* 7:2 (Summer 2000), pp. 155–70.

"Spring," "Too Much of a Good Thing," "Custom," "Invasions," "Roots," "Mi Tío Baca El Poeta de Socorro," and "Black Mesa," by Jimmy Santiago Baca, from *Black Mesa Poems,* copyright © 1989 by Jimmy Santiago Baca. Reprinted by permission of New Directions Publishing Corp.

"Martín," by Jimmy Santiago Baca, from *Martín and Meditations on the South Valley,* copyright © 1987 by Jimmy Santiago Baca. Reprinted by permission of New Directions Publishing Corp.

"Poem about My Rights," by June Jordan, from *Naming Our Destiny: New and Selected Poems,* copyright © 1989 by June Jordan. Reprinted by permission of Thunder's Mouth Press.

"Trying to Talk with a Man," by Adrienne Rich, from *Diving into the Wreck: Poems, 1971–1972,* copyright © 1973 by Adrienne Rich. Reprinted by permission of W. W. Norton and Company.

"Salmon Return," by Phil George, from *Kautsa,* copyright © 1984 by Phil George. Reprinted by permission of Confluence Press.

CONTRIBUTORS

Joni Adamson is Associate Professor of American Literature and Folklore at the south campus of the University of Arizona. Her essays on Native American literature have appeared in *Studies in American Indian Literatures* and in *Reading the Earth: New Directions in the Study of Literature and the Environment*. She is the author of *American Indian Literature, Environmental Justice, and Ecocriticism: The Middle Place*.

Steve Chase is Director of the new master's program in Environmental Advocacy and Organizing at the Antioch New England Graduate School. He has long worked as an activist, adult educator, publisher, and writer. Steve was the coeditor of the "Nature and Justice" special issue of *Orion Magazine* and the editor of the book *Defending the Earth*. His articles have appeared in *Z Magazine; Race, Poverty, and the Environment; The Journal of Multicultural Environmental Education; Orion; Whole Terrain; The Trumpeter;* and the *Hungry Mind Review*. He lives with his partner and youngest son in Arlington, Massachusetts. He can be contacted at Steven__Chase@antiochne.edu.

Jia-Yi Cheng-Levine is Assistant Professor of English at the University of Houston-Downtown, where she teaches courses on gender studies, ethnic American minorities, American literature, and writing. Her primary teaching and research interests lie in ecofeminism, environmental justice, minority discourse, and teaching methodology.

Susan Comfort is an Associate Professor in the English Department at Indiana University of Pennsylvania, where she teaches courses in Third World literature and women's studies, as well as introductory literature and writing courses. Her research and activism focus on environmental justice issues, globalization, and human rights. Currently, she is involved in an effort to establish an activist center in the city of Indiana that will serve as a clearinghouse for social justice, green, and feminist activism.

Giovanna Di Chiro is Assistant Professor of Environmental Science at Allegheny College. Her research focuses on the participation of nontraditional actors in environmental science and sustainable development. Currently she is writing a book, *Uncommon Expertise: Women, Science, and Environmental Politics.* Di Chiro's recent work involves developing community partnerships linking public art, community revitalization, and environmental justice through the cultural practices of "placemaking."

Nelta Edwards is an Assistant Professor in the Sociology Department at the University of Alaska Anchorage. She teaches courses in sociology and women's studies and her research concerns feminist theory, science, and the environment.

Mei Mei Evans is Assistant Professor of English and Director of the Master of Arts degree program at Alaska Pacific University. Her scholarly research concerns the naturalization of sexual, racial, and gender identities in U.S. cultural productions. A published fiction writer and longtime activist, she was the statewide coordinator of the Oil Reform Alliance, a coalition of environmental activists, fishermen, artists, and educators that formed in the wake of the Exxon Valdez oil spill to lobby successfully for legislation governing the extraction and transport of petroleum in Alaska and the United States.

Robert Figueroa is Visiting Assistant Professor in the Department of Philosophy and Religion at Colgate University, where he teaches courses on environmental justice, environmental philosophy, and social ethics. He is currently writing a textbook, *The Philosophy of Environmental Justice: An Introduction to the Issues and Problems,* and he has completed a manuscript entitled, *Whose Environment, Which Justice: Environmental Justice and Social Philosophy.* Also, he is presently coediting with Sandra Harding a volume on diversity and the philosophy of science and technology. His recent research extends into global environmental justice, the links between identity politics and environmental values, heritage and values of technology, and social equity in climate affairs.

Janis Johnson was born and raised in Lewiston, Idaho. She received a Ph.D. from Tulane University in New Orleans, where she currently teaches American Indian and environmental studies. Her dissertation, "Hidden Nation: Nez Perce Identity and American Indian Sovereignty," examines the ways in which popular representations of the Nez Perce Tribe have romanticized the tribe and effaced its sovereignty. "Hidden Nation" argues that the tribe's own cultural expressions, such as literature, dance, and even dance regalia, challenge and resist mythologization by the mainstream culture.

Valerie Kuletz is Lecturer in American Studies at the University of Canterbury in New Zealand. She has worked on various aspects of nuclear colonialism with Native American communities, culminating in her book *The Tainted Desert: Environmental and Social Ruin in the American West*. She is currently doing field work in Tahiti and the Marshall Islands on the political ecology of postnuclear spaces, and is a research fellow at the Institute for International Studies at the University of California, Berkeley.

Tom Lynch resides in Las Cruces, New Mexico, where he teaches Southwestern literature as an adjunct at New Mexico State University. He has been involved in numerous political activities, including campaigns to halt the nuclear power industry in the Pacific Northwest. For several years he organized civil disobedience protests at the Nevada Test Site. He is currently involved in efforts to restore the natural integrity of the Rio Grande in southern New Mexico and is compiling an anthology of writings about the Mexican Gray Wolf in support of the wolf restoration program. He has published numerous creative essays and scholarly articles, including studies of Silko, Thoreau, Abbey, and Vizenor, and is currently at work on an ecocritical study of Southwestern literature.

Devon Peña is Professor of Anthropology and Ethnic Studies at the University of Washington, where he coordinates the Ph.D. program in Environmental Anthropology. Professor Peña is a research associate and member of the Colorado Acequia Association where he works on acequia natural assets and environmental justice and is active in the programs for land and water trusts, watershed protection and restoration, and cooperative economic development. Peña serves on the national planning committee of the Second National People of Color Environmental Leadership Summit. He is currently completing work on a book about Mexican Americans and the environment (forthcoming from the University of Arizona Press in fall of 2003).

T. V. Reed is Director of American Studies and Professor of English at Washington State University. His publications include *Fifteen Jugglers, Five Believers: Literary Politics and the Poetics of American Social Movements* (University of California, 1992) and *Social Movements and Cultural Studies* (University of Minnesota, forthcoming). His widely used essay on "Theory and Method in American Cultural Studies" is now available in updated and expanded form online (www.wsu.edu/~amerstu/tm/bib.html). He also maintains the website "Cultural Environmental Studies" (www.wsu.edu/~amerstu/ce/ce.html).

Andrea Simpson is an Associate Professor at the University of Washington. Her book, *The Tie that Binds: Identity and Political Attitudes in the Post-Civil Rights Generation* (New York University Press, 1998) was selected as the "Best Book of 1998 on Racial Identity" by the American Political Science Association's Race and Ethnicity section. She is currently researching women in the environmental justice movement for a forthcoming book from Oxford University Press entitled, *In Shadowed Spaces: Women in the Environmental Justice Movement.*

Rachel Stein is Associate Professor of American Literature and Director of Women's and Multicultural Studies at Siena College, where she teaches courses on African American, Native American and other multicultural American literatures, as well as courses on gender and sexuality. Her articles on race, gender, sexuality, and nature in American literature have appeared in *Women's Studies; Interdisciplinary Studies in Literature and Environment; Reading Under the Sign of Nature;* and elsewhere. She is the author of *Shifting the Ground: American Women Writers' Revisions of Nature, Gender and Race.*

Julie Sze is an urban and environmental justice activist and scholar. She is currently a Ph.D. candidate in the American Studies Program at New York University. She has worked with New York City Environmental Justice Alliance around transportation, solid waste, and open space issues in low-income communities and communities of color, and as an Associate at the Community Academic Partnership for the Environment on community-based environmental justice research. Her scholarly work focuses on environmental justice, and on how ideas and practices concerning "race" and "nature" manifest in the culture and politics of the urban environment.

Jim Tarter is an Assistant Professor of English at Lewis-Clark State College in Lewiston, Idaho. He is teaching courses in environmental studies, multi-ethnic fiction, and Native American literature, and working in the College's Indian Bridge Program. His essays have appeared in *ISLE: Interdisciplinary*

Studies in Literature and Environment; Reading Under the Sign of Nature; and *The Greening of Literary Studies* (forthcoming). He is currently finishing a book called *Locating Environmental Justice in Contemporary American Fiction.*

Soenke Zehle is a Ph.D. candidate in Comparative Literature/American Studies at the State University of New York at Binghamton. He has been active in a variety of grassroots efforts and has taught interdisciplinary courses on ethnic studies, labor history, and environmental justice. He is currently completing his dissertation entitled, "Ecology and Empire: Indigenous Peoples in the Biodiversity Process."

INDEX